BUSINESS
ASSOCIATIONS
LAW AND CONTEXT

SECOND EDITION

EDITED BY ROBERT ILLIG
University of Oregon

cognella®
academic publishing

Bassim Hamadeh, CEO and Publisher
Carrie Montoya, Manager, Revisions and Author Care
Kaela Martin, Project Editor
Christian Berk, Associate Production Editor
Jess Estrella, Senior Graphic Designer
Alexa Lucido, Licensing Associate
Natalie Piccotti, Director of Marketing
Kassie Graves, Vice President of Editorial
Jamie Giganti, Director of Academic Publishing

Cover image copyright© Depositphotos/bst2012

Printed in the United States of America.

ISBN: 978-1-5165-3194-3 (pbk) / 978-1-5165-3195-0 (br)

www.cognella.com   800-200-3908

CONTENTS

INTRODUCTION

As the 19th Century faded into the 20th, Christopher Columbus Langdell and his colleagues at Harvard Law School perfected the case method. Their goal was to elevate legal education to the status of a discipline, earning it a coveted place in the academy alongside the sciences and humanities.[1] In order to imbue the study of law with a stature greater than that attributed to a mere trade school, they constructed a critique. They posited that the law was more than a mere collection of laws; the miscellaneous musings of judges, upon closer study, coalesce into more than a jumble of *ex post* rationalizations, more than the principled if incoherent delivery of *ad hoc* justice. Instead, Langdell and his colleagues asserted, law represents a coherent body of philosophic thought that is both worthy and capable of study. By applying a close reading to the text and meticulously parsing distinctions, lawyers, as scholars, can not only dissect and describe the law but also predict how it is likely to evolve and be interpreted by others. Much as climatologists and economists seek to extrapolate coming events from existing data, lawyers use the precedent embedded in legal opinions to discern future judicial behavior. We can thus approach appellate court decisions the way archeologists approach new and unusual artifacts: as direct evidence, the meaning of which may be ambiguous or contested.

All this explains why legal educators use casebooks, not textbooks. Our goal is not to provide a litany of rules and regulations for students to memorize. Rather, we seek to train the mind to solve problems. We excel not at imparting an encyclopedic knowledge of laws. Rather, we demonstrate to students, through repetition and group discussion, the tools and methods that lawyers use to uncover facts, deduce legal doctrine, and predict the application of precedent. We prepare them not for the known, but for the unknown. When a medical student dissects a cadaver, her purpose is to master its anatomy—to uncover the fixed laws of the physical-biological world. When a law student dissects a judicial opinion, by contrast, her goal is not merely to expose the judge's legal reasoning, because the structure of law is not a constant. Her goal is to learn *how* to decipher legal

---

1   For a more detailed and nuanced history of the developments that led to the academy's modern approach to law school pedagogy, see Robert Stevens, Law School: Legal Education in America from the 1850s to the 1980s (1983).

reasoning. The next case, unlike the next cadaver, will be composed of different parts in different places and a lawyer must know how to approach each new body of facts.

It is for this reason that legal pedagogy, at its best, focuses not on amassing knowledge but on the development of instinct. Law differs from the humanities and sciences. The laws of men change, whereas the laws of nature and the events of the past are fixed. Historical events, notwithstanding historians' evolving perspectives and novel interpretations, remain at some level immutable. Astronomers may once have believed the sun and planets revolved around the earth. But it was their understanding that changed, not the path of those celestial orbs. The laws of nature and the substance of the past can be challenging to uncover, yet the natural world observes fixed rules and historical events cannot be unwound. *Something* cures cancer, and *someone* assassinated JFK, even if that cure or that person at present eludes us.

But legal rules do change. They change because they are the inventions of human civilization. Even now, judges across America are handing down opinions that differ in their reasoning or outcome from past precedent; legislators are gaining or losing the political traction necessary to reverse or further the work of their predecessors; and regulators are adapting the law to new circumstances, changing societal values, and evolving technologies and behaviors. When you finish this course, laws will be different than they are now. Thirty years hence, when you reach your prime as advocates, laws will have evolved to a degree and in such a manner that is today difficult to imagine. And so legal pedagogy places its focus on process, not outcome. The legal academy prepares students to parse, interpret, and comprehend, rather than to memorize and categorize. We ask students *why* and *how*, not *what*. We challenge students to contextualize their learning and defend their conclusions.

* * *

The market for casebooks has led the academy astray. Instead of honing focused instruments for learning, faculty members now produce encyclopedic tomes that embed cases within an ever-expanding compendium of data. We confuse casebooks with horn books. No exception is unremarked on, no topic is too trivial to ignore, and no text is left unencumbered to speak for itself. In the contest for marketplace success, authors believe they must craft casebooks that are so broad and inclusive that they appeal in some respect to every professor, no matter how idiosyncratic her approach. Like the big-firm litigators they once were, casebook authors compete for dominance by burying their competitors in paper.

Yet by attempting to cater to every possible taste, these tomes unintentionally present students with a warped vision of legal pedagogy. Lost in the endless repetition of detail are the unifying themes that provide the law with both its coherence and its moral authority. Indeed, the typical casebook's emphasis on coverage leads many students to mistakenly focus their efforts on remembering outcomes rather than mastering process. For them, the law as a discipline splinters into a pre-Langdell cataloguing of rules and precedent. They gain knowledge but not wisdom.

This dim assessment of the industry doesn't even begin to address the added costs that encyclo-pedic casebooks and excessively long statutory supplements place on the backs of our already debt-strapped students. Legal educators should reject this detail-minded approach in favor of exposing for students the power that comes with identifying for oneself the meaning, context, structure, and logic of the law.

This casebook is an attempt to return to the logic of Langdell's revolutionary critique. It is composed almost entirely of legal decisions and statutes, the primary source material of our profession. Where context is absolutely necessary, as with a basic understanding of business law history, theory, and finance, it presents scholarly work in place of stale textbook explanation. The goal is to let the text speak for itself and so challenge students not only to parse meaning but also to learn to expose context and anticipate exceptions. This forces the students to do the hard work themselves, leaving it to the instructor to answer questions and clarify understanding in the classroom.

The business of law professors is not to "hide the ball," as we sometimes are accused of doing. Gamesmanship that serves merely to feed a professor's ego cannot be defended. Nor should we hand the proverbial ball to students, polished, elegant, and complete. Rather, the best legal educa-tors seek to guide students as they learn to parse texts with the same critical approach that we take, to learn to ask the questions that we ask. Undergraduate students may learn history from textbook explanations, but graduate students examine direct evidence—letters, diaries, census records—each with its own story to tell. Our role as authors and instructors is to act as advisors, not managers, in the educational process of each student. Accordingly, this casebook presents a selection of texts that require careful dissection and contemplation; texts from which readers learn to extrapolate technique; texts that speak for themselves. Some are old gems, some may not be a professor's favorite, some may even be wrong or, worse, wrongheaded. But they were selected for their pedagogical value and above all for the questions they raise. Master *how* to approach these texts, and you will have mastered the law of business associations.

* * *

Note concerning the text: the materials in this casebook were selected and edited solely for the purpose of pedagogy. To make them as readable as possible, they have been substantially abridged, and traditional but distracting indicators, such as ellipses and brackets, have been excluded from these abridgements. They are intended to serve as useful tools of learning rather than as a complete or accurate record of the underlying case law. For that, you must visit the law library.

* * *

Finally, I wish to convey my sincere thanks to my wonderful student researchers at the University of Oregon—as well as to the fine folks at Cognella—without whom this book would not have been possible. I also owe a special debt of gratitude to the inestimable Esther Sherman for her superb counsel and precision editing.

CHAPTER ONE

THE CONTEXT OF BUSINESS LAW

INTRODUCTION

The study of law is the study of history. Ours is an inherently backward-looking discipline—we examine the past to forecast the future. We scrutinize the logic and biases contained in yesterday's cases in order to predict tomorrow's decisions. We seek to understand the law's historical context in order to appreciate the arc of its evolution.

Thus, before we can grapple with the caselaw and statutes governing American business entities, we must survey the American economy from colonial days to the present. In doing so, we focus on events that impacted the opinions and attitudes of policymakers and set the stage for the manner in which our nation approaches the regulation of commerce.

Our particular concern is the development of the corporation during and after the Industrial Revolution as well as the ideas and innovations that were necessary preconditions to its invention. We further trace our nation's history in relation to a series of economic catastrophes that begins with the Great Depression in the 1930s and extends through the dotcom crash of 2001 and the 2008 mortgage crisis.

As you read the section on the historical context of corporate law, consider your own knowledge of American history. In particular, reflect on whether we can discern a direction to the development of business law. Policymakers adopt laws in real time in reaction to the events unfolding around them. Has the law simply lurched from one crisis to another, responding as best it could with the tools at hand? Or can we identify trends and imperatives that helped guide our commercial jurisprudence from the ancient to the modern? And can we extrapolate its trajectory into the future?

Historical context, of course, is not solely comprised of actions and events. Equally important is the development of the ideas that ground the law and fix its contours. Facts on their own lack significance. It is how facts are interpreted that matters—the interaction of events with observers' preconditioned biases and systems of belief. As students of corporate law, we must examine the theoretical framework utilized by past (and future) judges. What were the beliefs and objectives that lay behind the invention of the corporation? What tensions impacted its evolution?

With this in mind, we commence our study in Part A with the famous duo of Adolf Berle and Gardiner Means. Their classic treatise on "The Modern Corporation and Private Property" served as the lodestar that guided the development and interpretation of corporate law for close to a century. From its publication in 1932 until the mid-1990s, legal scholars (and policymakers) followed their lead and framed corporate law as a problem of agency costs. As the law-and-economics movement came into its own, however, legal scholars have questioned the importance of the underlying framework laid out by Berle and Means.

Given the prominence of such competing approaches, we consider in Part B the theories of more recent thinkers, including those who view the corporation as a "public good" whose sole purpose is to enhance commerce. It is through an understanding of these theoretical disputes that we can finally unpack the logic—and future—of corporate law.

Having thus set the stage with an understanding of theory, we delve into the history of corporate law in Part C.

At the end of this chapter, you will have a basic understanding of the theoretical constructs and historical developments that led to the evolution of the modern business form. As a result, you will be ready to engage with the legal principles that regulate most modern American business organizations.

PART A   THE CHALLENGE

THE MODERN CORPORATION AND PRIVATE PROPERTY[1]

Corporations have ceased to be merely legal devices through which the private business transactions of individuals may be carried on. Though still much used for this purpose, the corporate

---

1   Adolfe A. Berle, Jr. & Gardiner C. Means, "Chapter 1: Property In Transition," *The Modern Corporation and Private Property*, pp. 1-9. Copyright © 1932 by Transaction Publishers. Reprinted with permission.

form has acquired a larger significance. The corporation has, in fact, become both a method of property tenure and a means of organizing economic life. Grown to tremendous proportions, there may be said to have evolved a "corporate system"—as there was once a feudal system—which has attracted to itself a combination of attributes and powers, and has attained a degree of prominence entitling it to be dealt with as a major social institution.

We are examining this institution probably before it has attained its zenith. Spectacular as its rise has been, every indication seems to be that the system will move forward to proportions which would stagger imagination today; just as the corporate system of today was beyond the imagination of most statesmen and business men at the opening of the present century. For that reason, if for no other, it is desirable to examine this system, bearing in mind that its impact on the life of the country and of every individual is certain to be great; it may even determine a large part of the behaviour of most men living under it.

The typical business unit of the 19th century was owned by individuals or small groups; was managed by them or their appointees; and was, in the main, limited in size by the personal wealth of the individuals in control. These units have been supplanted in ever greater measure by great aggregations in which tens and even hundreds of thousands of workers and property worth hundreds of millions of dollars, belonging to tens or even hundreds of thousands of individuals, are combined through the corporate mechanism into a single producing organization under unified control and management. Such a unit is the American Telephone and Telegraph Company, perhaps the most advanced development of the corporate system. With assets of almost five billions of dollars, with 454,000 employees, and stockholders to the number of 567,694, this company may indeed be called an economic empire—an empire bounded by no geographical limits, but held together by centralized control.

Such an organization of economic activity rests upon two developments, each of which has made possible an extension of the area under unified control. The factory system, the basis of the industrial revolution, brought an increasingly large number of workers directly under a single management. Then, the modern corporation, equally revolutionary in its effect, placed the wealth of innumerable individuals under the same central control. By each of these changes the power of those in control was immensely enlarged and the status of those involved, worker or property owner, was radically changed. The independent worker who entered the factory became a wage laborer surrendering the direction of his labor to his industrial master. The property owner who invests in a modern corporation so far surrenders his wealth to those in control of the corporation that he has exchanged the position of independent owner for one in which he may become merely recipient of the wages of capital.

Corporations where this separation has become an important factor may be classed as quasi-public in character in contradistinction to the private, or closely held corporation in which no important separation of ownership and control has taken place.

Growing out of this separation are two characteristics, almost as typical of the quasi-public corporation as the separation itself—mere size and the public market for its securities. It is precisely this separation of control from ownership which makes possible tremendous aggregations of property. The Fords and the Mellons, whose personal wealth is sufficient to finance great enterprises, are so few, that they only emphasize the dependence of the large enterprise on the wealth of more than the individual or group of individuals who may be in control. The quasi-public corporation commands its supply of capital from a group of investors frequently described as the "investing public." It draws these savings to itself either directly, as individuals purchase stocks or bonds, or indirectly, as insurance companies, banks, and investment trusts receive these savings and invest them in corporate securities. To secure these funds it must commonly avail itself of an open market in its securities—usually by listing shares on a stock exchange, or, less importantly, by maintaining a private or "unlisted" market. So essential, in fact, is the open market to the quasi-public corporation that it may be considered almost as characteristic of that type of corporation as the separation of ownership from control and the great aggregation of wealth.

Though the American law makes no distinction between the private corporation and the quasi-public, the economics of the two are essentially different. The separation of ownership from control produces a condition where the interests of owner and of ultimate manager may, and often do, diverge, and where many of the checks which formerly operated to limit the use of power disappear. Size alone tends to give these giant corporations a social significance not attached to the smaller units of private enterprise. By the use of the open market for securities, each of these corporations assumes obligations towards the investing public which transform it from a legal method clothing the rule of a few individuals into an institution at least nominally serving investors who have embarked their funds in its enterprise. New responsibilities towards the owners, the workers, the consumers, and the State thus rest upon the shoulders of those in control. In creating these new relationships, the quasi-public corporation may fairly be said to work a revolution. It has destroyed the unity that we commonly call property—has divided ownership into nominal ownership and the power formerly joined to it. Thereby the corporation has changed the nature of profit-seeking enterprise.

Outwardly the change is simple enough. Men are less likely to own the physical instruments of production. They are more likely to own pieces of paper, loosely known as stocks, bonds, and other securities, which have become mobile through the machinery of the public markets. Beneath this, however, lies a more fundamental shift. Physical control over the instruments of production has been surrendered in ever growing degree to centralized groups who manage property in bulk, supposedly, but by no means necessarily, for the benefit of the security holders. Power over industrial property has been cut off from the beneficial ownership of this property—or, in less technical language, from the legal right to enjoy its fruits. Control of physical assets has passed from the individual owner to those who direct the quasi-public institutions, while the owner retains an interest in their product and increase. There has resulted the dissolution of the old atom of ownership into its component parts, control and beneficial ownership. This dissolution of the atom of property destroys the very foundation on which the economic order of the past three centuries has rested. Private enterprise, which has molded economic life since the close of the middle ages, has been rooted in the institution of private property.

Under the feudal system, its predecessor, economic organization grew out of mutual obligations and privileges. Private enterprise, on the other hand, has assumed an owner of the instruments of production with complete property rights over those instruments. Whereas the organization of feudal economic life rested upon an elaborate system of binding customs, the organization under the system of private enterprise has rested upon the self-interest of the property owner—a self-interest held in check only by competition and the conditions of supply and demand. Such self-interest has long been regarded as the best guarantee of economic efficiency. It has been assumed that, if the individual is protected in the right both to use his own property as he sees fit and to receive the full fruits of its use, his desire for personal gain can be relied upon as an effective incentive to his efficient use of any industrial property he may possess. In the quasi-public corporation, such an assumption no longer holds. As we have seen, it is no longer the individual himself who uses his wealth. Those in control of that wealth, and therefore in a position to secure industrial efficiency and produce profits, are no longer, as owners, entitled to the bulk of such profits. Those who control the destinies of the typical modern corporation own so insignificant a fraction of the company's stock that the returns from running the corporation profitably accrue to them in only a very minor degree. The stock-holders, on the other hand, to whom the profits of the corporation go, cannot be motivated by those profits to a more efficient use of the property, since they have surrendered all disposition of it to those in control of the enterprise. The explosion of the atom of property destroys the basis of the old assumption that the quest for profits will spur the owner of industrial property to its effective use. It consequently challenges the fundamental economic principle of individual initiative in industrial enterprise. It raises for reexamination the ends for which the modern corporation can be or will be run.

CORPORATE IRRESPONSIBILITY: AMERICA'S NEWEST EXPORT[2]

The modern American business corporation has been a subject of wonder and horror for much of the past century. Wonder for the limited liability and liquid shares that have given entrepreneurs and professional managers the power to concentrate and use capital for innovative and risky projects that create technological miracles and human comforts. Wonder for the corporation's

---

2   Lawrence Mitchell, "Selection," *Corporate Irresponsibility*, pp. 1-3. Copyright © 2001 by Yale University Press. Reprinted with permission.

specialized structure, which encourages millions of people to invest their money and go about their daily lives, leaving to skilled managers and workers the responsibility for the businesses they have financed. Wonder for the fabulous wealth that this protected capital has produced.

But the business corporation has also been a subject of horror. Horrors for the way its limited liability permits it to dump the costs of production onto those who are powerless to affect the corporation's conduct. Horror as corporate political pressure distorts democratic processes, as corporate welfare in the form of tax breaks and subsidies deforms the course of the economy. Horror as the fabulous wealth produced by business corporations ever more exaggerates the difference between the haves and the have nots.

American corporations and American capital have extraordinary power. The *New York Times* recently identified twenty-two American corporations which had market capitalizations greater than the gross domestic products of twenty-two individual countries, including Spain, Kuwait, Argentina, Poland, and Thailand. Public perception and reported facts tell us that American capital is overwhelming traditional and culturally diverse ways of thinking about, organizing, and conducting business throughout the world.

I will argue that the main problem with American corporations is their drive to maximize short-term stock prices, a result that no thoughtful person really wants. The root of the problem is the corporate structure itself: the corporation's legal structure encourages managers to aim for exactly this short-term result, and it does so by constraining their freedom to act responsibly and morally. Compounding the problems caused by the short-termism built into the corporate structure is the fact that for almost all legal purposes we treat the corporation as if it were a natural person, granting it the freedoms of a natural person to increase stock price however it likes, but without the moral and social conscience that leads real people to care about how they do business.

PART B THE THEORY

CORPORATIONS, CORPORATE LAW, AND NETWORKS OF CONTRACTS[3]

In the contractarian paradigm, firm managers are conceptualized as selecting a set of charter terms that capital markets price and that investors, in effect, purchase when they purchase a firm's securities. Because they have incentives to obtain the highest value for their firm's shares,

---

3   Michael Klausner, "Corporations, Corporate Law, and Networks of Contracts," *Virginia Law Review*, vol. 81, no. 8, pp. 767-771. Copyright © 1995 by Virginia Law Review. Reprinted with permission.

managers attempt to offer terms that maximize share values by minimizing agency costs and signaling to investors valuable information about the firm. Those terms might define shareholder voting rights, managers' duties of care and loyalty, shareholders' rights to dividends, or other aspects of the relationships among shareholders and managers. The same logic applies with respect to other components of the corporate contract. For instance, to the extent that the terms of a bond indenture can reduce the agency cost of debt, the corporation can reduce its interest expense and hence increase the value of its shares by skillful selection of indenture terms.

In this view, competition in capital markets (and indirectly in product markets) provides the selection mechanism that powers a quasi-Darwinian process for corporate contract terms. Terms that prove to be efficient are imitated and inferior terms are dropped. The aggregate value of all firms is thus maximized. Moreover, as long as there are no adverse effects on third parties, the process of maximizing firm value through the choice of charter terms also maximizes societal wealth. In this story, what is optimal for the firm is optimal for society.

If the incentives of managers and investors lead them to select corporate contract terms that maximize firm value, and if the maximization of firm value generally maximizes social wealth, then what is the role of corporate law? Why not let managers and investors write out their own contracts and have the law of contracts govern the process? The primary answer that the contractarian paradigm offers is well stated by Judge Frank Easterbrook and Professor Daniel Fischel: "Corporate law is a set of terms available off-the-rack so that participants in corporate ventures can save the cost of contracting. Corporate codes and existing judicial decisions supply these terms 'for free' to every corporation, enabling the venturers to concentrate on matters that are specific to their undertaking."

Although there are disagreements at the margin among scholars working within the contractarian paradigm, the general view is that socially optimal corporate law would provide a set of "default" terms, any or all of which a firm could adopt by inaction or reject by explicitly customizing an alternative term. The content of default terms, in this view, should be governed by a judgment regarding the terms that firms would select in the absence of transaction costs. Thus, as a starting point, an optimal default rule would be one that a majority of firms would adopt if contracting costs were zero. Because contracting costs are not zero, however, and because some terms may be more difficult to contract around than others, a refinement of this majoritarian starting point is commonly accepted: an efficient default rule is one that minimizes the aggregate cost of contracting.

To inform the judgment of courts and legislatures regarding the selection of default rules, the contractarian paradigm directs these bodies to look to the contract terms that corporations have adopted explicitly. These terms have survived the evolutionary process described above. If such terms continue to be widely used, the argument goes, they are likely to be worthy candidates for use as defaults.

From a contractarian perspective, the law should impose mandatory terms on relationships among corporate managers and investors only if market failure infects the process by which those terms are adopted. Possible market failures include collective action problems, externalities, and information imperfections that impair the ability of the capital market to price contract terms. Debates within the contractarian paradigm center on these market failures. "Strong-form" contractarians question their significance; to them, the contracts that exist are socially optimal, or at least close to optimal. Others are not so sanguine, but their primary concern is with midstream amendments, which are not pertinent to my analysis. When a corporation is formed or goes public, a regime of free contracting is thus expected to yield socially optimal corporate contracts.

In sum, the contractarian paradigm maintains that market forces tend to lead management to adopt corporate contracts that maximize firm values. Furthermore, consistent with the basic precepts of welfare economics, these competitive forces are seen as optimizing not only the value of individual firms but also social wealth, except in limited situations of market failure. Consequently, in the contractarian paradigm, the role of corporate law, at least at the stage of a firm's initial formation, is to facilitate the drafting of corporate contracts by providing a set of off-the-rack default terms that corporations can accept or reject at their option. Competition among states is expected to lead corporate law in this direction.

DIRECTOR PRIMACY: THE MEANS AND ENDS OF CORPORATION GOVERNANCE[4]

Since Ronald Coase's famous article "The Nature of the Firm" appeared over six decades ago, both economists and legal scholars have devoted considerable attention to the theory of the firm. Over time, this body of work generated a substantial literature providing both positive and normative insights into, *inter alia*, the internal governance institutions of firms. Although the various theories of the firm developed in that literature can be classified in various ways, and while some defy classification, two basic systems of classification capture most of the competing theories (see Figure 1). Along one axis (the "Means Axis"), theories of the firm are plotted according to whether they emphasize managerial or shareholder primacy. Older theories at the shareholder primacy end of the spectrum posit that shareholders own the corporation. Accordingly, directors and officers are mere stewards of the shareholders' interests. A more recent

4   Stephen M. Bainbridge, "Director Primacy: The Means and Ends of Corporation Governance," *Northwestern University Law Review*, vol. 97, no. 2, pp. 547-550. Copyright © 2003 by Northwestern University School of Law. Reprinted with permission.

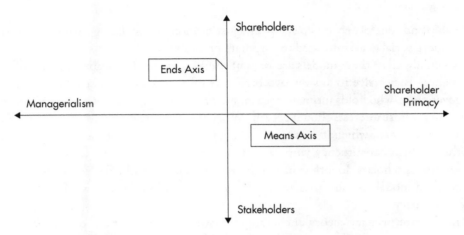

FIGURE 1: PLOTTING MODELS OF THE FIRM

variant, known as the "nexus of contracts" or "contractarian" model, which is one of Coase's many progeny, denies that shareholders own the corporation.

Instead, it argues that shareholders are merely one of many factors of production bound together in a complex web of explicit and implicit contracts. Contractarian theory nevertheless continues to treat directors and officers as contractual agents of the shareholders, with fiduciary obligations to maximize shareholder wealth. Shareholders therefore retain a privileged position among the corporation's various constituencies, enjoying a contract with the firm granting shareholders ownership-like rights, such as the vote and the protection of fiduciary obligations by directors and officers.

At the other end of the means axis lies managerialism. Managerialism perceives the corporation as a bureaucratic hierarchy dominated by professional managers. Directors are figureheads, while shareholders are nonentities. Thus, under managerialist models, managers are autonomous actors free to pursue whatever interests they choose (or society directs). Although the managerialist model long dominated corporate law scholarship and remains influential in some other disciplines, it no longer has much traction in the legal academy. Along the other axis (the "Ends Axis"), models can be plotted according to the interests the corporation is said to serve. At one end of the spectrum are models contending that corporations should be run so as to maximize shareholder wealth. At the other end are stakeholderist models arguing that directors and managers should consider the interests of all corporate constituencies in making corporate decisions. Not surprisingly, this axis reflects the division in corporate law scholarship along public-private lines. Proponents of shareholder wealth maximization typically treat corporate governance as a species of private law, such that the separation of ownership and control does not in and of itself justify state intervention in corporate governance. In contrast, stakeholderists commonly treat corporate governance as a species of public law, such that the separation of ownership and control becomes principally a justification for regulating corporate governance so as to achieve social goals unrelated to corporate profitability.

Essentially, all of these models are ways of thinking about the means and ends of corporate governance. They strive to answer two basic sets of questions: (1) as to the means of corporate governance, who holds ultimate decisionmaking power? and (2) as to the ends of corporate governance, whose interests should prevail? When the ultimate decisionmaker is presented with a zero-sum game, in which it must prefer the interests of one constituency class over those of all others, which constituency wins? Any model that commands the loyalty of one or more generations of scholars doubtless has more than a grain of truth. Yet, as we shall see, none of the standard models is fully satisfactory. There remains room for a new competitor—namely, director primacy.

The director primacy theory offers unique answers to the questions of the means and ends of corporate governance. As noted earlier, shareholder primacy models assume that shareholders both control the corporation, at least in some ultimate fashion, and are the appropriate beneficiaries of director fiduciary duties. Managerialist models assume that top management controls the corporation, but differ as to the interests managers should pursue. Stakeholderist models rarely focus on control issues, but instead emphasize that shareholders should not be the sole beneficiaries of director and officer fiduciary duties. The director primacy model, on the other hand, splits the baby rather differently. As to the means axis, director primacy asserts that neither end of the spectrum gets it right. Neither shareholders nor managers control corporations—boards of directors do. As to the ends axis, director primacy claims that shareholders are the appropriate beneficiaries of director fiduciary duties. Hence, director accountability for maximizing shareholder wealth remains an important component of director primacy.

PART C THE CONTEXT

THE AMERICAN CORPORATION[5]

Questions about the actions and purposes of American corporations have been with us as long as corporations themselves.

Why, during the ongoing financial and economic crises that broke out beginning in 2007, did large financial institutions and industrial firms teetering on the brink of failure—often because of their own misguided strategies and decisions—get bailed out by the federal government?

---

5 Ralph Gomory & Richard Sylla, "The American Corporation," *Daedalus*, pp. 102-110. Copyright © 2013 by MIT Press. Reprinted with permission.

Why did the government seemingly do much less for homeowners facing foreclosures on houses now worth less than the mortgage debt incurred to buy them, perhaps because they had lost their jobs in the economic downturn and could not afford the mortgage payments due?

Why do the profits of American corporations and the compensations of their executives stay high and even rise in some cases while jobs disappear and both economic growth and median family incomes stagnate? Why does the judicial branch join in to strengthen the influence of corporations?

It is not the first time in U.S. history that people have wondered whether ours is a government of the people or a government of the corporations. Such fears are as old as the republic. They were present in the 1790s, when the United States began to lead the world in the development of the corporation as the most dynamic form of modern business enterprise. They arose again in the financial and economic crises of the late 1830s and early 1840s, after state legislatures had created thousands of corporations. In the decades around the turn of the twentieth century, when many corporations became very large, the fear of corporate power resurfaced, leading to antitrust laws and federal regulation. The crises of the Great Depression led to further restraints on the financial and economic powers of corporations.

If there is any surprise about the current crisis, it is not that worries about corporate power and its abuse are once again being raised, but that so little is being done about them in comparison with the reforms of the 1840s, the Progressive Era, and the New Deal.

Americans have always viewed corporations with mixed feelings. On the one hand, a corporation with limited liability and endowed with a long life is an attractive vehicle for numerous investors to pool their individual capitals, receiving tradable shares of the company in return. Pooling of capital makes possible large, long-term investments that can achieve economies of scale and scope in the production and distribution of goods and services that are beyond the capabilities of sole proprietorships and partnerships. Indeed, one of the less appreciated reasons for the rapid rise of the U.S. economy in the nineteenth century in comparison to other nations was the relative ease of obtaining a corporate charter in America.

On the other hand, inherent in the corporate form are problems of conflicting goals. Will the managers of corporations manage them in the interests of the shareholder-owners? Or will the managers act in their self-interest? Will corporate managers take into account the interests of employees, customers, suppliers, lenders, and the polity that made the corporation possible?

In the period from the 1790s to the 1860s, the United States led the world in modern corporate development. Recent research provides the first comprehensive look at corporate development, revealing that U.S. states from 1790 to 1860 chartered 22,419 business corporations under special legislative acts and several thousand more under general incorporation laws that were introduced mostly in the 1840s and 1850s. These totals far exceed the number of corporations created in any other country (most likely in all other countries combined) during that time.

Most of the early American corporations, operating within a state or in a city or town, were small by later standards. The largest were banks and insurance companies, joined later in the era by railroads and manufacturers. Stockholders, often locals, could monitor corporate operations firsthand, and they were more directly involved in corporate affairs than would later be the case. Stockholders' meetings were frequent and actually provided guidance for management. Passive stockholders could keep an eye on their investments by checking prices in securities markets and by observing the dividends they received, which in this era accounted for the lion's share of corporate net earnings.

Legislative chartering meant that charters could be tailor-made for each corporation, with its powers, responsibilities—including those to the community—and basic governance provisions carefully specified. Most charters were not perpetual, but rather had set terms of years and had to come up periodically for renewal. Voting rules for shareholders in elections of directors and other corporate matters varied. They were not always the modern norm of one vote per share, which favors large-block shareholders. Legislative chartering could easily be corrupted, however, with incumbent corporations using money and influence to defeat charters for potential competitors, and would-be corporations using the same tools to gain charters.

General incorporation laws, also a modern norm, were introduced late in the antebellum era as a way to avoid the corruption involved in legislative chartering as well as what was perceived as too close a relationship between corporations and the states. Under general laws, any group of incorporators meeting the specifications of the law could receive a charter, the granting of which became an administrative rather than legislative function of government. Access to the corporate form became more open—a gain for society. But state oversight of the creation and monitoring of corporations was reduced.

From the 1860s to the 1930s, most corporations remained small (as is still true), but growing numbers of them became very large and operated nationwide and even multi-nationally. Large corporations required professional managers, who often had limited or no ownership shares. These "Berle-Means" corporations, so named after the authors of a famous 1932 book, *The Modern Corporation and Private Property*, effectively separated ownership (shareholders) from control (management), marginalizing the influence of owner-shareholders in corporate affairs.

In this era, external checks on the possibility that managers would behave opportunistically against the interests of owners and anti-socially against the larger interests of the country came in two forms: investment bankers and government. Large corporations often had to access capital markets by selling shares and bonds, a process in which investment bankers served as intermediaries. These bankers had an interest in corporate governance to assure the investors who had purchased corporate securities from them that their investments were sound and secure. They exercised that interest by monitoring their corporate clients, even going so far as to place bank representatives on corporate boards. To many Americans, however, such banker influence was suspect, and charges of banker dominance and a "money trust" caused investment bankers late in this era to retreat from their monitoring and oversight roles in corporate affairs. That, of course, served to increase the powers of corporate managers.

Americans' suspicions about large banks and investment bankers were also directed at large corporations. The Gilded Age of the late nineteenth century featured the rise of the Robber Barons, both the business leaders who amassed great power and wealth in the rise of mass-production and mass-distribution industries, and the great financiers of Wall Street who collaborated with them. Popular politicians, such as trust-busting Theodore Roosevelt, adopted ordinary Americans' concerns about the concentration of wealth and power, leading to the passage of antitrust laws and corporate regulation at both the federal and state levels.

The period from the 1930s to the 1980s began with the Great Depression, which put the financial and corporate sectors under a cloud, resulting in a host of New Deal reforms. In finance, the Glass-Steagall Act (1933) separated investment banks and commercial banks, ramped up federal regulation, and introduced deposit insurance. A series of securities acts (1933, 1934, and 1940) compelled publicly traded corporations to disclose more (and more timely) information to their stockholders and the general public. The acts also provided regulatory oversight of securities trading and investment companies.

Corporations recovered much of the prestige they lost during the Depression through their contributions to the successful outcome of World War II. The lessons about the economy learned from World War II varied with the eye of the beholder. To some, the overwhelming factor in the U.S. contribution to the war effort was our immense ability to manufacture. That capacity was certainly there: already by the 1920s, the United States not only led the world in production of the key industrial products, steel and electricity, but also led in their per-capita production. When the United States entered the war, President Franklin Roosevelt created the War Production Board, comprised of industry leaders. Under their command, the country moved with incredible speed from civilian to military production. Airplanes in enormous numbers were produced in place of cars. U.S. shipbuilding capacity produced carrier-led fleets whose eventual scale dwarfed those of America's enemies.

For two decades after 1945, large American corporations were subject to little international or domestic competition because of their oligopolistic market structures. Dividend payouts declined as corporations retained more and more of their profits to fund much of their investment. Because of New Deal reforms and profit retention, the financial sector, which earlier had both financed and strongly influenced corporate affairs, was essentially reduced to advisory and service roles. Stockholders did not mind lower dividends because prosperous times increased the value of their shares, and regulation by the Securities and Exchange Commission increased investor confidence that Wall Street provided a level playing field.

Managers still controlled corporations, and they exercised their power by choosing directors. Often these included top managers themselves. Outside directors chosen by management were obviously beholden to management. Stockholders, the putative owners, had little say. The

Berle-Means corporation remained alive and well, enjoying its heyday in the two decades after World War II. Corporations did so well in this period because of a strong American economy, a worldwide demand for American products and know-how, and a lack of competition from abroad. A widespread, though not unanimous, view was that corporate and country prosperity were closely linked. It was during this period of prosperity in the 1950s that General Motors CEO Charles Wilson, in hearings related to his nomination by Eisenhower to be Secretary of Defense, made his famous statement that "what was good for our country was good for General Motors and vice versa."

In the early postwar decades, the problem of corporate goals seemed under control. Managers in general did not feather their own nests at the expense of owners and other stakeholders. J. K. Galbraith, a keen observer of corporate America, explained that the system worked as well as it did because managerial power was faced by countervailing powers in the form of big labor and big government. Unions were at their strongest in these decades, in part because of New Deal labor reforms, and they pushed for higher wages as well as health care and retirement benefits from corporate employers. As for big government, federal regulatory and antitrust laws put in place from the 1880s through the 1930s remained on the books, and postwar Congresses and administrations added a host of new laws.

The interests of managers, stockholders, workers, consumers, and society seemed well aligned. And they needed to be. Aside from purely economic issues, the United States and the Soviet Union were fighting a Cold War that was in significant part a war of ideas. Communism as practiced and advocated by the U.S.S.R. asserted that it would deliver the workers of the world from the slavery of capitalism and raise their standard of living. Soviet ideology dominated states of Eastern Europe, engulfed China and Cuba, and supported strong Communist parties in many parts of the world, including important West European countries such as France and Italy.

Fortunately, the widely shared growth and prosperity in the United States supported the idea that capitalism could be both effective and benign. Even the Soviet leader Nikita Khrushchev, in a widely quoted remark on a visit to the United States, admitted grudgingly that "the slaves of capitalism live well."

Corporations for some decades after World War II were willing to accept a mix of goals; they aimed for good products, satisfied customers, a good effect on the community and nation, and a steady return to the shareholders. But that was about to change.

The economies of the rest of the non-Communist world began to revive. Foreign competition for the American market mattered more than ever because of the tremendous evolution of sea-borne commerce in the form of container ships. Goods of every size made in one country could be shipped around the world to another nation at greatly reduced cost. Later, airborne freight also entered the picture for goods of more value per pound. The *de facto* protectionism provided by the oceans was being repealed by the march of transport technology.

Japan in particular, by providing government support and direction, emphasized manufacturing for export. It developed and adopted new and better manufacturing techniques, forging rapidly ahead in key industries ranging from automobiles, once the U.S. stronghold, to consumer electronics and, later, computer memories. American industry, used to easy success in an environment with limited competition, was slow to respond. Rising inflation and energy-price shocks further eroded American competitiveness. The U.S. dollar lost value compared to other leading currencies. The stock market languished. The easy years were over, and the 1970s saw a major slowdown in what had been steadily rising U.S. productivity, economic growth, and prosperity. Corporate America was in trouble.

The period from the 1980s to the present has been marked by a major shift away from a broad view of stakeholder interests to an almost exclusive focus on shareholder value. Galbraith's countervailing powers had in fact begun to break down by the 1970s. Declining union membership gradually reduced the influence of big labor on corporate managers. Corporations hastened the trend by closing factories in the old manufacturing belt of the Northeast and Midwest, where unions were strong, shifting production to Sun Belt states that had long anti-union traditions. The old manufacturing areas became known as the Rust Belt.

Countervailing power weakened further as academics and others began to attack government antitrust and regulatory policies as misguided. They called for deregulation and increasingly placed government itself under scrutiny. Instead of working in the public interest, many argued, government practiced interest-group politics. Bureaucrats had their own interests—larger budgets, more authority, more employees—which had little to do with the public interest. Ronald Reagan, the popular president from 1981 to 1989, epitomized this new view when he famously said government wasn't the solution, it was the problem.

Academics came to the rescue of corporations, or so it seemed, with new theories of what corporate managers should do. Instead of catering to the interests of various stakeholders, as they had done in the good old days of the postwar era, managers would best serve owners and society in general, the academics argued, by single-mindedly working to maximize shareholder value. The stakeholder view was complicated; actions that are in the interests of some stakeholders may be counter to the interests of others. Higher wages may mean lower profits, and lower wages may mean higher profits.

In contrast, shareholder value was determined daily in the stock market, which the efficient-markets hypothesis showed to be good for measuring that value. The stock market, academics further argued, would identify good corporate managers—those who increased share prices—and would expose bad ones: those who didn't. Managers who failed to maximize shareholder value would be disciplined and even jettisoned by the market for corporate control, which featured hostile takeovers and leveraged buyouts financed by a rejuvenated and innovative financial sector. Society supposedly benefited because the corporate goal was now to make the total value of the enterprise, as measured by what it would take to buy it on the open market, as large as possible.

This academic doctrine fell on receptive ears. From a shareholder perspective, it put their interests in the driver's seat; the success of the company was to be measured by their return. From the point of view of corporate management, it was a mixed blessing. After all, corporate leadership was used to a great deal of independence, they took pride in having good products and being respected members of the community, and they dealt with their fellow workers and managers every day. Shareholders, in contrast, were a distant and uninformed mass to be dealt with by dividends. But in a world of profit maximization, profits could be measured every day and had to be reported every quarter.

This gap in the natural orientation of shareholders and corporate managers was well recognized in academia: it was simply the old principal-agent problem. And, the academics argued, it was not that hard a problem to solve. The solution was to give corporate leadership major stock options. When the stock went up, management benefited hugely. This approach aligned the interests of managers with those of the shareholders.

The stock-options solution cost the company and its shareholders nothing if the stock did not go up, so it was possible to vote the corporate leadership amounts of options that overcame any hesitancy. In fact, CEO compensation soared to previously unheard-of heights. And under many circumstances, a CEO did not have to be exceptional to profit from stock options. In the rising stock market of the 1980s and 1990s, compensations for all CEOs rose together. Certain practices in corporate governance helped generate this result. CEOs sometimes served simultaneously as chairmen of their boards. They invited other CEOs to serve on their boards and possibly chair the compensation committee, a favor that often was returned. CEOs and boards hired compensation consultants that, perhaps unsurprisingly, seldom if ever recommended reducing CEO compensation.

Criticisms of CEO compensation usually elicited a response such as, "He created $2 billion of increased value, why shouldn't he get $100 million of it?" This attitude implied that the efforts of an entire company, with tens of thousands of employees, were the result of a single CEO or top-management team. John F. Welch, CEO of General Electric from 1981 to 2001, is a prominent example. In the 1980s, Welch was dubbed "Neutron Jack" for reducing GE employment by more than one hundred thousand (of about four hundred thousand) and for firing each year the bottom 10 percent of his managers. Welch also led the old manufacturing company into financial services, which came to account for a large proportion of GE's profits. Shareholder value and profits soared under Welch, whose stock options made him a very wealthy man. In 1999, *Fortune* magazine named him Manager of the Century. But Welch's initiatives would lead to problems for GE and his successor after he retired.

The principal-agent problem often did seem to be solved by the stock-option form of remuneration. Employees, however, were not discussed in the stock-option solution to the principal-agent problem, although they were affected by it. Wages, executive compensation, and profits all come out of the total "value added" by a corporation. With the extensive use of stock options, executive compensation and profit, which is reflected in stock price, are linked together. Both improve if wages can be held down. Thus, holding down wages became in the interest of both management and shareholders.

The path that the division of corporate value added has taken since 1980 is reflected in data on productivity, pay, and income shares. From 1947 to 1979, productivity rose 119 percent, average compensation of production and non-supervisory workers (who constitute more than four-fifths of the private-sector labor force) grew 100 percent, and the share of national income received by the top 1 percent of earners (which would include most of top corporate management) ranged from 9 to 13 percent. From 1979 to 2009, in contrast, productivity rose 80 percent, worker compensation rose 8 percent, and the top 1 percent of earners increased their share of national income to more than 23 percent.

The most recent (pre-crisis) data show that the wealthiest 1 percent of Americans own roughly one-third of the value of all shares, that the wealthiest 5 percent hold more than two-thirds of the value of all shares, with the other third spread over the remaining 95 percent.

Currently, the dominant motivation of the American corporation is to maximize profits and raise stock price in the interest of shareholders. While this is often regarded as a legal requirement, it is not. Corporate directors owe their fiduciary duties not to the shareholders, as is often thought, but to the corporation. Indeed, it would be surprising if the law prescribed shareholder value as the only goal given that the Business Roundtable, as recently as 1981, publicly urged the consideration of many other factors.

Despite its lack of legal standing, the sway of "maximizing shareholder value" appears absolute. In today's large corporations, shareholders are distant from the company and their sole attachment is to the shares they hold, although they usually hold them for only a short time. Corporate results, if the goal is shareholder value, are easily measured; companies that do not measure up will see a change of CEO or of the board, or possibly a hostile takeover.

CHAPTER TWO

UNDERSTANDING AGENCY

INTRODUCTION

A generation ago, the study of business associations was almost universally divided into two subject areas. One course was offered on "Agency and Partnerships," while another was offered on "Corporations." The two were considered to be separate subjects worthy of independent study. However, modern law schools combined the study of the available business forms into a single subject area and christened it "Business Associations."

The reason for this change is that observers have come to see agency, partnerships, corporations, and other business entities as existing not in isolation but along a continuum. In each case, the entity's structure addresses the same questions but provides different answers. Who controls the entity's conduct, and what limitations are placed on that control? Who "owns" the entity and stands to benefit from its actions? How is the entity formed? How is it terminated? Who is liable for its negligence or other misdeeds? How are the profits (or losses) distributed?

With this theoretical approach in mind, a newcomer to the subject might assume that the best way to organize a course on business associations would be topic by topic rather than entity by entity. Experience, however, suggests that such an approach would be exceedingly confusing and thus counterproductive. As a result, our study of business associations takes on a hybrid form. We consider all of the entities in a single course, but we address them sequentially. This means that we begin our study of legal doctrine with an examination of the two traditional unincorporated entities—agency and partnership. Only then will we move on to address the corporate form and other more modern entity types.

This chapter provides a brief introduction to the regulation of agency. Although important for our purposes, agency is in fact a universal construct that is not limited to the realm of business law. Rather, it exists in and is relevant to almost all areas of law. Although, by custom, agency principles are examined most thoroughly in the context of business regulation, you will encounter them throughout your study and practice.

Agency is the term used to describe the relationship whereby one person (or entity) acts on behalf of another—the so-called "principal." As such, it requires no state filing or other formal action in order to arise. Rather, agency serves as a default association that establishes the parties' respective legal rights in the absence of other business entities. In this sense, it is a subset of the law of contracts. Indeed, agents are sometimes referred to as employees and their principals as employers.

In most situations, the two parties have agreed purposefully to act as agent and principal, in which case there is little that the law of business associations need add. However, because it is a default form, agency can be created inadvertently. The parties may have intended to create a relationship—meaning that their intent to act in concert was both mutual and consensual—but they may have left its particulars undefined. In such cases, it is up to the law to determine whether their relationship is one of agency or whether it can best be described legally in some other fashion. One of our most significant challenges is distinguishing between agency relationships and relationships like those between lenders and borrowers or suppliers and purchasers. This question is the subject of the material presented in Part A.

In Part B, we assess a series of cases that demonstrate the extent of the liability of the agent and principal to third parties. As between themselves, agents and principals act under the guise of contract law. The terms and conditions of their employment are unremarkable and do not require any special legal analysis. As between the parties and unrelated third persons, however, different rules apply. Generally speaking, principals are liable for the contracts (and torts) of their agents when such agents are acting within the scope of their authority. Thus, Part B considers the nature and extent of agent authority.

At the end of this chapter, you will have the tools to identify and evaluate circumstances that give rise to an agency relationship such that the principal becomes liable for the debts of the agent. This will enable you to advise businesses—such as banks and franchises—that frequently run the risk that they will be asked to answer for the liabilities of their insolvent or wayward business partners. Your goal will be to help them structure their dealings in a manner that avoids the liability associated with agency.

AGENCY FORMATION PART A

A. GAY JENSON FARMS CO. V. CARGILL, INC.

SUPREME COURT OF MINNESOTA (PETERSON, J.)
309 N.W. 2D 285 (1981)

Plaintiffs, 86 individual, partnership or corporate farmers, brought this action against defendant Cargill, Inc. and defendant Warren Grain & Seed Co. to recover losses sustained when Warren defaulted on the contracts made with plaintiffs for the sale of grain. After a trial by jury, judgment was entered in favor of plaintiffs, and Cargill brought this appeal. We affirm.

Warren was operated by Lloyd Hill and his son, Gary Hill.

Lloyd Hill decided in 1964 to apply for financing from Cargill. Cargill's officials from the Moorhead regional office investigated Warren's operations and recommended that Cargill finance Warren.

Under this contract, Warren would receive funds and pay its expenses by issuing drafts drawn on Cargill through Minneapolis banks. The drafts were imprinted with both Warren's and Cargill's names. Proceeds from Warren's sales would be deposited with Cargill and credited to its account. In return for this financing, Warren appointed Cargill as its grain agent for transaction with the Commodity Credit Corporation. Cargill was also given a right of first refusal to purchase market grain sold by Warren to the terminal market.

A new contract was negotiated in 1967, extending Warren's credit line to $300,000 and incorporating the provisions of the original contract. It was also stated in the contract that Warren would provide Cargill with annual financial statements and that either Cargill would keep the books for Warren or an audit would be conducted by an independent firm. Cargill was given the right of access to Warren's books for inspection.

In addition, the agreement provided that Warren was not to make capital improvements or repairs in excess of $5,000 without Cargill's prior consent. Further, it was not to become liable as guarantor on another's indebtedness, or encumber its assets except with Cargill's permission. Consent by Cargill was required before Warren would be allowed to declare a dividend or sell and purchase stock.

Officials from Cargill's regional office made a brief visit to Warren shortly after the agreement was executed. They examined the annual statement and the accounts receivable, expenses, inventory, seed, machinery and other financial matters. Warren was informed that it would be reminded periodically to make the improvements recommended by Cargill. At approximately this time, a memo was given to the Cargill official in charge of the Warren account, Erhart Becker, which stated in part: "This organization (Warren) needs very strong paternal guidance."

21

In 1970, Cargill contracted with Warren and other elevators to act as its agent to seek growers for a new type of wheat called Bounty 208. Warren, as Cargill's agent for this project, entered into contracts for the growing of the wheat seed, with Cargill named as the contracting party. Farmers were paid directly by Cargill for the seed and all contracts were performed in full. In 1971, pursuant to an agency contract, Warren contracted on Cargill's behalf with various farmers for the growing of sunflower seeds for Cargill. The arrangements were similar to those made in the Bounty 208 contracts, and all those contracts were also completed. Both these agreements were unrelated to the open account financing contract. In addition, Warren, as Cargill's agent in the sunflower seed business, cleaned and packaged the seed in Cargill bags.

During this period, Cargill continued to review Warren's operations and expenses and recommend that certain actions should be taken.[1] Warren purchased from Cargill various business forms printed by Cargill and received sample forms from Cargill which Warren used to develop its own business forms.

Cargill wrote to its regional office in 1970 expressing its concern that the pattern of increased use of funds allowed to develop at Warren was similar to that involved in two other cases in which Cargill experienced severe losses. Cargill did not refuse to honor drafts or call the loan, however. A new security agreement which increased the credit line to $750,000 was executed in 1972, and a subsequent agreement which raised the limit to $1,250,000 was entered into in 1976.

Warren was at that time shipping Cargill 90% of its cash grain. When Cargill's facilities were full, Warren shipped its grain to other companies. Approximately 25% of Warren's total sales was seed grain which was sold directly by Warren to its customers.

As Warren's indebtedness continued to be in excess of its credit line, Cargill began to contact Warren daily regarding its financial affairs. Cargill headquarters informed its regional office in 1973 that, since Cargill money was being used, Warren should realize that Cargill had the right to make some critical decisions regarding the use of the funds. Cargill headquarters also told Warren that a regional manager would be working with Warren on a day-to-day basis as well as in monthly planning meetings. In 1975, Cargill's regional office began to keep a daily debit position on Warren. A bank account was opened in Warren's name on which Warren could draw checks in 1976. The account was to be funded by drafts drawn on Cargill by the local bank.

In early 1977, it became evident that Warren had serious financial problems. Several farmers, who had heard that Warren's checks were not being paid, inquired or had their agents inquire

---

1   Between 1967 and 1973, Cargill suggested that Warren take a number of steps, including: (1) a reduction of seed grain and cash grain inventories; (2) improved collection of accounts receivable; (3) reduction or elimination of its wholesale seed business and its speciality grain operation; (4) marketing fertilizer and steel bins on consignment; (5) a reduction in withdrawals made by officers; (6) a suggestion that Warren's bookkeeper not issue her own salary checks; and (7) cooperation with Cargill in implementing the recommendations. These ideas were apparently never implemented, however.

at Cargill regarding Warren's status and were initially told that there would be no problem with payment. In April 1977, an audit of Warren revealed that Warren was $4 million in debt. After Cargill was informed that Warren's financial statements had been deliberately falsified, Warren's request for additional financing was refused. In the final days of Warren's operation, Cargill sent an official to supervise the elevator, including disbursement of funds and income generated by the elevator.

After Warren ceased operations, it was found to be indebted to Cargill in the amount of $3.6 million. Warren was also determined to be indebted to plaintiffs in the amount of $2 million, and plaintiffs brought this action in 1977 to seek recovery of that sum. Plaintiffs alleged that Cargill was jointly liable for Warren's indebtedness as it had acted as principal for the grain elevator.

The court determined that Cargill was the disclosed principal of Warren. It was concluded that Cargill was jointly liable with Warren for plaintiffs' losses, and judgment was entered for plaintiffs.

Cargill seeks a reversal of the jury's findings or, if the jury findings are upheld, a reversal of the trial court's determination that Cargill was a disclosed principal.

The major issue in this case is whether Cargill, by its course of dealing with Warren, became liable as a principal on contracts made by Warren with plaintiffs. Cargill contends that no agency relationship was established with Warren, notwithstanding its financing of Warren's operation and its purchase of the majority of Warren's grain. However, we conclude that Cargill, by its control and influence over Warren, became a principal with liability for the transactions entered into by its agent Warren.

Agency is the fiduciary relationship that results from the manifestation of consent by one person to another that the other shall act on his behalf and subject to his control, and consent by the other so to act. In order to create an agency there must be an agreement, but not necessarily a contract between the parties. An agreement may result in the creation of an agency relationship although the parties did not call it an agency and did not intend the legal consequences of the relation to follow. The existence of the agency may be proved by circumstantial evidence which shows a course of dealing between the two parties. When an agency relationship is to be proven by circumstantial evidence, the principal must be shown to have consented to the agency since one cannot be the agent of another except by consent of the latter.

Cargill contends that the prerequisites of an agency relationship did not exist because Cargill never consented to the agency, Warren did not act on behalf of Cargill, and Cargill did not exercise control over Warren. We hold that all three elements of agency could be found in the particular circumstances of this case. By directing Warren to implement its recommendations, Cargill manifested its consent that Warren would be its agent. Warren acted on Cargill's behalf in procuring grain for Cargill as the part of its normal operations which were totally financed

23

Cargill got involved

by Cargill.[2] Further, an agency relationship was established by Cargill's interference with the internal affairs of Warren, which constituted de facto control of the elevator.

A creditor who assumes control of his debtor's business may become liable as principal for the acts of the debtor in connection with the business. It is noted in comment a to Restatement (Second) of Agency section 14 O that:

> A security holder who merely exercises a veto power over the business acts of his debtor by preventing purchases or sales above specified amounts does not thereby become a principal. However, if he takes over the management of the debtor's business either in person or through an agent, and directs what contracts may or may not be made, he becomes a principal, liable as a principal for the obligations incurred thereafter in the normal course of business by the debtor who has now become his general agent. The point at which the creditor becomes a principal is that at which he assumes de facto control over the conduct of his debtor, whatever the terms of the formal contract with his debtor may be.

A number of factors indicate Cargill's control over Warren, including the following:

1. Cargill's constant recommendations to Warren by telephone;
2. Cargill's right of first refusal on grain;
3. Warren's inability to enter into mortgages, to purchase stock or to pay dividends without Cargill's approval;
4. Cargill's right of entry onto Warren's premises to carry on periodic checks and audits;
5. Cargill's correspondence and criticism regarding Warren's finances, officers salaries and inventory;
6. Cargill's determination that Warren needed "strong paternal guidance";
7. Provision of drafts and forms to Warren upon which Cargill's name was imprinted;
8. Financing of all Warren's purchases of grain and operating expenses; and
9. Cargill's power to discontinue the financing of Warren's operations.

We recognize that some of these elements, as Cargill contends, are found in an ordinary debtor-creditor relationship. However, these factors cannot be considered in isolation, but, rather, they must be viewed in light of all the circumstances surrounding Cargill's aggressive financing of Warren.

---

2 Although the contracts with the farmers were executed by Warren, Warren paid for the grain with drafts drawn on Cargill. While this is not in itself significant, it is one factor to be taken into account in analyzing the relationship between Warren and Cargill.

It is also Cargill's position that the relationship between Cargill and Warren was that of buyer-supplier rather than principal-agent. Restatement (Second) of Agency section 14 K compares an agent with a supplier as follows:

> One who contracts to acquire property from a third person and convey it to another is the agent of the other only if it is agreed that he is to act primarily for the benefit of the other and not for himself.

According to the Restatement, factors indicating that one is a supplier, rather than an agent, are:

> (1) That he is to receive a fixed price for the property irrespective of price paid by him. This is the most important. (2) That he acts in his own name and receives the title to the property which he thereafter is to transfer. (3) That he has an independent business in buying and selling similar property.

The *amici curiae* assert that, if the jury verdict is upheld, firms and banks which have provided business loans to county elevators will decline to make further loans. The decision in this case should give no cause for such concern. We deal here with a business enterprise markedly different from an ordinary bank financing, since Cargill was an active participant in Warren's operations rather than simply a financier. Cargill's course of dealing with Warren was, by its own admission, a paternalistic relationship in which Cargill made the key economic decisions and kept Warren in existence.

Although considerable interest was paid by Warren on the loan, the reason for Cargill's financing of Warren was not to make money as a lender but, rather, to establish a source of market grain for its business. As one Cargill manager noted, "We were staying in there because we wanted the grain." For this reason, Cargill was willing to extend the credit line far beyond the amount originally allocated to Warren. It is noteworthy that Cargill was receiving significant amounts of grain and that, notwithstanding the risk that was recognized by Cargill, the operation was considered profitable.

On the whole, there was a unique fabric in the relationship between Cargill and Warren which varies from that found in normal debtor-creditor situations. We conclude that, on the facts of this case, there was sufficient evidence from which the jury could find that Cargill was the principal of Warren within the definitions of agency set forth in Restatement (Second) of Agency.

Affirmed.

GIZZI V. TEXACO, INC.

UNITED STATES COURT OF APPEALS, THIRD CIRCUIT (MCLAUGHLIN, J.)
437 F.2D 308 (1971)

The question posed on this appeal is whether the trial judge properly granted appellee Texaco's motion for a directed verdict in this personal injury action. Jurisdiction in the district court was based on diversity of citizenship and requisite amount in controversy.

Appellant Augustine Gizzi was a steady patron of a Texaco service station located on Route 130 and Chestnut Street, Westville, New Jersey. The real estate upon which the station was situated was owned by a third party and was leased to the operator of the station, Russell Hinman. Texaco owned certain pieces of equipment and also supplied the operator with the normal insignia to indicate that Texaco products were being sold there.

In June of 1965, the station operator, Hinman, interested Gizzi in a 1958 Volkswagen van, which Hinman offered to put in good working order and sell for $400. Gizzi agreed to make the purchase and Hinman commenced his work on the vehicle. The work took about two weeks and included the installation of a new master braking cylinder and a complete examination and testing of the entire braking system. On June 18, 1965 Gizzi came to the station and paid the $400. He was given a receipt for the payment and was told that the car would be ready that evening. Gizzi returned at about six o'clock, accompanied by appellant Anthony Giaccio. They took the van and then departed for Philadelphia, Pennsylvania, to pick up and deliver some air-conditioning equipment. While driving on the Schuylkill Expressway, Gizzi attempted to stop the vehicle by applying the brakes. He discovered that the brakes did not work and, as a result, the vehicle collided with the rear end of a tractor trailer causing serious injuries to both Gizzi and Giaccio.

With regard to the sale of this vehicle, no actual agency existed between Texaco and Hinman. Although most of the negotiations involved in the transaction took place at the Texaco station, the record indicates that Hinman was selling the van on his own behalf, and not on behalf of Texaco. Texaco received no portion of the proceeds. The corporation was not designated the seller on the bill of sale, title to the vehicle being listed in the name of a company located in Atlantic City, New Jersey. Gizzi did receive a Texaco credit invoice as a receipt for the cash he paid. It would seem that this was an available convenience utilized by Hinman to record the transaction.

The repair work performed by Hinman was incidental to the sale of the vehicle. He offered to put the vehicle into good working order to further induce Gizzi to purchase it. Some work was done on the van after the money had been paid on June 18 and all work on the braking system was completed prior to that date.

The theory of liability advanced by appellants below was that Texaco had clothed Hinman with apparent authority to make the necessary repairs and sell the vehicle on its behalf and that Gizzi reasonably assumed that Texaco would be responsible for any defects, especially defects in those portions of the van which were repaired or replaced by Hinman. It was further contended that Gizzi entered into the transaction relying on this apparent authority, thereby creating a situation in which Texaco was estopped from denying that an agency did in fact exist.

[handwritten margin note: Appellant wants to hold Texaco liable]

The concepts of apparent authority, and agency by estoppel are closely related. Both depend on manifestations by the alleged principal to a third person, and reasonable belief by the third person that the alleged agent is authorized to bind the principal. The manifestations of the principal may be made directly to the third person, or may be made to the community, by signs or advertising. In order for the third person to recover against the principal, he must have relied on the indicia of authority originated by the principal, and such reliance must have been reasonable under the circumstances.

In support of their theory of liability, appellants introduced evidence to show that Texaco exercised control over the activities of the service station in question. They showed that Texaco insignia and the slogan "Trust your car to the man who wears the star" were prominently displayed. It was further established that Texaco engaged in substantial national advertising, the purpose of which was to convey the impression that Texaco dealers are skilled in automotive servicing, as well as to promote Texaco products, and that this advertising was not limited to certain services or products. The record reveals that approximately 30 per cent of the Texaco dealers in the country engage in the selling of used cars and that this activity is known to and acquiesced in by the corporation. Actually, Texaco had a regional office located directly opposite the service station in question and Texaco personnel working in this office were aware of the fact that used vehicles were being sold from the station. It was further established that there were signs displayed indicating that an "Expert foreign car mechanic" was on the premises.

Appellant Gizzi testified that he was aware of the advertising engaged in by Texaco and that it had instilled in him a certain sense of confidence in the corporation and its products.

In granting Texaco's motion for a directed verdict, the court stated:

> I am convinced that as a matter of law there could not be any apparent authority on the basis of what I heard so far or what I have had the slightest glimmer that you could show, no apparent authority on the part of this operator to bind Texaco in connection with the sale of this used Volkswagen bus.
>
> In short, nobody could reasonably interpret any of these slogans or representations or indicia of control as dealing with anything more than the servicing of automobiles, and to the extent of putting gas in them and the ordinary things that are done at service stations.

That 'Trust your car to the man who wears the star' could not possibly be construed to apply to installing new brake systems or selling used cars.

We are of the opinion that the court below erred in granting the motion. Questions of apparent authority are questions of fact and are therefore for the jury to determine. On a motion for a directed verdict, and on appeal from the granting of such a motion, all evidence and testimony must be viewed in a light most favorable to the party against whom such motion is made and that party is entitled to all reasonable inferences that could be drawn from the evidence. While the evidence on behalf of appellants by no means amounted to an overwhelming case of liability, we are of the opinion that reasonable men could differ regarding it and that the issue should have been determined by the jury, after proper instructions from the court.

For the reasons stated herein, the order of the district court will be vacated and the case remanded for further proceedings consistent with this opinion.

PART B AGENCY AUTHORITY AND LIABILITY

MILL STREET CHURCH OF CHRIST V. HOGAN

COURT OF APPEALS OF KENTUCKY (HOWARD, J.)
785 S.W.3D 263 (1990)

Mill Street Church of Christ and State Automobile Mutual Insurance Company petition for review of a decision of the New Workers' Compensation Board [hereinafter "New Board"] which had reversed an earlier decision by the Old Workers' Compensation Board [hereinafter "Old Board"]. The Old Board had ruled that Samuel J. Hogan was not an employee of the Mill Street Church of Christ and was not entitled to any workers' compensation benefits. The New Board reversed and ruled that Samuel Hogan was an employee of the church.

In 1986, the Elders of the Mill Street Church of Christ decided to hire church member, Bill Hogan, to paint the church building. The Elders decided that another church member, Gary Petty, would be hired to assist if any assistance was needed. In the past, the church had hired Bill Hogan for similar jobs, and he had been allowed to hire his brother, Sam Hogan, the respondent, as a helper. Sam Hogan had earlier been a member of the church but was no longer a member.

Dr. David Waggoner, an Elder of the church, soon contacted Bill Hogan, and he accepted the job and began work. Apparently Waggoner made no mention to Bill Hogan of hiring a helper at that time. Bill Hogan painted the church by himself until he reached the baptistry portion of the church. This was a very high, difficult portion of the church to paint, and he decided that he needed help. After Bill Hogan had reached this point in his work, he discussed the matter of a helper with Dr. Waggoner at his office. According to both Dr. Waggoner and Hogan, they discussed the possibility of hiring Gary Petty to help Hogan. None of the evidence indicates that Hogan was told that he had to hire Petty. In fact, Dr. Waggoner apparently told Hogan that Petty was difficult to reach. That was basically all the discussion that these two individuals had concerning hiring a helper. None of the other Elders discussed the matter with Bill Hogan.

On December 14, 1986, Bill Hogan approached his brother, Sam, about helping him complete the job. Bill Hogan told Sam the details of the job, including the pay, and Sam accepted the job. On December 15, 1986, Sam began working. A half hour after he began, he climbed the ladder to paint a ceiling corner, and a leg of the ladder broke. Sam fell to the floor and broke his left arm. Sam was taken to the Grayson County Hospital Emergency Room where he was treated. The church Elders did not know that Bill Hogan had approached Sam Hogan to work as a helper until after the accident occurred.

After the accident, Bill Hogan reported the accident and resulting injury to Charles Payne, a church Elder and treasurer. Payne stated in a deposition that he told Bill Hogan that the church had insurance. At this time, Bill Hogan told Payne the total number of hours worked which included a half hour that Sam Hogan had worked prior to the accident. Payne issued Bill Hogan a check for all of these hours. Further, Bill Hogan did not have to use his own tools and materials in the project. The church supplied the tools, materials, and supplies necessary to complete the project. Bill purchased needed items from Dunn's Hardware Store and charged them to the church's account.

It is undisputed in this case that Mill Street Church of Christ is an insured employer under the Workers' Compensation Act. Sam Hogan filed a claim under the Workers' Compensation Act.

As part of their argument, petitioners argue the New Board also erred in finding that Bill Hogan possessed implied authority as an agent to hire Sam Hogan. Petitioners contend there was neither implied nor apparent authority in the case at bar.

It is important to distinguish implied and apparent authority before proceeding further. Implied authority is actual authority circumstantially proven which the principal actually intended the agent to possess and includes such powers as are practically necessary to carry out the duties actually delegated. Apparent authority on the other hand is not actual authority but is the authority the agent is held out by the principal as possessing. It is a matter of appearances on which third parties come to rely.

29

Petitioners attack the New Board's findings concerning implied authority. In examining whether implied authority exists, it is important to focus upon the agent's understanding of his authority. It must be determined whether the agent <u>reasonably believes</u> because of present or past conduct of the principal that the principal wishes him to act in a certain way or to have certain authority. The nature of the task or job may be another factor to consider. Implied authority may be necessary in order to implement the <u>express authority</u>. The existence of prior similar practices is one of the most important factors. Specific conduct by the principal in the past permitting the agent to exercise similar powers is crucial.

The person alleging agency and resulting authority has the burden of proving that it exists. Agency cannot be proven by a mere statement, but it can be established by circumstantial evidence including the acts and conduct of the parties such as the continuous course of conduct of the parties covering a number of successive transactions.

In considering the above factors in the case at bar, Bill Hogan had implied authority to hire Sam Hogan as his helper. First, in the past the church had allowed Bill Hogan to hire his brother or other persons whenever he needed assistance on a project. Even though the Board of Elders discussed a different arrangement this time, no mention of this discussion was ever made to Bill or Sam Hogan. In fact, the discussion between Bill Hogan and Church Elder Dr. Waggoner, indicated that Gary Petty would be difficult to reach and Bill Hogan could hire whomever he pleased. Further, Bill Hogan needed to hire an assistant to complete the job for which he had been hired. The interior of the church simply could not be painted by one person. Maintaining a safe and attractive place of worship clearly is part of the church's function, and one for which it would designate an agent to ensure that the building is properly painted and maintained.

Finally, in this case, Sam Hogan believed that Bill Hogan had the authority to hire him as had been the practice in the past. To now claim that Bill Hogan could not hire Sam Hogan as an assistant, especially when Bill Hogan had never been told this fact, would be very unfair to Sam Hogan. Sam Hogan relied on Bill Hogan's representation. The church treasurer in this case even paid Bill Hogan for the half hour of work that Sam Hogan had completed prior to the accident. Considering the above facts, we find that Sam Hogan was within the employment of the Mill Street Church of Christ at the time he was injured.

The decision of the New Workers' Compensation Board is affirmed.

THREE-SEVENTY LEASING CORPORATION V. AMPEX CORPORATION

UNITED STATES COURT OF APPEALS, FIFTH CIRCUIT (DYER, J.)
528 F.2D 993 (1976)

Three-Seventy Leasing Corporation (370) seeks damages from Ampex Corporation (Ampex) for breach of a contract to sell six computer core memories. The district court, sitting without a jury, found that there was an enforceable contract between 370 and Ampex.

Three-Seventy Leasing Corporation was formed by Joyce, at all times its only active employee, for the purpose of purchasing computer hardware from various manufacturers for lease to endusers. In August of 1972, Kays, as salesman of Ampex and friend of Joyce, initiated discussions with Joyce regarding the possibility of 370 purchasing computer equipment from Ampex. A meeting was arranged between Kays, Joyce, and Mueller, Kays' superior at Ampex. Joyce was informed at this meeting that Ampex could sell to 370 only if 370 could pass Ampex's credit requirements. Joyce informed the two that he did not think this would be a problem.

At approximately the same time, Joyce began negotiations with Electronic Data Systems (EDS), which resulted in EDS's verbal commitment to lease six units of Ampex computer core memory from 370. Desiring to close the two transactions simultaneously, Joyce continued negotiations with Kays. These negotiations resulted in a written document submitted by Kays to Joyce at the direction of Mueller. The document provided for the purchase by Joyce of six core memory units at a price of $100,000 each, with a down payment of $150,000 and the remainder to be paid over a five-year period. The document specified that delivery was to be made to EDS. The document also contained a signature block for a representative of 370 and a signature block for a representative of Ampex.

Joyce received this document about November 3, 1972, and executed it on November 6, 1972. The document was never executed by a representative of Ampex. This document forms the core of the present controversy. 370 argues that the document was an offer to sell by Ampex, which was accepted upon Joyce's signature. Ampex contends that the document was nothing more than a solicitation which became an offer to purchase upon execution by Joyce, and that this offer was never accepted by Ampex. 370 counters by arguing in the alternative that even if the document when signed by Joyce was only an offer to purchase, the offer was later accepted by representatives of Ampex.

The district court, in concluding that there existed an enforceable contract, made no determination as to whether the document described above was an offer to sell accepted by Joyce's signature, or an offer to purchase when signed by Joyce which was later accepted by Ampex.

We reject the first alternative as being without evidentiary support. Elemental principles demand that there be a meeting of the minds and a communication that each party has consented to the terms of the agreement in order for a contract to exist. There is no evidence, either written or oral, other than the document itself, which shows that Ampex had the requisite intent necessary to the formation of a contract prior to November 6, 1972, the date the document was executed by Joyce. And the document on its face does not supply that intent. Rather, the fact that the document had a signature block for a representative of Ampex which was unsigned at the time it was submitted to Joyce, in the absence of other evidence, negates any interpretation that Ampex intended this to be an offer to Joyce, without any further acts necessary on the part of Ampex.

Thus, the document, when signed by Joyce, at most constituted an offer by him to purchase. In order for there to be a valid contract, we must therefore find some act of acceptance on the part of Ampex. On November 9, 1972, Mueller issued an intra-office memorandum which stated in part that "on November 3, 1972, Ampex was awarded an Agreement by Three-Seventy Leasing, Dallas, Texas, for the purchase of six (6) ARM-3360 Memory Units", to be installed at EDS. This memorandum further informed those concerned at Ampex of Joyce's request that all contact with 370 be handled through Kays. On November 17, 1972, Kays sent a letter to Joyce which confirmed the delivery dates for the memory units.[3] We conclude, in light of the circumstances surrounding these negotiations, that the district court was not clearly erroneous when it found that Kays had apparent authority to accept Joyce's offer on behalf of Ampex, and we further conclude that the November 17 letter, in these circumstances, can reasonably be interpreted to be an <u>acceptance</u>.

An agent has apparent authority sufficient to bind the principal when the principal acts in such a manner as would lead a reasonably prudent person to suppose that the agent had the authority he purports to exercise. Further, absent knowledge on the part of third parties to the contrary, an agent has the apparent authority to do those things which are <u>usual and proper</u> to the conduct of the business which he is employed to conduct.

In this case, Kays was employed by Ampex in the capacity of a salesman. It is certainly reasonable for third parties to presume that one employed as salesman has the authority to bind his

---

3   That letter stated:

   Dear John:

         With regard to delivery of equipment purchased by Three-Seventy Leasing: Ampex will ship three (3) million bytes of ARM-3360 magnetic core in sufficient time to install 1 1/2 million bytes the weekend of December 16, 1972. The remaining balance of 1 1/2 million bytes will be installed by the weekend of December 30, 1972.

         The equipment will be installed in Camphill, Pennsylvania at a predetermined site by Electronic Data Systems.

   Regards,

   Thomas C. Kays

   Sales Representative

32

employer to sell. And Ampex did nothing to dispel this reasonable inference. Rather, its actions and inactions provided a further basis for this belief. First, Kays, at the direction of Mueller, submitted the controversial document to Joyce for signature. The document contained a space for signature by an Ampex representative. Nothing in the document suggests that Kays did not have authority to sign it on behalf of Ampex.[4] Second, Joyce indicated to Kays and Mueller that he wished all communications to be channeled through Kays. Mueller agreed, and acknowledged this in the November 9 intra-company memorandum. Neither Mueller, nor anyone else at Ampex ever informed Joyce that communication regarding acceptance would come through anyone other than Kays. In light of this request and Ampex's agreement, Joyce could reasonably expect that Kays would speak for the company.

Various individuals in the Ampex hierarchy testified at trial that only the contract manager or other supervisor in the company's contract department had authority to sign a contract on behalf of Ampex. However, there is no evidence that this limitation was ever communicated to Joyce in any manner. Absent knowledge of such a limitation by third parties, that limitation will not bar a claim of apparent authority.

Thus, when Joyce received Kays' November 17 letter, he had every reason to believe, based upon Ampex's prior actions, that Kays spoke on behalf of the company. We thus agree with the district court's finding that Kays had apparent authority to act for Ampex.

Having determined that Kays had apparent authority to bind Ampex, we further conclude that his letter of November 17, in light of the pattern of negotiations, could reasonably be interpreted as a promise to ship the six memory units on the dates specified in the letter and on the terms previously set out in the document executed by Joyce and submitted to Ampex. The district court's finding that a contract was formed is therefore not clearly erroneous.

Affirmed in part and reversed in part.

WATTEAU V. FENWICK

HIGH COURT OF ENGLAND & WALES
QUEEN'S BENCH DIVISION (COLERIDGE, C.J.)
1 Q.B. 346 (1892)

APPEAL from the decision of the county court judge of Middlesborough.

---

4   It would have been an easy matter to provide in the document that only certain officers of Ampex had authority to sign on its behalf. Any inference to the contrary resulting from Ampex's failure to specify such a limitation must weigh against Ampex.

From the evidence it appeared that one Humble had carried on business at a beerhouse called the Victoria Hotel, at Stockton-on-Tees, which business he had transferred to the defendants, a firm of brewers, some years before the present action. After the transfer of the business, Humble remained as defendants' manager; but the licence was always taken out in Humble's name, and his name was painted over the door. Under the terms of the agreement made between Humble and the defendants, the former had no authority to buy any goods for the business except bottled ales and mineral waters; all other goods required were to be supplied by the defendants themselves. The action was brought to recover the price of goods delivered at the Victoria Hotel over some years, for which it was admitted that the plaintiff gave credit to Humble only: they consisted of cigars, bovril, and other articles. The learned judge allowed the claim for the cigars and bovril only, and gave judgment for the plaintiff for 22l. 12s. 6d. The defendants appealed.

Finlay, Q.C., for the defendants: The decision of the county court judge was wrong. The liability of a principal for the acts of his agent, done contrary to his secret instructions, depends upon his holding him out as his agent—that is, upon the agent being clothed with an apparent authority to act for his principal. Where, therefore, a man carries on business in his own name through a manager, he holds out his own credit, and would be liable for goods supplied even where the manager exceeded his authority. But where, as in the present case, there is no holding out by the principal, but the business is carried on in the agent's name and the goods are supplied on his credit, a person wishing to go behind the agent and make the principal liable must [show] an agency in fact.

Lord Coleridge, C.J.: Cannot you, in such a case, sue the undisclosed principal on discovering him?

Finlay, Q.C., for the defendants: Only where the act done by the agent is within the scope of his agency; not where there has been an excess of authority. Where any one has been held out by the principal as his agent, there is a contract with the principal by estoppel, however much the agent may have exceeded his authority; where there has been no holding out, proof must be given of an agency in fact in order to make the principal liable.

Boydell Houghton, for the plaintiff: The defendants are liable in the present action. They are in fact undisclosed principals, who instead of carrying on the business in their own names employed a manager to carry it on for them, and clothed him with authority to do what was necessary to carry on the business. The case depends upon the same principles as *Edmunds v. Bushell*, where the manager of a business which was carried on in his own name with the addition "and Co." accepted a bill of exchange, notwithstanding a stipulation in the agreement with his principal that he should not accept bills; and the Court held that the principal was liable to an indorsee who took the bill without any knowledge of the relations between the principal and agent. In that case there was no holding out of the manager as an agent; it was the simple case of an agent being allowed to act as the ostensible principal without any disclosure to the world of there being any one behind him. Here the defendants have so conducted themselves as to enable their agent to hold himself out to the world as the proprietor of their business, and they are clearly undisclosed principals: *Ramazotti v. Bowring.* All that the plaintiff has to do, therefore, in order to charge the principals, is to [show] that the goods supplied were such as were ordinarily used in the business—that is to say, that they were within the reasonable scope of the agent's authority.

LORD COLERIDGE, C.J.
WILLS, J.
The plaintiff sues the defendants for the price of cigars supplied to the Victoria Hotel, Stockton-upon-Tees. The house was kept, not by the defendants, but by a person named Humble, whose name was over the door. The plaintiff gave credit to Humble, and to him alone, and had never heard of the defendants. The business, however, was really the defendants', and they had put Humble into it to manage it for them, and had forbidden him to buy cigars on credit. The cigars, however, were such as would usually be supplied to and dealt in at such an establishment. The learned county court judge held that the defendants were liable. I am of the opinion that he was right.

There seems to be less of direct authority on the subject than one would expect. But I think that the Lord Chief Justice during the argument laid down the correct principle, viz., once it is established that the defendant was the real principal, the ordinary doctrine as to principal and agent applies—that the principal is liable for all the acts of the agent which are within the authority usually confided to an agent of that character, notwithstanding limitations, as between the principal and the agent, put upon that authority. It is said that it is only so where there has been a holding out of authority—which cannot be said of a case where the person supplying the goods knew nothing of the existence of a principal. But I do not think so. Otherwise, in every case of undisclosed principal, or at least in every case where the fact of there being a principal was undisclosed, the secret limitation of authority would prevail and defeat the action of the person dealing with the agent and then discovering that he was an agent and had a principal.

But in the case of a dormant partner it is clear law that no limitation of authority as between the dormant and active partner will avail the dormant partner as to things within the ordinary authority of a partner. The law of partnership is, on such a question, nothing but a branch of the general law of principal and agent, and it appears to me to be undisputed and conclusive on the point now under discussion.

The principle laid down by the Lord Chief Justice, and acted upon by the learned county court judge, appears to be identical with that enunciated in the judgments of Cockburn, C.J., and Mellor, J., in *Edmunds v. Bushell,* the circumstances of which case, though not identical with those of the present, come very near to them. There was no holding out, as the plaintiff knew nothing of the defendant. I appreciate the distinction drawn by Mr. Finlay in his argument, but the principle laid down in the judgments referred to, if correct, abundantly covers the present case. I cannot find that any doubt has ever been expressed that it is correct, and I think it is right, and that very mischievous consequences would often result if that principle were not upheld.

In my opinion this appeal ought to be dismissed with costs.

Appeal dismissed.

BOTTICELLO V. STEFANOVICZ

SUPREME COURT OF CONNECTICUT (PETERS, J.)
411 A.2D 16 (1979)

This case concerns the enforceability of an agreement for the sale of real property when that agreement has been executed by a person owning only an undivided half interest in the property. The plaintiff brought an action for specific performance against the defendants to compel conveyance of their land in accordance with the terms of a lease and option-to-purchase agreement signed by one of the defendants.

The finding of the trial court discloses the following undisputed facts: The defendants, Mary and Walter Stefanovicz in 1943 acquired as tenants in common a farm situated in the towns of Colchester and Lebanon. In the fall of 1965, the plaintiff, Anthony Botticello, became interested in the property. When he first visited the farm, Walter advised him that the asking price was $100,000. The following January, the plaintiff again visited the farm and made a counteroffer of $75,000. At that time, Mary stated that there was "no way" she could sell it for that amount. Ultimately the plaintiff and Walter agreed upon a price of $85,000 for a lease with an option to purchase; during these negotiations, Mary stated that she would not sell the property for less than that amount.

The informal agreement was finalized with the assistance of counsel for both Walter and the plaintiff. The agreement was drawn up by Walter's attorney after consultation with Walter and the plaintiff; it was then sent to, and modified by, the plaintiff's attorney. The agreement was signed by Walter and by the plaintiff. Neither the plaintiff nor his attorney, nor Walter's attorney, was then aware of the fact that Walter did not own the property outright. The plaintiff, although a successful businessman with considerable experience in real estate never requested his attorney to do a title search of any kind, and consequently no title search was done. Walter never represented to the plaintiff or the plaintiff's attorney, or to his own attorney, that he was acting for his wife, as her agent. Mary's part ownership came to light in 1968, when a third party sought an easement over the land in question.

Shortly after the execution of the lease and option-to-purchase agreement, the plaintiff took possession of the property. He made substantial improvements on the property and, in 1971, properly exercised his option to purchase. When the defendants refused to honor the option agreement, the plaintiff commenced the present action against both Mary and Walter, seeking specific performance, possession of the premises, and damages.

The trial court found the issues for the plaintiff and ordered specific performance of the option-to-purchase agreement. In their appeal, the defendants claim that Mary was never a party to the agreement, and its terms may therefore not be enforced as to her.

The plaintiff alleged, and the trial court agreed, that although Mary was not a party to the lease and option-to-purchase agreement, its terms were nonetheless binding upon her because Walter acted as her authorized agent in the negotiations, discussions, and execution of the written agreement. The defendants have attacked several findings of fact and conclusions of law, claiming that the underlying facts and applicable law do not support the court's conclusion of agency. We agree.

Agency is defined as the fiduciary relationship which results from manifestation of consent by one person to another that the other shall act on his behalf and subject to this control, and consent by the other so to act. Thus, the three elements required to show the existence of an agency relationship include: (1) a manifestation by the principal that the agent will act for him; (2) acceptance by the agent of the undertaking; and (3) an understanding between the parties that the principal will be in control of the undertaking.

agency elements

The existence of an agency relationship is a question of fact. The burden of proving agency is on the plaintiff and it must be proven by a fair preponderance of the evidence. Marital status cannot in and of itself prove the agency relationship. Nor does the fact that the defendants owned the land jointly make one the agent for the other.

marriage ≠ agency

The facts set forth in the court's finding are wholly insufficient to support the court's conclusion that Walter acted as Mary's authorized agent in the discussions concerning the sale of their farm and in the execution of the written agreement. The finding indicates that when the farm was purchased, and when the couple transferred property to their sons, Walter handled many of the business aspects, including making payments for taxes, insurance, and mortgage. The finding also discloses that Mary and Walter discussed the sale of the farm, and that Mary remarked that she would not sell it for $75,000, and would not sell it for less than $85,000. A statement that one will not sell for less than a certain amount is by no means the equivalent of an agreement to sell for that amount. Moreover, the fact that one spouse tends more to business matters than the other does not, absent other evidence of agreement or authorization, constitute the delegation of power as to an agent. What is most damaging to the plaintiff's case is the court's uncontradicted finding that, although Mary may have acquiesced in Walter's handling of many business matters, Walter never signed any documents as agent for Mary prior to 1966. Mary had consistently signed any deed, mortgage, or mortgage note in connection with their jointly held property.

Mary always signed things that involved her

In light of the foregoing, it is clear that the facts found by the court fail to support its conclusion that Walter acted as Mary's authorized agent, and the conclusion therefore cannot stand.

The plaintiff argues, alternatively, that even if no agency relationship existed at the time the agreement was signed, Mary was bound by the contract executed by her husband because she ratified its terms by her subsequent conduct. The trial court accepted this alternative argument as well, concluding that Mary had ratified the agreement by receiving and accepting payments from the plaintiff, and by acquiescing in his substantial improvements to the farm. The underlying facts, however, do not support the conclusion of ratification.

Ratification is defined as the affirmance by a person of a prior act which did not bind him but which was done or professedly done on his account. Ratification requires acceptance of the results of the act with an intent to ratify, and with full knowledge of all the material circumstances.

The finding neither indicates an intent by Mary to ratify the agreement, nor establishes her knowledge of all the material circumstances surrounding the deal. At most, Mary observed the plaintiff occupying and improving the land, received rental payments from the plaintiff from time to time, knew that she had an interest in the property, and knew that the use, occupancy, and rentals were pursuant to a written agreement she had not signed. None of these facts is sufficient to support the conclusion that Mary ratified the agreement and thus bound herself to its terms. It is undisputed that Walter had the power to lease his own undivided one-half interest in the property and the facts found by the trial court could be referable to that fact alone. Moreover, the fact that the rental payments were used for "family" purposes indicates nothing more than one spouse providing for the other.

The plaintiff makes the further argument that Mary ratified the agreement simply by receiving its benefits and by failing to repudiate it. The plaintiff fails to recognize that before the receipt of benefits may constitute ratification, the other requisites for ratification must first be present. Thus if the original transaction was not purported to be done on account of the principal, the fact that the principal receives its proceeds does not make him a party to it. Since Walter at no time purported to be acting on his wife's behalf, as is essential to effective subsequent ratification, Mary is not bound by the terms of the agreement, and specific performance cannot be ordered as to her.

We turn now to the question of relief. In view of our holding that Mary never authorized her husband to act as her agent for any purpose connected with the lease and option-to-purchase agreement, recovery against her is precluded. As to Walter, the fact that his ownership was restricted to an undivided one-half interest in no way limited his capacity to contract. He contracted to convey full title and for breach of that contract he may be held liable. The facts of the case are sufficient to furnish a basis for relief to the plaintiff by specific performance or by damages.

There is error as to the judgment against the defendant Mary Stefanovicz; the judgment as to her is set aside and the case remanded with direction to render judgment in her favor. As to the defendant Walter Stefanovicz, there is error only as to the remedy ordered. The judgment as to him is set aside and the case remanded for a new trial limited to the form of relief.

38

HODDESON V. KOOS BROS.

SUPREME COURT OF NEW JERSEY, APPELLATE DIVISION (JAYNE, J.)
135 A.2D 702 (1957)

The occurrence which engages our present attention is a little more than conventionally unconventional in the common course of trade. Old questions appear in new styles. A digest of the story told by Mrs. Hoddeson will be informative and perhaps admonitory to the unwary shopper.

The plaintiff Mrs. Hoddeson was acquainted with the spacious furniture store conducted by the defendant, Koos Bros., a corporation. On a previous observational visit, her eyes had fallen upon certain articles of bedroom furniture which she ardently desired to acquire for her home. It has been said that 'the sea hath bounds but deep desire hath none.' Her sympathetic mother liberated her from the grasp of despair and bestowed upon her a gift of $165 with which to consummate the purchase.

It was in the forenoon of August 22, 1956 that Mrs. Hoddeson, accompanied by her aunt and four children, happily journeyed from her home in South River to the defendant's store to attain her objective. Upon entering, she was greeted by a tall man with dark hair frosted at the temples and clad in a light gray suit. He inquired if he could be of assistance, and she informed him specifically of her mission. Whereupon he immediately guided her, her aunt, and the flock to the mirror then on display and priced at $29 which Mrs. Hoddeson identified, and next to the location of the designated bedroom furniture which she had described.

Upon confirming her selections the man withdrew from his pocket a small pad or paper upon which he presumably recorded her order and calculated the total purchase price to be $168.50. Mrs. Hoddeson handed to him the $168.50 in cash. He informed her the articles other than those on display were not in stock, and that reproductions would upon notice be delivered to her in September. Alas, she omitted to request from him a receipt for her cash disbursement. The transaction consumed in time a period from 30 to 40 minutes.

Mrs. Hoddeson impatiently awaited the delivery of the articles of furniture, but a span of time beyond the assured date of delivery elapsed, which motivated her to inquire of the defendant the cause of the unexpected delay. Sorrowful, indeed, was she to learn from the defendant that its records failed to disclose any such sale to her and any such monetary credit in payment.

It eventuated that Mrs. Hoddeson and her aunt were subsequently unable positively to recognize among the defendant's regularly employed salesmen the individual with whom Mrs. Hoddeson had arranged for the purchase, although when she and her aunt were afforded the opportunities to gaze intently at one of the five salesmen assigned to that department of the store, both indicated a resemblance of one of them to the purported salesman, but frankly acknowledged the incertitude of their identification. The defendant's records revealed that the salesman bearing the alleged resemblance was on vacation and hence presumably absent from the store during the week of August 22, 1956.

As you will at this point surmise, the insistence of the defendant at the trial was that the person who served Mrs. Hoddeson was an impostor deceitfully impersonating a salesman of the defendant without the latter's knowledge.

It was additionally disclosed by the testimony that a relatively large number of salesmen were employed at the defendant's store, and that since they were remunerated in part on a sales commission basis, there existed considerable rivalry among them to serve incoming customers; hence the improbability of the unnoticed intrusion of an impersonator.

Fortifying the defense, each of the five salesmen, but not every salesman, denied that he had attended Mrs. Hoddeson on the stated occasion, and the defendant's comptroller and credit manager verified the absence in the store records of any notation of the alleged sale and of the receipt of the stated cash payment.

Where a party seeks to impose liability upon an alleged principal on a contract made by an alleged agent, as here, the party must assume the obligation of proving the agency relationship. It is not the burden of the alleged principal to disprove it.

Concisely stated, the liability of a principal to third parties for the acts of an agent may be shown by proof disclosing (1) express or real authority which has been definitely granted; (2) implied authority, that is, to do all that is proper, customarily incidental and reasonably appropriate to the exercise of the authority granted; and (3) apparent authority, such as where the principal by words, conduct, or other indicative manifestations has 'held out' the person to be his agent.

Obviously the plaintiffs' evidence in the present action does not substantiate the existence of any basic express authority or project any question implicating implied authority. The point here debated is whether or not the evidence circumstantiates the presence of apparent authority, and it is at this very point we come face to face with the general rule of law that the apparency and appearance of authority must be shown to have been created by the manifestations of the alleged principal, and not alone and solely by proof of those of the supposed agent. Assuredly the law cannot permit apparent authority to be established by the mere proof that a mountebank in fact exercised it.

The plaintiffs here prosecuted an action in assumpsit, alleging a privity of contract with the defendant through the relationship of agency between the latter and the salesman. The inadequacy of the evidence to prove the alleged essential element of agency obliges us to reverse the judgment.

no evidence of privity between D & salesman

But prelude, as we may do here, a case in which a reconciliation of the factual circumstances disclosed by the evidence of both the plaintiffs and the defendant exhibits an unalleged and an undetermined justiciable cause of action, should the plaintiffs, by our reversal of the judgment, be conclusively denied the opportunity, auspicious or not, appropriately and not mistakenly, to seek judicial relief?

Let us hypothesize for the purposes of our present comments that the acting salesman was not in fact an employee of the defendant, yet he behaved and deported himself during the stated period in the business establishment of the defendant in the manner described by the evidence adduced on behalf of the plaintiffs, would the defendant be immune as a matter of law from liability for the plaintiffs' loss? The tincture of estoppel that gives color to instances of apparent authority might in the law operate likewise to preclude a defendant's denial of liability. It matters little whether for immediate purposes we entitle or characterize the principle of law in such cases as "agency by estoppel" or "a tortious dereliction of duty owed to an invited customer." That which we have in mind are the unique occurrences where solely through the lack of the proprietor's reasonable surveillance and supervision an impostor falsely impersonates in the place of business an agent or servant of his. Certainly the proprietor's duty of care and precaution for the safety and security of the customer encompasses more than the diligent observance and removal of banana peels from the aisles. Broadly stated, the duty of the proprietor also encircles the exercise of reasonable care and vigilance to protect the customer from loss occasioned by the deceptions of an apparent salesman. The rule that those who bargain without inquiry with an apparent agent do so at the risk and peril of an absence of the agent's authority has a patently impracticable application to the customers who patronize our modern department stores.

Our concept of the modern law is that where a proprietor of a place of business by his dereliction of duty enables one who is not his agent conspicuously to act as such and ostensibly to transact the proprietor's business with a patron in the establishment, the appearances being of such a character as to lead a person of ordinary prudence and circumspection to believe that the impostor was in truth the proprietor's agent, in such circumstances the law will not permit the proprietor defensively to avail himself of the impostor's lack of authority and thus escape liability for the consequential loss thereby sustained by the customer.

Let it not be inferred from our remarks that we have derived from the record before us a conviction that the defendant in the present case was heedless of its duty, that Mrs. Hoddeson acted with ordinary prudence, or that the factual circumstances were as represented at the trial.

In reversing the judgment under review, the interests of justice seem to us to recommend the allowance of a new trial with the privilege accorded the plaintiffs to reconstruct the architecture of their complaint appropriately to project for determination the justiciable issue to which, in view of the inquisitive object of the present appeal, we have alluded. We do not in the exercise of our modern processes of appellate review permit the formalities of a pleading of themselves to defeat the substantial opportunities of the parties.

Reversed and new trial allowed.

CHAPTER THREE

UNDERSTANDING PARTNERSHIPS

INTRODUCTION

Having concluded our introduction to the law of agency, we now turn our attention to the second of what are traditionally thought of as "unincorporated entities"—namely, partnerships.

Like agency, partnerships are created and maintained through intent; they do not require legal notice or other formal action to exist. Indeed, partnerships comprise a sort of super-agency. It is an oft-repeated adage that every partner is both the agent and principal of every other partner. Ominously, this means that every partner can bind the partnership and that every partner is liable for the debts (and torts) of every other associated partner. In practice, this can mean that a wealthy partner serves as the de *facto* guarantor of her poorer partners' far-flung business affairs—an unpleasant prospect indeed.

With this background in mind, we begin our study of partnerships where we began our study of agency. We examine the rules that determine when the law should deem a relationship between two or more persons to constitute something greater than the sum of its parts. Of course, business actors can become partners purposefully by shaking hands and saying something obvious like "Let's be partners." However, they can also become partners by behaving as such, whether or not they intended the particular legal consequences that ensue. In order to better understand the application of these principles, we address in Part A a question similar to that posed at the beginning of Chapter Two: when should two parties be considered partners, such that the one partner becomes liable for the debts of the other?

In the remaining parts of this chapter, we turn to the default rules that govern the relationship between partners. Here, we look at the management rights of partners, their duties toward one another, the manner in which profits and losses are allocated among the partners, and the allowable methods for transferring partnership interests and/or terminating a partnership.

As you read this material, consider the architecture of business law. The logic of partnerships, for example, appears reasonable on its face. Indeed, it can be difficult to imagine any alternative regime. However, when taken to its natural conclusion, partnership logic often creates results that neither party would have elected had they considered the matter. What is it about partnership law that seems to lead inexorably to a negative outcome? Why establish and enforce default rules that the parties invariably find surprising (and usually unpleasant)?

Consider, as well, the significance of the fiduciary duties established in the pivotal case of *Meinhard v. Salmon.* Judge Cardozo's opinion predates the publication of the Berle and Means theory of agency costs yet appears to address the same concerns. Regardless of any other rule or agreement, Cardozo mandates that all partners must treat one another with "the punctilio of an honor the most sensitive." This is a concept he borrows from the law of trusts and incorporates whole cloth into the regulation of for-profit businesses. Ask yourself why (and whether) such a rule is necessary and how it impacts the behavior of business partners. Also of importance is the question of whether fiduciary duties should be waivable, and if so, when, and by whom?

At the end of this chapter, you will be able to identify the factors that give rise to an involuntary partnership, thus enabling you to advise clients about how to properly structure relationships so as to avoid an undesirable result. You will also have an understanding of the default rules that apply to partners vis-à-vis one another. This latter set of rules tends to be of most interest to litigators, as it is seldom advisable to choose to form a partnership. Rather, these rules generally come into play when two parties, acting as partners, enter into a dispute with one another or with a third party. In such a case, because there are no agreed-upon contract terms, the dispute must be resolved with reference to the default rules contained in the law of partnerships.

PARTNERSHIP FORMATION PART A

REVISED UNIFORM PARTNERSHIP ACT[1]

SECTION 101(6). DEFINITIONS

"Partnership" means an association of two or more persons to carry on as co-owners a business for profit formed under Section 202, predecessor law, or comparable law of another jurisdiction.

SECTION 202(a). FORMATION OF PARTNERSHIP

Except as otherwise provided ... the association of two or more persons to carry on as co-owners a business for profit forms a partnership, whether or not the persons intend to form a partnership.

MARTIN V. PEYTON

COURT OF APPEALS OF NEW YORK (PER CURIAM)
246 N.Y. 213 (1927)

Partnership results from contract, express or implied. If denied it may be proved by the production of some written instrument; by testimony as to some conversation; by circumstantial evidence. If nothing else appears the receipt by the defendant of a share of the profits of the business is enough.

Assuming some written contract between the parties the question may arise whether it creates a partnership. If it be complete; if it expresses in good faith the full understanding and obligation of the parties, then it is for the court to say whether a partnership exists.

In the case before us the claim that the defendants became partners in the firm of Knauth, Nachod & Kuhne, doing business as bankers and brokers, depends upon the interpretation of certain instruments. There is nothing in their subsequent acts determinative of or indeed material upon this question. And we are relieved of questions that sometimes arise. "The plaintiff's position is not," we are told, "that the agreements of June 4, 1921, were a false expression or incomplete expression of the intention of the parties. We say that they express defendants' intention and that that intention was to create a relationship which as a matter of law constitutes a partnership."

Nor may the claim of the plaintiff be rested on any question of estoppel. "The plaintiff's claim," he stipulates, "is a claim of actual partnership, not of partnership by estoppel."

Remitted then, as we are, to the documents themselves, we refer to circumstances surrounding their execution only so far as is necessary to make them intelligible. And we are to remember that although the intention of the parties to avoid liability as partners is clear, although in language precise and definite they deny any design to then join the firm of K. N. & K.; although they say their interests in profits should be construed merely as a measure of compensation for loans, not an interest in profits as such; although they provide that they shall not be liable for any losses or treated as partners, the question still remains whether in fact they agree to so associate themselves with the firm as to "carry on as co-owners a business for profit."

In the spring of 1921 the firm of K. N. & K. found itself in financial difficulties. John R. Hall was one of the partners. He was a friend of Mr. Peyton. From him he obtained the loan of almost $500,000 of Liberty bonds, which K. N. & K. might use as collateral to secure bank advances. This, however, was not sufficient. The firm and its members had engaged in unwise speculations, and it was deeply involved. Mr. Hall was also intimately acquainted with George W. Perkins, Jr., and with Edward W. Freeman. He also knew Mrs. Peyton and Mrs. Perkins and Mrs. Freeman. All were anxious to help him. He, therefore, representing K. N. & K., entered into negotiations with them. While they were pending a proposition was made that Mr. Peyton, Mr. Perkins and Mr. Freeman or some of them should become partners. It met a decided refusal. Finally an agreement was reached. It is expressed in three documents, executed on the same day, all a part of the one transaction. They were drawn with care and are unambiguous. We shall refer to them as "the agreement," "the indenture," and "the option."

We have no doubt as to their general purpose. The respondents were to loan K. N. & K. $2,500,000 worth of liquid securities, which were to be returned to them on or before April 15, 1923. The firm might hypothecate them to secure loans totalling $2,000,000, using the proceeds as its business necessities required. To insure respondents against loss K. N. & K. were to turn over to them a large number of their own securities which may have been valuable, but which were of so speculative a nature that they could not be used as collateral for bank loans. In compensation for the loan the respondents were to receive 40 per cent of the profits of the firm until the return was made, not exceeding, however, $500,000 and not less than $100,000. Merely because the transaction involved the transfer of securities and not of cash does not prevent its being a loan within the meaning of section 11. The respondents also were given an option to join the firm if they or any of them expressed a desire to do so before June 4, 1923.

Many other detailed agreements are contained in the papers. Are they such as may be properly inserted to protect the lenders? Or do they go further? Whatever their purpose, did they in truth associate the respondents with the firm so that they and it together thereafter carried on as co-owners a business for profit? The answer depends upon an analysis of these various provisions.

As representing the lenders, Mr. Peyton and Mr. Freeman are called "trustees." The loaned securities when used as collateral are not to be mingled with other securities of K. N. & K., and the trustees at all times are to be kept informed of all transactions affecting them. To them shall be paid all dividends and income accruing therefrom. They may also substitute for any of the securities loaned securities of equal value. With their consent the firm may sell any of its securities held by the respondents, the proceeds to go, however, to the trustees. In other similar ways the trustees may deal with these same securities, but the securities loaned shall always be sufficient in value to permit of their hypothecation for $2,000,000. If they rise in price the excess may be withdrawn by the defendants. If they fall they shall make good the deficiency.

So far there is no hint that the transaction is not a loan of securities with a provision for compensation. Later a somewhat closer connection with the firm appears. Until the securities are returned the directing management of the firm is to be in the hands of John R. Hall, and his life is to be insured for $1,000,000, and the policies are to be assigned as further collateral security to the trustees. These requirements are not unnatural. Hall was the one known and trusted by the defendants. Their acquaintance with the other members of the firm was of the slightest. These others had brought an old and established business to the verge of bankruptcy. As the respondents knew, they also had engaged in unsafe speculation. The respondents were about to loan $2,500,000 of good securities. As collateral they were to receive others of problematical value. What they required seems but ordinary caution. Nor does it imply an association in the business.

The trustees are to be kept advised as to the conduct of the business and consulted as to important matters. They may inspect the firm books and are entitled to any information they think important. Finally they may veto any business they think highly speculative or injurious. Again we hold this but a proper precaution to safeguard the loan. The trustees may not initiate any transaction as a partner may do. They may not bind the firm by any action of their own. Under the circumstances the safety of the loan depended upon the business success of K. N. & K. This success was likely to be compromised by the inclination of its members to engage in speculation. No longer, if the respondents were to be protected, should it be allowed. The trustees, therefore, might prohibit it, and that their prohibition might be effective, information was to be furnished them. Not dissimilar agreements have been held proper to guard the interests of the lender.

As further security each member of K. N. & K. is to assign to the trustees their interest in the firm. No loan by the firm to any member is permitted and the amount each may draw is fixed. No other distribution of profits is to be made. So that realized profits may be calculated the existing capital is stated to be $700,000, and profits are to be realized as promptly as good business practice will permit. In case the trustees think this is not done, the question is left to them and to Mr. Hall, and if they differ then to an arbitrator. There is no obligation that the firm shall continue the business. It may dissolve at any time. Again we conclude there is nothing here not properly adapted to secure the interest of the respondents as lenders. If their compensation is dependent on a percentage of the profits still provision must be made to define what these profits shall be.

The "indenture" is substantially a mortgage of the collateral delivered by K. N. & K. to the trustees to secure the performance of the "agreement." It certainly does not strengthen the claim that the respondents were partners.

Finally we have the "option." It permits the respondents or any of them or their assignees or nominees to enter the firm at a later date if they desire to do so by buying 50 per cent or less of the interests therein of all or any of the members at a stated price. Or a corporation may, if the respondents and the members agree, be formed in place of the firm. Meanwhile, apparently with the design of protecting the firm business against improper or ill-judged action which might render the option valueless, each member of the firm is to place his resignation in the hands of Mr. Hall. If at any time he and the trustees agree that such resignation should be accepted, that member shall then retire, receiving the value of his interest calculated as of the date of such retirement.

This last provision is somewhat unusual, yet it is not enough in itself to show that on June 4, 1921, a present partnership was created nor taking these various papers as a whole do we reach such a result. It is quite true that even if one or two or three like provisions contained in such a contract do not require this conclusion, yet it is also true that when taken together a point may come where stipulations immaterial separately cover so wide a field that we should hold a partnership exists. As in other branches of the law a question of degree is often the determining factor. Here that point has not been reached.

The judgment appealed from should be affirmed, with costs.

PART B PARTNERSHIP MANAGEMENT

REVISED UNIFORM PARTNERSHIP ACT[2]

SECTION 301. PARTNER AGENT OF PARTNERSHIP

(1) Each partner is an agent of the partnership for the purpose of its business. An act of a partner, including the execution of an instrument in the partnership name, for apparently carrying on in the ordinary course the partnership business or business of the kind carried on by the partnership binds the partnership, unless the partner had no authority to act for the partnership in the particular matter and the person with whom the partner was dealing knew or had received a notification that the partner lacked authority.

---

2   National Conference of Commissioners on Uniform State Laws, "Revised Uniform Partnership Act." Copyright © 1997 by National Conference of Commissioners on Uniform State Laws. Reprinted with permission.

(2) An act of a partner which is not apparently for carrying on in the ordinary course the partnership business or business of the kind carried on by the partnership binds the partnership only if the act was authorized by the other partners.

SECTION 306. PARTNER'S LIABILITY

(a) Except as otherwise provided … all partners are liable jointly and severally for all obligations of the partnership unless otherwise agreed by the claimant or provided by law.

(b) A person admitted as a partner into an existing partnership is not personally liable for any partnership obligation incurred before the person's admission as a partner.

SECTION 401(j). PARTNER'S RIGHTS AND DUTIES

A difference arising as to a matter in the ordinary course of business of a partnership may be decided by a majority of thee partners. An act outside the ordinary course of business of a partnership and an amendment to the partnership agreement may be undertaken only with the consent of all the partners.

SMITH V. DIXON

SUPREME COURT OF ARKANSAS (HOLT, J.)
386 S.W.2D 244 (1965)

The appellee, as purchaser, brought this action against appellants, as sellers, for the specific performance of a contract for the sale of realty and in the alternative sought damages for nonperformance of the contract.

The appellants are E. F. Smith, his wife, and their children and spouses. This entire family constitutes a business firm known as E. F. Smith & Sons, A Partnership. The "Contract For Sale Of Realty With Lease" was signed by one of the appellants, W. R. Smith, on behalf of the family partnership.

By the terms of the contract, executed in March 1962, the partnership agreed to sell the 750 acre "Cracraft" plantation for $200,000.00 and convey title to the appellee on January 3, 1963. In the interim, by the lease provisions, the appellee took possession, farmed, and improved a portion of the property. Upon refusal of the appellants to convey the land as recited in the contract, the appellee instituted this action. The chancellor denied specific performance and awarded appellee special damages in the amount of $11,512.73.

The partnership was created a short time after the lands in controversy were acquired by the family in 1951. The court found that:

> Soon after the purchase of "Cracraft" and the "Sterling Place," the Smiths, at the suggestion and on the recommendation of the financial institutions, who were to finance the farming operations for them on the farms, organized and formed a partnership known as E. F. Smith & Sons. They term the partnership an "operating partnership". The general purpose of the firm was to engage in farming operations on the farms, including direct cultivation and renting to others. The operation was later expanded to engage in the general farming business in the area. The partnership agreement was oral and has never been reduced to writing. Mr. W. R. Smith is the predominent member of both the partnership and the Smiths. He serves as the managing partner with general powers, with Mr. Charles Smith in charge of production. The other members of the partnership did not, nor at the present time, appear to have any direct participation or responsibility in the operation. The firm, by and through its managing partner, Mr. W. R. Smith, has acted as agent for or under contract with, the Smiths in the sale of the "Sterling Place" to Mr. Rankin, in a similar capacity in another land conveyance and as trustee for another purchase.

It appears undisputed that appellant W. R. Smith was authorized by the members of the partnership to negotiate for the sale of the lands in question to the appellee. However, it is claimed that his authorization was based upon different terms of sale, mainly, a price of $225,000.00 instead of $200,000.00. Therefore, it is urged that the contract is unenforceable since it was not signed nor ratified by other members of the family.

In the case of *May v. Ewan*, we held that a partnership is bound by the acts of a partner when he acts within the scope or *apparent* scope of his authority. There we quoted with approval:

> In order to determine the apparent scope of the authority of a partner, recourse may frequently be had to past transactions indicating a custom or course of dealing peculiar to the firm in question.

In the case at bar it was customary in past transactions, as in the present one, for the partnership to rely upon the co-partner, W. R. Smith, to transact the business affairs of the firm. We agree with the chancellor that appellant W. R. Smith was acting within the apparent scope of his authority as a partner when he signed the contract and that it is binding and enforceable upon the partnership.

NATIONAL BISCUIT CO. V. STROUD

SUPREME COURT OF NORTH CAROLINA (PARKER, J.)
249 N.C. 467 (1959)

C. N. Stroud and Earl Freeman entered into a general partnership to sell groceries under the firm name of Stroud's Food Center. There is nothing in the agreed statement of facts to indicate or suggest that Freeman's power and authority as a general partner were in any way restricted or limited by the articles of partnership in respect to the ordinary and legitimate business of the partnership. Certainly, the purchase and sale of bread were ordinary and legitimate business of Stroud's Food Center during its continuance as a going concern.

Several months prior to February 1956 Stroud advised plaintiff that he personally would not be responsible for any additional bread sold by plaintiff to Stroud's Food Center. After such notice to plaintiff, it from 6 February 1956 to 25 February 1956, at the request of Freeman, sold and delivered bread in the amount of $171.04 to Stroud's Food Center.

In *Johnson v. Bernheim*, this Court said: "A and B are general partners to do some given business; the partnership is, by operation of law, a power to each to bind the partnership in any manner legitimate to the business. If one partner goes to a third person to buy an article on time for the partnership, the other partner cannot prevent it by writing to the third person not to sell to him on time; or, if one party attempts to buy for cash, the other has no right to require that it shall be on time. And what is true in regard to buying is true in regard to selling. What either partner does with a third person is binding on the partnership. It is otherwise where the partnership is not general, but is upon special terms, as that purchases and sales must be with and for cash. There the power to each is special, in regard to all dealings with third persons at least who have notice of the terms." There is contrary authority. However, this text of C.J.S. does not mention the effect of the provisions of the Uniform Partnership Act.

The General Assembly of North Carolina in 1941 enacted a Uniform Partnership Act, which became effective 15 March 1941.

G.S.§ 59-39 is entitled "Partner Agent of Partnership as to Partnership Business", and subsection (1) reads:

> Every partner is an agent of the partnership for the purpose of its business, and the act of every partner, including the execution in the partnership name of any instrument, for apparently carrying on in the usual way the business of the partnership of which he is a member binds the partnership, unless the partner so acting has in fact no authority to act for the partnership in the particular matter, and the person with whom he is dealing has knowledge of the fact that he has no such authority.

G.S. § 59-39(4) states: "No act of a partner in contravention of a restriction on authority shall bind the partnership to persons having knowledge of the restriction."

G.S. § 59-45 provides that "all partners are jointly and severally liable for the acts and obligations of the partnership."

G.S. § 59-48 is captioned "Rules Determining Rights and Duties of Partners". Subsection (e) thereof reads: "All partners have equal rights in the management and conduct of the partnership business." Subsection (h) hereof is as follows: "Any difference arising as to ordinary matters connected with the partnership business may be decided by a majority of the partners; but no act in contravention of any agreement between the partners may be done rightfully without the consent of all the partners."

Freeman as a general partner with Stroud, with no restrictions on his authority to act within the scope of the partnership business so far as the agreed statement of facts shows, had under the Uniform Partnership Act "equal rights in the management and conduct of the partnership business." Under G.S. § 59-48(h) Stroud, his co-partner, could not restrict the power and authority of Freeman to buy bread for the partnership as a going concern, for such a purchase was an "ordinary matter connected with the partnership business," for the purpose of its business and within its scope, because in the very nature of things Stroud was not, and could not be, a majority of the partners. Therefore, Freeman's purchases of bread from plaintiff for Stroud's Food Center as a going concern bound the partnership and his co-partner Stroud. The quoted provisions of our Uniform Partnership Act, in respect to the particular facts here, are in accord with the principle of law stated in *Johnson v. Bernheim.*

At the close of business on 25 February 1956 Stroud and Freeman by agreement dissolved the partnership. By their dissolution agreement all of the partnership assets, including cash on hand, bank deposits and all accounts receivable, with a few exceptions, were assigned to Stroud, who bound himself by such written dissolution agreement to liquidate the firm's assets and discharge its liabilities. It would seem a fair inference from the agreed statement of facts that the partnership got the benefit of the bread sold and delivered by plaintiff to Stroud's Food Center, at Freeman's request, from 6 February 1956 to 25 February 1956. But whether it did or not, Freeman's acts, as stated above, bound the partnership and Stroud.

Affirmed.

MEINHARD V. SALMON

COURT OF APPEALS OF NEW YORK (CARDOZO, C.J.)
249 N.Y. 458 (1928)

On April 10, 1902, Louisa M. Gerry leased to the defendant Walter J. Salmon the premises known as the Hotel Bristol at the northwest corner of Forty-Second street and Fifth avenue in the city of New York. The lease was for a term of 20 years, commencing May 1, 1902, and ending

April 30, 1922. The lessee undertook to change the hotel building for use as shops and offices at a cost of $200,000. Alterations and additions were to be accretions to the land.

Salmon, while in course of treaty with the lessor as to the execution of the lease, was in course of treaty with Meinhard, the plaintiff, for the necessary funds. The result was a joint venture with terms embodied in a writing. Meinhard was to pay to Salmon half of the moneys requisite to reconstruct, alter, manage, and operate the property. Salmon was to pay to Meinhard 40 per cent. of the net profits for the first five years of the lease and 50 per cent. for the years thereafter. If there were losses, each party was to bear them equally. Salmon, however, was to have sole power to "manage, lease, underlet and operate" the building. There were to be certain pre-emptive rights for each in the contingency of death.

They were coadventures, subject to fiduciary duties akin to those of partners. As to this we are all agreed. The heavier weight of duty rested, however, upon Salmon. He was a coadventurer with Meinhard, but he was manager as well. During the early years of the enterprise, the building, reconstructed, was operated at a loss. If the relation had then ended, Meinhard as well as Salmon would have carried a heavy burden. Later the profits became large with the result that for each of the investors there came a rich return. For each the venture had its phases of fair weather and of foul. The two were in it jointly, for better or for worse.

When the lease was near its end, Elbridge T. Gerry had become the owner of the reversion. He owned much other property in the neighborhood, one lot adjoining the Bristol building on Fifth avenue and four lots on Forty-Second street. He had a plan to lease the entire tract for a long term to some one who would destroy the buildings then existing and put up another in their place. In the latter part of 1921, he submitted such a project to several capitalists and dealers. He was unable to carry it through with any of them. Then, in January, 1922, with less than four months of the lease to run, he approached the defendant Salmon. The result was a new lease to the Midpoint Realty Company, which is owned and controlled by Salmon, a lease covering the whole tract, and involving a huge outlay. The term is to be 20 years, but successive covenants for renewal will extend it to a maximum of 80 years at the will of either party. The existing buildings may remain unchanged for seven years. They are then to be torn down, and a new building to cost $3,000,000 is to be placed upon the site. The rental, which under the Bristol lease was only $55,000, is to be from $350,000 to $475,000 for the properties so combined. Salmon personally guaranteed the performance by the lessee of the covenants of the new lease until such time as the new building had been completed and fully paid for.

The lease between Gerry and the Midpoint Realty Company was signed and delivered on January 25, 1922. Salmon had not told Meinhard anything about it. Whatever his motive may have been, he had kept the negotiations to himself. Meinhard was not informed even of the bare existence of a project. The first that he knew of it was in February, when the lease was an accomplished fact. He then made demand on the defendants that the lease be held in trust as an asset of the venture, making offer upon the trial to share the personal obligations incidental

53

to the guaranty. The demand was followed by refusal, and later by this suit. A referee gave judgment for the plaintiff, limiting the plaintiff's interest in the lease, however, to 25 per cent. The limitation was on the theory that the plaintiff's equity was to be restricted to one-half of so much of the value of the lease as was contributed or represented by the occupation of the Bristol site. Upon cross-appeals to the Appellate Division, the judgment was modified so as to enlarge the equitable interest to one-half of the whole lease. With this enlargement of plaintiff's interest, there went, of course, a corresponding enlargement of his attendant obligations. The case is now here on an appeal by the defendants.

Joint adventurers, like copartners, owe to one another, while the enterprise continues, the duty of the finest loyalty. Many forms of conduct permissible in a workaday world for those acting at arm's length, are forbidden to those bound by fiduciary ties. A trustee is held to something stricter than the morals of the market place. Not honesty alone, but the punctilio of an honor the most sensitive, is then the standard of behavior. As to this there has developed a tradition that is unbending and inveterate. Uncompromising rigidity has been the attitude of courts of equity when petitioned to undermine the rule of undivided loyalty by the "disintegrating erosion" of particular exceptions. Only thus has the level of conduct for fiduciaries been kept at a level higher than that trodden by the crowd. It will not consciously be lowered by any judgment of this court.

The owner of the reversion, Mr. Gerry, had vainly striven to find a tenant who would favor his ambitious scheme of demolition and construction. Baffled in the search, he turned to the defendant Salmon in possession of the Bristol, the keystone of the project. He figured to himself beyond a doubt that the man in possession would prove a likely customer. To the eye of an observer, Salmon held the lease as owner in his own right, for himself and no one else. In fact he held it as a fiduciary, for himself and another, sharers in a common venture. If this fact had been proclaimed, if the lease by its terms had run in favor of a partnership, Mr. Gerry, we may fairly assume, would have laid before the partners, and not merely before one of them, his plan of reconstruction. The pre-emptive privilege, or, better, the pre-emptive opportunity, that was thus an incident of the enterprise, Salmon appropriated to himself in secrecy and silence. He might have warned Meinhard that the plan had been submitted, and that either would be free to compete for the award. If he had done this, we do not need to say whether he would have been under a duty, if successful in the competition, to hold the lease so acquired for the benefit of a venture then about to end, and thus prolong by indirection its responsibilities and duties. The trouble about his conduct is that he excluded his coadventurer from any chance to compete, from any chance to enjoy the opportunity for benefit that had come to him alone by virtue of his agency. This chance, if nothing more, he was under a duty to concede. The price of its denial is an extension of the trust at the option and for the benefit of the one whom he excluded.

No answer is it to say that the chance would have been of little value even if seasonably offered. Such a calculus of probabilities is beyond the science of the chancery. Meinhard might have offered better terms, or reinforced his offer by alliance with the wealth of others. He knew that Salmon was the manager. As the time drew near for the expiration of the lease, he would naturally assume from silence, if from nothing else, that the lessor was willing to extend it for a term of years, or at least to let it stand as a lease from year to year. In the absence of such notice, the matter of an extension was one that would naturally be attended to by the manager of the enterprise, and not neglected altogether. The very fact that Salmon was in control with exclusive powers of direction charged him the more obviously with the duty of disclosure, since only through disclosure could opportunity be equalized. If he might cut off renewal by a purchase for his own benefit when four months were to pass before the lease would have an end, he might do so with equal right while there remained as many years. He might steal a march on his comrade under cover of darkness, and then hold the captured ground. Loyalty and comradeship are not so easily abjured.

We have no thought to hold that Salmon was guilty of a conscious purpose to defraud. Very likely he assumed in all good faith that with the approaching end of the venture he might ignore his coadventurer and take the extension for himself. He had given to the enterprise time and labor as well as money. He had made it a success. Meinhard, who had given money, but neither time nor labor, had already been richly paid. There might seem to be something grasping in his insistence upon more. Such recriminations are not unusual when coadventurers fall out. They are not without their force if conduct is to be judged by the common standards of competitors. That is not to say that they have pertinency here. Salmon had put himself in a position in which thought of self was to be renounced, however hard the abnegation. He was much more than a coadventurer. He was a managing coadventurer. For him and for those like him the rule of undivided loyalty is relentless and supreme. A different question would be here if there were lacking any nexus of relation between the business conducted by the manager and the opportunity brought to him as an incident of management. For this problem, as for most, there are distinctions of degree. If Salmon had received from Gerry a proposition to lease a building at a location far removed, he might have held for himself the privilege thus acquired, or so we shall assume. Here the subject-matter of the new lease was an extension and enlargement of the subject-matter of the old one. A managing coadventurer appropriating the benefit of such a lease without warning to his partner might fairly expect to be reproached with conduct that was underhand, or lacking, to say the least, in reasonable candor, if the partner were to surprise him in the act of signing the new instrument. Conduct subject to that reproach does not receive from equity a healing benediction.

We agree with the Appellate Division that the plaintiff's equitable interest is to be measured by the value of half of the entire lease, and not merely by half of some undivided part. A single building covers the whole area. Physical division is impracticable along the lines of the Bristol site, the keystone of the whole. Division of interests and burdens is equally impracticable.

The judgment should be modified by providing that at the option of the defendant Salmon there may be substituted for a trust attaching to the lease a trust attaching to the shares of stock, with the result that one-half of such shares together with one additional share will in that event be allotted to the defendant Salmon and the other shares to the plaintiff, and as so modified the judgment should be affirmed with costs.

ANDREWS, J. (dissenting).

Fair dealing and a scrupulous regard for honesty is required. But nothing more. It may be stated generally that a partner may not for his own benefit secretly take a renewal of a firm lease to himself. In short, as we once said, "the elements of actual fraud—of the betrayal by secret action of confidence reposed, or assumed to be reposed, grows in importance as the relation between the parties falls from an express to an implied or a quasi trust, and on to those cases where good faith alone is involved."

With this view of the law I am of the opinion that the issue here is simple. Was the transaction, in view of all the circumstances surrounding it, unfair and inequitable? I reach this conclusion for two reasons. There was no general partnership, merely a joint venture for a limited object, to end at a fixed time. The new lease, covering additional property, containing many new and unusual terms and conditions, with a possible duration of 80 years, was more nearly the purchase of the reversion than the ordinary renewal with which the authorities are concerned.

The referee finds that this arrangement did not create a partnership between Mr. Salmon and Mr. Meinhard. In this he is clearly right. He is equally right in holding that while no general partnership existed the two men had entered into a joint adventure and that while the legal title to the lease was in Mr. Salmon, Mr. Meinhard had some sort of an equitable interest therein. Mr. Salmon was to manage the property for their joint benefit. He was bound to use good faith. He could not willfully destroy the lease, the object of the adventure, to the detriment of Mr. Meinhard.

In many respects, besides the increase in the land demised, the new lease differs from the old. Instead of an annual rent of $55,000 it is now from $350,000 to $475,000. Instead of a fixed term of twenty years it may now be, at the lessee's option, eighty. Instead of alterations in an existing structure costing about $200,000 a new building is contemplated costing $3,000,000. Of this sum $1,500,000 is to be advanced by the lessor to the lessee, "but not to its successors or assigns," and is to be repaid in installments. Again no assignment or sale of the lease may be made without the consent of the lessor.

Under these circumstances the referee has found and the Appellate Division agrees with him, that Mr. Meinhard is entitled to an interest in the second lease, he having promptly elected to assume his share of the liabilities imposed thereby.

Were this a general partnership between Mr. Salmon and Mr. Meinhard, I should have little doubt as to the correctness of this result, assuming the new lease to be an offshoot of the old. Such a situation involves questions of trust and confidence to a high degree; it involves questions of goodwill; many other considerations. As has been said, rarely if ever may one partner without the knowledge of the other acquire for himself the renewal of a lease held by the firm, even if the new lease is to begin after the firm is dissolved. Warning of such an intent, if he is managing partner, may not be sufficient to prevent the application of this rule.

We have here a different situation governed by less drastic principles.

The one complaint made is that Mr. Salmon obtained the new lease without informing Mr. Meinhard of his intention. Nothing else. There is no claim of actual fraud. No claim of misrepresentation to anyone.

What then was the scope of the adventure into which the two men entered?

It seems to me that the venture so inaugurated had in view a limited object and was to end at a limited time. There was no intent to expand it into a far greater undertaking lasting for many years. The design was to exploit a particular lease. Doubtless in it Mr. Meinhard had an equitable interest, but in it alone. This interest terminated when the joint adventure terminated.

So far I have treated the new lease as if it were a renewal of the old. As already indicated, I do not take that view. Such a renewal could not be obtained. Any expectancy that it might be had vanished. What Mr. Salmon obtained was not a graft springing from the Bristol lease, but something distinct and different—as distinct as if for a building across Fifth avenue. No fraud, no deceit, no calculated secrecy is found. Simply that the the arrangement was made without the knowledge of Mr. Meinhard. I think this not enough.

The judgment of the courts below should be reversed and a new trial ordered, with costs in all courts to abide the event.

PARTNERSHIP DISSOLUTION PART C
AND TERMINATION

REVISED UNIFORM PARTNERSHIP ACT[3]

SECTION 502. PARTNER'S TRANSFERABLE INTEREST IN PARTNERSHIP

The only transferable interest of a partner in the partnership is the partner's share of the profits and losses of the partnership and the partner's right to receive distributions. The interest is personal property.

---

3   National Conference of Commissioners on Uniform State Laws, "Revised Uniform Partnership Act." Copyright © 1997 by National Conference of Commissioners on Uniform State Laws. Reprinted with permission.

SECTION 701. PURCHASE OF DISSOCIATED PARTNER'S INTEREST

(a) If a partner is dissociated from a partnership without resulting in a dissolution and winding up of the partnership business ... the partnership shall cause the dissociated partner's interest in the partnership to be purchased for a buyout price determined pursuant to subsection (b).

(b) The buyout price of a dissociated partner's interest is the amount that would have been distributable to the dissociating partner ... if, on the date of dissociation, the assets of the partnership were sold at a price equal to or greater than the liquidation value or the value based on a sale of the entire business as a going concern without the dissociated partner and the partnership were wound up as of that date. Interest must be paid from the date of dissociation to the date of payment.

SECTION 703(a). DISSOCIATED PARTNER'S LIABILITY TO OTHER PERSONS

A partner's dissociation does not of itself discharge the partner's liability for a partnership obligation incurred before dissociation. A dissociated partner is not liable for a partnership obligation incurred after dissociation, except as otherwise provided.

8182 MARYLAND ASSOCIATES, LIMITED PARTNERSHIP

SUPREME COURT OF MISSOURI (PRICE, C.J.)
14 S.W.3D 576 (2000)

On April 5, 1984, the Missouri general partnership of Popkin, Stern, Heifitz, Lurie, Sheehan, Reby & Chervitz, a law firm, entered into a lease agreement with 8182 Maryland. Defendant Richard J. Sheehan, a general partner of Popkin, Stern, Heifitz, Lurie, Sheehan, Reby & Chervitz, signed the lease along with the other thirteen general partners.[4] This lease was for the use of two floors and space in the parking garage of an office building that had yet to be constructed. The term of the lease was 120 months and commenced on the date the space was made "ready for occupancy" by 8182 Maryland. Rent was to be paid on the first day of each month. The lease was silent as to liability for incoming or withdrawing partners from Popkin, Stern, Heifitz, Lurie, Sheehan, Reby & Chervitz. The lease did, however, contain a clause requiring the written consent of the landlord for assignment of the lease.

---

4   Sheehan passed away on March 11, 1996. His wife and estate administrator, Kathryn Sheehan, has been substituted as a party in this suit.

In October of 1985, Sheehan withdrew from the partnership.[5] On December 31, 1985, Sheehan assigned his interest in the partnership to the remaining partners. Neither this document nor the partnership agreement was made a part of the record on appeal. In January of 1986, Sheehan's resignation became effective and the partnership formally adopted the shorter name of "Popkin & Stern." Apparently, the lease with 8182 Maryland was not expressly assigned in writing by the old partnership of Popkin, Stern, Heifitz, Lurie, Sheehan, Reby & Chervitz to the new partnership of Popkin & Stern, nor did Popkin & Stern assume the obligations of the lease in writing. On or before April 26, 1986, Popkin & Stern began occupancy of the leased premises.

[handwritten margin note: change partnership to Popkin & Stern but didn't assign lease to new partnership name]

At varying points between January 1, 1985, and January 1, 1986, Defendants Timothy Noelker, Douglas Burdette, Barbara Lageson, and Jeffrey Klar became partners of Popkin & Stern. There is no evidence in the record that any partnership agreement signed by these partners contained language concerning personal liability on the lease for incoming partners. None were asked to sign the lease agreement or any assumption agreement. It does not appear that the lease agreement was ever expressly assigned in writing to any of the new partnerships that resulted from the changing composition of the firm, or that any of these new partnerships assumed the obligation of the lease in writing. Noelker, Burdette, Lageson, and Klar all withdrew from the firm on or before December 1, 1989. None entered into a withdrawal agreement with any Popkin & Stern partnership or 8182 Maryland.

In September of 1991, Popkin & Stern defaulted on its lease obligation to 8182 Maryland and subsequently filed for bankruptcy in 1992. The third amended petition in this case, filed on January 13, 1993, alleged that 8182 Maryland suffered damages in the amount of $865,488.53 for past-due rent and the partnership's pro rata share of the building's operating expenses and parking garage expenses and $4,891,975.91 for the "present value of the Premises for the remainder of the stated term over the reasonable value of the Premises for the remainder of the stated term," a remedy the lease expressly allowed to the landlord upon the partnership's default. 8182 Maryland named as defendants all past and present general partners of the firm since April 4, 1984, but has dismissed thirty-six of those defendants.

Noelker and Klar filed partial motions for summary judgment seeking to limit any recovery of damages to partnership assets, not their individual assets. The trial court entered an order of partial summary judgment in favor of Noelker on January 22, 1993, and in favor of Klar on February 10, 1993. Later, Sheehan, Noelker, Klar, Burdette, and Harris filed separate motions for summary judgment requesting the circuit court dismiss, in all respects, the third amended petition against each of them. The trial court granted these motions and it is from the granting of these motions that 8182 Maryland appeals.

---

5   Sheehan resigned from the firm to become the Assistant Chief Litigation Counsel, Division of Enforcement, Securities and Exchange Commission in Washington, D.C. He subsequently joined the New York Stock Exchange as vice president for enforcement and became first vice president and assistant general counsel for Dean Witter.

Partnership law in Missouri is governed by the Uniform Partnership Law. The UPL is nearly identical to the Uniform Partnership Act, adopted in most states.

Central to the determination of personal liability for Defendant Sheehan and Defendants Noelker, Burdette, Lageson, and Klar is the legal effect the withdrawal of existing partners and the addition of incoming partners has on a partnership. The withdrawal of an existing partner dissolves the partnership. Dissolution, however, is not a termination of the partnership business. A partner's personal liability is not discharged merely by the dissolution of the partnership. However, a partner may be discharged from any existing liability upon dissolution of the partnership by an agreement to that effect between himself, the partnership creditor and the person or partnership continuing the business. Under certain circumstances, such an agreement may even be inferred.

The remaining partners may choose not to terminate and wind up, but to continue the partnership business. The Uniform Partnership Law contemplates that dissolved partnerships may continue in business for a short, long or indefinite period of time so long as none of the partners insist on a winding up and final termination of the partnership business. The result is that the old firm continues until its affairs are wound up and a new partnership is formed, consisting of the remaining members of the old partnership. Any creditors of the old partnership also become creditors of the new partnership continuing the business.

The UPL does not expressly make the admission of a new partner a ground for dissolution. However, it is universally admitted that any change in membership dissolves a partnership, and creates a new partnership.

Defendant Sheehan was a partner who personally signed the lease, but withdrew from the partnership of Popkin, Stern, Heifitz, Lurie, Sheehan, Reby & Chervitz before the lease agreement commenced or was breached by Popkin & Stern. There is no doubt Sheehan was personally liable for the lease while still a partner at Popkin, Stern, Heifitz, Lurie, Sheehan, Reby & Chervitz. When Sheehan and the other general partners of Popkin, Stern, Heifitz, Lurie, Sheehan, Reby & Chervitz signed the lease agreement with 8182 Maryland, each partner of the partnership became personally liable on the agreement.

Sheehan first claims his withdrawal from the partnership terminated his personal liability because his withdrawal became effective before the lease agreement "commenced." We do not agree. A party becomes liable on a contractual agreement, even a lease agreement with a future date of commencement, at the moment it is executed. Commencement, under the terms of this lease, was merely the starting point for the collection of rent and the possibility of occupancy, not the beginning of contractual liability. Once Sheehan signed the lease agreement, he became jointly and severally liable for all existing and future obligations under that lease.

Sheehan also claims his liability terminated at withdrawal because he withdrew before any breach of the lease occurred. We again disagree. When Sheehan withdrew from Popkin, Stern, Heifitz, Lurie, Sheehan, Reby & Chervitz, the partnership was dissolved, and the new partnership of Popkin & Stern resulted among the remaining partners. Dissolution, however, of the partnership does not of itself discharge the existing liability of any partner. Liability for partnership obligations does not die simply by disassociating oneself from the partnership business.

Moreover, withdrawing partners retain personal liability after withdrawal, even for contingent obligations.

Defendants Noelker, Burdette, Lageson, and Klar became partners of Popkin & Stern at various times subsequent to the lease agreement, but all left the partnership before the breach occurred. Defendants rely exclusively on UPA (1914) § 17 for the proposition that their liability can only be satisfied out of partnership assets.

We have not had occasion to interpret section 17. Several other states, however, have adopted identical language in their partnership laws and have analyzed the implications of that section in the context of lease agreements. Generally, these states have approached the issue of liability by focusing upon when the obligation of a lease "arises."

Ellingson v. Walsh, however, approached the question by interpreting California's version of UPA section 17 in the dual context of property and contract law theories, traditionally referred to as privity of contract and privity of estate. In *Ellingson*, a partner who joined a partnership after the execution of a lease agreement contested his personal liability for a breach of the lease. The court, however, found that trying to determine when the obligation of a lease agreement arises, overlooks the fact that a tenant of real property is not liable for rent solely by reason of the contract of lease. One may become a tenant at will or a periodic tenant under an invalid lease, or without any lease at all, by occupancy with consent. Such tenancies carry with them the incidental obligation of rent, and the liability therefore arises not from contract but from the relationship of landlord and tenant. The tenant is liable by operation of law.

Thus, a party that signs a lease agreement is liable not only contractually for the covenants of the agreement by privity of contract, but also for rent under the creation of a tenancy by privity of estate.

The court also found that although the original partnership expressly assumed the lease and was, therefore, liable both under the lease contract and as a tenant, the addition of a new partner caused the first partnership to be dissolved and a new partnership came into being composed of the old members and the new partner. This second partnership did not expressly assume the obligations of the lease, but it occupied the premises. Whether it was liable contractually on the lease is immaterial; it became liable for rent as a tenant. Thus, the members of the new partnership were liable for rent not because of when the obligation of a lease arose, but because they were in occupation of the premises. This liability arises and binds continually throughout the period of occupation.

The analysis set out in *Ellingson* provides the clearest framework for determining the personal liability of partners relative to a partnership lease consistent with the UPA and Missouri landlord/tenant law. In Missouri, a lease agreement has a dual nature; it is both a conveyance and a contract. As between the lessor and lessee, a lease creates a contractual relationship, privity of contract, as well as being a conveyance of an estate in land which creates privity of estate. Privity of contract carries with it the obligations in the written lease agreement, while privity of estate carries with it liability for rent and any other covenants running with the land.

Thus, the original partnership of Popkin, Stern, Heifitz, Lurie, Sheehan, Reby & Chervitz had privity of contract upon signing the lease agreement. When Sheehan withdrew, however, the original partnership was dissolved and a new one, Popkin & Stern, comprised of the remaining members of the original partnership, was formed. This new partnership continued the partnership business, acquiring the creditors of the old partnership. Although not a party to the lease between Popkin, Stern, Heifitz, Lurie, Sheehan, Reby & Chervitz and 8182 Maryland, Popkin & Stern occupied the leased premises and paid the rent. Unfortunately, there was no assignment and/or assumption agreement specifically defining the relationship of the old partnership and its partners, the new partnership and its partners, and 8182 Maryland.

When a party other than a tenant is shown to be in possession of the premises, and paying rent therefor, there is a presumption that the lease has been assigned to him. The lease was, therefore, presumably assigned to the resulting partnership. Over the years, each time an old partner left or a new partner joined the partnership, a similar dissolution occurred, and when the remaining partners joined by any incoming partners continued to occupy the leased premises and pay rent, another assignment of the lease to the resulting partnership was presumed.

Due to its occupation of the premises and the presumed assignment, Popkin & Stern, and each partnership thereafter, was in privity of estate with 8182 Maryland. Privity of estate creates liability only for payment of rent and other covenants running with the land while the tenant is in possession. Thus, each succeeding Popkin & Stern partnership, and each of the partnerships' varying partners, became jointly and severally liable for rent payments only during the period their partnerships were in privity of estate with 8182 Maryland. When each Defendant withdrew from the partnership they were a member of, that partnership ceased to exist and ceased to occupy the land. Its privity of estate ended, and thus the withdrawing partner's personal liability for rent ended as well.

Defendants Noelker, Burdette, Lageson, and Klar are not personally liable for rent arising subsequent to the time they were members of a partnership in occupation of the premises when the lease breach occurred subsequent to their withdrawal. We affirm the judgments entered in their favor.

PAGE V. PAGE

SUPREME COURT OF CALIFORNIA (TRAYNOR, J.)
359 P.2D 41 (1961)

Plaintiff and defendant are partners in a linen supply business in Santa Maria, California. Plaintiff appeals from a judgment declaring the partnership to be <u>for a term</u> rather than <u>at will.</u>

The partners entered into an oral partnership agreement in 1949. Within the first two years each partner contributed approximately $43,000 for the purchase of land, machinery, and linen needed to begin the business. From 1949 to 1957 the enterprise was unprofitable, losing approximately $62,000. The partnership's major creditor is a corporation, wholly owned by plaintiff, that supplies the linen and machinery necessary for the day-to-day operation of the business. This corporation holds a $47,000 demand note of the partnership. The partnership operations began to improve in 1958. The partnership earned $3,824.41 in that year and $2,282.30 in the first three months of 1959. Despite this improvement plaintiff wishes to terminate the partnership.

The Uniform Partnership Act provides that a partnership may be dissolved "By the express will of any partner when no definite term or particular undertaking is specified." The trial court found that the partnership is for a term, namely, "such reasonable time as is necessary to enable said partnership to repay from partnership profits, indebtedness incurred for the purchase of land, buildings, laundry and delivery equipment and linen for the operation of such business." Plaintiff correctly contends that this finding is without support in the evidence.

Defendant testified that the terms of the partnership were to be similar to former partnerships of plaintiff and defendant, and that the understanding of these partnerships was that "we went into partnership to start the business and let the business operation pay for itself – put in so much money, and let the business pay itself out." There was also testimony that one of the former partnership agreements provided in writing that the profits were to be retained until all obligations were paid.

Upon cross-examination defendant admitted that the former partnership in which the earnings were to be retained until the obligations were repaid was substantially different from the present partnership. The former partnership was a limited partnership and provided for a definite term of five years and a partnership at will thereafter. Defendant insists, however, that the method of operation of the former partnership showed an understanding that all obligations were to be repaid from profits. He nevertheless concedes that there was no understanding as to the term of the present partnership in the event of losses.

Viewing this evidence most favorable for defendant, it proves only that the partners expected to meet current expenses from current income and to recoup their investment if the business were successful.

Defendant contends that such an expectation is sufficient to create a partnership for a term under the rule of *Owen v. Cohen.* In that case we held that when a partner advances a sum of money to a partnership with the understanding that the amount contributed was to be a loan to the partnership and was to be repaid as soon as feasible from the prospective profits of the business, the partnership is for the term reasonably required to repay the loan. It is true that *Owen v. Cohen* and other cases hold that partners may impliedly agree to continue in business until a certain sum of money is earned, or one or more partners recoup their investments, or until certain debts are paid, or until certain property could be disposed of on favorable terms. In each of these cases, however, the implied agreement found support in the evidence.

In the instant case, however, defendant failed to prove any facts from which an agreement to continue the partnership for a term may be implied. The understanding to which defendant testified was no more than a common hope that the partnership earnings would pay for all the necessary expenses. Such a hope does not establish even by implication a "definite term or particular undertaking." All partnerships are ordinarily entered into with the hope that they will be profitable, but that alone does not make them all partnerships for a term and obligate the partners to continue in the partnerships until all of the losses over a period of many years have been recovered.

Defendant contends that plaintiff is acting in bad faith and is attempting to use his superior financial position to appropriate the now profitable business of the partnership. Defendant has invested $43,000 in the firm, and owing to the long period of losses his interest in the partnership assets is very small. The fact that plaintiff's wholly owned corporation holds a $47,000 demand note of the partnership may make it difficult to sell the business as a going concern. Defendant fears that upon dissolution he will receive very little and that plaintiff, who is the managing partner and knows how to conduct the operations of the partnership, will receive a business that has become very profitable because of the establishment of Vandenberg Air Force Base in its vicinity. Defendant charges that plaintiff has been content to share the losses but now that the business has become profitable he wishes to keep all the gains.

There is no showing in the record of bad faith or that the improved profit situation is more than temporary. In any event these contentions are irrelevant to the issue whether the partnership is for a term or at will. Since, however, this action is for a declaratory judgment and will be the basis for future action by the parties, it is appropriate to point out that defendant is amply protected by the fiduciary duties of copartners.

Even though the Uniform Partnership Act provides that a partnership at will may be dissolved by the express will of any partner, this power, like any other power held by a fiduciary, must be exercised in good faith.

We have often stated that "Partners are trustees for each other, and in all proceedings connected with the conduct of the partnership every partner is bound to act in the highest good faith to his copartner and may not obtain any advantage over him in the partnership affairs by the slightest misrepresentation, concealment, threat or adverse pressure of any kind."

A partner at will is not bound to remain in a partnership, regardless of whether the business is profitable or unprofitable. A partner may not, however, by use of adverse pressure "freeze out" a copartner and appropriate the business to his own use. A partner may not dissolve a partnership to gain the benefits of the business for himself, unless he fully compensates his copartner for his share of the prospective business opportunity. In this regard, his fiduciary duties are at least as great as those of a shareholder of a corporation.

In the instant case, plaintiff has the power to dissolve the partnership by express notice to defendant. If, however, it is proved that plaintiff acted in bad faith and violated his fiduciary duties by attempting to appropriate to his own use the new prosperity of the partnership without adequate compensation to his copartner, the dissolution would be wrongful and the plaintiff would be liable for violation of the implied agreement not to exclude defendant wrongfully from the partnership business opportunity.

The judgment is reversed.

PARTNERSHIP ACCOUNTING PART D AND FINANCE

REVISED UNIFORM PARTNERSHIP ACT[6]

SECTION 401(a). PARTNER'S RIGHTS AND DUTIES

Each partner is deemed to have an account that is:

(1) credited with an amount equal to the money plus the value of any other property, net of the amount of any liabilities, the partner contributes to the partnership and the partner's share of the partnership profits; and

(2) charged with an amount equal to the money plus the value of any other property, net of the amount of any liabilities, distributed by the partnership to the partner and the partner's shares of the partnership losses.

---

6   National Conference of Commissioners on Uniform State Laws, "Revised Uniform Partnership Act." Copyright © 1997 by National Conference of Commissioners on Uniform State Laws. Reprinted with permission.

RICHERT V. HANDLY

SUPREME COURT OF WASHINGTON (ROSELLINI, J.)
311 P.2D 417 (1957)

This is an action for an accounting, wherein the plaintiff alleged that he entered into a partnership agreement with the defendant husband (hereafter referred to as the defendant), under the terms of which he, the plaintiff, was to purchase a stand of timber and the defendant was to log it, using his equipment, and the two were to share equally in the profits or losses resulting from the venture. He further alleged that the undertaking was unsuccessful; that after the payment of all operating expenses, the partnership suffered a loss of $9,825.12; that he had advanced $26,842 but had been repaid only $10,000 for his advances; and that he was entitled to $16,842 less $4,912.56 (one half of the net loss), or $11,929.44. In his amended answer, the defendant admitted that the parties had contracted with each other, but alleged that "there was no settled agreement between the partners as to recovery by the plaintiff for loss upon his capital contribution, nor as to the priority of any right to recover upon his capital contribution." In addition, he claimed certain offsets and asked that the complaint be dismissed.

The cause was tried to the court, which found in favor of the defendant in the amount of $1,494.51, plus costs.

The facts found by the trial court are as follows:

"I That defendants C. C. Handly and Mildred Handly are husband and wife constituting a marital community resident in Mason County, Washington.

"II During the month of April 1953 plaintiff Richert advised defendant Handly that he had available for purchase according to his cruise 1,700,000 feet of timber in the State of Oregon, that he, Richert proposed to purchase said timber with his funds and requested Handly to log said timber on the basis that the two of them would share the profit or loss on the transaction.

"III Prior to the purchase of the timber by the plaintiff the parties inspected the same and defendant Handly advised Richert that there was no more than approximately 1,000,000 feet of timber on the tract in question, and that the cruise was in error.

"IV The plaintiff Richert purchased the timber for a price of $24,300.00 after the parties had inspected it as aforesaid, and Handly proceeded to log the same under an oral working agreement. The essential elements of this agreement were as follows: Handly was to furnish a tractor for which he was to be paid rental at the rate of $13.00 per hour and was to haul the logs on his trucks at the rate of $8.00 per thousand. He was also to manage the operation, keep the records and handle and account for the funds received and expended during the course of the same. The profit or loss resulting from this single logging venture was to be borne equally. There was no requirement that Handly contribute to Richert for the purchase price of the timber in the event of loss.

"V The tract involved yielded between 800,000 and 900,000 feet of timber and the transaction resulted in a loss, the loss being caused by the deficiency in timber.

"V The defendant Handly employed a bookkeeper and accountant in the State of Oregon to keep the records of this venture.

"VII The gross receipts of the venture amounted to $41,629.83. These funds were banked and accounted for by Handly. There was no concealment nor unlawful withholding or conversion of any of the funds.

"VIII Handly drew from the proceeds of the sale of the timber the sum of $7,016.88. Richert received from the proceeds of the sale of the timber the sum of $10,000.00.

"IX There was no agreement express or implied on the part of Handly to repay Richert for his investment in the timber.

"X A partnership income tax was prepared for the year 1953 by Elliott B. Spring, accountant in Shelton, Washington. This return was signed by Handly after he protested the accounting shown thereon. The accounting appearing on said return was set up on the basis of Spring's understanding and opinion as to what the legal relationship of the parties was with reference to this single logging transaction.

"XI The $10,000.00 received by Richert and the $7,016.88 drawn by Handly are unexpended gross revenues of the undertaking."

Upon these facts, the court entered the following conclusions of law:

"I The arrangement of the parties hereto with reference to the single transaction involved constitutes a joint venture.

"II The defendant Handly is in no way responsible for plaintiff's loss on the purchase of the timber involved.

"III Of the total amount of $17,016.88 heretofore identified as unexpended gross revenue of the undertaking each party hereto is entitled to $8,508.44. Richert has been overpaid in the amount of $1491.56, and Handly is entitled to judgment against him in the amount of $1491.56.

"IV Plaintiff is entitled to take nothing by his complaint."

Although the plaintiff maintains that the court erred in holding the undertaking to be a "joint venture" rather than a "partnership," we think the distinction is immaterial in this action. Deciding whether the relationship between the parties was that of partners or joint venturers does not determine their rights and duties under their contract or the status of their account. We will disregard, therefore, the conclusion of law that the arrangement constituted a joint venture.

On the other hand, it is manifest that the findings are inadequate to support the judgment entered, or any other judgment. There is a finding that the parties to the contract had agreed to share the profits or losses equally; but there is a further finding that the defendant had not agreed to contribute to the plaintiff for his investment in the timber in the event of loss; in other words, that they had not agreed to share the losses equally. Aside from the finding that the profit or loss was to be borne equally, which is inconsistent with the further finding that the defendant was not to contribute to the plaintiff for the purchase price of the timber in the event of loss, the findings are silent as to the basis on which the profit or loss was to be shared, whether proportionately to the contribution of each party, or otherwise. The mere fact that the defendant was not to be personally liable to the plaintiff for his losses does not mean that the plaintiff was not to be reimbursed out of the proceeds of the venture.

The findings also fail to reveal whether there was an understanding that the defendant was to be compensated for his services in managing the operation, apart from his share in the profits, and if so, in what amount. The only allegation contained in the amended answer pertaining to an agreement to reimburse the defendant for his services, was that he was owed $400 for maintaining fire watch and $25 for running property lines; and yet inherent in the court's disposition of the matter is a finding that these services were worth the full amount of the plaintiff's investment, or $26,842; for the court treated all of the "unexpended gross revenues" as profits and divided them equally between the parties, one of whom had lost nothing (unless his claimed offsets in the total amount of $4,800 were valid), while the other had lost an investment of $26,842.

The court appears to have lost sight of the fact that there could be no profits until the expenses of the operation were paid, including the cost of the timber. The conclusion that all of the "unexpended gross revenues" were to be divided equally between the parties could only be reached if it had been agreed that the plaintiff would not be reimbursed for his contribution. Such an intention cannot be inferred from any of the findings entered.

Since the findings are inadequate to support the conclusions and judgment, or any judgment on the matter in question, the cause must be remanded with directions to make findings regarding the basis on which the parties agreed that the losses were to be shared and whether the claims of one partner were to take priority over the claims of the other; the amount contributed by each (including cost of timber, and equipment rental, and also including services if there was an agreement that the defendant was to be compensated for his services, in addition to his share in the profits, if any); the total receipts and the authorized disbursements; the amount which each of the parties has received to date; and the amount due each on the basis of their agreement.

The judgment is reversed and the cause is remanded with directions to enter findings on the matters indicated above, conclusions, and judgment based thereon.

RICHERT V. HANDLY

SUPREME COURT OF WASHINGTON (HUNTER, J.)
330 P.2D 1079 (1958)

At the hearing on this matter pursuant to the remittitur, counsel for the respective parties agreed that no additional proof would be produced. Therefore, the trial court, after hearing argument of counsel, entered the following additional findings of fact in compliance with the remittitur:

"XII. The parties *did not agree upon or specify the basis* upon which losses were to be shared, nor whether the claims of *one partner* were to take priority over the claims of *the other*.

"XIII. Richert contributed a total of $26,842 for cost of timber and incidental advancements. Handly used his own equipment to haul logs, as agreed by the parties, and was paid $8,673.84 for this service. Handly used his own tractor, as agreed by the parties, and was paid $9,240 for this service. *There was no agreement that Handly was to be compensated for his services, in addition to his share in the profits, if any, (and except for the equipment and tractor services as last hereinbefore stated), and the accounting between the parties does not disclose any such compensation.*

"XIV. The gross receipts from the sale of logs were $41,629.83. The disbursements were hauling, $8,673.84; falling and bucking, $3,474.21; tractor, $9,240.00; payroll and taxes, $4,786.56; cruising, $35.00; right of way, $200.00; commission, $500.00; paid to Richert, $10,000.00; withdrawn by Handly, $7,016.88; Total, $43,926.49.

"XV. *There was no agreement* of the parties as to how a loss of the capital contributed by Richert in the amount of $26,842.00 was to be borne, and *accordingly it cannot be determined the amount due each on the basis of their agreement.*"

On the basis of such findings, the court concluded neither party was entitled to judgment against the other, that the complaint should be dismissed, and that the costs should abide the ultimate outcome of the case as provided by remittitur.

Mr. Richert has again appealed to this court from the judgment entered.

Since the trial court found that the parties had not agreed upon or specified the basis upon which losses were to be shared, or whether the claims of *one partner* were to take priority over the claims of the *other*, the provisions of the uniform partnership act are controlling. RCW 25.04.180 provides:

"The rights and duties of the partners in relation to the partnership shall be determined, *subject to any agreement between them*, by the following rules:

"(1) *Each partner shall be repaid his contributions, whether by way of capital or advances to the partnership property and share equally in the profits and surplus remaining after all liabilities,* including those to partners, are satisfied; and *must contribute toward the losses, whether of capital or otherwise, sustained by the partnership according to his share in the profits.*

"*(6) No partner is entitled to remuneration for acting in the partnership business,* except that a surviving partner is entitled to reasonable compensation for his services in winding up the partnership affairs."

Therefore, applying the statute to the additional facts found by the trial court, to which no error was assigned, we find the following account established:

Capital Contribution:	
Appellant Richert	$26,842.00
Respondent Handly	None
Gross Receipts From Sale of Timber:	$41,629.83
Expenses:	
Tractor	9,240.00
Hauling	8,673.84
Falling & Bucking	3,474.21
Payroll & Taxes	4,786.56
Cruising	35.00
Right of Way	200.00
Commission	500.00
	$26,909.61
Gross Receipts	41,629.83
Less Expenses	26,909.61
Net Receipts	$14,720.22
Appellant's Capital Contribution	26,842.00
Less Net Receipts	14,720.22
Net Loss	$12,121.78

Appellant has received $10,000 from the venture leaving a balance on his Capital Contribution of	$16,842.00
Less 1/2 of net loss ($12,121.78)	6,060.89
Amount respondent must reimburse appellant for loss resulting from logging venture	$10,781.11

It follows that the judgment of the trial court is incorrect, as a matter of law, under the facts found. Therefore, the judgment is reversed, and the cause remanded with directions to enter judgment in favor of the appellant in accordance with the views expressed herein.

[handwritten margin note: logger pay back land buyer]

KOVACIK V. REED

SUPREME COURT OF CALIFORNIA (SCHAUER, J.)
315 P.2D 314 (1957)

In this suit for dissolution of a joint venture and for an accounting, defendant appeals from a judgment that plaintiff recover from defendant one half the losses of the venture. We have concluded that inasmuch as the parties agreed that plaintiff was to supply the money and defendant the labor to carry on the venture, defendant is correct in his contention that the trial court erred in holding him liable for one half the monetary losses, and that the judgment should therefore be reversed.

The appeal is taken upon a settled statement under the provisions of subdivisions (b), (c), and (d) of rule 7, Rules on Appeal. From the "condensed statement of the oral proceedings" included in the settled statement, it appears that plaintiff, a licensed building contractor in San Francisco, operated his contracting business as a sole proprietorship under the fictitious name of "Asbestos Siding Company." Defendant had for a number of years worked for various building contractors in that city as a job superintendent and estimator.

Early in November, 1952, "Kovacik told Reed that Kovacik had an opportunity to do kitchen remodeling work for Sears Roebuck Company in San Francisco and asked Reed to become his job superintendent and estimator in this venture. Kovacik said that he had about $10,000.00 to invest in the venture and that, if Reed would superintend and estimate the jobs, Kovacik would share the profits with Reed on a 50-50 basis. Kovacik did not ask Reed to agree to share any loss that might result and Reed did not offer to share any such loss. The subject of a possible loss was not discussed in the inception of this venture. Reed accepted Kovacik's proposal and commenced work for the venture shortly after November 1, 1952. Reed's only contribution was his own labor. Kovacik provided all of the venture's financing through the credit of Asbestos Siding Company, although at times Reed purchased materials for the jobs in his own name or on his account for which he was reimbursed.

"The venture bid on and was awarded a number of remodeling jobs in San Francisco. Reed worked on all of the jobs as job superintendent. During August, 1953, Kovacik, who at that time had all of the financial records of the venture in his possession, informed Reed that the venture had been unprofitable and demanded contribution from Reed as to amounts which Kovacik claimed to have advanced in excess of the income received from the venture. Reed at no time promised, represented or agreed that he was liable for any of the venture's losses, and he consistently and without exception refused to contribute to or pay any of the loss resulting from the venture. The venture was terminated on August 31, 1953."

Kovacik thereafter instituted this proceeding, seeking an accounting of the affairs of the venture and to recover from Reed one half of the losses. Despite the evidence above set forth from the statement of the oral proceedings, showing that at no time had defendant agreed to be liable for any of the losses, the trial court "found"—more accurately, we think, concluded as a matter of law—that "plaintiff and defendant were to share equally all their joint venture profits and losses between them," and that defendant "agreed to share equally in the profits and losses of said joint venture." Following an accounting taken by a referee appointed by the court, judgment was rendered awarding plaintiff recovery against defendant of some $4,340, as one half the monetary losses[7] found by the referee to have been sustained by the joint venture.

It is the general rule that in the absence of an agreement to the contrary the law presumes that partners and joint adventurers intended to participate equally in the profits and losses of the common enterprise, irrespective of any inequality in the amounts each contributed to the capital employed in the venture, with the losses being shared by them in the same proportions as they share the profits.

However, it appears that in the cases in which the above stated general rule has been applied, each of the parties had contributed capital consisting of either money or land or other tangible property, or else was to receive compensation for services rendered to the common undertaking

---

7 The record is silent as to the factors taken into account by the referee in determining the "loss" suffered by the venture. However, there is no contention that defendant's services were ascribed any value whatsoever. It may also be noted that the trial court "found" that "neither plaintiff nor defendant was to receive compensation for their services rendered to said joint venture, but plaintiff and defendant were to share equally all their joint venture profits and losses between them." Neither party suggests that plaintiff actually rendered services to the venture in the same sense that defendant did. And, as is clear from the settled statement, plaintiff's proposition to defendant was that plaintiff would provide the money as against defendant's contribution of services as estimator and superintendent.

which was to be paid before computation of the profits or losses. Where, however, as in the present case, one partner or joint adventurer contributes the money capital as against the other's skill and labor, all the cases cited, and which our research has discovered, hold that neither party is liable to the other for contribution for any loss sustained. Thus, upon loss of the money the party who contributed it is not entitled to recover any part of it from the party who contributed only services. The rationale of this rule, as expressed in *Heran v. Hall* and *Meadows v. Mocquot*, is that where one party contributes money and the other contributes services, then in the event of a loss each would lose his own capital—the one his money and the other his labor. Another view would be that in such a situation the parties have, by their agreement to share equally in profits, agreed that the values of their contributions—the money on the one hand and the labor on the other—were likewise equal; it would follow that upon the loss, as here, of both money and labor, the parties have shared equally in the losses. Actually, of course, plaintiff here lost only some $8,680—or somewhat less than the $10,000 which he originally proposed and agreed to invest.

The judgment is reversed.

[handwritten margin note: if you only contribute services, you can't be held liable for $$$ loss]

[handwritten notes:

R
−15,000
+4,000
+6,000

O
−15,000
+4,000
]

CHAPTER FOUR

BUSINESS PLANNING

INTRODUCTION

Some readers may be familiar with entity types other than corporations and partnerships. For example, many small businesses are organized as limited liability companies, or LLCs. Law firms, meanwhile, are now frequently structured as limited liability partnerships. You may also have heard of so-called S corporations or perhaps even the more recent invention of "benefit corporations." If you scan the table of contents of this book, however, you will notice that we do not attempt to study any of these alternative entity forms in a substantive fashion. This is because each is really just an adaptation or recombination of the features of the two basic forms—partnerships and corporations.

An LLC statute, for example, combines partnership-style taxation with corporate limited liability. Thus, the best way to study the attributes of an LLC is to study them in the context in which they were developed—as traits of partnerships and corporations. These elements developed over years or even centuries, and their jurisprudence is rich and nuanced. Moreover, there are countless examples to study as well as a sufficient breadth of cases to explicate almost any conceivable circumstance. The law governing LLCs, by contrast, is shallow or sometimes nonexistent. Moreover, a typical LLC legal decision might aspire to nothing more complicated than ratifying the relevant partnership or corporate law and formally adopting it for use by LLCs. Thus, to understand taxation or limited liability (or any other attribute) in the LLC context, it is best that we study them in the context of partnerships and corporations.

Note that there are really two questions that must be asked by anyone who seeks to form a business. The first is known as "choice of law" or "choice of jurisdiction," while the second is known as "choice of entity." Part A addresses choice of jurisdiction by examining the legal concepts that enable practitioners to select the law of the state that will govern the proposed business. Part A also provides background on Delaware law and the reasons why the nation's second-smallest state became and remains the host jurisdiction for a sizable majority of America's largest corporations.

Of course, the trick to business planning is becoming familiar with the alphabet soup of available entities and understanding how each uniquely combines the attributes taken from partnerships and corporations. Part B therefore addresses the choice-of-entity question by comparing and contrasting the attributes of the most popular business forms side by side. Our goal is to identify which entity is best suited for any given business case. It is, in other words, a game of mix and match: collaborate with the client to select the most desirable elements for her business goals and then work backwards to determine which entity best combines them. For example, startup companies with high growth potential tend to be organized as corporations, whereas startup companies that do not anticipate dramatic and immediate growth are better suited to the LLC form.

At the end of this chapter, you will have the tools necessary to advise a client on how and where to organize a new business venture. You will also be able to draw upon the knowledge gained in this chapter to discern benefits and drawbacks of the various entity types as well as begin to understand how these types relate to one another.

PART A CHOICE OF JURISDICTION

Coca-Cola is headquartered in Georgia. The Ford Motor Company has its base of operations in Michigan, Walmart in Arkansas, and Apple in California. Yet all four—along with approximately two-thirds of America's largest publicly traded companies—are incorporated in Delaware. To understand the truly bizarre nature of this discrepancy, consider that Delaware's population is less than half that of Portland, Oregon. Geographically, Delaware could fit comfortably within the boundaries of Lane County, Oregon, where I reside.

This almost surreal state of affairs poses for us four important questions: How, from a legal standpoint, can it be possible that so much of American business is regulated by so small a state as Delaware? Why did this situation arise? Why has it continued to the present day? And is it a good thing?

LEGAL AUTHORITY

Corporations are legal fictions that cannot exist absent government sanction. They require a grant of authority—sometimes referred to as a "concession"—from one or another state in order to be recognized as a legal entity. This is in contrast to a run-of-the-mill contract, which may be made privately and does not require government authorization to become enforceable. A corporation, before it will be treated as a collective entity, must make a public filing that both gives notice of its manifestation and adopts and ratifies the regulatory scheme by which it will be bound.

Surprisingly, however, there is no requirement that a corporation obtain its authority from any particular state. In fact, the law is quite the opposite. Article IV, Section 1 of the US Constitution reads as follows:

> Full Faith and Credit shall be given in each State to the public Acts, Records, and judicial Proceedings of every other State.

In practice, this means that if a corporation is organized pursuant to the laws of, say, New York, its existence and construction must be recognized by the other forty-nine states. According to the "internal affairs doctrine," the governance structure of a corporation is determined by the laws of its state of incorporation, not the state in which it is geographically located. Such matters might include the method by which it divides profits and assigns liabilities, its voting procedures, and its distribution of managerial authority.

Of course, matters not affecting the internal affairs of a corporation remain in the purview of whatever state exercises jurisdiction. For example, a company incorporated in New York but conducting business only in Oregon would be subject to Oregon's laws regarding subjects such as fair labor practices, environmental protection, and property and income taxation. If it also had operations in California and New York, those operations would be subject to the external regulations of California and New York, respectively.

The legal impact of this system is twofold. First, it means that corporations can select the laws by which their internal governance will be regulated. In most other circumstances, one must abide by the law of the jurisdiction in which one lives or operates. It is not possible, for example, to choose one's tax laws. Nor can a violent criminal choose to be tried in a state that has no death penalty. A corporation, however, can select which state's regulatory scheme it finds to be most advantageous.

The second impact of the internal affairs doctrine has been the emergence of a contest among the states for corporate charters. When a business incorporates in a particular state, it must pay that state an annual fee, known as a "franchise tax." For a small state like Delaware, this stream of revenue can have significant financial benefits—approximately one-fourth of its annual budget is currently funded by income from franchise fees. As a result, scholars have long observed that states are in competition with one another to attract the revenue that comes with corporate charters.

HISTORICAL DEVELOPMENT

Prior to 1875, most states had adopted so-called "restrictive pattern acts" that reflected Americans' deep distrust of corporate enterprises. These statutes granted authority for corporations to exist but placed severe restrictions on the manner in which they could be operated. In particular, corporations were subject to four major limitations. First, they were generally limited in their size, scope, and purpose. Second, managers had relatively limited operational discretion and could not take many actions—such as borrowing money, leasing property, or raising additional capital—without (often unanimous) shareholder approval. Third, shareholders were personally liable for employee wages and certain other categories of debt. Fourth, and perhaps most significant, corporations were not permitted to own shares of other corporations.

Prior to the Industrial Revolution, most American businesses were small, operated locally, and had relatively modest capital needs. As the nation industrialized in the years following the Civil War and businesses grew in size and complexity, the need for more efficient management structures became acute. Because the law could not keep pace with the rate of change, creative lawyers conceived of clever means to evade its constraints. For example, Standard Oil—then the world's largest energy company—was organized not as a corporation but as a trust that held shares of its subsidiaries for the benefit of its investors. This structure allowed it to evade the rules against a corporation owning stock.

During the last two decades of the nineteenth century, however, New Jersey enacted a series of laws that liberalized its approach to corporate regulation. In 1889, it adopted the first of what are now known as "enabling statutes." Its laws attempted to foster entrepreneurship and to support, rather than regulate, business growth. Under New Jersey's system, the legislature would continue to regulate the external affairs of corporations, but the rules governing their internal affairs would from that point forward be designed to maximize efficiency rather than constrain behavior that the legislature deemed undesirable.

The business world's reaction to New Jersey's plan of deregulation was both swift and enthusiastic. In fact, so many corporations chose to adopt its regulatory scheme—and to pay its franchise taxes—that it was able to eliminate altogether both its property and income taxes. But among Progressive Era critics of corporate excess, the reaction was quite the opposite. In 1913, after a long political struggle, then-governor Woodrow Wilson signed back into law many of the restrictions that New Jersey had taken the lead in abolishing.

What happened next became a sort of origin myth regarding would-be corporate watchdogs. Delaware adopted New Jersey's deregulatory approach and emerged as the capital of American business law. During the era of New Jersey's prominence, Delaware (along with Maine, South Dakota, and West Virginia) had copied its corporation statute. When New Jersey opted to return to its regulatory past, Delaware eagerly took possession of its mantle as America's least-regulated jurisdiction. Rather than conforming to New Jersey's new laws, most businesses simply reincorporated in the Blue Hen State. To the dismay of New Jersey and the delight of Delaware, corporate America had defeated the reformers and demonstrated the power of regulatory arbitrage.

MAINTAINING ITS PROMINENCE

Having learned from what it believes to be New Jersey's grand mistake, Delaware today works diligently to preserve its pro-business reputation. It accomplishes this in several ways. First, its legislature makes it a priority to constantly update the Delaware General Corporation Law, thereby ensuring that its legal system remains on the cutting edge of deregulation. Second, the Delaware Secretary of State's office is extremely courteous and efficient, a true model of how government should run. Third, pursuant to Delaware's constitution, the DGCL can be amended only by a two-thirds majority of both houses of the legislature. Thus, it would be extremely difficult for a corporate governance reformer to shift the direction of Delaware law back toward more extensive regulation, as happened in New Jersey in 1913.

Delaware's leadership position is also a result of three structural advantages that it does not control. First, as a small state, it has a relatively small tax base. Indeed, it is home to more business entities than people. This means that the income it earns from corporate franchise fees makes up a much larger percentage of its total tax revenue than would be the case in a more populous state. Corporate managers can therefore trust that Delaware will never risk increasing regulation without endangering this revenue stream. It is, in other words, held hostage by its reliance on income from corporate charters.

A second structural advantage enjoyed by Delaware comes under the rubric of what economists call "network externalities." These are benefits that accrue from the fact that so many corporations are incorporated in Delaware. A business that follows the crowd and chooses Delaware lowers the risk that it will be singled out for any wrongdoing. Its choice of Delaware law also signals to investors that its managers are savvy enough to know the unwritten best practices of corporate governance. Finally, because the characteristics of Delaware law are so familiar to business leaders the world over, its selection facilitates communication and increases transparency and efficiency.

Delaware's third structural advantage arises from the large number of corporate law disputes that are settled there. Because of its remarkably low person-to-business ratio, a significant proportion of its court cases involve questions of corporate governance. This is a plus for corporations

DE would die w/o corps

because it means that many Delaware judges have become experts regarding business law, making it more likely that their decisions will correctly identify and balance the business realities of any given case. It is also a plus in that its large number of decisions means that Delaware's caselaw is quite robust. Whatever the issue, no matter how obscure, it is likely that there already exists helpful precedent. As a result, Delaware law is highly predictable, even regarding its arcana.

In practical terms, Delaware's pro-business approach means that a large majority of American businesses find it desirable to incorporate pursuant to Delaware law. Note, however, that every state in which a business conducts active operations will require the business to register there as a "foreign corporation" and pay a modest annual fee.

A RACE TO ... WHERE?

As long ago as 1933, in *Liggett v. Lee,* Supreme Court Justice Louis Brandeis famously described America's system of regulatory competition as "one not of diligence but of laxity." He and other critics of corporate excess argued that, since it is corporate managers who make the decision as to where to incorporate, state legislatures have every incentive to pander to those managers (at the expense of both shareholders and society at large). The result is a deregulatory spiral—a "race to the bottom."

In the 1980s and 1990s, however, as the law-and-economics movement gained traction, conservative scholars argued that the opposite was true. They agreed with liberal observers that states were engaged in a contest to see which could become the most pro-business. However, they believed in the benefits of unfettered competition. For them, a contest to see which state could most fully deregulate constituted a "race to the top."

More recently, scholars have added an additional observation: the competition among states may in fact be something of a myth. On most issues of importance to managers, corporation law differs little from state to state; all state's laws are enabling. Because of the combination of Delaware's first-mover advantage and its gains from network externalities, any real competition ceased to exist long ago.

Delaware does, however, face one formidable competitor—the federal government. A business can reincorporate so as to avoid a given state's regulatory scheme, but no business can afford to forgo the American marketplace altogether. Congress will always have jurisdiction, should it choose to exercise its prerogative. Indeed, beginning at least as far back as the 1930s, Washington has responded to business scandals with new laws, while Delaware has remained silent. For example, in the wake of the Great Depression, Congress enacted a far-reaching system of federal securities regulation (which is the subject of Chapter Ten). Congress further extended its regulatory reach following, among other financial disasters, the dotcom crash of 2001 and the mortgage crisis of 2008.

Thus, the *status quo* appears to be little or no regulation of corporate governance by Delaware coupled with slowly increasing regulation by the federal government. Whether this is a positive or a negative depends on your political preference—and perhaps your stock portfolio.

CHOICE OF ENTITY PART B

Entrepreneurs and others who organize a new business must do more than select the state in which to incorporate. They must also select the form of entity they wish to utilize. Traditionally, the two basic choices have been corporations and partnerships. In fact, until at least the late 1990s, law school courses on business entities were commonly named "Corporations" and "Partnerships." There are, however, a number of other choices that now exist, including, most importantly, limited liability companies (or LLCs).

The nuances of the various entities are complex and require a full reading of the caselaw. Set forth below, however, are the general mechanics applicable to the different business forms that help determine entity choice.

CORPORATIONS

Corporations are governed by statute, with each state having its own corporate code. Prominent business states like Delaware and New York have unique statutory formats. Many other states have adopted versions of the Model Business Corporation Act. Lawyers should always consult the most up-to-date version of the applicable state's statute rather than relying on memory or a general summary such as the one below. Corporate statutes have many small variations across the states and are subject to frequent revisions.

Corporations are licensed by the state. They are formed by filing papers—Articles or a Certificate of Incorporation (known colloquially as the corporation's "charter")—and paying a modest fee to the Secretary of State of the state whose laws are to govern. Generally, the charter is quite basic and includes only the corporation's name, an address at which legal papers may be served, the nature or purpose of the business to be conducted (which may be as broad as "to engage in any lawful act or activity"), the number of shares the corporation is authorized to issue, and the name and address of the incorporator. For larger and more complex businesses, other information may also be included in the charter, such as the granting of special rights to shareholders and the waiver of certain liabilities of the corporation's directors. If a corporation is to be located or conduct business in states other than the state of its incorporation, a similar filing and fee must be paid in each such state to register it as a "foreign corporation."

Each corporation is controlled by a board of directors who are charged with managing its "business and affairs." The board may consist of any number of persons and may also delegate its powers to one or more committees and/or to officers. Traditionally, many states required that every corporation have both a president and secretary, and that these positions be held by different human beings. However, this requirement is less frequent today, and it is generally possible to have a corporation with a single officer. The board of directors may from time to time adopt by-laws and resolutions that govern the conduct of its business and the powers and responsibilities of the corporation's various agents.

Corporations are sometimes said to be "owned" by their shareholders. This means that the equity of the corporation—its residual value after all debts are paid—is allocated among its shareholders in proportion to the number of shares each shareholder purchased. One vote is assigned to each share, such that a single shareholder owning many shares would be entitled to many votes. A corporation may have multiple classes or series of shares, each with its own set of rights, privileges, and restrictions.

Corporations have perpetual life. The death or other exit of a shareholder, director, or officer does not terminate or alter the nature or existence of a corporation. In order to dissolve a corporation, one must generally obtain either a court order or the consent of the holders of a majority of its outstanding shares. Failure to pay annual taxes, known as "franchise fees," will result in a corporation's involuntary dissolution.

Corporations are treated as distinct legal persons. They can own property, sue and be sued, and generally enjoy the rights and privileges of legal persons. They are responsible for their own debts and must pay their own taxes. Such treatment yields two important results: limited liability and so-called "double taxation."

Corporate shareholders enjoy limited liability. Except in unusual circumstances, shareholders are shielded from the debts of the corporations in which they invest. If a corporation enters into a contract or commits a tort, it is only the assets of the corporation that may be seized to pay the debt. Its shareholders' personal assets are protected because they and the corporation each constitute a distinct legal person, and the law does not generally require one person to stand for the debts of another. Thus, if a corporation becomes insolvent, it may enter into bankruptcy and its shareholders may lose the value of their investment, but creditors cannot generally seize any of the shareholders' personal belongings.

Corporate profits are subject to a system of double taxation. As a distinct legal person, a corporation must pay federal income taxes on the profits it earns from the conduct of its business. This generally represents a specified portion of the corporation's gross earnings after deducting expenses. However, a second layer of tax is applied to a corporation's earnings if they are paid out to its shareholders in the form of a cash dividend or in-kind distribution. Again, this occurs because the corporation and its shareholders are treated as distinct legal persons. Thus, when a corporation distributes money to its shareholders, the shareholders realize income of their own from their investment in the corporation. In this respect, the same dollar of corporate profit is subject to federal income tax twice as it travels through the corporation and into the coffers of its shareholders.

As an illustration, imagine that a corporation earns exactly $1,000 and pays income tax at a flat rate of 30%. Imagine too that it has a single shareholder who is also subject to income tax at a flat rate of 30%. The corporation must pay $300 (30% of the $1,000) to the IRS when taxes are due. If the corporation's directors then choose to pay out the remaining $700 to its shareholder, she will be deemed to have profited to the extent of the $700, just as if she had earned the money from some other source. She must therefore pay $210 (30% of $700) to the IRS when taxes are due. In the end, she will be enriched to the extent of $490, whereas she would have been enriched by $700 had she earned the money directly and not utilized the corporate form.

This example is oversimplified, and the tax rates applied to corporate dividends (the second layer of tax) have generally been substantially lower than the rates applied to ordinary income such as that earned by the corporation. However, avoidance of the impact of double taxation is generally an important factor for entrepreneurs to consider when making a choice of entity. The resulting conventional wisdom has been that a corporation is highly valued for the limited liability it confers upon its shareholders, but with the tradeoff that it produces lower after-tax profits. As a result, many entrepreneurs who have chosen to form corporations have sought ways to dampen the impact of the second layer of tax.

One prominent method for limiting the bite of double taxation is for small business owners to withdraw profits from a corporation in the form of salary. Remember that a corporation pays taxes only to the extent it realizes profits *after deducting expenses*. One common business expense is the salary paid to employees. Therefore, if a corporation pays a salary to its shareholders in their guise *as employees*—a common situation among small businesses where the owners are typically also the managers—those payments will put money into the shareholders' pockets while simultaneously reducing the corporation's net profits by an equal amount. The employee-shareholders must still pay taxes on the monies they receive, but such monies will be taxed only once because they are exempt from corporate-level tax. Many other strategies, including the lending of money and the leasing of property to the corporation, can also be used to limit corporate-level taxes. Alternatively, profits can be accumulated or reinvested inside the corporation such that they are never subject to a shareholder-level tax because they are never distributed to shareholders. Indeed, the somewhat shocking reality is that most corporations enjoy limited liability while actually paying little or no federal income tax.

PARTNERSHIPS

Existing on the opposite end of the spectrum from incorporated entities are unincorporated partnerships. Generally speaking, they represent the default business form for entrepreneurs who forget or choose not to incorporate. Indeed, for the most part, they are organized today only by accident. Entrepreneurs who actively plan for the formation of their business typically select a different entity structure. Generally speaking, whereas corporations are formal and hierarchical, partnerships are informal and egalitarian.

Partnerships are formed when two or more persons express their intent to join forces in a business for profit. Thus, no filing is needed since no state sanction is necessary. As a result, partnerships are highly unstable. If a partner dies or otherwise severs her intent to remain a partner, the partnership is immediately ended. For this reason, creditors are sometimes unwilling to extend favorable terms to a partnership.

Partnerships are governed by a partnership agreement. This agreement may be explicit or implicit, and may divide management and profits in any manner the partners prefer. In the absence of evidence of an agreement, the default rules contained in the applicable state statute will control the partnership. Although every state has adopted a version of either the Uniform Partnership Act (1914) or the Revised Uniform Partnership Act (1993 or 1997), partnerships can perhaps be better understood as having grown out of the common law.

Pursuant to the default partnership rules, each partner has an equal number of votes and the same management powers, regardless of the amount of money or time she contributes. Partners are deemed to be both agents and principals of the partnership. As a result, each partner can individually bind the partnership to contracts in the ordinary course. Likewise, each partner is entitled to an equal portion of any profits and is responsible for an equal portion of any partnership debts.

Partnership law is both uneasy and equivocal regarding the nature of a partnership as a distinct legal entity. Partnerships can own property, sue and be sued, and enjoy other rights and privileges of legal persons. However, partnerships are not treated as distinct legal entities for purposes of federal income taxes and they do not confer limited liability upon their owners.

Partnerships do not protect partners from liability for business debts. If a partnership cannot pay a debt, the creditor in question has the right to go after the personal assets of the individual partners. In fact, a partner's liability is joint and several, meaning that each partner effectively guarantees all of the partnership's debts. Investing even one dollar in a partnership is therefore equivalent to risking one's entire estate. That being said, if a particular partner is singled out and sued for more than her proportionate share of the debt, she can force the other partners to contribute their proportionate share. On the other hand, this may turn out to be a false hope. If one or more partners are left out of a lawsuit, it may be because they lack sufficient personal funds to pay (or contribute their proportionate share to) the debt. It is therefore extremely risky to be the only wealthy partner in a partnership, a hazard that should be clear in the minds of anyone doing business without forming an incorporated entity. This is especially true because partnerships can be formed by a mere expression of intent and because each partner, absent agreement to the contrary, shares equal power in the management of the business.

For federal income tax purposes, partnerships do not exist other than for recordkeeping purposes (partners must file a Schedule K reporting partnership profits so that the IRS can ensure that all partners are reporting the same amount of profit). Thus, when a partnership realizes taxable profits, those profits are immediately attributable to the individual partners as if they themselves were the direct earners of the money. As a result, partners receive business income without the impact of the corporate double tax. Returning to the illustration above, partners of a partnership that earned $1,000 in profits would be entitled to the full $700 of after-tax profit (the total profit less a single layer of $300 of tax). In addition, it should be noted that any special tax attributes attached to the partnership's income due to the manner in which such income was earned will be retained and attributed to the partner. Thus, for example, ordinary income or investment income earned by a partnership will be treated as ordinary income or investment income, as applicable, in the hands of its partners.

Although this system of "flow-through" or "pass-through" taxation appears to be more favorable than the tax system applied to corporations, one dark side does exist. There is the potential for a disconnect to arise between taxation and profit. Taxes are assessed when they are realized (although we generally pay this assessment only once a year for administrative convenience). However, it is not necessarily the case that a partnership will pay out profits to its shareholders at any particular time or at all. Instead, profits may be retained or re-invested in the business, meaning that a partner may be subject to tax on monies she never received. One common solution for this potential risk is for the partners to agree to cause an automatic annual distribution of profits to the extent necessary for the partners to pay their federal income taxes associated with the partnership's business. On the other hand, if the partners are savvy enough to engage in this level of tax planning, they are unlikely to want to form a partnership.

To return again to the conventional wisdom of business planning, partnerships are desirable because of their favorable tax treatment, but their lack of limited liability makes them anathema to most entrepreneurs. Traditionally, then, those planning a new business venture were forced to select between the limited liability of incorporated entities and the pass-through tax treatment of disregarded entities. The law was crying out for a structure that would allow entrepreneurs to have it both ways.

SUBCHAPTER S CORPORATIONS

If corporations and partnerships were the only two choices facing an entrepreneur, there would be a strong desire among the business community for an alternative that combined the best attributes of both entities. In fact, both Congress and state legislatures have taken steps to provide such alternatives. However, the manner in which their respective powers are limited by notions of federalism has impacted the development of these alternatives. Congress can change the taxation of business entities, but not their underlying corporate structure. State legislatures, by contrast, have the power to alter the nature and governance of the different business entities, but not their federal tax treatment.

The taxation of most corporations is governed by Subchapter C of the Internal Revenue Code. As a result, traditional corporations are sometimes known as "C corporations." This is to contrast them with so-called "S corporations." S corporations are creatures of the Internal Revenue Code and are thus exactly the same as C corporations for all purposes of state corporate law. Indeed, S corporations begin their existence as C corporations, but make a special tax election (within one year of their incorporation) by which they agree to be subject to Subchapter S of the Internal Revenue Code.

For most business lawyers, Subchapter S can be understood as conferring upon certain corporations the tax status of a flow-through entity. The mechanics of how this works are slightly different from the mechanics of partnership taxation and, for tax attorneys, these differences can sometimes be quite important. However, for the most part, the overall impact of Subchapter S is to tax small corporations like partnerships. In this manner, Congress in 1958 used its power over the tax code to provide a hybrid entity that granted favorable federal tax treatment to corporations upon which state legislatures had previously conferred limited liability. As a result, until the emergence of LLCs in the late 1990s, small businesses were frequently organized as S corporations.

Not every corporation can elect to be taxed pursuant to Subchapter S, however. To qualify, the corporation must (1) be a domestic corporation, (2) have only a single class of stock, (3) have only individuals (or certain trusts and estates) as shareholders, (4) have no non-resident alien shareholders, and (5) have only a limited number of shareholders. Initially, the permitted number of shareholders was limited to ten. That number has crept upward over the years, however, and S corporations are currently allowed to have up to one hundred shareholders. Notwithstanding this liberalizing trend, the restrictions on S corporation status have limited the usefulness of this vehicle for many complex business structures.

LIMITED PARTNERSHIPS

While Congress was experimenting with ways of giving corporations favorable tax treatment, state legislatures were experimenting with ways of giving partnerships limited liability. The most prominent result is the limited partnership.

Limited partnerships are generally exactly like normal or "general" partnerships, with two key differences. First, in order to obtain a grant of limited liability from the state, there must be a filing (and a fee must be paid). Typically, this takes the form of a very basic Certificate of Limited Partnership that includes little more than the name of the partnership, the name of the general partners, and an address at which process may be served. Limited partnerships, in other words, are like corporations in that they are creatures of statute with perpetual life. They cannot be formed or dissolved merely by the presence or absence of intent, but rather require an affirmative act of incorporation or dissolution. Foreign LPs likewise must be registered in each state in which they carry on a business.

The second difference is the manner in which management and liability are apportioned. In a limited partnership, the structure of management is set forth in a Limited Partnership Agreement, an often lengthy document that addresses many of the same questions (although with different answers) as do a corporate charter and bylaws. The partners are divided into two classes, and there must be at least one partner of each class type. General partners are treated exactly the same as partners in a general partnership. They manage the affairs of the partnership and face joint and severable liability for its debts. Often, limited partnerships are structured such that there is only a single general partner who guarantees all of the firm's debts. Limited partners, on the other hand, have no role in the day-to-day management of the business but enjoy corporate-like limited liability. For the limited partners, then, LPs combine the benefits of both pass-through tax treatment and limited liability.

Note that limited partnerships divide power in a way that S corporations, with their single class of stock, cannot. The result is that, while S corporations have long been the preferred vehicle for small, "mom and pop" businesses, LPs have been quite popular as vehicles for joint investment, such as venture capital and hedge funds. A bank or other professional investor—usually an entity with limited liability of its own—typically serves as the general partner, controlling the business and its investments, while passive investors contribute money in exchange for limited partnership interests. Their personal assets are protected by limited liability, but their earnings are subject to only a single layer of tax.

LIMITED LIABILITY COMPANIES

Although limited partnerships and S corporations represent significant steps forward for entrepreneurs, they both have drawbacks. In a limited partnership, someone—usually the professional manager—must retain full personal liability for the entity's debts. And with regard to S corporations, the prohibitions against corporate shareholders and multiple classes of stock narrow the range of circumstances in which they can be used.

In 1977, the State of Wyoming adopted the nation's first true limited liability company statute, modeled after German law. It combined limited liability for all investors with the true pass-through tax treatment of a partnership. In 1982, Florida adopted a similar statute. Yet there remained a problem. The states of Wyoming and Florida lacked the power to determine the application of federal income tax. They could declare that LLCs should be taxed as disregarded entities, but could not make it so. The question hung in the air: what would the IRS make of these new entities?

In 1988, the IRS adopted a four-part resemblance test. It stated that the key attributes of a corporation could be summarized as (1) limited liability, (2) continuity of life, (3) centralized management, and (4) free transferability of ownership shares. Henceforth, the IRS would examine any new entity structure according to these four factors. An entity that satisfied three or more would be taxed like a corporation; one that satisfied two or fewer would be taxed as a partnership pursuant to Subchapter K of the Internal Revenue Code.

With this clarification in tax status, the race was now on. Within a very few years, all fifty states had adopted a version of LLC statute, and today LLCs make up over two-thirds of all new entity formations in Delaware. However, the IRS ruling was not without its own limitations. First, it applied only to multi-member firms. Second, and more importantly, it did not serve to sort business entities according to their tax attributes so much as to regulate their internal governance structure. Predictably, perhaps, corporate lawyers did not passively organize new LLCs and wait to see how the IRS would categorize them in accordance with its four-part test. Rather, they read up on the tax rules and structured new LLCs in a manner that garnered them the tax treatment they preferred. Generally speaking, they made sure that any new LLC had a limited life (often either 30 or 99 years, depending on the aggressiveness of the lawyer) and that ownership interests were not freely transferable.

The result was that the IRS found itself in the position of dictating the governance structure of a state-law entity, an unintended role to which it was not suited. Recognizing this, the IRS in 1997 adopted its so-called "check-the-box" regulations. From that point on, a non-traditional entity like an LLC, regardless of the number of members, could simply make an election—check the box to be treated as a disregarded entity and taxed like a partnership; don't check the box to be taxed as a C corporation or S corporation. In effect, the IRS had teamed up with state legislatures to grant entrepreneurs their ultimate goal, an entity choice that combined the flow-through tax treatment of a partnership with the limited liability of a corporation. Single-member LLCs were also granted the same preferential tax status.

LLCs, like limited partnerships and corporations, are creatures of statute with perpetual life that require formal filings (and fees) to be organized. Typically, this takes the form of a very basic Certificate of Formation that need contain only the name of the LLC and the name and address of its agent for service of process. Dissolution, likewise, generally requires a majority vote of the members or a court order. Foreign LLCs must register in each state in which they carry on business.

In terms of management and ownership structure, LLCs offer incredible flexibility, the details of which are spelled out by the parties in an Operating Agreement that is often quite similar in content to a Limited Partnership Agreement. Generally speaking, LLCs may be either member-managed or manager-managed. Member-managed LLCs operate like partnerships. Management and ownership are shared equally among the equity owners, who take a direct role in managing the business.

By contrast, manager-managed LLCs can operate like either a limited partnership or a corporation. If there is a single manager, charged with managing the business on behalf of the members, then the result will look and feel like a limited partnership, especially if the manager is also a member. If there is a board of managers, with several individuals charged with managing the business as a group, the result will look and feel like a corporation with a board of directors. In each case, voting power and equity ownership is divided among one or more classes of "units" or "membership interests" instead of shares, and the managers may appoint officers and/or committees to whom they delegate power.

With their combination of pass-through taxation and limited liability for all investors, LLCs have begun to crowd out the field. For most purposes, they have replaced S corporations[1] and limited partnerships and may someday make up the bulk of all business entities. So why is more attention not paid to them in law school? First, their unique history means that most states adopted one or another form of LLC statute prior to the passage of any sort of model act. As a result, there is a relative lack of uniformity among the nation's LLC statutes, making it difficult to generalize about their specifics. Second, because they are comparatively new on the scene, there simply is not enough caselaw to study in depth. Third, and most importantly for students, LLCs are hybrid entities that borrow concepts from both corporate and partnership law. As a result, the best way to learn about an LLC's corporate-like attributes, such as limited liability, is to study the development of limited liability in the context of corporations. Likewise, the best way to learn about its partnership-like attributes, such as pass-through taxation, is to study the taxation of partnerships. Thus, although the typical Business Associations curriculum appears not to address LLCs in any depth, the reality is that students learn all they need to know about LLCs from this brief summary coupled with a careful study of corporations and partnerships.

---

1   Surprisingly, there appears to exist a fair degree of uncertainty regarding whether S corporations confer tax benefits superior to LLCs in the realm of self-employment taxes. Although it appears that the IRS proposed rules in 1997 that provide clarification for how LLC members can avoid the unnecessary imposition of self-employment taxes, these rules are relatively unknown and many practitioners remain concerned enough to recommend that certain small-business owners form an S corporation rather than an LLC.

OTHER MISCELLANEOUS ENTITY TYPES

When an individual engages in business transactions on her own, with no partner and no formal entity structure, she is known as a sole proprietor. She is responsible for her own debts and is the sole beneficiary of any profits she earns. She likewise pays her own taxes directly on any such profits.

In addition to the five most significant entities described above, there exist a variety of other entity forms and structures that are typically designed with a particular industry or profession in mind. Because they generally borrow concepts from corporations and partnerships, and because they have limited applicability, they do not deserve as much attention as do the other main entity types. All, however, are creatures of statute with perpetual life that require specific filings (and fees) in order to be organized or dissolved.

One example of a specialized vehicle is the statutory business trust. This entity form is used almost exclusively by the mutual-fund industry. Because mutual funds are regulated as "investment companies" under the federal securities laws, they are not well suited to most business structures. Indeed, because so many of the nation's large mutual funds are based in Boston, these entities are generally known as "Massachusetts business trusts," even if they are organized pursuant to the laws of Delaware or another state.

Another example is the limited liability partnership, or LLP. This entity structure was designed for lawyers, accountants, and architects and, in many states, may not be organized for use by non-professionals. LLPs are for the most part similar to limited partnerships, but with two main differences. First, there is no general partner, such that all partners enjoy limited liability for business debts that are not attributable to their own personal negligence. Second, all partners face unlimited personal liability for debts that arise due to their own malpractice. Thus, in an LLP, each partner effectively guarantees the quality of her own work but not that of her partners.

Other entity forms include national banks, such as Citibank, N.A., which are federally chartered by the Office of the Comptroller of Currency; federally chartered credit unions and savings banks; limited liability limited partnerships, or LLLPs, which combine aspects of limited partnerships and LLPs; professional corporations, or PCs, which tailor the corporate form for use by professional firms; professional limited liability companies, or PLLCs, which combine aspects of PCs and LLCs; consumer and worker cooperatives; and many more. Indeed, the National Football League claims that it is not an entity at all, but rather an "unincorporated association."

BENEFIT CORPORATIONS

During the last decade or so, a number of socially responsible investors have become increasingly frustrated by what they perceive as the antisocial purposes of corporations. As a result, they have engaged in a highly successful nationwide lobbying effort to pass one or more variations of benefit corporation statutes. The idea behind most of these efforts is to require corporations formed pursuant to such a statute to operate with the express purpose of benefitting one or more "stakeholders" in addition to its traditional shareholders. Examples of such stakeholders include employees, the environment, and the community or society at large. Often, these so-called "B corporations" are required to publish an annual report regarding their socially responsible activities.

As of 2014, twenty-eight states, including Delaware, had adopted some version of benefit corporation statue, although with a wide degree of variance among them. Prominent B corporations include Etsy, Patagonia, and Seventh Generation.

Benefit corporations are too new on the scene for an adequate understanding of their impact, and many questions remain. For example, can the directors of a B corporation that treats its employees well be sued by representatives of the environment for going too far and failing to create a sufficient surplus that can be donated to environmental charities? Likewise, can a B corporation that pays dividends be sued by representatives of the local community who believe too much has been paid to shareholders and not enough invested in local schools and parks? Or vice versa? And if such suits are not possible, what limitations actually exist on the social responsibility of a B corporation's managers? What ensures that they will actually behave in a manner that is any more "beneficial" than does a regular corporation?

Despite a number of lingering questions, the most significant challenge to B corporations is that they do not appear to be in any way necessary. Corporations organized under traditional statutes already have the express power to make donations to charity, and many corporate statutes permit or even mandate that a corporation's board of directors consider a wide range of stakeholder interests under a variety of circumstances. Indeed, the business judgment rule grants management significant latitude to act in whatever manner they select. Many progressive commentators assume that this latitude allows only for manager indiscretion, but in fact it permits managers to act in the public interest as well. It is not the structure of corporate law that drives our current obsession with shareholder wealth maximization, but the national conversation regarding the role and responsibilities of corporate America.

The resulting criticism is that B corporation statutes may amount to nothing more than a marketing gimmick promulgated by the very groups that would be paid annually to certify each B corporation's status. Even worse, many commentators worry that socially responsible investors will now withdraw from the ongoing debate over the purpose and function of traditional corporations in order to focus on B corporations. The result will be that traditional corporations—which will always account for the great bulk of America's economic output—will feel less pressure to act in a manner that is socially responsible. Indeed, they may even interpret the division of corporations into two categories, beneficial and regular, as a license for traditional corporations to ignore the public interest. Ironically, then, there is real potential for B corporation statutes to backfire and result in fewer (and smaller), rather than more, socially responsible businesses.

CONCLUSION

Having now considered the range of entity choices facing an entrepreneur, the question arises as to what extent the law controls. Put differently, is it the law or the market (or something else) that will dictate the reality facing a new business? In fact, upon closer inspection, it appears that the choice of entity may have little bearing on the two most important legal questions facing an entrepreneur—the entity's tax status and the liability of its investors.

In general, the investors in any small enterprise, regardless of entity choice, are likely to bear unlimited personal liability for the debts of the firm. If the organizers select to form a partnership, liability will, by law, be joint and several and unlimited. If they instead elect to form a corporation, LLC or limited partnership, the law will assign them limited liability, but they are unlikely to enjoy it.

In most small business enterprises, the two most significant contract liabilities are likely to be a lease and a loan (for start-up costs and working capital). Landlords and lenders, however, are unlikely to extend credit to a business with little or no operating history and little in the way of assets. As a result, they are all but certain to require that the investors guaranty the firm's debts. Limited liability, while available on paper, will not survive the negotiation process.

In terms of the other main source of small business liability—tort law claims for negligence and malpractice—the situation is similar. Although the investors will benefit from limited liability *as shareholders*, they are themselves likely in many cases to be the cause of any tort liability. In a small business where the owners are the managers, it is they who are most likely to engage in malpractice or in conduct that is deemed to be negligent. In such cases, they can be sued directly for their own misconduct. Limited liability shields investors, not employees, and small business owner-managers serve in both roles and so are vulnerable to suit based on either theory.

The tax situation is similarly likely to be unaffected by the choice of entity. Certainly, if the organizers of a firm select a disregarded entity like a limited partnership or LLC, its profits will be subject to only a single layer of tax. On the other hand, with sufficient planning, the profits of most small corporations can be withdrawn as a combination of salary, fringe benefits, rent, and interest on loans—all typical business expenses that reduce a corporation's profits. Often, these will result in zero corporate-level tax and hence no double taxation. After all, zero profit means zero tax.

So what about firms on the other end of the spectrum? Does the choice of entity by large enterprises with many shareholders have important tax and liability implications? Again, the answer is generally no, although here the reasons reside primarily in the Internal Revenue Code.

Regardless of form, any entity that is deemed to be a "publicly traded partnership" will be subject to double taxation. A publicly traded partnership is one whose ownership interests are regularly traded on an established securities market or readily tradable on a secondary market (or its substantial equivalent), *unless* the partnership has one hundred or fewer partners or more than 90% of its income arises from passive investments in securities. Thus, any pass-through entity with even minimal operations runs the risk that it will be retroactively subjected to a second layer of entity-level tax, a truly devastating result with a myriad of complex implications beyond just the higher tax rates, if it has more than one hundred equity owners. With this in mind, practitioners generally assume that any LLC or limited partnership that has more than one hundred investors will be taxed like a corporation. In addition, any LLC or limited partnership that attempts to sell its shares via Nasdaq or the New York Stock Exchange, regardless of its size, will be subject to double taxation.

The tax rules for publicly traded partnerships remove any incentive for an enterprise with a large number of investors to organize as a flow-through entity. As a result, they are almost invariably organized as corporations (or as limited partnerships, with an LLC serving as the general partner, in the case of venture capital and hedge funds). In any case, if a creditor were to try to obtain a guaranty from the shareholders of say, Microsoft, it would face the daunting facts that Microsoft currently has more than eight billion shares outstanding and that almost twenty-six million of its shares change hands in any given ten-day period. Simply put, even if one could sue the investors of Microsoft as a legal matter, it is not at all clear *how* this could be accomplished on a practical level.

Large enterprises, then, are likely to benefit from limited liability for the same reason that they are likely to be subjected to double taxation—the tax code removes any incentive to organize as a flow-through entity. Yet note that even here the story is more complex, for many large enterprises are able to reduce their U.S. federal income tax burden to almost zero as a result of creative and aggressive tax-planning techniques. Indeed, corporate tax experts sometimes like to joke that for most business enterprises, paying income tax is optional.

This discussion has three major implications. First, although the choice of entity matters, market realities are likely to force most small business owners to forego the benefits of limited liability, while the realities of our tax system mean that only large enterprises will be subject to a system of double taxation; and even then the true tax bite is likely to be small. Second, the real distinction among entity structures may reside in the extent of the transaction costs involved in their formation and operation. Small corporations may be able to avoid entity-level tax equally as often as do small LLCs, but only after incurring potentially hefty accounting and recordkeeping costs. Third, lawyers as planners should remain ever humble in the face of market forces and social norms. The law is not an automatic trump card, and we must advise our clients based on more than an understanding of its intricacies and possibilities. We must consider the context in which our clients operate and advise them based on an understanding of practical reality as much as of legal theory. Both are necessary, yet neither is sufficient.

CHAPTER FIVE

FUNDAMENTALS OF CORPORATION LAW

INTRODUCTION

Although many small businesses are organized as LLCs or partnerships, nearly all big business in the United States is conducted through the corporate form. The law governing corporations therefore takes on a particularly public interest. Their conduct and operations—for good or for ill—have implications for the nation's political economy that extend far beyond the interests of their owners and employees. Whether or not you are invested in Wall Street, you have a stake in how its business is conducted.

It is therefore worth stepping back for a moment to contemplate both the dominance and achievements of the corporate form. Without a doubt, corporations can wreak much havoc in the world, as can any assembly of well-organized people, given sufficient resources. However, corporations have also given us miracles of modern invention. They make the cars we drive and the mobile phones with which we communicate. They provide the medicines that keep us healthy and the food that keeps us nourished. In our capitalist society, corporations serve as the organizing structure for the efforts of more than one hundred million workers. Rather than planning our economy in a top-down manner, we rely on a decentralized network of private corporations to produce close to $20 trillion of goods annually.

For perspective regarding the scope of the corporate enterprise, consider that in 2018, Apple Computers had a market valuation that exceeded the nominal GDP of all but sixteen of the world's independent nations. Indeed, put together, the value of Apple and Microsoft exceeded the GDP of *Russia*. And with close to two million registered corporations, there is no part of modern American society that survives untouched by their influence.

We therefore begin our study of corporations in this chapter with an examination of what makes this invention of nineteenth-century America so special. What is it about the corporate form that has led to its dominance? Although corporations have existed in the United States for more than two centuries, its fundamental nature has remained surprisingly contentious right up to the present day. In fact, we remain divided over two existential questions: What exactly *are* corporations? And what are they *for?*

In Part A, we compare the Supreme Court's approach to two famous disputes. The first attempted to dissect the quasi-public nature of Dartmouth College in what became one of the first federal court decisions to overturn a state statute. The second involved highly controversial campaign finance laws and the Constitutional rights (or lack thereof) of business entities. In both cases, though separated by almost two centuries, the court's decision turned on its understanding of the fundamental nature of the corporate form.

In Part B, we delve into the even more contentious issue of the purpose of corporations. Are they merely profit-maximizing machines whose sole aim is to benefit their owners? Or do corporations and their managers owe a broader duty to society as a whole? For whose benefit, in other words, do corporations exist? In order to answer these questions, we turn to the proponents of corporate social responsibility as well as the theories and influence of legendary industrialist Henry Ford.

Finally, in Part C, we take a brief look at the powers of corporations. Are there any limits to what they are permitted to do? We place this question in the legal context in order to discern the relationship between corporations and other institutions.

At the end of this chapter, you will have a deeper understanding of how and for what purposes corporations exist and operate. Such an understanding will enable you to represent not only corporate clients in planning and structuring their affairs but also others in their dealings with corporations. Most importantly, your knowledge of the nuances of these debates will make you a better-informed citizen who can take a leadership role in helping shape the future of America's political economy.

NATURE OF CORPORATIONS PART A

TRUSTEES OF DARTMOUTH COLLEGE V. WOODWARD

SUPREME COURT OF THE UNITED STATES (MARSHALL, C.J.)
17 U.S. 518 (1819)

This is an action of trover, brought by the Trustees of Dartmouth College against William H. Woodward, in the state court of New Hampshire, for the book of records, corporate seal, and other corporate property, to which the plaintiffs allege themselves to be entitled. A special verdict, after setting out the rights of the parties, finds for the defendant. The single question now to be considered is, do the acts to which the verdict refers violate the constitution of the United States?

This court can be insensible neither to the magnitude nor delicacy of this question. But the American people have said, in the constitution of the United States, that "no state shall pass any bill of attainder, *ex post facto* law, or law impairing the obligation of contracts." In the same instrument, they have also said, "that the judicial power shall extend to all cases in law and equity arising under the constitution." On the judges of this court, then, is imposed the high and solemn duty of protecting, from even legislative violation, those contracts which the constitution of our country has placed beyond legislative control; and, however irksome the task may be, this is a duty from which we dare not shrink.

The title of the plaintiffs originates in a charter dated the 13th day of December, in the year 1769, incorporating twelve persons therein mentioned, by the name of "The Trustees of Dartmouth College," granting to them and their successors the usual corporate privileges and powers, and authorizing the trustees, who are to govern the college, to fill up all vacancies which may be created in their own body.

The defendant claims under three acts of the legislature of New Hampshire, the most material of which was passed on the 27th of June 1816, and is entitled, "an act to amend the charter, and enlarge and improve the corporation of Dartmouth College." Among other alterations in the charter, this act increases the number of trustees to twenty-one, gives the appointment of the additional members to the executive of the state, and creates a board of overseers, with power to inspect and control the most important acts of the trustees. This board consists of twenty-five persons. The president of the senate, the speaker of the house of representatives, of New Hampshire, and the governor and lieutenant-governor of Vermont, for the time being, are to be members *ex officio*. The board is to be completed by the governor and council of New Hampshire, who are also empowered to fill all vacancies which may occur. The acts of the 18th and 26th of December are supplemental to that of the 27th of June, and are principally intended to carry that act into effect. The majority of the trustees of the college have refused to accept this amended charter, and have brought this suit for the corporate property, which is in possession of a person holding by virtue of the acts which have been stated.

It can require no argument to prove, that the circumstances of this case constitute a contract. An application is made to the crown for a charter to incorporate a religious and literary institution. In the application, it is stated, that large contributions have been made for the object, which will be conferred on the corporation, as soon as it shall be created. The charter is granted, and on its faith the property is conveyed. Surely, in this transaction every ingredient of a complete and legitimate contract is to be found. The points for consideration are, 1. Is this contract protected by the constitution of the United States? 2. Is it impaired by the acts under which the defendant holds?

1. On the first point, is has been argued, that the word "contract," in its broadest sense, would comprehend the political relations between the government and its citizens, would extend to offices held within a state, for state purposes, and to many of those laws concerning civil institutions, which must change with circumstances, and be modified by ordinary legislation; which deeply concern the public, and which, to preserve good government, the public judgment must control.

That the framers of the constitution did not intend to restrain the states in the regulation of their civil institutions, adopted for internal government, and that the instrument they have given us, is not to be so construed, may be admitted. The provision of the constitution never has been understood to embrace other contracts, than those which respect property, or some object of value, and confer rights which may be asserted in a court of justice.

The parties in this case differ less on general principles, less on the true construction of the constitution in the abstract, than on the application of those principles to this case, and on the true construction of the charter of 1769. This is the point on which the cause essentially depends. If the act of incorporation be a grant of political power, if it create a civil institution, to be employed in the administration of the government, or if the funds of the college be public property, or if the state of New Hampshire, as a government, be alone interested in its transactions, the subject is one in which the legislature of the state may act according to its own judgment, unrestrained by any limitation of its power imposed by the constitution of the United States.

But if this be a private eleemosynary institution, endowed with a capacity to take property, for objects unconnected with government, whose funds are bestowed by individuals, on the faith of the charter; if the donors have stipulated for the future disposition and management of those funds, in the manner prescribed by themselves; there may be more difficulty in the case, although neither the persons who have made these stipulations, nor those for whose benefit they were made, should be parties to the cause. Those who are no longer interested in the property, may yet retain such an interest in the preservation of their own arrangements, as to have a right to insist, that those arrangements shall be held sacred. Or, if they have themselves disappeared, it becomes a subject of serious and anxious inquiry, whether those whom they have legally empowered to represent them for ever, may not assert all the rights which they possessed, while in being; whether, if they be without personal representatives, who may feel injured by a violation of the compact, the trustees be not so completely their representatives, in the eye of the law, as to stand in their place, not only as respects the government of the college, but also as respects the maintenance of the college charter. It becomes then the duty of the court, most seriously to examine this charter, and to ascertain its true character.

From the instrument itself, it appears, that about the year 1754, the Rev. Eleazer Wheelock established, at his own expense, and on his own estate, a charity school for the instruction of Indians in the Christian religion. The success of this institution inspired him with the design of soliciting contributions in England, for carrying on and extending his undertaking. In this pious work, he employed the Rev. Nathaniel Whitaker, who, by virtue of a power of attorney from Dr. Wheelock, appointed the Earl of Dartmouth and others, trustees of the money, which had been, and should be, contributed; which appointment Dr. Wheelock confirmed by a deed of trust, authorizing the trustees to fix on a site for the college. They determined to establish the school on Connecticut river, in the western part of New Hampshire; that situation being supposed favorable for carrying on the original design among the Indians, and also for promoting learning among the English; and the proprietors in the neighborhood having made large offers of land, on condition, that the college should there be placed. Dr. Wheelock then applied to the crown for an act of incorporation; and represented the expediency of appointing those whom he had, by his last will, named as trustees in America, to be members of the proposed corporation. "In consideration of the premises," "for the education and instruction of the youth of the Indian tribes," &c., "and also of English youth, and any others," the charter was granted, and the trustees of Dartmouth College were, by that name, created a body corporate, with power, for the use of the said college, to acquire real and personal property, and to pay the president, tutors and other officers of the college, such salaries as they shall allow.

This charter was accepted, and the property, both real and personal, which had been contributed for the benefit of the college, was conveyed to, and vested in, the corporate body.

From this brief review of the most essential parts of the charter, it is apparent, that the funds of the college consisted entirely of private donations. The probability is, that the Earl of Dartmouth, and the other trustees in England, were, in fact, the largest contributors. Yet the legal conclusion, from the facts recited in the charter, would probably be, that Dr. Wheelock was the founder of the college. The origin of the institution was, undoubtedly, the Indian charity school, established by Dr. Wheelock, at his own expense. It was at his insistance, and to enlarge this school, that contributions were solicited in England. Dartmouth College is really endowed by private individuals, who have bestowed their funds for the propagation of the Christian religion among the Indians, and for the promotion of piety and learning generally. It is then an eleemosynary, and so far as respects its funds, a private corporation.

Do its objects stamp on it a different character? Are the trustees and professors public officers, invested with any portion of political power, partaking in any degree in the administration of civil government, and performing duties which flow from the sovereign authority? Is education altogether in the hands of government? Does every teacher of youth become a public officer, and do donations for the purpose of education necessarily become public property, so far that the will of the legislature, not the will of the donor, becomes the law of the donation?

Doctor Wheelock, as the keeper of his charity-school, instructing the Indians in the art of reading, and in our holy religion; sustaining them at his own expense, and on the voluntary contributions of the charitable, could scarcely be considered as a public officer, exercising any portion of those duties which belong to government; nor could the legislature have supposed, that his private funds, or those given by others, were subject to legislative management, because they were applied to the purposes of education. When, afterwards, his school was enlarged, and the liberal contributions made in England, and in America, enabled him to extend his care to the education of the youth of his own country, no change was wrought in his own character, or in the nature of his duties.

Whence, then, can be derived the idea, that Dartmouth College has become a public institution, and its trustees public officers, exercising powers conferred by the public for public objects? Not from the source whence its funds were drawn; for its foundation is purely private and eleemosynary—not from the application of those funds; for money may be given for education, and the persons receiving it do not, by being employed in the education of youth, become members of the civil government. Is it from the act of incorporation?

A corporation is an artificial being, invisible, intangible, and existing only in contemplation of law. Being the mere creature of law, it possesses only those properties which the charter of its creation confers upon it, either expressly, or as incidental to its very existence. Among the most important are immortality, and, if the expression may be allowed, individuality; properties, by which a perpetual succession of many persons are considered as the same, and may act as a single individual. They enable a corporation to manage its own affairs, and to hold property, without the perplexing intricacies, the hazardous and endless necessity, of perpetual conveyances for the purpose of transmitting it from hand to hand. It is chiefly for the purpose of clothing bodies of men, in succession, with these qualities and capacities, that corporations were invented, and are in use. By these means, a perpetual succession of individuals are capable of acting for the promotion of the particular object, like one immortal being. But this being does not share in the civil government of the country, unless that be the purpose for which it was created. Its immortality no more confers on it political power, or a political character, than immortality would confer such power or character on a natural person. It is no more a state instrument, than a natural person exercising the same powers would be.

The objects for which a corporation is created are universally such as the government wishes to promote. They are deemed beneficial to the country; and this benefit constitutes the consideration, and in most cases, the sole consideration of the grant. The benefit to the public is considered as an ample compensation for the faculty it confers, and the corporation is created. If the advantages to the public constitute a full compensation for the faculty it gives, there can be no reason for exacting a further compensation, by claiming a right to exercise over this artificial being, a power which changes its nature, and touches the fund, for the security and application of which it was created.

From the fact, then, that a charter of incorporation has been granted, nothing can be inferred, which changes the character of the institution, or transfers to the government any new power over it. The character of civil institutions does not grow out of their incorporation, but out of the manner in which they are formed, and the objects for which they are created. The right to change them is not founded on their being incorporated, but on their being the instruments of government, created for its purposes.

We are next led to the inquiry, for whose benefit the property given to Dartmouth College was secured? The counsel for the defendant have insisted, that the beneficial interest is in the people of New Hampshire.

The particular interests of New Hampshire never entered into the mind of the donors, never constituted a motive for their donation. The propagation of the Christian religion among the savages, and the dissemination of useful knowledge among the youth of the country, were the avowed and the sole objects of their contributions. In these, New Hampshire would participate; but nothing particular or exclusive was intended for her. Even the site of the college was selected, not for the sake of New Hampshire, but because it was "most subservient to the great ends in view," and because liberal donations of land were offered by the proprietors, on condition that the institution should be there established. The clause which constitutes the incorporation, and expresses the objects for which it was made, declares those objects to be the instruction of the Indians, "and also of English youth, and any others." So that the objects of the contributors, and the incorporating act, were the same; the promotion of Christianity, and of education generally, not the interests of New Hampshire particularly.

From this review of the charter, it appears, that Dartmouth College is an eleemosynary institution, incorporated for the purpose of perpetuating the application of the bounty of the donors, to the specified objects of that bounty; that its trustees or governors were originally named by the founder, and invested with the power of perpetuating themselves; that they are not public officers, nor is it a civil institution, participating in the administration of government; but a charity-school, or a seminary of education, incorporated for the preservation of its property, and the perpetual application of that property to the objects of its creation.

Yet a question remains to be considered, of more real difficulty, on which more doubt has been entertained, than on all that have been discussed. The founders of the college, at least, those whose contributions were in money, have parted with the property bestowed upon it, and their representatives have no interest in that property. The donors of land are equally without interest, so long as the corporation shall exist. The students are fluctuating, and no individual among our youth has a vested interest in the institution, which can be asserted in a court of justice. Neither the founders of the college, nor the youth for whose benefit it was founded, complain of the alteration made in its charter, or think themselves injured by it. The trustees alone complain, and the trustees have no beneficial interest to be protected.

An artificial, immortal being, was created by the crown, capable of receiving and distributing for ever, according to the will of the donors, the donations which should be made to it. On this being, the contributions which had been collected were immediately bestowed. These gifts were made, not indeed to make a profit for the donors, or their posterity, but for something, in their opinion, of inestimable value; for something which they deemed a full equivalent for the money with which it was purchased. The consideration for which they stipulated, is the perpetual application of the fund to its object, in the mode prescribed by themselves. Their descendants may take no interest in the preservation of this consideration. But in this respect their descendants are not their representatives; they are represented by the corporation. The corporation is the assignee of their rights, stands in their place, and distributes their bounty, as they would themselves have distributed it, had they been immortal. So, with respect to the students who are to derive learning from this source; the corporation is a trustee for them also. Their potential rights, which, taken distributively, are imperceptible, amount collectively to a most important interest. These are, in the aggregate, to be exercised, asserted and protected, by the corporation. They were as completely out of the donors, at the instant of their being vested in the corporation, and as incapable of being asserted by the students, as at present.

Had parliament, immediately after the emanation of this charter, and the execution of those conveyances which followed it, annulled the instrument, so that the living donors would have witnessed the disappointment of their hopes, the perfidy of the transaction would have been universally acknowledged. Yet, then, as now, the donors would have no interest in the property; then, as now, those who might be students would have had no rights to be violated; then, as now, it might be said, that the trustees, in whom the rights of all were combined, possessed no private, individual, beneficial interests in the property confided to their protection. Yet the contract would, at that time, have been deemed sacred by all. What has since occurred, to strip it of its inviolability? Circumstances have not changed it. In reason, in justice, and in law, it is now, what is was in 1769.

This is plainly a contract to which the donors, the trustees and the crown (to whose rights and obligations New Hampshire succeeds) were the original parties. It is a contract made on a valuable consideration. It is a contract for the security and disposition of property. It is a contract, on the faith of which, real and personal estate has been conveyed to the corporation. It is, then, a contract within the letter of the constitution, and within its spirit also.

Almost all eleemosynary corporations, those which are created for the promotion of religion, of charity or of education, are of the same character. The law of this case is the law of all. These eleemosynary institutions do not fill the place, which would otherwise be occupied by government, but that which would otherwise remain vacant.

The opinion of the court, after mature deliberation, is, that this is a contract, the obligation of which cannot be impaired, without violating the constitution of the United States. This opinion appears to us to be equally supported by reason, and by the former decisions of this court.

2. We next proceed to the inquiry, whether its obligation has been impaired by those acts of the legislature of New Hampshire, to which the special verdict refers?

On the part of the crown, it was expressly stipulated, that this corporation, thus constituted, should continue for ever; and that the number of trustees should for ever consist of twelve, and no more. By this contract, the crown was bound, and could have made no violent alteration in its essential terms, without impairing its obligation.

By the revolution, the duties, as well as the powers, of government devolved on the people of New Hampshire. It is too clear, to require the support of argument, that all contracts and rights respecting property, remained unchanged by the revolution. The obligations, then, which were created by the charter to Dartmouth College, were the same in the new, that they had been in the old government. The power of the government was also the same. A repeal of this charter, at any time prior to the adoption of the present constitution of the United States, would have been an extraordinary and unprecedented act of power, but one which could have been contested only by the restrictions upon the legislature, to be found in the constitution of the state. But the constitution of the United States has imposed this additional limitation, that the legislature of a state shall pass no act "impairing the obligation of contracts."

It results from this opinion, that the acts of the legislature of New Hampshire, which are stated in the special verdict found in this cause, are repugnant to the constitution of the United States; and that the judgment on this special verdict ought to have been for the plaintiffs. The judgment of the state court must, therefore, be reversed.

STORY, J. (concurring).

An aggregate corporation, at common law, is a collection of individuals, united into one collective body, under a special name, and possessing certain immunities, privileges and capacities, in its collective character, which do not belong to the natural persons composing it. Among other things, it possesses the capacity of perpetual succession, and of acting by the collected vote or will of its component members, and of suing and being sued in all things touching its corporate rights and duties. It is, in short, an artificial person, existing in contemplation of law, and endowed with certain powers and franchises which, though they must be exercised through the medium of its natural members, are yet considered as subsisting in the corporation itself, as distinctly as if it were a real personage. Hence, such a corporation may sue and be sued by its own members, and may contract with them in the same manner, as with any strangers. A great variety of these corporations exist, in every country governed by the common law; in some of which, the corporate existence is perpetuated by new elections, made from time to time; and in others, by a continual accession of new members, without any corporate act. Some of these corporations are, from the particular purposes to which they are devoted, denominated spiritual, and some lay; and the latter are again divided into civil and eleemosynary corporations. It is unnecessary, in this place, to enter into any examination of civil corporations. Eleemosynary corporations are such as are constituted for the perpetual distribution of the free-alms and bounty of the founder, in such manner as he has directed; and in this class, are ranked hospitals for the relief of poor and impotent persons, and colleges for the promotion of learning and piety, and the support of persons engaged in literary pursuits.

Another division of corporations is into public and private. Public corporations are generally esteemed such as exist for public political purposes only, such as towns, cities, parishes and counties; and in many respects, they are so, although they involve some private interests; but strictly speaking, public corporations are such only as are founded by the government, for public purposes, where the whole interests belong also to the government. If, therefore, the foundation be private, though under the charter of the government, the corporation is private, however extensive the uses may be to which it is devoted, either by the bounty of the founder, or the nature and objects of the institution. For instance, a bank created by the government for its own uses, whose stock is exclusively owned by the government, is, in the strictest sense, public corporation. So, a hospital created and endowed by the government for general charity. But a bank, whose stock is owned by private persons, is a private corporation, although it is erected by the government, and its objects and operations partake of a public nature. The same doctrine may be affirmed of insurance, canal, bridge and turnpike companies. In all these cases, the uses may, in a certain sense, be called public, but the corporations are private; as much so, indeed, as if the franchises were vested in a single person.

This reasoning applies in its full force to eleemosynary corporations. A hospital, founded by a private benefactor, is, in point of law, a private corporation, although dedicated by its charter to general charity. So, a college, founded and endowed in the same manner, although, being for the promotion of learning and piety, it may extend its charity to scholars from every class in the community, and thus acquire the character of a public institution.

When a private eleemosynary corporation is thus created, by the charter of the crown, it is subject to no other control on the part of the crown, than what is expressly or implicitly reserved by the charter itself. Unless a power be reserved for this purpose, the crown cannot, in virtue of its prerogative, without the consent of the corporation, alter or amend the charter, or divest the corporation of any of its franchises, or add to them, or add to, or diminish, the number of the trustees, or remove any of the members, or change or control the administration of the charity, or compel the corporation to receive a new charter. This is the uniform language of the authorities, and forms one of the most stubborn, and well settled doctrines of the common law.

In my judgment, it is perfectly clear, that any act of a legislature which takes away any powers or franchises vested by its charter in a private corporation, or its corporate officers, or which restrains or controls the legitimate exercise of them, or transfers them to other persons, without its assent, is a violation of the obligations of that charter. If the legislature mean to claim such an authority, it must be reserved in the grant. The charter of Dartmouth College contains no such reservation; and I am, therefore, bound to declare, that the acts of the legislature of New Hampshire, now in question, do impair the obligations of that charter, and are, consequently, unconstitutional and void.

CITIZENS UNITED V. FEDERAL ELECTION COMMISSION

SUPREME COURT OF THE UNITED STATES (KENNEDY, J.)
588 U.S. 310 (2010)

Federal law prohibits corporations and unions from using their general treasury funds to make independent expenditures for speech defined as an "electioneering communication" or for speech expressly advocating the election or defeat of a candidate.

Citizens United is a nonprofit corporation. It has an annual budget of about $12 million. Most of its funds are from donations by individuals; but, in addition, it accepts a small portion of its funds from for-profit corporations.

In January 2008, Citizens United released a film entitled *Hillary: The Movie*. It is a 90-minute documentary about then-Senator Hillary Clinton, who was a candidate in the Democratic Party's 2008 Presidential primary elections. The movie mentions Senator Clinton by name and depicts interviews with political commentators and other persons, most of them quite critical of Senator Clinton.

Before the Bipartisan Campaign Reform Act of 2002, federal law prohibited—and still does prohibit—corporations and unions from using general treasury funds to make direct contributions to candidates or independent expenditures that expressly advocate the election or defeat of a candidate, through any form of media, in connection with certain qualified federal elections.

Citizens United wanted to make the movie available through video-on-demand within 30 days of the 2008 primary elections. It feared, however, that both the film and the ads would be covered by the federal ban on corporate-funded independent expenditures, thus subjecting the corporation to civil and criminal penalties. In December 2007, Citizens United sought declaratory and injunctive relief against the Federal Election Commission.

Speech is an essential mechanism of democracy, for it is the means to hold officials accountable to the people. For these reasons, political speech must prevail against laws that would suppress it, whether by design or inadvertence. Laws that burden political speech are "subject to strict scrutiny," which requires the Government to prove that the restriction "furthers a compelling interest and is narrowly tailored to achieve that interest."

Corporations have 1A rights too

The Court has recognized that First Amendment protection extends to corporations. This protection has been extended by explicit holdings to the context of political speech. "The identity of the speaker is not decisive in determining whether speech is protected. Corporations and other associations, like individuals, contribute to the 'discussion, debate, and the dissemination of information and ideas' that the First Amendment seeks to foster". The Court has thus rejected the argument that political speech of corporations or other associations should be treated differently under the First Amendment simply because such associations are not "natural persons."

It is irrelevant for purposes of the First Amendment that corporate funds may "have little or no correlation to the public's support for the corporation's political ideas." All speakers, including individuals and the media, use money amassed from the economic marketplace to fund their speech. The First Amendment protects the resulting speech, even if it was enabled by economic transactions with persons or entities who disagree with the speaker's ideas.

The Government contends that corporate independent expenditures can be limited because of its interest in protecting dissenting shareholders from being compelled to fund corporate political speech. There is little evidence of abuse that cannot be corrected by shareholders "through the procedures of corporate democracy."

Those reasons are sufficient to reject this shareholder-protection interest; and, moreover, the statute is both underinclusive and overinclusive. As to the first, if Congress had been seeking to protect dissenting shareholders, it would not have banned corporate speech in only certain media within 30 or 60 days before an election. A dissenting shareholder's interests would be implicated by speech in any media at any time. As to the second, the statute is overinclusive because it covers all corporations, including nonprofit corporations and for-profit corporations with only single shareholders. As to other corporations, the remedy is not to restrict speech but to consider and explore other regulatory mechanisms. The regulatory mechanism here, based on speech, contravenes the First Amendment.

Shareholder objections raised through the procedures of corporate democracy can be more effective today because modern technology makes disclosures rapid and informative. With the advent of the Internet, prompt disclosure of expenditures can provide shareholders and citizens with the information needed to hold corporations and elected officials accountable for their positions and supporters. Shareholders can determine whether their corporation's political speech advances the corporation's interest in making profits, and citizens can see whether elected officials are "'in the pocket' of so-called moneyed interests." The First Amendment protects political speech; and disclosure permits citizens and shareholders to react to the speech of corporate entities in a proper way. This transparency enables the electorate to make informed decisions and give proper weight to different speakers and messages.

SCALIA, J. (concurring).

I write separately to address JUSTICE STEVENS' discussion of "Original Understandings". This section of the dissent purports to show that today's decision is not supported by the original understanding of the First Amendment.

Despite the corporation-hating quotations the dissent has dredged up, it is far from clear that by the end of the 18th century corporations were despised. If so, how came there to be so many of them? The dissent's statement that there were few business corporations during the eighteenth century—"only a few hundred during all of the 18th century"—is misleading. There were approximately 335 charters issued to business corporations in the United States by the end of the 18th century. This was a "considerable extension of corporate enterprise in the field of business," and represented "unprecedented growth". Moreover, what seems like a small number by today's standards surely does not indicate the relative importance of corporations when the Nation was considerably smaller. As I have previously noted, "by the end of the eighteenth century the corporation was a familiar figure in American economic life."

Most of the Founders' resentment towards corporations was directed at the state-granted monopoly privileges that individually chartered corporations enjoyed. Modern corporations do not have such privileges, and would probably have been favored by most of our enterprising Founders— excluding, perhaps, Thomas Jefferson and others favoring perpetuation of an agrarian society. Moreover, if the Founders' specific intent with respect to corporations is what matters, why does the dissent ignore the Founders' views about other legal entities that have more in common with modern business corporations than the founding-era corporations? At the time of the founding, religious, educational, and literary corporations were incorporated under general incorporation statutes, much as business corporations are today. There were also small unincorporated business associations, which some have argued were the " 'true progenitors' " of today's business corporations. Were all of these silently excluded from the protections of the First Amendment?

The lack of a textual exception for speech by corporations cannot be explained on the ground that such organizations did not exist or did not speak. To the contrary, colleges, towns and cities, religious institutions, and guilds had long been organized as corporations at common law and under the King's charter, and as I have discussed, the practice of incorporation only expanded in the United States. Both corporations and voluntary associations actively petitioned the Government and expressed their views in newspapers and pamphlets. For example: An antislavery Quaker corporation petitioned the First Congress, distributed pamphlets, and communicated through the press in 1790. The New York Sons of Liberty sent a circular to colonies farther south in 1766. And the Society for the Relief and Instruction of Poor Germans circulated a biweekly paper from 1755 to 1757. The dissent offers no evidence—none whatever—that the First Amendment's unqualified text was originally understood to exclude such associational speech from its protection.

The dissent says that when the Framers "constitutionalized the right to free speech in the First Amendment, it was the free speech of individual Americans that they had in mind." That is no doubt true. All the provisions of the Bill of Rights set forth the rights of individual men and women—not, for example, of trees or polar bears. But the individual person's right to speak includes the right to speak in association with other individual persons. Surely the dissent does not believe that speech by the Republican Party or the Democratic Party can be censored because it is not the speech of "an individual American." It is the speech of many individual Americans, who have associated in a common cause, giving the leadership of the party the right to speak on their behalf. The association of individuals in a business corporation is no different—or at least it cannot be denied the right to speak on the simplistic ground that it is not "an individual American."

The Amendment is written in terms of "speech," not speakers. Its text offers no foothold for excluding any category of speaker, from single individuals to partnerships of individuals, to unincorporated associations of individuals, to incorporated associations of individuals—and the dissent offers no evidence about the original meaning of the text to support any such exclusion.

STEVENS, J. (concurring).

The basic premise underlying the Court's ruling is its iteration, and constant reiteration, of the proposition that the First Amendment bars regulatory distinctions based on a speaker's identity, including its "identity" as a corporation. While that glittering generality has rhetorical appeal, it is not a correct statement of the law. Nor does it tell us when a corporation may engage in electioneering that some of its shareholders oppose. It does not even resolve the specific question whether Citizens United may be required to finance some of its messages with the money in its PAC. The conceit that corporations must be treated identically to natural persons in the political sphere is not only inaccurate but also inadequate to justify the Court's disposition of this case.

Although they make enormous contributions to our society, corporations are not actually members of it. They cannot vote or run for office. Because they may be managed and controlled by nonresidents, their interests may conflict in fundamental respects with the interests of eligible voters. The financial resources, legal structure, and instrumental orientation of corporations raise legitimate concerns about their role in the electoral process.

We have held that speech can be regulated differentially on account of the speaker's identity, when identity is understood in categorical or institutional terms. The Government routinely places special restrictions on the speech rights of students, prisoners, members of the Armed Forces, foreigners, and its own employees.

If taken seriously, our colleagues' assumption that the identity of a speaker has no relevance to the Government's ability to regulate political speech would lead to some remarkable conclusions. It would appear to afford the same protection to multinational corporations controlled by foreigners as to individual Americans. Under the majority's view, I suppose it may be a First Amendment problem that corporations are not permitted to vote, given that voting is, among other things, a form of speech.

Those few corporations that existed at the founding were authorized by grant of a special legislative charter. Corporate sponsors would petition the legislature, and the legislature, if amenable, would issue a charter that specified the corporation's powers and purposes and "authoritatively fixed the scope and content of corporate organization," including "the internal structure of the corporation." Corporations were created, supervised, and conceptualized as quasi-public entities, "designed to serve a social function for the state." It was "assumed that they were legally privileged organizations that had to be closely scrutinized by the legislature because their purposes had to be made consistent with public welfare."

The individualized charter mode of incorporation reflected the "cloud of disfavor under which corporations labored" in the early years of this Nation. Thomas Jefferson famously fretted that corporations would subvert the Republic. General incorporation statutes, and widespread acceptance of business corporations as socially useful actors, did not emerge until the 1800's.

The Framers thus took it as a given that corporations could be comprehensively regulated in the service of the public welfare. Unlike our colleagues, they had little trouble distinguishing corporations from human beings, and when they constitutionalized the right to free speech in the First Amendment, it was the free speech of individual Americans that they had in mind. While individuals might join together to exercise their speech rights, business corporations, at least, were plainly not seen as facilitating such associational or expressive ends. Even "the notion that business corporations could invoke the First Amendment would probably have been quite a novelty," given that "at the time, the legitimacy of every corporate activity was thought to rest entirely in a concession of the sovereign."

In light of these background practices and understandings, it seems to me implausible that the Framers believed "the freedom of speech" would extend equally to all corporate speakers, much less that it would preclude legislatures from taking limited measures to guard against corporate capture of elections.

Nothing in Justice Scalia's account dislodges my basic point that members of the founding generation held a cautious view of corporate power and a narrow view of corporate rights (not that they "despised" corporations), and that they conceptualized speech in individualistic terms. If no prominent Framer bothered to articulate that corporate speech would have lesser status than individual speech, that may well be because the contrary proposition—if not also the very notion of "corporate speech"—was inconceivable.

The fact that corporations are different from human beings might seem to need no elaboration, except that the majority opinion almost completely elides it. *Austin* set forth some of the basic differences. Unlike natural persons, corporations have "limited liability" for their owners and managers, "perpetual life," separation of ownership and control, "and favorable treatment of the accumulation and distribution of assets that enhance their ability to attract capital and to deploy their resources in ways that maximize the return on their shareholders' investments." Unlike voters in U.S. elections, corporations may be foreign controlled. Unlike other interest groups, business corporations have been "effectively delegated responsibility for ensuring society's economic welfare"; they inescapably structure the life of every citizen. "The resources in the treasury of a business corporation,'" furthermore, "'are not an indication of popular support for the corporation's political ideas."

"'They reflect instead the economically motivated decisions of investors and customers. The availability of these resources may make a corporation a formidable political presence, even though the power of the corporation may be no reflection of the power of its ideas.'" It might also be added that corporations have no consciences, no beliefs, no feelings, no thoughts, no desires. Corporations help structure and facilitate the activities of human beings, to be sure, and their "personhood" often serves as a useful legal fiction. But they are not themselves members of "We the People" by whom and for whom our Constitution was established.

These basic points help explain why corporate electioneering is not only more likely to impair compelling governmental interests, but also why restrictions on that electioneering are less likely to encroach upon First Amendment freedoms. One fundamental concern of the First Amendment is to "protect the individual's interest in self-expression." Corporate speech, however, is derivative speech, speech by proxy.

It is an interesting question "who" is even speaking when a business corporation places an advertisement that endorses or attacks a particular candidate. Presumably it is not the customers or employees, who typically have no say in such matters. It cannot realistically be said to be the shareholders, who tend to be far removed from the day-to-day decisions of the firm and whose political preferences may be opaque to management. Perhaps the officers or directors of the corporation have the best claim to be the ones speaking, except their fiduciary duties generally prohibit them from using corporate funds for personal ends. Some individuals associated with the corporation must make the decision to place the ad, but the idea that these individuals are thereby fostering their self expression or cultivating their critical faculties is fanciful. It is entirely possible that the corporation's electoral message will conflict with their personal convictions. Take away the ability to use general treasury funds for some of those ads, and no one's autonomy, dignity, or political equality has been impinged upon in the least.

The legal structure of corporations allows them to amass and deploy financial resources on a scale few natural persons can match. The structure of a business corporation, furthermore, draws a line between the corporation's economic interests and the political preferences of the individuals associated with the corporation; the corporation must engage the electoral process with the aim "to enhance the profitability of the company, no matter how persuasive the arguments for a broader or conflicting set of priorities." Consequently, when corporations grab up the prime broadcasting slots on the eve of an election, they can flood the market with advocacy that bears "little or no correlation" to the ideas of natural persons or to any broader notion of the public good. The opinions of real people may be marginalized.

There is yet another way in which laws such as § 203 can serve First Amendment values. Interwoven with our concern to protect the integrity of the electoral process is a concern to protect the rights of shareholders from a kind of coerced speech: electioneering expenditures that do not "reflect their support." When corporations use general treasury funds to praise or attack a particular candidate for office, it is the shareholders, as the residual claimants, who are effectively footing the bill. Those shareholders who disagree with the corporation's electoral message may find their financial investments being used to undermine their political convictions. A rule that privileges the use of PACs thus does more than facilitate the political speech of like-minded shareholders; it also curbs the rent seeking behavior of executives and respects the views of dissenters. Our contested precedent's acceptance of restrictions on general treasury spending "simply allows people who have invested in the business corporation for purely economic reasons"—the vast majority of investors, one assumes—"to avoid being taken advantage of, without sacrificing their economic objectives."

The Court dismisses this interest on the ground that abuses of shareholder money can be corrected "through the procedures of corporate democracy," and, it seems, through Internet-based disclosures. I fail to understand why the Court is so confident in these mechanisms. By "corporate democracy," presumably the Court means the rights of shareholders to vote and to bring derivative suits for breach of fiduciary duty. In practice, however, many corporate lawyers will tell you that "these rights are so limited as to be almost nonexistent," given the internal authority wielded by boards and managers and the expansive protections afforded by the business judgment rule. Modern technology may help make it easier to track corporate activity, including electoral advocacy, but it is utopian to believe that it solves the problem. Most American households that own stock do so through intermediaries such as mutual funds and pension plans, which makes it more difficult both to monitor and to alter particular holdings. Studies show that a majority of individual investors make no trades at all during a given year.

In a democratic society, the longstanding consensus on the need to limit corporate campaign spending should outweigh the wooden application of judge-made rules.

PART B PURPOSE OF CORPORATIONS

DODGE V. FORD MOTOR CO.

SUPREME COURT OF MICHIGAN (OSTRANDER, J.)
170 N.W. 668 (1919)

The case for plaintiffs must rest upon the claim, and the proof in support of it, that the proposed expansion of the business of the corporation, involving the further use of profits as capital, ought to be enjoined because inimical to the best interests of the company and its shareholders, and upon the further claim that in any event the withholding of the special dividend asked for by plaintiffs is arbitrary action of the directors requiring judicial interference.

The rule which will govern courts in deciding these questions is not in dispute. It is, of course, differently phrased by judges and by authors, and, as the phrasing in a particular instance may seem to lean for or against the exercise of the right of judicial interference with the actions of corporate directors, the context, or the facts before the court, must be considered. This court, in *Hunter v. Roberts, Throp & Co.*, recognized the rule in the following language:

> It is a well-recognized principle of law that the directors of a corporation, and they alone, have the power to declare a dividend of the earnings of the corporation, and to determine its amount. Courts of equity will not interfere in the management of the directors unless it is clearly made to appear that they are guilty of fraud or misappropriation of the corporate funds, or refuse to declare a dividend when the corporation has a surplus of net profits which it can, without detriment to its business, divide among its stockholders, and when a refusal to do so would amount to such an abuse of discretion as would constitute a fraud, or breach of that good faith which they are bound to exercise towards the stockholders.

When plaintiffs made their complaint and demand for further dividends, the Ford Motor Company had concluded its most prosperous year of business. The demand for its cars at the price of the preceding year continued. It could make and could market in the year beginning August 1, 1916, more than 500,000 cars. Sales of parts and repairs would necessarily increase. The cost of materials was likely to advance, and perhaps the price of labor; but it reasonably might have expected a profit for the year of upwards of $60,000,000. It had assets of more than $132,000,000, a surplus of almost $112,000,000, and its cash on hand and municipal bonds were nearly $54,000,000. Its total liabilities, including capital stock, was a little over $20,000,000. It had declared no special dividend during the business year except the October, 1915, dividend. It had been the practice, under similar circumstances, to declare larger dividends. Considering only these facts, a refusal to declare and pay further dividends appears to be not an exercise of discretion on the part of the directors, but an arbitrary refusal to do what the circumstances required to be done. These facts and others call upon the directors to justify their action, or failure or refusal to act. In justification, the defendants have offered testimony tending to prove, and which does prove, the following facts: It had been the policy of the corporation for a considerable time to annually reduce the selling price of cars, while keeping up, or improving, their quality. As early as in June, 1915, a general plan for the expansion of the productive capacity of the concern by a practical duplication of its plant had been talked over by the executive officers and directors and agreed upon; not all of the details having been settled, and no formal action of directors having been taken. The erection of a smelter was considered, and engineering and other data in connection therewith secured. In consequence, it was determined not to reduce the selling price of cars for the year beginning August 1, 1915, but to maintain the price and to accumulate a large surplus to pay for the proposed expansion of plant and equipment, and perhaps to build a plant for smelting ore. It is hoped, by Mr. Ford, that eventually 1,000,000 cars will be annually produced. The contemplated changes will permit the increased output.

The plan, as affecting the profits of the business for the year beginning August 1, 1916, and thereafter, calls for a reduction in the selling price of the cars. It is true that this price might be at any time increased, but the plan called for the reduction in price of $80 a car. The capacity of the plant, without the additions thereto voted to be made (without a part of them at least), would produce more than 600,000 cars annually. This number, and more, could have been sold for $440 instead of $360, a difference in the return for capital, labor, and materials employed of at least $48,000,000. In short, the plan does not call for and is not intended to produce immediately a more profitable business, but a less profitable one; not only less profitable than formerly, but less profitable than it is admitted it might be made. The apparent immediate effect will be to diminish the value of shares and the returns to shareholders.

It is the contention of plaintiffs that the apparent effect of the plan is intended to be the continued and continuing effect of it, and that it is deliberately proposed, not of record and not by official corporate declaration, but nevertheless proposed, to continue the corporation henceforth as a semi-eleemosynary institution and not as a business institution. In support of this contention, they point to the attitude and to the expressions of Mr. Henry Ford.

Mr. Henry Ford is the dominant force in the business of the Ford Motor Company. No plan of operations could be adopted unless he consented, and no board of directors can be elected whom he does not favor. One of the directors of the company has no stock. One share was assigned to him to qualify him for the position, but it is not claimed that he owns it. A business, one of the largest in the world, and one of the most profitable, has been built up. It employs many men, at good pay.

"My ambition," said Mr. Ford, "is to employ still more men, to spread the benefits of this industrial system to the greatest possible number, to help them build up their lives and their homes. To do this we are putting the greatest share of our profits back in the business."

With regard to dividends, the company paid sixty per cent on its capitalization of two million dollars, or $1,200,000, leaving $58,000,000 to reinvest for the growth of the company. This is Mr. Ford's policy at present, and it is understood that the other stockholders cheerfully accede to this plan.

He had made up his mind in the summer of 1916 that no dividends other than the regular dividends should be paid, "for the present."

"Q. For how long? Had you fixed in your mind any time in the future, when you were going to pay –
"A. No.
"Q. That was indefinite in the future?
"A. That was indefinite; yes, sir."

The record, and especially the testimony of Mr. Ford, convinces that he has to some extent the attitude towards shareholders of one who has dispensed and distributed to them large gains and that they should be content to take what he chooses to give. His testimony creates the impression, also, that he thinks the Ford Motor Company has made too much money, has had too large profits, and that, although large profits might be still earned, a sharing of them with the public, by reducing the price of the output of the company, ought to be undertaken. We have no doubt that certain sentiments, philanthropic and altruistic, creditable to Mr. Ford, had large influence in determining the policy to be pursued by the Ford Motor Company—the policy which has been herein referred to.

It is said by his counsel that—

"Although a manufacturing corporation cannot engage in humanitarian works as its principal business, the fact that it is organized for profit does not prevent the existence of implied powers to carry on with humanitarian motives such charitable works as are incidental to the main business of the corporation."

And again:

"As the expenditures complained of are being made in an expansion of the business which the company is organized to carry on, and for purposes within the powers of the corporation as hereinbefore shown, the question is as to whether such expenditures are rendered illegal because influenced to some extent by humanitarian motives and purposes on the part of the members of the board of directors."

114

In discussing this proposition, counsel have referred to decisions such as *Hawes v. Oakland.* These cases, after all, like all others in which the subject is treated, turn finally upon the point, the question, whether it appears that the directors were not acting for the best interests of the corporation. We do not draw in question, nor do counsel for the plaintiffs do so, the validity of the general proposition stated by counsel nor the soundness of the opinions delivered in the cases cited. The case presented here is not like any of them. The difference between an incidental humanitarian expenditure of corporate funds for the benefit of the employees, like the building of a hospital for their use and the employment of agencies for the betterment of their condition, and a general purpose and plan to benefit mankind at the expense of others, is obvious. There should be no confusion (of which there is evidence) of the duties which Mr. Ford conceives that he and the stockholders owe to the general public and the duties which in law he and his codirectors owe to protesting, minority stockholders. A business corporation is organized and carried on primarily for the profit of the stockholders. The powers of the directors are to be employed for that end. The discretion of directors is to be exercised in the choice of means to attain that end, and does not extend to a change in the end itself, to the reduction of profits, or to the nondistribution of profits among stockholders in order to devote them to other purposes.

[handwritten margin note: corporations are supposed to make $ for stockholders]

There is committed to the discretion of directors, a discretion to be exercised in good faith, the infinite details of business, including the wages which shall be paid to employees, the number of hours they shall work, the conditions under which labor shall be carried on, and the price for which products shall be offered to the public.

It is said by appellants that the motives of the board members are not material and will not be inquired into by the court so long as their acts are within their lawful powers. As we have pointed out, and the proposition does not require argument to sustain it, it is not within the lawful powers of a board of directors to shape and conduct the affairs of a corporation for the merely incidental benefit of shareholders and for the primary purpose of benefiting others, and no one will contend that, if the avowed purpose of the defendant directors was to sacrifice the interests of shareholders, it would not be the duty of the courts to interfere.

We are not, however, persuaded that we should interfere with the proposed expansion of the business of the Ford Motor Company. In view of the fact that the selling price of products may be increased at any time, the ultimate results of the larger business cannot be certainly estimated. The judges are not business experts. It is recognized that plans must often be made for a long future, for expected competition, for a continuing as well as an immediately profitable venture. The experience of the Ford Motor Company is evidence of capable management of its affairs. It may be noticed, incidentally, that it took from the public the money required for the execution of its plan, and that the very considerable salaries paid to Mr. Ford and to certain executive officers and employees were not diminished. We are not satisfied that the alleged motives of the directors, in so far as they are reflected in the conduct of the business, menace the interests of shareholders. It is enough to say, per-haps, that the court of equity is at all times open to complaining shareholders having a just grievance.

Defendants say, and it is true, that a considerable cash balance must be at all times carried by such a concern. But, as has been stated, there was a large daily, weekly, monthly, receipt of cash. The output was practically continuous and was continuously, and within a few days, turned into cash. Moreover, the contemplated expenditures were not to be immediately made. The large sum appropriated for the smelter plant was payable over a considerable period of time. So that, without going further, it would appear that, accepting and approving the plan of the directors, it was their duty to distribute on or near the first of August, 1916, a very large sum of money to stockholders.

A.P. SMITH MFG. CO. V. BARLOW

SUPREME COURT OF NEW JERSEY (JACOBS, J.)
98 A.2D 581 (1953)

The Chancery Division, in a well-reasoned opinion by Judge Stein, determined that a donation by the plaintiff The A. P. Smith Manufacturing Company to Princeton University was *intra vires*. Because of the public importance of the issues presented, the appeal duly taken to the Appellate Division has been certified directly to this court under Rule 1:5-1(a).

The company was incorporated in 1896 and is engaged in the manufacture and sale of valves, fire hydrants and special equipment, mainly for water and gas industries. Its plant is located in East Orange and Bloomfield and it has approximately 300 employees. Over the years the company has contributed regularly to the local community chest and on occasions to Upsala College in East Orange and Newark University, now part of Rutgers, the State University. On July 24, 1951 the board of directors adopted a resolution which set forth that it was in the corpo-ration's best interests to join with others in the 1951 Annual Giving to Princeton University, and appropriated the sum of $1,500 to be transferred by the corporation's treasurer to the university as a contribution towards its maintenance. When this action was questioned by stockholders the corporation instituted a declaratory judgment action in the Chancery Division and trial was had in due course.

Mr. Hubert F. O'Brien, the president of the company, testified that he considered the contri-bution to be a sound investment, that the public expects corporations to aid philanthropic and benevolent institutions, that they obtain good will in the community by so doing, and that their charitable donations create a favorable environment for their business operations. In addition, he expressed the thought that in contributing to liberal arts institutions, corporations were further-ing their self-interest in assuring the free flow of properly trained personnel for administrative and other corporate employment. Mr. Frank W. Abrams, chairman of the board of the Standard

Oil Company of New Jersey, testified that corporations are expected to acknowledge their public responsibilities in support of the essential elements of our free enterprise system. He indicated that it was not "good business" to disappoint "this reasonable and justified public expectation," nor was it good business for corporations "to take substantial benefits from their membership in the economic community while avoiding the normally accepted obligations of citizenship in the social community." Mr. Irving S. Olds, former chairman of the board of the United States Steel Corporation, pointed out that corporations have a self-interest in the maintenance of liberal education as the bulwark of good government. He stated that "Capitalism and free enterprise owe their survival in no small degree to the existence of our private, independent universities" and that if American business does not aid in their maintenance it is not "properly protecting the long-range interest of its stockholders, its employees and its customers." Similarly, Dr. Harold W. Dodds, President of Princeton University, suggested that if private institutions of higher learning were replaced by governmental institutions our society would be vastly different and private enterprise in other fields would fade out rather promptly. Further on he stated that "democratic society will not long endure if it does not nourish within itself strong centers of non-governmental fountains of knowledge, opinions of all sorts not governmentally or politically originated. If the time comes when all these centers are absorbed into government, then freedom as we know it, I submit, is at an end."

The objecting stockholders have not disputed any of the foregoing testimony nor the showing of great need by Princeton and other private institutions of higher learning and the important public service being rendered by them for democratic government and industry alike. Similarly, they have acknowledged that for over two decades there has been state legislation on our books which expresses a strong public policy in favor of corporate contributions such as that being questioned by them. Nevertheless, they have taken the position that (1) the plaintiff's certificate of incorporation does not expressly authorize the contribution and under common-law principles the company does not possess any implied or incidental power to make it, and (2) the New Jersey statutes which expressly authorize the contribution may not constitutionally be applied to the plaintiff, a corporation created long before their enactment.

In his discussion of the early history of business corporations Professor Williston refers to a 1702 publication where the author stated flatly that "The general intent and end of all civil incorporations is for better government." And he points out that the early corporate charters, particularly their recitals, furnish additional support for the notion that the corporate object was the public one of managing and ordering the trade as well as the private one of profit for the members. However, with later economic and social developments and the free availability of the corporate device for all trades, the end of private profit became generally accepted as the controlling one in all businesses other than those classed broadly as public utilities. As a concomitant the common-law rule developed that those who managed the corporation could not disburse any corporate funds for philanthropic or other worthy public cause unless the expenditure would benefit the corporation. During the 19th Century when corporations were relatively few and small and did not dominate the country's wealth, the common-law rule did not significantly interfere with the public interest. But the 20th Century has presented a different climate. Control of economic wealth has passed largely from individual entrepreneurs to dominating corporations, and calls upon the corporations for reasonable philanthropic donations have come to be made with increased public support. In many instances such contributions have been sustained by the courts within the common-law doctrine upon liberal findings that the donations tended reasonably to promote the corporate objectives.

When the wealth of the nation was primarily in the hands of individuals they discharged their responsibilities as citizens by donating freely for charitable purposes. With the transfer of most of the wealth to corporate hands and the imposition of heavy burdens of individual taxation, they have been unable to keep pace with increased philanthropic needs. They have therefore, with justification, turned to corporations to assume the modern obligations of good citizenship in the same manner as humans do. Congress and state legislatures have enacted laws which encourage corporate contributions, and much has recently been written to indicate the crying need and adequate legal basis therefore. In actual practice corporate giving has correspondingly increased. Thus, it is estimated that annual corporate contributions throughout the nation aggregate over 300 million dollars, with over 60 million dollars thereof going to universities and other educational institutions. Similarly, it is estimated that local community chests receive well over 40% of their contributions from corporations; these contributions and those made by corporations to the American Red Cross, to Boy Scouts and Girl Scouts, to 4-H Clubs and similar organizations have almost invariably been unquestioned.

During the first world war corporations loaned their personnel and contributed substantial corporate funds in order to insure survival; during the depression of the '30s they made contributions to alleviate the desperate hardships of the millions of unemployed; and during the second world war they again contributed to insure survival. They now recognize that we are faced with other, though nonetheless vicious, threats from abroad which must be withstood without impairing the vigor of our democratic institutions at home and that otherwise victory will be pyrrhic indeed. More and more they have come to recognize that their salvation rests upon sound economic and social environment which in turn rests in no insignificant part upon free and vigorous nongovernmental institutions of learning. It seems to us that just as the conditions prevailing when corporations were originally created required that they serve public as well as private interests, modern conditions require that corporations acknowledge and discharge social as well as private responsibilities as members of the communities within which they operate. Within this broad concept there is no difficulty in sustaining, as incidental to their proper objects and in aid of the public welfare, the power of corporations to contribute corporate funds within reasonable limits in support of academic institutions.

In 1930 a statute was enacted in our State which expressly provided that any corporation could cooperate with other corporations and natural persons in the creation and maintenance of community funds and charitable, philanthropic or benevolent instrumentalities conducive to public welfare, and could for such purposes expend such corporate sums as the directors "deem expedient and as in their judgment will contribute to the protection of the corporate interests." Under the terms of the statute donations in excess of 1% of the capital stock required 10 days' notice to stockholders and approval at a stockholders' meeting if written objections were made by the holders of more than 25% of the stock; in 1949 the statute was amended to increase the limitation to 1% of capital and surplus.

The appellants contend that the foregoing New Jersey statutes may not be applied to corporations created before their passage. Fifty years before the incorporation of The A. P. Smith Manufacturing Company our Legislature provided that every corporate charter thereafter granted "shall be subject to alteration, suspension and repeal, in the discretion of the legislature." A similar reserved power was placed into our State Constitution in 1875, and is found in our present Constitution. In the early case of *Zabriskie v. Hackensack & New York Railroad Company*, the court was called upon to determine whether a railroad could extend its line, above objection by a stockholder, under a legislative enactment passed under the reserve power after the incorporation of the railroad. Notwithstanding the breadth of the statutory language and persuasive authority elsewhere, it was held that the proposed extension of the company's line constituted a vital change of its corporate object which could not be accomplished without unanimous consent. The court announced the now familiar New Jersey doctrine that although the reserved power permits alterations in the public interest of the contract between the state and the corporation, it has no effect on the contractual rights between the corporation and its stockholders and between stockholders *Inter se*. Unfortunately, the court did not consider whether it was not contrary to the public interest to permit the single minority stockholder before it to restrain the railroad's normal corporate growth and development as authorized by the Legislature and approved, reasonably and in good faith, by the corporation's managing directors and majority stockholders. Although the later cases in New Jersey have not disavowed the doctrine of the *Zabriskie* case, it is noteworthy that they have repeatedly recognized that where justified by the advancement of the public interest the reserved power may be invoked to sustain later charter alterations even though they affect contractual rights between the corporation and its stockholders and between stockholders *inter se*.

State legislation adopted in the public interest and applied to pre-existing corporations under the reserved power has repeatedly been sustained by the United States Supreme Court above the contention that it impairs the rights of stockholders and violates constitutional guarantees under the Federal Constitution.

It seems clear to us that the public policy supporting the statutory enactments under consideration is far greater and the alteration of pre-existing rights of stockholders much lesser than in the cited cases sustaining various exercises of the reserve power. In encouraging and expressly authorizing reasonable charitable contributions by corporations, our State has not only joined with other states in advancing the national interest but has also specially furthered the interests of its own people who must bear the burdens of taxation resulting from increased state and federal aid upon default in voluntary giving. It is significant that in its enactments the State has not in anywise sought to impose any compulsory obligations or alter the corporate objectives. And since in our view the corporate power to make reasonable charitable contributions exists under modern conditions, even apart from express statutory provision, its enactments simply constitute helpful and confirmatory declarations of such power, accompanied by limiting safeguards.

In the light of all of the foregoing we have no hesitancy in sustaining the validity of the donation by the plaintiff. There is no suggestion that it was made indiscriminately or to a pet charity of the corporate directors in furtherance of personal rather than corporate ends. On the contrary, it was made to a preeminent institution of higher learning, was modest in amount and well within the limitations imposed by the statutory enactments, and was voluntarily made in the reasonable belief that it would aid the public welfare and advance the interests of the plaintiff as a private corporation and as part of the community in which it operates. We find that it was a lawful exercise of the corporation's implied and incidental powers under common-law principles and that it came within the express authority of the pertinent state legislation. As has been indicated, there is now widespread belief throughout the nation that free and vigorous non-governmental institutions of learning are vital to our democracy and the system of free enterprise and that withdrawal of corporate authority to make such contributions within reasonable limits would seriously threaten their continuance. Corporations have come to recognize this and with their enlightenment have sought in varying measures, as has the plaintiff by its contribution, to insure and strengthen the society which gives them existence and the means of aiding themselves and their fellow citizens. Clearly then, the appellants, as individual stockholders whose private interests rest entirely upon the well-being of the plaintiff corporation, ought not be permitted to close their eyes to present-day realities and thwart the long-visioned corporate action in recognizing and voluntarily discharging its high obligations as a constituent of our modern social structure.

The judgment entered in the Chancery Division is in all respects
Affirmed.

POWERS OF CORPORATIONS PART C

WISWALL V. THE GREENVILLE AND RALEIGH PLANK ROAD COMPANY

SUPREME COURT OF NORTH CAROLINA (CAUSE, J.)
56 N.C. 183 (1857)

The bill in this case set forth that the plaintiffs are stockholders in the Greenville and Raleigh plank-road company, which was chartered by the General Assembly at its session of 1850, and was duly organized by complying with the terms of the said Act; that the said company was incorporated for "the purpose of effecting a communication by means of a plank road from within the limits of the town of Greenville in Pitt County, to the city of Raleigh;" that in accordance with the said charter a plank road has been built from the said town of Greenville to the town of Wilson in Wilson county, which is in the most direct and practical line towards the city of Raleigh, but that the same has not been extended further, for the want of the necessary funds. The bill goes on to recite the various clauses of the act of incorporation, prescribing the nature and extent of the duties of the company, the extent of its powers and privileges, and the object of its incorporation, which clauses are fully set forth in the opinion of the court, and therefore need not be stated here. It further sets forth that the said company has been for several years in operation, and has, from the tolls received, accumulated a fund of about $4000; that the individuals named in the bill are the president and directors of the said road for the time being, and as such have the control and management of the affairs of the said company; that the said president and directors, or a majority of them, with the sanction and approbation of a majority of the stockholders, have adopted a resolution to purchase with the said funds a line of stages with the necessary appurtenances, to be run as their property upon the said road, and further to procure a contract from the U. S. government for carrying the public mail by such stage line upon the said road; and that they have appointed one of their number, the defendant Johnston, an agent, to effectuate these purposes, and that the said president and directors, through their agent, the said Johnston, are taking measures to accomplish both these purposes. They insist in their bill that this would be a misapplication of the funds which are needed for the repair of the road, which is in a worn and dilapidated condition, or should be divided amongst the stockholders; that such enterprises are foreign to the purpose for which the company was instituted, and not authorized by their charter; that besides exposing the company to the risk of loss from the undertaking, these measures will expose them to the danger of a forfeiture of their corporate privileges; they, therefore, pray for an injunction.

To this bill the defendants demurred. There was a joinder in demurrer; and the cause being set down for argument, was sent to this Court.

PEARSON, J.

It was conceded in the argument that a corporation has a right to restrain by injunction the corporators from doing any act which is not embraced within the scope and purpose for which the corporate body was created, and which would be a violation of the charter; not only on the ground that such act would operate injuriously upon the rights and interests of the corporators, but on the further ground that a forfeiture of the charter would be thereby incurred.

So, the only question made by the demurrer is this: Has the company power to purchase stages and horses to be run upon the said road?—and has it likewise power to enter into a contract to carry the United States mail on the road by means of such stages?

This question must be decided by a construction of the charter. We have examined it, and declare our opinion to be, that no such power is given to the company.

The first section sets out the object of the incorporation, to wit, "for the purpose of effecting a communication by means of a plank road from Greenville to Raleigh."

The third section grants the franchise of incorporation, and gives all the powers, rights and privileges necessary "for the purposes mentioned in this act."

The ninth section invests the president and directors of the company "with all the rights and powers necessary for the *construction, repairs and maintaining* of a plank road to be located as aforesaid."

The fourteenth section provides for the erection of *toll-houses and gates*.

The fifteenth section provides for the collection of toll to be "*demanded and received from all persons using the said plank road,*" with a proviso that the tolls shall be so regulated that the profits shall not exceed twenty-five per cent on the capital in any one year.

These sections contain the substantive provisions; the others merely embrace the details necessary for the formation of the company, etc.

The mere statement makes the question too plain for observation. If, under the power to construct, repair and maintain a plank road, a power can be implied to buy stages and horses and become a mail contractor, the company, by a parity of reasoning, has an implied power to set up establishments at convenient points along the road for the purchase of produce to be carried over its road. Besides, how are tolls to be demanded and received, and how are the profits of this enlarged operation to be regulated? How are losses from such speculations to be guarded against?

It may as well be contended that a turn-pike company, from its power to construct, repair and maintain the road, has, by implication, power to embark in the business of mail contractor, or in buying and selling horses, cattle, or produce, under the suggestion that the road would be subservient to these purposes.

Let the demurrer be overruled.

CHAPTER SIX

UNDERSTANDING CORPORATIONS

INTRODUCTION

In this chapter, we examine the nuts and bolts of corporate law—the machinery that makes them run. Like a cognitive psychologist trying to understand the mind's inner workings, we seek to unlock the proverbial "black box" that will illuminate the nuances of corporate decision-making. How are corporations formed, operated, and dissolved? Who exercises control, and how is such control limited? To answer these questions, we follow the money and encounter the underlying architecture of how resources and workers are put to use in the American economy.

Part A explains the process through which corporations are formed by examining several examples of failed attempts at formation. Part B turns to the distribution of decision-making authority among corporate managers and directors. Part C provides a famous example of the complex mechanics involved in shareholder voting. Part D then brings us full circle to the legal issues implicated by attempts to dissolve and liquidate a corporation.

As you engage with this material, notice the formalistic manner with which courts approach the rules governing business operations. Neither intent nor traditional matters of justice seem to be of great import. Courts rarely attempt to look beyond the surface description of a transaction to identify and grapple with its true essence. Rather, in corporate law, a thing is what it says it is; form actually does trump substance.

It can be tempting, therefore, to dismiss the rules of corporate governance as being simplistic or lacking in moral integrity. However, it is worth asking why this would be the case. What is it about the rules that govern the internal workings of corporations that lead courts to such an approach? Why, for example, will judges aggressively recharacterize a transaction for tax law purposes but not for corporate law purposes? Why honor form over substance?

Finally, in Part E, we turn to the question of corporation finance. How is money invested in corporations, and—more importantly—how are profits and losses divided among investors? Our goal in this section is not to learn to identify a good or bad investment opportunity. (We'll leave that endeavor to the business schools.) Rather, we seek to understand how corporate law gives effect to investor preferences. How are corporations valued, and how are such valuations recorded in their financial statements? What kinds of stock exist, and what are their rights and preferences? In what ways are investors vulnerable to manipulation by management?

At the end of this chapter, you will understand the rules and mechanisms that comprise our system of corporate governance. This will enable you to help translate your clients' legitimate objectives into valid and enforceable actions.

PART A CORPORATE FORMATION

COOPERS & LYBRAND V. FOX

COLORADO COURT OF APPEALS (KELLY, C.J.) 758 P.2D 683 (1988)

In an action based on breach of express and implied contracts, the plaintiff, Coopers & Lybrand, appeals the judgment of the trial court in favor of the defendant, Garry J. Fox. . Coopers contends that the trial court erred in ruling that Fox, a corporate promoter, could not be held liable on a pre-incorporation contract in the absence of an agreement that he would be so liable, and that Coopers had, and failed to sustain, the burden of proving any such agreement. We reverse.

On November 3, 1981, Fox met with a representative of Coopers, a national accounting firm, to request a tax opinion and other accounting services. Fox informed Coopers at this meeting that he was acting on behalf of a corporation he was in the process of forming, G. Fox and Partners, Inc. Coopers accepted the "engagement" with the knowledge that the corporation was not yet in existence.

G. Fox and Partners, Inc., was incorporated on December 4, 1981. Coopers completed its work by mid-December and billed "Mr. Garry R. Fox, Fox and Partners, Inc." in the amount of $10,827. When neither Fox nor G. Fox and Partners, Inc., paid the bill, Coopers sued Garry Fox, individually, for breach of express and implied contracts based on a theory of promoter liability.

Fox argued at trial that, although Coopers knew the corporation was not in existence when he engaged the firm's services, it either expressly or impliedly agreed to look solely to the corporation for payment. Coopers argued that its client was Garry Fox, not the corporation. The parties stipulated that Coopers had done the work, and Coopers presented uncontroverted testimony that the fee was fair and reasonable.

The trial court failed to make written findings of fact and conclusions of law. However, in its bench findings at the end of trial, the court found that there was no agreement, either express or implied, that would obligate Fox, individually, to pay Coopers' fee, in effect, because Coopers had failed to prove the existence of any such agreement. The court entered judgment in favor of Fox.

As a preliminary matter, we reject Fox's argument that he was acting only as an agent for the future corporation. One cannot act as the agent of a nonexistent principal. On the contrary, the uncontroverted facts place Fox squarely within the definition of a promoter. A promoter is one who, alone or with others, undertakes to form a corporation and to procure for it the rights, instrumentalities, and capital to enable it to conduct business.

When Fox first approached Coopers, he was in the process of forming G. Fox and Partners, Inc. He engaged Coopers' services for the future corporation's benefit. In addition, though not dispositive on the issue of his status as a promoter, Fox became the president, a director, and the principal shareholder of the corporation, which he funded, only nominally, with a $100 contribution. Under these circumstances, Fox cannot deny his role as a promoter.

Coopers asserts that the trial court erred in finding that Fox was under no obligation to pay Coopers' fee in the absence of an agreement that he would be personally liable. We agree.

As a general rule, promoters are personally liable for the contracts they make, though made on behalf of a corporation to be formed. The well-recognized exception to the general rule of promoter liability is that if the contracting party knows the corporation is not in existence but nevertheless agrees to look solely to the corporation and not to the promoter for payment, then the promoter incurs no personal liability. In the absence of an express agreement, the existence of an agreement to release the promoter from liability may be shown by circumstances making it reasonably certain that the parties intended to and did enter into the agreement.

Here, the trial court found there was *no* agreement, either express or implied, regarding Fox's liability. Thus, in the absence of an agreement releasing him from liability, Fox is liable.

It is undisputed that the defendant, Garry J. Fox, engaged Coopers' services, that G. Fox and Partners, Inc., was not in existence at that time, that Coopers performed the work, and that the fee was reasonable. The only dispute, as the trial court found, is whether Garry Fox is liable for payment of the fee. We conclude that Fox is liable, as a matter of law, under the doctrine of promoter liability.

CRANSON V. INTERNATIONAL BUSINESS MACHINES CORPORATION

COURT OF APPEALS OF MARYLAND (HORNEY, J.)
200 A.2D 33 (1964)

On the theory that the Real Estate Service Bureau was neither a *de jure* nor a *de facto* corporation and that Albion C. Cranson, Jr., was a partner in the business conducted by the Bureau and as such was personally liable for its debts, the International Business Machines Corporation brought this action against Cranson for the balance due on electric typewriters purchased by the Bureau. At the same time it moved for summary judgment and supported the motion by affidavit. In due course, Cranson filed a general issue plea and an affidavit in opposition to summary judgment in which he asserted in effect that the Bureau was a *de facto* corporation and that he was not personally liable for its debts.

The agreed statement of facts shows that in April 1961, Cranson was asked to invest in a new business corporation which was about to be created. Towards this purpose he met with other interested individuals and an attorney and agreed to purchase stock and become an officer and director. Thereafter, upon being advised by the attorney that the corporation had been formed under the laws of Maryland, he paid for and received a stock certificate evidencing ownership of shares in the corporation, and was shown the corporate seal and minute book. The business of the new venture was conducted as if it were a corporation, through corporate bank accounts, with auditors maintaining corporate books and records, and under a lease entered into by the corporation for the office from which it operated its business. Cranson was elected president and all transactions conducted by him for the corporation, including the dealings with I.B.M., were made as an officer of the corporation. At no time did he assume any personal obligation or pledge his individual credit to I.B.M. Due to an oversight on the part of the attorney, of which Cranson was not aware, the certificate of incorporation, which had been signed and acknowledged prior to May 1, 1961, was not filed until November 24, 1961. Between May 17 and November 8, the Bureau purchased eight typewriters from I.B.M., on account of which partial payments were made, leaving a balance due of $4,333.40, for which this suit was brought.

The fundamental question presented by the appeal is whether an officer[1] of a defectively incorporated association may be subjected to personal liability under the circumstances of this case. We think not.

Traditionally, two doctrines have been used by the courts to clothe an officer of a defectively incorporated association with the corporate attribute of limited liability. The first, often referred to as the doctrine of de facto corporations, has been applied in those cases where there are elements showing: (1) the existence of law authorizing incorporation; (2) an effort in good faith to incorporate under the existing law; and (3) actual use or exercise of corporate powers. The second, the doctrine of estoppel to deny the corporate existence, is generally employed where the person seeking to hold the officer personally liable has contracted or otherwise dealt with the association in such a manner as to recognize and in effect admit its existence as a corporate body.

It is not at all clear what Maryland has done with respect to the two doctrines. There have been no recent cases in this State on the subject and some of the seemingly irreconcilable earlier cases offer little to clarify the problem.

I.B.M. contends that the failure of the Bureau to file its certificate of incorporation debarred all corporate existence. But, in spite of the fact that the omission might have prevented the Bureau from being either a corporation *de jure* or *de facto*,[2] we think that I.B.M. having dealt with the Bureau as if it were a corporation and relied on its credit rather than that of Cranson, is estopped to assert that the Bureau was not incorporated at the time the typewriters were purchased. In 1 Clark and Marshall, Private Corporations, § 89, it is stated:

> The doctrine in relation to estoppel is based upon the ground that it would generally be inequitable to permit the corporate existence of an association to be denied by persons who have represented it to be a corporation, or held it out as a corporation, or by any persons who have recognized it as a corporation by dealing with it as such; and by the overwhelming weight of authority, therefore, a person may be estopped to deny the legal incorporation of an association which is not even a corporation de facto.

---

1   Although we are concerned with the liability of an "officer" in this case, the principles of law stated herein might under other circumstances be applicable to a determination of the liability of a member or shareholder of a defectively organized corporation.

2   Those states which recognize the *de facto* doctrine are not in accord as to whether a corporation *de facto* may be created in spite of the failure to file the necessary papers. Some courts, without making clear in every instance whether a *de facto* corporation was meant or not, have stated that failure to file the required papers prevented the organizations from becoming a corporation and have held in effect that the persons acting as a corporation are a mere association or partnership. Other courts, without expressly deciding whether a *de facto* corporation was created, hold that the statutes of the state imply corporate existence prior to the filing of articles of incorporation. Still other courts hold that a *de facto* existence is not precluded by failure to file the articles of incorporation.

In cases similar to the one at bar, involving a failure to file articles of incorporation, the courts of other jurisdictions have held that where one has recognized the corporate existence of an association, he is estopped to assert the contrary with respect to a claim arising out of such dealings.

Since I.B.M. is estopped to deny the corporate existence of the Bureau, we hold that Cranson was not liable for the balance due on account of the typewriters.

Judgment reversed; the appellee to pay the costs.

PART B CORPORATE MANAGEMENT

IN THE MATTER OF DRIVE-IN DEVELOPMENT CORP.

UNITED STATES COURT OF APPEALS, SEVENTH CIRCUIT
(SWYGERT, J.)
371 F.2D 215 (1966)

The principal question in this appeal relates to the circumstances which may bind a corporation to a guaranty of the obligations of a related corporation when it is contended that the corporate officer who executed the guaranty had no authority to do so. The facts giving rise to the question underlie a claim filed by the National Boulevard Bank of Chicago in an arrangement proceeding under chapter XI of the Bankruptcy Act, in which the Drive In Development Corporation was the debtor. National Boulevard's claim was disallowed by the referee, whose decision was confirmed by the district court.

Drive In was one of four subsidiary companies controlled by Tastee Freez Industries, Inc., a holding company that conducted no business of its own. Each of the subsidiaries performed one phase of the operation of an integrated business which franchised and supplied soft ice-cream stores and mobile units.

The guaranty by Drive In which forms the basis of the claim in this proceeding was given National Boulevard in connection with an April 1962 undertaking by which Allied Business agreed to sell and assign to the bank conditional sales contracts generated by Freez King. Allied Business had entered similar financing arrangements in lesser amounts with National Boulevard since 1960 which had included guaranties by the various Tastee Freez subsidiaries, but Drive In had not been a guarantor in any of them. On April 9, 1962, Allied Business entered into a contract with the bank that set forth the terms by which conditional sales contracts would be assigned to National Boulevard. Two days later, on April 11, 1962, Tastee Freez,

Harlee, Freez King, Carrols, and Drive In executed an instrument whereby they jointly and severally guaranteed Allied Business' obligations under its contract with National Boulevard. Maranz signed the guaranty on behalf of Drive In as "Chairman" and Dick attested to its execution as secretary.

National Boulevard requested a copy of the resolution by the board of directors of each of the guarantors authorizing the execution of the guaranty. Copies of these resolutions were furnished by all guarantors except Tastee Freez. Drive In's copy was certified, with the corporate seal affixed, by Dick, the corporation's secretary. No such resolution, however, was contained in Drive In's corporate minute book.[3]

On September 4, 1963, Tastee Freez and each of its subsidiaries, including Drive In, filed voluntary petitions under chapter XI of the Bankruptcy Act. National Boulevard filed a claim against Drive In before the referee, asserting the guaranty executed on April 11, 1962 as the basis for it.

Turning to the merits of the objections to National Boulevard's claim, the referee found that Drive In's minute book did not show that a resolution authorizing Maranz to sign the guaranty was adopted by the directors and that Dick could not recall a specific directors' meeting at which such a resolution was approved. From these findings, the referee concluded that Maranz, who signed the guaranty on behalf of Drive In, had no authority, "either actual or implied or apparent," to bind Drive In. This conclusion was erroneous. Drive In was estopped to deny Maranz' express authority to sign the guaranty because of the certified copy of a resolution of Drive In's board of directors purporting to grant such authority furnished to the bank by Dick, whether or not such a resolution was in fact formally adopted. Dick was the secretary of the corporation. Generally, it is the duty of the secretary to keep the corporate records and to make proper entries of the actions and resolutions of the directors. Therefore it was within the authority of Dick to certify that a resolution such as challenged here was adopted. Statements made by an officer or agent in the course of a transaction in which the corporation is engaged and which are within the scope of his authority are binding upon the corporation. Consequently Drive In was estopped to deny the representation made by Dick in the certificate forwarded to National Boulevard, in the absence of actual or constructive knowledge on the part of the bank that the representation was untrue.

The objectors argue that since William Schneider, a vice president of National Boulevard, requested Dick to furnish the certified copy of a resolution granting authority to execute the guaranty, and since Hugh Driscoll, another vice president of National Boulevard, was also a

---

3   At the hearing before the referee, Dick testified that he did not remember a board of directors' meeting at which a resolution authorizing the execution of the guaranty was presented, although he stated that a number of informal meetings of the directors were held and that such a resolution was discussed at one of the meetings. Dick also testified that Leo Maranz and Bernard Spira and Sylvan Spira were aware of the fact that between 1960 and 1963 National Boulevard on several occasions asked for guaranties from several of the companies; further, he testified that he didn't recall any of them objecting to the fact that he had given a guaranty.

director of Tastee Freez and was familiar with the organization of the subsidiaries, the bank was somehow in a position to know that no resolution had in fact been adopted by Drive In's board of directors. These facts, however, fall far short of proving such knowledge on the part of National Boulevard.

Although intercorporate contracts of guaranty do not usually occur in the regular course of commercial business, here the interrelationship of Tastee Freez and its subsidiaries presented a situation in which the guaranty was not so unusual as would ordinarily obtain. Furthermore, the realities of modern corporate business practices do not contemplate that those who deal with officers or agents acting for a corporation should be required to go behind the representations of those who have authority to speak for the corporation and who verify the authority of those who presume to act for the corporation.

The order of the district court confirming the referee's order is reversed in part and affirmed in part.

LEE V. JENKINS BROTHERS

UNITED STATES COURT OF APPEALS, SECOND CIRCUIT (MEDINA, J.) 268 F.2D 357 (1959)

Bernard J. Lee appeals from a judgment dismissing his complaint in two consolidated actions against Jenkins Brothers, a corporation, and against Farnham Yardley, to recover pension payments allegedly due under an oral agreement by Yardley on behalf of the corporation and for his own account, made in 1920.

Assuming, arguendo, that there was evidence sufficient to support a finding that Yardley promised Lee a pension of not to exceed $1500 at the age of 60, even if not employed by Jenkins at that time, we find that, while there is no proof of actual authority, the combination of circumstances here present would, if we assume such a promise was made, make the question of apparent authority an issue for the jury.

The following is a summary of Lee's testimony. At the time of the alleged contract Lee was in the employ of the Crane Company, a large manufacturer of valves, fittings and plumbing supplies, at the company's Bridgeport plant. He had been with the Crane Company for thirteen years and had risen to the post of business manager, earning a salary of $4,000 per year. In December, 1919, the Crane Company agreed to sell its Bridgeport plant to Jenkins Brothers, a New Jersey corporation and a defendant in one of these actions. The transaction was consummated June 1, 1920 when Jenkins took over Crane's Bridgeport plant.

First, Lee testified:

130

As far as the pension that I had earned with Crane Company he said the company (Jenkins Brothers) would pay that pension (and) if they didn't or, if anything came up, he would assume the liability himself he would guarantee payment of the pension; and in consideration of that promise I agreed to go to work for Jenkins Bros. on June 1, 1920.

The amount of the pension referred to by Mr. Yardley was a maximum of $1500 a year and that would be paid me when I reached the age of 60 years; regardless of what happened in the meantime, if I were with the company or not, I would be given a credit for those 13 years of service with the maximum pension of $1500.

Later Lee put it this way:

Mr. Farnham Yardley said that Jenkins would assume the obligation for my credit pension record with Crane Company and, if anything happened and they did not pay it, he would guarantee it himself.

Mr. Yardley's words were 'regardless of what happens, you will get that pension if you join our company.

Finally, Lee summarized his position:

My claim is that the company through the chairman of the board of directors and the president, promised me credit for my 13 years of service with Crane Company, regardless of what happened I would receive a pension at the age of 60, not to exceed $1,500 a year. If I was discharged in 1921 or 1922 or left I would still get that pension. That is what I am asking for.

This agreement was never reduced to writing.

Lee's prospects with Jenkins turned out to be just about as bright as he had hoped. He subsequently became vice president and general manager in charge of manufacturing and a director of the company. At that time he was receiving a salary of $25,000 from Jenkins, $8,000 more from an affiliate, plus an annual 10 per cent bonus. In 1945, however, after 25 years with Jenkins, Lee was discharged at the age of 55.

In the discussion which follows we assume, *arguendo*, that there was evidence sufficient to support a finding that Yardley orally agreed on behalf of the corporation that Lee would be paid at the age of 60 a pension not to exceed $1500, and that Yardley's words "regardless of what happens" were, as Lee contends, to be interpreted as meaning that Lee would receive this pension even if he were not working for Jenkins at the time the pension became payable. Jenkins asserts that Yardley had no authority to bind it to such an "extraordinary" contract, express, implied, or apparent and

[handwritten margin note: Yardley promised Lee he would match his current pension if he came to work @ Jenkin Bros.]

131

the trial court so found. There is nothing in the proofs submitted by Lee to warrant any finding of actual authority in Yardley. The Certificate of Incorporation and By-Laws of Jenkins are not in evidence nor was any course of conduct shown as between the corporation and Yardley. Accordingly, on the phase of the case now under discussion, we are dealing only with apparent authority.

Our question on this phase of the case then boils itself down to the following: can it be said as a matter of law that Yardley as president, chairman of the board, substantial stockholder and trustee and son-in-law of the estate of the major stockholder, had no power in the presence of the company's most interested vice president to secure for a "reasonable" length of time badly needed key personnel by promising an experienced local executive a life pension to commence in 30 years at the age of 60, even if Lee were not then working for the corporation, when the maximum liability to Jenkins under such a pension was $1500 per year.

A survey of the law on the authority of corporate officers does not reveal a completely consistent pattern. For the most part the courts perhaps have taken a rather restrictive view on the extent of powers of corporate officials, but the dissatisfaction with such an approach has been manifested in a variety of exceptions such as ratification, estoppel, and promissory estoppel.

Such an assumption is ill-founded. The circumstances and facts known to exist between officer and corporation, from which actual authority may be implied, may be entirely different from those circumstances known to exist as between the third party and the corporation. The two concepts are separate and distinct even though the state of the proofs in a given case may cause considerable overlap.

The rule most widely cited is that the president only has authority to bind his company by acts arising in the usual and regular course of business but not for contracts of an "extraordinary" nature. The substance of such a rule lies in the content of the term "extraordinary" which is subject to a broad range of interpretation.

The growth and development of this rule occurred during the late nineteenth and early twentieth centuries when the potentialities of the corporate form of enterprise were just being realized. As the corporation became a more common vehicle for the conduct of business it became increasingly evident that many corporations, particularly small closely held ones, did not normally function in the formal ritualistic manner hitherto envisaged. While the boards of directors still nominally controlled corporate affairs, in reality officers and managers frequently ran the business with little, if any, board supervision. The natural consequence of such a development was that third parties commonly relied on the authority of such officials in almost all the multifarious transactions in which corporations engaged. The pace of modern business life was too swift to insist on the approval by the board of directors of every transaction that was in any way "unusual."

The judicial recognition given to these developments has varied considerably. Whether termed "apparent authority" or an "estoppel" to deny authority, many courts have noted the injustice caused by the practice of permitting corporations to act commonly through their executives and then allowing them to disclaim an agreement as beyond the authority of the contracting officer, when the contract no longer suited its convenience. Other courts, however, continued to cling to the past with little attempt to discuss the unconscionable results obtained or the doctrine of apparent authority. Such restrictive views have been generally condemned by the commentators.

The summary of holdings pro and con in general on the subject of what are and what are not "extraordinary" agreements is inconclusive at best. But the pattern becomes more distinct when we turn to the more limited area of employment contracts.

It is generally settled that the president as part of the regular course of business has authority to hire and discharge employees and fix their compensation. In so doing he may agree to hire them for a specific number of years if the term selected is deemed reasonable. But employment contracts for life or on a "permanent" basis are generally regarded as "extraordinary" and beyond the authority of any corporate executive if the only consideration for the promise is the employee's promise to work for that period. Jenkins would have us analogize the pension agreement involved herein to these generally condemned lifetime employment contracts because it extends over a long period of time, is of indefinite duration, and involves an indefinite liability on the part of the corporation.

It is not surprising that lifetime employment contracts have met with substantial hostility in the courts, for these contracts are often oral, uncorroborated, vague in important details and highly improbable. However, at times such contracts have been enforced where the circumstances tended to support the plausibility of plaintiff's testimony. All this is a not uncommon indication that the law in a particular area is in a state of evolution, and there seems every reason to believe that the law affecting numerous features of employer-employee relationship, is far from static.

In this case Lee was hired at a starting salary of $4,000 per year plus a contemplated pension of $1500 per year in thirty years. Had Lee been hired at a starting salary of $10,000 per year the cost to the corporation over the long run would have been substantially greater, yet no one could plausibly contend that such an employment contract was beyond Yardley's authority.

Apparent authority is essentially a question of fact. It depends not only on the nature of the contract involved, but the officer negotiating it, the corporation's usual manner of conducting business, the size of the corporation and the number of its stockholders, the circumstances that give rise to the contract, the reasonableness of the contract, the amounts involved, and who the contracting third party is, to list a few but not all of the relevant factors. In certain instances a given contract may be so important to the welfare of the corporation that outsiders would naturally suppose that only the board of directors (or even the shareholders) could properly handle it. It is in this light that the "ordinary course of business" rule should be given its content. Beyond such 'extraordinary' acts, whether or not apparent authority exists is simply a matter of fact.

Accordingly, we hold that, assuming there was sufficient proof of the making of the pension agreement, Connecticut, in the particular circumstances of this case, would probably take the view that reasonable men could differ on the subject of whether or not Yardley had apparent authority to make the contract, and that the trial court erred in deciding the question as a matter of law.

133

MCQUADE V. STONEHAM

COURT OF APPEALS OF NEW YORK (POUND, C.J.)
263 N.Y. 323 (1934)

The action is brought to compel specific performance of an agreement between the parties, entered into to secure the control of National Exhibition Company, also called the Baseball Club (New York Nationals or "Giants"). This was one of Stoneham's enterprises which used the New York polo grounds for its home games. McGraw was manager of the Giants. McQuade was at the time the contract was entered into a city magistrate. He resigned December 8, 1930.

Defendant Stoneham became the owner of 1,306 shares, or a majority of the stock of National Exhibition Company. Plaintiff and defendant McGraw each purchased 70 shares of his stock. Plaintiff paid Stoneham $50,338.10 for the stock he purchased. As a part of the transaction, the agreement in question was entered into. It was dated May 21, 1919. Some of its pertinent provisions are

"VIII. The parties hereto will use their best endeavors for the purpose of continuing as directors of said Company and as officers thereof the following:

"**Directors:**
"Charles A. Stoneham,
"John J. McGraw,
"Francis X. McQuade,
"with the right to the party of the first part [Stoneham] to name all additional directors as he sees fit:

"**Officers:**
"Charles A. Stoneham, President,
"John J. McGraw, Vice-President,
"Francis X. McQuade, Treasurer.

"IX. No salaries are to be paid to any of the above officers or directors, except as follows:
"President $45,000
"Vice-President 7,500
"Treasurer 7,500

"X. There shall be no change in said salaries, no change in the amount of capital, or the number of shares, no change or amendment of the by-laws of the corporation or any matters regarding the policy of the business of the corporation or any matters which may in anywise affect, endanger or interfere with the rights of minority stockholders, excepting upon the mutual and unanimous consent of all of the parties hereto.

"XIV. This agreement shall continue and remain in force so long as the parties or any of them or the representative of any, own the stock referred to in this agreement, to wit, the party of the first part, 1,166 shares, the party of the second part 70 shares and the party of the third part 70 shares, except as may otherwise appear by this agreement."

In pursuance of this contract Stoneham became president and McGraw vice president of the corporation. McQuade became treasurer. In June, 1925, his salary was increased to $10,000 a year. He continued to act until May 2, 1928, when Leo J. Bondy was elected to succeed him. The board of directors consisted of seven men. The four outside of the parties hereto were selected by Stoneham and he had complete control over them. At the meeting of May 2, 1928, Stoneham and McGraw refrained from voting, McQuade voted for himself, and the other four voted for Bondy. Defendants did not keep their agreement with McQuade to use their best efforts to continue him as treasurer. On the contrary, he was dropped with their entire acquiescence. At the next stockholders' meeting he was dropped as a director although they might have elected him.

The courts below have refused to order the reinstatement of McQuade, but have given him damages for wrongful discharge, with a right to sue for future damages.

The cause for dropping McQuade was due to the falling out of friends. McQuade and Stoneham had disagreed. The trial court has found in substance that their numerous quarrels and disputes did not affect the orderly and efficient administration of the business of the corporation; that plaintiff was removed because he had antagonized the dominant Stoneham by persisting in challenging his power over the corporate treasury and for no misconduct on his part. The court also finds that plaintiff was removed by Stoneham for protecting the corporation and its minority stockholders. We will assume that Stoneham put him out when he might have retained him, merely in order to get rid of him.

Defendants say that the contract in suit was void because the directors held their office charged with the duty to act for the corporation according to their best judgment and that any contract which compels a director to vote to keep any particular person in office and at a stated salary is illegal. Directors are the exclusive executive representatives of the corporation, charged with administration of its internal affairs and the management and use of its assets. They manage the business of the corporation. "An agreement to continue a man as president is dependent upon his continued loyalty to the interests of the corporation." So much is undisputed.

Plaintiff contends that the converse of this proposition is true and that an agreement among directors to continue a man as an officer of a corporation is not to be broken so long as such

[handwritten margin notes: guys make an agreement to vote for one another to keep their positions but then Stoneham, McQuade breakup Stoneham gets McQuade booted McQuade sues Stoneham for violating agreement]

[handwritten note at bottom: can a director enter an agreement that limits his vote? no, it's unenforceable]

135

officer is loyal to the interests of the corporation and that, as plaintiff has been found loyal to the corporation, the agreement of defendants is enforceable.

Although it has been held that an agreement among stockholders whereby it is attempted to divest the directors of their power to discharge an unfaithful employee of the corporation is illegal as against public policy, it must be equally true that the stockholders may not, by agreement among themselves, control the directors in the exercise of the judgment vested in them by virtue of their office to elect officers and fix salaries. Their motives may not be questioned so long as their acts are legal. The bad faith or the improper motives of the parties does not change the rule. Directors may not by agreements entered into as stockholders abrogate their independent judgment.

Stockholders may, of course, combine to elect directors. That rule is well settled. As Holmes, C. J., pointedly said: "If stockholders want to make their power felt, they must unite. There is no reason why a majority should not agree to keep together". The power to unite is, however, limited to the election of directors and is not extended to contracts whereby limitations are placed on the power of directors to manage the business of the corporation by the selection of agents at defined salaries.

The minority shareholders whose interests McQuade says he has been punished for protecting, are not, aside from himself, complaining about his discharge. He is not acting for the corporation or for them in this action. It is impossible to see how the corporation has been injured by the substitution of Bondy as treasurer in place of McQuade. As McQuade represents himself in this action and seeks redress for his own wrongs, "we prefer to listen to [the corporation and the minority stockholders] before any decision as to their wrongs."

It is urged that we should pay heed to the morals and manners of the market place to sustain this agreement and that we should hold that its violation gives rise to a cause of action for damages rather than base our decision on any outworn notions of public policy. Public policy is a dangerous guide in determining the validity of a contract and courts should not interfere lightly with the freedom of competent parties to make their own contracts. We do not close our eyes to the fact that such agreements, tacitly or openly arrived at, are not uncommon, especially in close corporations where the stockholders are doing business for convenience under a corporate organization. We know that majority stockholders, united in voting trusts, effectively manage the business of a corporation by choosing trustworthy directors to reflect their policies in the corporate management. Nor are we unmindful that McQuade has, so the court has found, been shabbily treated as a purchaser of stock from Stoneham. We have said: "A trustee is held to something stricter than the morals of the market place," but Stoneham and McGraw were not trustees for McQuade as an individual. Their duty was to the corporation and its stockholders, to be exercised according to their unrestricted lawful judgment. They were under no legal obligation to deal righteously with McQuade if it was against public policy to do so.

136

The courts do not enforce mere moral obligations, nor legal ones either, unless someone seeks to establish rights which may be waived by custom and for convenience. We are constrained by authority to hold that a contract is illegal and void so far as it precludes the board of directors, at the risk of incurring legal liability, from changing officers, salaries, or policies or retaining individuals in office, except by consent of the contracting parties. On the whole, such a holding is probably preferable to one which would open the courts to pass on the motives of directors in the lawful exercise of their trust.

The judgment of the Appellate Division and that of the Trial Term should be reversed and the complaint dismissed, with costs in all courts.

LEHMAN, J. (concurring).

The defendant Stoneham owned the majority stock of the corporation and could exercise the control of the corporation which the holder of the majority stock possesses. He could choose the directors of the corporation who in turn would elect the officers and determine the corporate policies. The agreement between the defendant Stoneham, the plaintiff, McQuade, and McGraw provided, in effect, that, in consideration of the sale by Stoneham of part of his majority stock, the power of control which Stoneham had previously exercised should be shared with McQuade and McGraw, and, specifically, that mutual assurance should be given that this power of control would be used in concert to continue each of the three parties to the contract as directors and officers of the corporation at stipulated salaries and to preclude change without common consent in "matters regarding the policy of the business of the corporation or any matters which may in any wise affect, endanger or interfere with the rights of minority stockholders."

We have said: "An ordinary agreement, among a minority in number, but a majority in shares, for the purpose of obtaining control of the corporation by the election of particular persons as directors is not illegal." We are agreed that, if the contract had provided only for the election of directors, it would not have been illegal. Its vice, if any, is inherent in the provisions intended to give assurance that the directors so elected would act according to the prearranged design of the stockholders in apportioning the corporate offices and emoluments of such offices among the majority stockholders.

There can, I think, be no doubt that shareholders owning a majority of the corporate stock may combine to obtain and exercise any control which a single owner of such stock could exercise. What may lawfully be done by an individual may ordinarily be lawfully done by a combination, but no combination is legal if formed to accomplish an illegal object. No such combination or agreement may "contravene any express charter or statutory provision or contemplate any fraud, oppression or wrong against other stockholders or other illegal object."

In *Manson v. Curtis* we held invalid, on that ground, an agreement for the selection "of directors who should remain passive or mechanical to the will and word" of one of the parties to the agreement. Now it is said that, for the same reason, this agreement must be held unenforceable, though here the agreement contemplated no restriction upon the powers of the board of directors, and no dictation or interference by stockholders except in so far as concerns the election and remuneration of officers and the adhesion by the corporation to established policies.

It seems difficult to reconcile such a decision with the statements in the opinion in *Manson* that "it is not illegal or against public policy for two or more stockholders owning the majority of the shares of stock to unite upon a course of corporate policy or action, or upon the officers whom they will elect," and that "shareholders have the right to combine their interests and voting powers to secure such control of the corporation and the adoption of and adhesion by it to a specific policy and course of business." Obviously, a combination intended to effect the election of certain officers and to obtain control of the corporation and adhesion by it to a specific policy and course of business can accomplish its ends only to the extent that directors will bow to the will of those who united to elect them. The directors have the power and the duty to act in accordance with their own best judgment so long as they remain directors. The majority stockholders can compel no action by the directors, but at the expiration of the term of office of the directors the stockholders have the power to replace them with others whose actions coincide with the judgment or desires of the holders of a majority of the stock. The theory that directors exercise in all matters an independent judgment in practice often yields to the fact that the choice of directors lies with the majority stockholders and thus gives the stockholders a very effective control of the action by the board of directors. In truth the board of directors may check the arbitrary will of those who would otherwise completely control the corporation, but cannot indefinitely thwart their will.

A contract which destroys this check contravenes "express charter or statutory provisions" and is, therefore, illegal. A contract which merely provides that stockholders shall in combination use their power to achieve a legitimate purpose is not illegal. They may join in the election of directors who, in their opinion, will be in sympathy with the policies of the majority stockholders and who, in the choice of executive officers, will be influenced by the wishes of the majority stockholders. The directors so chosen may not act in disregard of the best interests of the corporation and its minority stockholders, but with that limitation they may and, in practice, usually are swayed by the wishes of the majority. Otherwise there would be no continuity of corporate policy and no continuity in management of corporate affairs.

The contract now under consideration provides, in a narrow field, for corporate action within these limitations

A contract which merely provides for the election of fit officers and adhesion to particular policy determined in advance constitutes an agreement by which men in combination exercise a power which could be lawfully exercised if lodged in a single man. It is legal, if designed to protect legitimate interests without wrong to others. Public policy should be governed by facts, not abstractions. The contract is, in my opinion, valid. It is unenforceable only because it resulted in an employment which was itself illegal.

CLARK V. DODGE

COURT OF APPEALS OF NEW YORK (CROUCH, J.)
199 N.E. 641 (1936)

The action is for the specific performance of a contract between the plaintiff, Clark, and the defendant Dodge, relating to the affairs of the two defendant corporations.

The facts, briefly stated, are as follows: The two corporate defendants are New Jersey corporations manufacturing medicinal preparations by secret formulae. The main office, factory, and assets of both corporations are located in the state of New York. In 1921, and at all times since, Clark owned 25 per cent and Dodge 75 per cent of the stock of each corporation. Dodge took no active part in the business, although he was a director, and through ownership of their qualifying shares, controlled the other directors of both corporations. He was the president of Bell & Co., Inc., and nominally general manager of Hollings-Smith Company, Inc. The plaintiff, Clark, was a director and held the offices of treasurer and general manager of Bell & Co., Inc., and also had charge of the major portion of the business of Hollings-Msith Company, Inc. The formulae and methods of manufacture of the medicinal preparations were known to him alone. Under date of February 15, 1921, Dodge and Clark, the sole owners of the stock of both corporations, entered into a written agreement under seal, which after reciting the stock ownership of both parties, the desire of Dodge that Clark should continue in the efficient management and control of the business of Bell & Co., Inc., so long as he should "remain faithful, efficient and competent to so manage and control the said business;" and his further desire that Clark should not be the sole custodian of a specified formula, but should share his knowledge thereof and of the method of manufacture with a son of Dodge, provided, in substance, as follows: That Dodge during his lifetime and, after his death, a trustee to be appointed by his will, would so vote his stock and so vote as a director that the plaintiff (a) should continue to be a director of Bell & Co., Inc.; and (b) should continue as its general manager so long as he should be "faithful, efficient and competent;" (c) should during his life receive one-fourth of the net income of the corporations either by way of salary or dividends; and (d) that no unreasonable or incommensurate salaries should be paid to other officers or agents which would so reduce the net income as materially to affect Clark's profits. Clark on his part agreed to disclose the specified formula to the son and to instruct him in the details and methods of manufacture; and, further, at the end of his life to bequeath his stock—if no issue survived him—to the wife and children of Dodge.

It was further provided that the provisions in regard to the division of net profits and the regulation of salaries should also apply to the Hollings-Smith Company.

The complaint alleges due performance of the contract by Clark and breach thereof by Dodge in that he has failed to use his stock control to continue Clark as a director and as general manager, and has prevented Clark from receiving his proportion of the income, while taking his own, by causing the employment of incompetent persons at excessive salaries, and otherwise.

The relief sought is reinstatement as director and general manager and an accounting by Dodge and by the corporations for waste and for the proportion of net income due plaintiff, with an injunction against further violations.

The only question which need be discussed is whether the contract is illegal as against public policy within the decision in *McQuade v. Stoneham*, upon the authority of which the complaint was dismissed by the Appellate Division.

"The business of a corporation shall be managed by its board of directors." That is the statutory norm. Are we committed by the *McQuade* Case to the doctrine that there may be no variation, however slight or innocuous, from that norm, where salaries or policies or the retention of individuals in office are concerned? There is ample authority supporting that doctrine and something may be said for it, since it furnishes a simple, if arbitrary, test. Apart from its practical administrative convenience, the reasons upon which it is said to rest are more or less nebulous. Public policy, the intention of the Legislature, detriment to the corporation, are phrases which in this connection mean little. Possible harm to bona fide purchasers of stock or to creditors or to stockholding minorities have more substance; but such harms are absent in many instances. If the enforcement of a particular contract damages nobody—not even, in any perceptible degree, the public—one sees no reason for holding it illegal, even though it impinges slightly upon the broad provision of section 27. Damage suffered or threatened is a logical and practical test, and has come to be the one generally adopted by the courts. Where the directors are the sole stockholders, there seems to be no objection to enforcing an agreement among them to vote for certain people as officers. There is no direct decision to that effect in this court, yet there are strong indications that such a rule has long been recognized. The opinion in *Manson v. Curtis*, closed its discussion by saying: "The rule that all the stockholders by their universal consent may do as they choose with the corporate concerns and assets, provided the interests of creditors are not affected, because they are the complete owners of the corporation, cannot be invoked here." That was because all the stockholders were not parties to the agreement there in question. So, where the public was not affected, "the parties in interest, might, by their original agreement of incorporation, limit their respective rights and powers," even where there was a conflicting statutory standard.

Except for the broad dicta in the *McQuade* opinion, we think there can be no doubt that the agreement here in question was legal and that the complaint states a cause of action. There was no attempt to sterilize the board of directors, as in the *Manson* and *McQuade* cases. The only restrictions on Dodge were (a) that as a stockholder he should vote for Clark as a director—a perfectly legal contract; (b) that as director he should continue Clark as general manager, so long as he proved faithful, efficient, and competent—an agreement which could harm nobody; (c) that Clark should always receive as salary or dividends one-fourth of the "net income." For the purposes of this motion, it is only just to construe that phrase as meaning whatever was left for distribution after the directors had in good faith set aside whatever they deemed wise; (d) that no salaries to other officers should be paid, unreasonable in amount or incommensurate with services rendered—a beneficial and not a harmful agreement.

If there was any invasion of the powers of the directorate under that agreement, it is so slight as to be negligible; and certainly there is no damage suffered by or threatened to anybody. The broad statements in the *McQuade* opinion, applicable to the facts there, should be confined to those facts.

The judgment of the Appellate Division should be reversed and the order of the Special Term affirmed, with costs in this court and in the Appellate Division.

[handwritten margin note: The agreement is legal as long as they aren't hurting anyone else bc it's between the 2 sole owners.]

SHAREHOLDER VOTING PART C

RINGLING BROS.-BARNUM & BAILEY COMBINED SHOWS, INC. V. EDITH CONWAY RINGLING

SUPREME COURT OF DELAWARE (PEARSON, J.)
53 A.2D 441 (1947)

The Court of Chancery was called upon to review an attempted election of directors at the 1946 annual stockholders meeting of the corporate defendant. The pivotal questions concern an agreement between two of the three present stockholders, and particularly the effect of this agreement with relation to the exercise of voting rights by these two stockholders. At the time of the meeting, the corporation had outstanding 1000 shares of capital stock held as follows: 315 by petitioner Edith Conway Ringling; 315 by defendant Aubrey B. Ringling Haley (individually or as executrix and legatee of a deceased husband); and 370 by defendant John Ringing North. The purpose of the meeting was to elect the entire board of seven directors. The shares could be voted cumulatively. Mrs. Ringling asserts that by virtue of the operation of an agreement between her and Mrs. Haley, the latter was bound to vote her shares for an adjournment of the meeting, or in the alternative, for a certain slate of directors. Mrs. Haley contends that she was not so bound for reason that the agreement was invalid, or at least revocable.

The two ladies entered into the agreement in 1941. It makes like provisions concerning stock of the corporate defendant and of another corporation, but in this case, we are concerned solely with the agreement as it affects the voting of stock of the corporate defendant. The agreement recites that each party was the owner "subject only to possible claims of creditors of the estates of Charles

Ringling and Richard Ringling, respectively" (deceased husbands of the parties), of 300 shares of the capital stock of the defendant corporation; that in 1938 these shares had been deposited under a voting trust agreement which would terminate in 1947, or earlier, upon the elimination of certain liability of the corporation; that each party also owned 15 shares individually; that the parties had "entered into an agreement in April 1934 providing for joint action by them in matters affecting their ownership of stock and interest in" the corporate defendant; that the parties desired "to continue to act jointly in all matters relating to their stock ownership or interest in" the corporate defendant (and the other corporation). The agreement then provides as follows:

"Now, therefore, in consideration of the mutual covenants and agreements hereinafter contained the parties hereto agree as follows:

1. "Neither party will sell any shares of stock or any voting trust certificates in either of said corporations to any other person whosoever, without first making a written offer to the other party hereto of all of the shares or voting trust certificates proposed to be sold, for the same price and upon the same terms and conditions as in such proposed sale, and allowing such other party a time of not less than 180 days from the date of such written offer within which to accept same.

2. "In exercising any voting rights to which either party may be entitled by virtue of ownership of stock or voting trust certificates held by them in either of said corporation, each party will consult and confer with the other and the parties will act jointly in exercising such voting rights in accordance with such agreement as they may reach with respect to any matter calling for the exercise of such voting rights.

3. "In the event the parties fail to agree with respect to any matter covered by paragraph 2 above, the question in disagreement shall be submitted for arbitration to Karl D. Loos, of Washington, D. C. as arbitrator and his decision thereon shall be binding upon the parties hereto. Such arbitration shall be exercised to the end of assuring for the respective corporations good management and such participation therein by the members of the Ringling family as the experience, capacity and ability of each may warrant. The parties may at any time by written agreement designate any other individual to act as arbitrator in lieu of said Loos.

4. "This agreement shall be in effect from the date hereof and shall continue in effect for a period of ten years unless sooner terminated by mutual agreement in writing by the parties hereto."

The Mr. Loos mentioned in the agreement is an attorney and has represented both parties since 1937, and, before and after the voting trust was terminated in late 1942, advised them with respect to the exercise of their voting rights. At the annual meetings in 1943 and the two following years, the parties voted their shares in accordance with mutual understandings arrived at as a result of discussions. In each of these years, they elected five of the seven directors. Mrs.

Ringling and Mrs. Haley each had sufficient votes, independently of the other, to elect two of the seven directors. By both voting for an additional candidate, they could be sure of his election regardless of how Mr. North, the remaining stockholder, might vote.[4]

Some weeks before the 1946 meeting, they discussed with Mr. Loos the matter of voting for directors. They were in accord that Mrs. Ringling should cast sufficient votes to elect herself and her son; and that Mrs. Haley should elect herself and her husband; but they did not agree upon a fifth director. The day before the meeting, the discussions were continued, Mrs. Haley being represented by her husband since she could not be present because of illness. In a conversation with Mr. Loos, Mr. Haley indicated that he would make a motion for an adjournment of the meeting for sixty days, in order to give the ladies additional time to come to an agreement about their voting. On the morning of the meeting, however, he stated that because of something Mrs. Ringling had done, he would not consent to a postponement. Mrs. Ringling then made a demand upon Mr. Loos to act under the third paragraph of the agreement "to arbitrate the disagreement" between her and Mrs. Haley in connection with the manner in which the stock of the two ladies should be voted. At the opening of the meeting, Mr. Loos read the written demand and stated that he determined and directed that the stock of both ladies be voted for an adjournment of sixty days. Mrs. Ringling then made a motion for adjournment and voted for it. Mr. Haley, as proxy for his wife, and Mr. North voted against the motion. Mrs. Ringling (herself or through her attorney, it is immaterial which,) objected to the voting of Mrs. Haley's stock in any manner other than in accordance with Mr. Loos' direction. The chairman ruled that the stock could not be voted contrary to such direction, and declared the motion for adjournment had carried. Nevertheless, the meeting proceeded to the election of directors. Mrs. Ringling stated that she would continue in the meeting "but without prejudice to her position with respect to the voting of the stock and the fact that adjournment had not been taken." Mr. Loos directed Mrs. Ringling to cast her votes

882 for Mrs. Ringling,
882 for her son, Robert, and
441 for a Mr. Dunn, who had been a member of the board for several years. She complied.

Mr. Loos directed that Mrs. Haley's votes be cast
882 for Mrs. Haley,

---

4   Each lady was entitled to cast 2205 votes (since each had the cumulative voting rights of 315 shares, and there were 7 vacancies in the directorate). The sum of the votes of both is 4410, which is sufficient to allow 882 votes for each of 5 persons. Mr. North, holding 370 shares, was entitled to cast 2590 votes, which obviously cannot be divided so as to give to more than two candidates as many as 882 votes each. It will be observed that in order for Mrs. Ringling and Mrs. Haley to be sure to elect five directors (regardless of how Mr. North might vote) they must act together in the sense that their combined votes must be divided among five different candidates and at least one of the five must be voted for by both Mrs. Ringling and Mrs. Haley.

882 for Mr. Haley, and
441 for Mr. Dunn.

Instead of complying, Mr. Haley attempted to vote his wife's shares
1103 for Mrs. Haley, and
1102 for Mr. Haley.

Mr. North voted his shares
864 for a Mr. Woods,
863 for a Mr. Griffin, and
863 for Mr. North.

The chairman ruled that the five candidates proposed by Mr. Loos, together with Messrs. Woods and North, were elected. The Haley-North group disputed this ruling insofar as it declared the election of Mr. Dunn; and insisted that Mr. Griffin, instead, had been elected. A director's meeting followed in which Mrs. Ringling participated after stating that she would do so "without prejudice to her position that the stockholders' meeting had been adjourned and that the directors' meeting was not properly held." Mr. Dunn and Mr. Griffin, although each was challenged by an opposing faction, attempted to join in voting as directors for different slates of officers. Soon after the meeting, Mrs. Ringling instituted this proceeding.

The Vice Chancellor determined that the agreement to vote in accordance with the direction of Mr. Loos was valid as a "stock pooling agreement" with lawful objects and purposes, and that it was not in violation of any public policy of this state. He held that where the arbitrator acts under the agreement and one party refuses to comply with his direction, "the Agreement constitutes the willing party an implied agent possessing the irrevocable proxy of the recalcitrant party for the purpose of casting the particular vote." It was ordered that a new election be held before a master, with the direction that the master should recognize and give effect to the agreement if its terms were properly invoked.

Before taking up defendants' objections to the agreement, let us analyze particularly what it attempts to provide with respect to voting, including what functions and powers it attempts to repose in Mr. Loos, the "arbitrator." The agreement recites that the parties desired "to continue to act jointly in all matters relating to their stock ownership or interest in" the corporation. The parties agreed to consult and confer with each other in exercising their voting rights and to act jointly—that is, concertedly; unitedly; towards unified courses of action—in accordance with such agreement as they might reach. Thus, so long as the parties agree for whom or for what their shares shall be voted, the agreement provides no function for the arbitrator. His role is limited to situations where the parties fail to agree upon a course of action. In such cases, the agreement directs that "the question in disagreement shall be submitted for arbitration" to Mr. Loos "as arbitrator and his decision thereon shall be binding upon the parties." These provisions are

144

designed to operate in aid of what appears to be a primary purpose of the parties, "to act jointly" in exercising their voting rights, by providing a means for fixing a course of action whenever they themselves might reach a stalemate.

The agreement does not describe the undertaking of each party with respect to a decision of the arbitrator other than to provide that it "shall be binding upon the parties." It seems to us that this language, considered with relation to its context and the situations to which it is applicable, means that each party promised the other to exercise her own voting rights in accordance with the arbitrator's decision.

Having examined what the parties sought to provide by the agreement, we come now to defendants' contention that the voting provisions are illegal and revocable. They say that the courts of this state have definitely established the doctrine "that there can be no agreement, or any device whatsoever, by which the voting power of stock of a Delaware corporation may be irrevocably separated from the ownership of the stock, except by an agreement which complies with Section 18" of the Corporation Law, and except by a proxy coupled with an interest.

The statute reads, in part, as follows:

> Sec. 18. Fiduciary Stockholders; Voting Power of; Voting Trusts: Persons holding stock in a fiduciary capacity shall be entitled to vote the shares so held, and persons whose stock is pledged shall be entitled to vote, unless in the transfer by the pledgor on the books of the corporation he shall have expressly empowered the pledgee to vote thereon, in which case only the pledgee, or his proxy may represent said stock and vote thereon.
>
> One or more stockholders may by agreement in writing deposit capital stock of an original issue with or transfer capital stock to any person or persons, or corporation or corporations authorized to act as trustee, for the purpose of vesting in said person or persons, corporation or corporations, who may be designated Voting Trustee or Voting Trustees, the right to vote thereon for any period of time determined by such agreement, not exceeding ten years, upon the terms and conditions stated in such agreement. Such agreement may contain any other lawful provisions not inconsistent with said purpose. Said Voting Trustees may vote upon the stock so issued or transferred during the period in such agreement specified; stock standing in the names of such Voting Trustees may be voted either in person or by proxy, and in voting said stock, such Voting Trustees shall incur no responsibility as stockholder, trustee or otherwise, except for their own individual malfeasance.

In our view, neither the cases nor the statute sustain the rule for which the defendants contend. Their sweeping formulation would impugn well-recognized means by which a shareholder may effectively confer his voting rights upon others while retaining various other rights. For example, defendants' rule would apparently not permit holders of voting stock to confer upon stockholders of another class, by the device of an amendment of the certificate of incorporation, the exclusive right to vote during periods when dividends are not paid on stock of the latter class. The broad prohibitory meaning which defendants find in Section 18 seems inconsistent with their concession that proxies coupled with an interest may be irrevocable, for the statute contains nothing about such proxies. The statute authorizes, among other things, the deposit or transfer of stock in trust for a specified purpose, namely, "vesting" in the transferee "the right to vote thereon" for a limited period; and prescribes numerous requirements in this connection. Accordingly, it seems reasonable to infer that to establish the relationship and accomplish the purpose which the statute authorizes, its requirements must be complied with. But the statute does not purport to deal with agreements whereby shareholders attempt to bind each other as to how they shall vote their shares. Various forms of such pooling agreements, as they are sometimes called, have been held valid and have been distinguished from voting trusts.

We think the particular agreement before us does not violate Section 18 or constitute an attempted evasion of its requirements, and is not illegal for any other reason. Generally speaking, a shareholder may exercise wide liberality of judgment in the matter of voting, and it is not objectionable that his motives may be for personal profit, or determined by whims or caprice, so long as he violates no duty owed his fellow shareholders. The ownership of voting stock imposes no legal duty to vote at all. A group of shareholders may, without impropriety, vote their respective shares so as to obtain advantages of concerted action. They may lawfully contract with each other to vote in the future in such way as they, or a majority of their group, from time to time determine. Reasonable provisions for cases of failure of the group to reach a determination because of an even division in their ranks seem unobjectionable. The provision here for submission to the arbitrator is plainly designed as a deadlock-breaking measure, and the arbitrator's decision cannot be enforced unless at least one of the parties (entitled to cast one-half of their combined votes) is willing that it be enforced. We find the provision reasonable. It does not appear that the agreement enables the parties to take any unlawful advantage of the outside shareholder, or of any other person. It offends no rule of law or public policy of this state of which we are aware.

Legal consideration for the promises of each party is supplied by the mutual promises of the other party. The undertaking to vote in accordance with the arbitrator's decision is a valid contract. The good faith of the arbitrator's action has not been challenged and, indeed, the record indicates that no such challenge could be supported. Accordingly, the failure of Mrs. Haley to exercise her voting rights in accordance with his decision was a breach of her contract. It is no extenuation of the breach that her votes were cast for two of the three candidates directed by the arbitrator. His directions to her were part of a single plan or course of action for the voting of the shares of both parties to the agreement, calculated to utilize an advantage of joint action by them which would bring about the election of an additional director. The actual voting of Mrs. Haley's shares frustrates that plan to such an extent that it should not be treated as a partial performance of her contract.

Throughout their argument, defendants make much of the fact that all votes cast at the meeting were by the registered shareholders. The Court of Chancery may, in a review of an election, reject votes of a registered shareholder where his voting of them is found to be in violation of rights of another person. It seems to us that upon the application of Mrs. Ringling, the injured party, the votes representing Mrs. Haley's shares should not be counted. Since no infirmity in Mr. North's voting has been demonstrated, his right to recognition of what he did at the meeting should be considered in granting any relief to Mrs. Ringling; for her rights arose under a contract to which Mr. North was not a party. With this in mind, we have concluded that the election should not be declared invalid, but that effect should be given to a rejection of the votes representing Mrs. Haley's shares. No other relief seems appropriate in this proceeding. Mr. North's vote against the motion for adjournment was sufficient to defeat it. With respect to the election of directors, the return of the inspectors should be corrected to show a rejection of Mrs. Haley's votes, and to declare the election of the six persons for whom Mr. North and Mrs. Ringling voted.

This leaves one vacancy in the directorate. The question of what to do about such a vacancy was not considered by the court below and has not been argued here. For this reason, and because an election of directors at the 1947 annual meeting (which presumably will be held in the near future) may make a determination of the question unimportant, we shall not decide it on this appeal. If a decision of the point appears important to the parties, any of them may apply to raise it in the Court of Chancery, after the mandate of this court is received there.

An order should be entered directing a modification of the order of the Court of Chancery in accordance with this opinion.

STROH V. BLACKHAWK HOLDING CORPORATION

SUPREME COURT OF ILLINOIS (DAVIS, J.)
272 N.E.2D 1 (1971)

The issue before this court is the validity of the 500,000 shares of Class B stock, which by the articles of incorporation of Blackhawk were limited in their rights by the provision "none of the shares of Class B stock shall be entitled to dividends either upon voluntary or involuntary liquidation or otherwise." It is the plaintiffs' contention that because of the foregoing limitation—depriving the Class B shares of the "economic" incidents of shares of stock, or of the proportionate interest in the corporate assets—the Class B shares do not in fact constitute shares of stock.

Blackhawk Holding Corporation was organized under the Illinois Business Corporation Act in November of 1963. Its articles of incorporation authorized the issuance of 3,000,000 shares of Class A stock with a par value of $1, and 500,000 shares of Class B stock without par value. In addition to the limitation placed on the Class B stock, set forth above, the articles also provided that neither the Class A nor Class B shares would carry preemptive rights. Pursuant to the preorganization subscription agreements, 21 promoters purchased 87,868 shares of the Class A stock at the price of $3.40 per share ($298,751.20), and the 500,000 shares of Class B stock at 1/4¢ per share ($1,250). Thereafter, the corporation registered the Class A shares with the securities division of the office of the Secretary of State of Illinois for the sale of 500,000 shares thereof to the general public at a price of $4 per share. The prospectus for the registration described the Class A and Class B stock, and quoted from the articles of incorporation relative to their respective rights and preferences. The prospectus explained that every share of each class of stock would be entitled to one vote on all general matters submitted to a vote of the shareholders and, that in the election of directors, the votes could be cumulated. The prospectus also explained that no Class B stock was being offered for sale in that all of such stock has been previously issued. Under the heading "Organization and Development," the prospectus also stated: "Subscriptions for a total of $300,001.20 were sold to twenty-one persons, representing 87,868 class A shares, the class now being offered, at the price of $3.40 per share ($298,751.20) and 500,000 class B shares, at a price of one-fourth of a cent per share ($1,250.00); thus said subscribers by virtue of a $300,001.20 investment, have control of the corporation having an initial capitalization of $2,000,000.00 after this offering."

In August of 1964, there was a 2 for 1 split of the Class A stock, increasing the shares outstanding from 587,863 to 1,175.736 shares. The corporation sold additional Class A stock to the public in 1965 for $4 a share. As of June 1968, there were 1,237,681 Class A shares and 500,000 Class B shares outstanding, the latter representing 28.78% of the total voting shares of the company.

A corporation is a creature of statute. It is a legal entity which owes its existence to the fiat of law. Its being and powers are from the sovereign State as its will is expressed through legislative enactment. The articles of incorporation of an Illinois corporation constitute a contract, threefold in nature. It is a contract between the corporation and the State and it creates powers and limitations, rights and duties as between the corporation and its shareholders, as well as between the shareholders themselves. The powers and limitations of a corporation are found in its articles of incorporation, the provisions of its stock certificates, its by-laws, and in the constitutional and statutory provisions in force when the articles of incorporation were adopted. The articles of incorporation of Blackhawk purport to create a Class B stock that possesses no rights in the assets or in the earnings of the corporation. Whether this can be done, and whether such shares have the requisite attributes of a valid share of stock, must be determined in accordance with the constitution of the State, the provision of the Business Corporation Act, and the common law of the State.

Under the Illinois constitution of 1870, a stockholder in an Illinois corporation is guaranteed the right to vote based upon the number of shares owned by him. Section 14 of the Business Corporation Act provides that shares of stock in an Illinois corporation may be divided into classes,

> "with such designations, preferences, qualifications, limitations, restrictions and such special or relative rights as shall be stated in the articles of incorporation. The articles of incorporation shall not limit or deny the voting power of the shares of any class.
>
> Without limiting the authority herein contained, a corporation when so provided in its articles of incorporation, may issue shares of preferred or special classes:
>
> (c) Having preference over any other class or classes of shares as to the payment of dividends.
>
> (d) Having preference as to the assets of the corporation over any other class or classes of shares upon the voluntary or involuntary liquidation of the corporation."

Section 2.6 of the Act, in defining "shares" states, "'Shares' means the units into which the proprietary interests in a corporation are divided." This was formerly section 2(f) of the Act which defined shares as "units into which shareholders' rights to participate in the control of a corporation, in its surplus or profits, or in the distribution of its assets, are divided."

To the plaintiffs, "proprietary," as used in the definition of shares, means a property right, and shares must then represent some economic interest, or interest in the property or assets of the corporation. However, the word "proprietary" does not necessarily denote economic or asset rights, although it has been defined as synonymous with ownership or to denote legal title. In *Colten*, the court defined "proprietary" as meaning ownership, exclusive title or dominion, and implying possession and physical control of a thing.

We agree with the defendants' construction. We interpret this statutory definition to mean that the proprietary rights conferred by the ownership of stock may consist of one or more of the rights to participate "in the control of the corporation, in its surplus or profits, or in the distribution of its assets." The use of the disjunctive conjunction "or," indicates that one or more of the three named rights may inure to a stockholder by virtue of his stock ownership.

We must here decide the extent to which economic attributes of shares of stock may be eliminated. This must be determined from the intent of the legislature which, in no small part, can be gathered from the language and words it chose to express that intent. The statutory definition of "shares" is of particular importance in that it governs the meaning of the word as used throughout the Business Corporation Act and controls in its construction. The legislature has the power to make any reasonable definition of the terms in a statute and such definition for the purposes of the Act, will be sustained.

Section 14 of the Act clearly expresses the intent of the legislature to be that parties to a corporate entity may create whatever restrictions and limitations they may want with regard to their corporate stock by expressing such restrictions and limitations in the articles of incorporation. These rights and powers granted by the legislature to the corporation to make the terms of its contract with its shareholders are limited only by the proviso that the articles may not limit or deny the voting power of any share. This section of the Act expressly confers the right to prefer a class of shares over another with regard to dividends and assets. Section 2.6 defines shares as "The units into which the proprietary interests in a corporation are divided."

In seeking the intent of the legislature, a statute should be construed as a whole and its separate parts considered together. Our present constitution requires only that a shareholder not be deprived of his voice in management. It does not require that a shareholder, in addition to the management aspect of ownership, must also have an economic interest.

Thus, section 14, like the constitution, limits the power of a corporation only as to the voting aspect of ownership.

When the relevant sections of the Act are read together with the constitution, it seems apparent that it was the intent of the legislature that the proprietary interests represented by the shares of stock consist of management or control rights, rights to earnings, and rights to assets. There are other rights which are incidental to these. Under our laws, the rights to earnings and the rights to assets—the "economic" rights—may be removed and eliminated from the other attributes of a share of stock. Only the management incident of ownership may not be removed.

The constitution requires only that the right to vote be proportionate to the number of shares owned, not to the investment made in a corporation. It has long been the common practice in Illinois to classify shares of stock such that one may invest less than another in a corporation, and yet have control. One of two shareholders may purchase ten shares of a class of stock issued at its par value of $1,000 per share, and his business partner may purchase 100 shares of another class of the corporate stock issued at its par value of $10 per share. The parties, for varying reasons, may be very willing that the party investing the $1,000 have control of the management of the corporation, as opposed to the party having the investment of $10,000.

If there is overreaching of fraud in establishing the different relative voting rights of shares, that is another matter and there is a remedy available. We are aware that the classification of shares, so as to enable one class to obtain greater voting rights with the same or lesser investment in a corporation than another class, may carry with it the possibility for wrongdoing. However, it also often serves a valid purpose and there is nothing inherently wrong in such a scheme.

We find nothing in the declared public policy of this State to condemn stock of this nature.

Affirmed and remanded, with directions.

SCHAEFER, J. (dissenting).
"Under our laws," say the majority, "the rights to earnings and the rights to assets—the 'economic' rights—may be removed and eliminated from the other attributes of a share of stock. Only the management incident of ownership may not be removed." This seems to me to be saying that the ownership incidents of ownership may be eliminated. What remains, then, is a disembodied right to manage the assets of a corporation, divorced from any financial interest in those assets except such as may accrue from the power to manage them. In my opinion, what is left after the economic rights are "removed and eliminated" is not a share of corporate stock under the law of Illinois.

BUSINESS ROUNDTABLE V. SECURITIES AND EXCHANGE COMMISSION

UNITED STATES COURT OF APPEALS, DC CIRCUIT (GINSBURG, J.) 647 F.3D. 1144 (2011)

The Business Roundtable and the Chamber of Commerce of the United States, each of which has corporate members that issue publicly traded securities, petition for review of Exchange Act Rule 14a-11. The rule requires public companies to provide shareholders with information about, and their ability to vote for, shareholder-nominated candidates for the board of directors. The petitioners argue the Securities and Exchange Commission promulgated the rule in violation of the Administrative Procedure Act because, among other reasons, the Commission failed adequately to consider the rule's effect upon efficiency, competition, and capital formation, as required. For these reasons and more, we grant the petition for review and vacate the rule.

The proxy process is the principal means by which shareholders of a publicly traded corporation elect the company's board of directors. Typically, incumbent directors nominate a candidate for each vacancy prior to the election, which is held at the company's annual meeting. Before the meeting the company puts information about each nominee in the set of "proxy materials" – usually comprising a proxy voting card and a proxy statement – it distributes to all shareholders.

The proxy statement concerns voting procedures and background information about the board's nominee(s); the proxy card enables shareholders to vote for or against the nominee(s) without attending the meeting. A shareholder who wishes to nominate a different candidate may separately file his own proxy statement and solicit votes from shareholders, thereby initiating a "proxy contest."

Rule 14a-11 provides shareholders an alternative path for nominating and electing directors. Concerned the current process impedes the expression of shareholders' right under state corporation laws to nominate and elect directors, the Commission proposed the rule with the goal of ensuring "the proxy process functions, as nearly as possible, as a replacement for an actual in-person meeting of shareholders." The rule requires a company subject to the Exchange Act proxy rules, including an investment company (such as a mutual fund) registered under the Investment Company Act of 1940, to include in its proxy materials "the name of a person or persons nominated by a qualifying shareholder or group of shareholders for election to the board of directors."

To use Rule 14a-11, a shareholder or group of shareholders must have continuously held "at least 3% of the voting power of the company's securities entitled to be voted" for at least three years prior to the date the nominating shareholder or group submits notice of its intent to use the rule, and must continue to own those securities through the date of the annual meeting. The nominating shareholder or group must submit the notice, which may include a statement of up to 500 words in support of each of its nominees, to the Commission and to the company. A company that receives notice from an eligible shareholder or group must include the proffered information about the shareholder(s) and his nominee(s) in its proxy statement and include the nominee(s) on the proxy voting card.

The Commission did place certain limitations upon the application of Rule 14a-11. The rule does not apply if applicable state law or a company's governing documents "prohibit shareholders from nominating a candidate for election as a director." Nor may a shareholder use Rule 14a-11 if he is holding the company's securities with the intent of effecting a change of control of the company. The company is not required to include in its proxy materials more than one shareholder nominee or the number of nominees, if more than one, equal to 25 percent of the number of directors on the board.

The Commission concluded that Rule 14a-11 could create "potential benefits of improved board and company performance and shareholder value" sufficient to "justify its potential costs." The agency rejected proposals to let each company's board or a majority of its shareholders decide whether to incorporate Rule 14a-11 in its bylaws, saying that "exclusive reliance on private ordering under State law would not be as effective and efficient" in facilitating shareholders' right to nominate and elect directors.

Under the APA, we will set aside agency action that is "arbitrary, capricious, an abuse of discretion, or otherwise not in accordance with law." We must assure ourselves the agency has "examined the relevant data and articulated a satisfactory explanation for its action including a rational connection between the facts found and the choices made." The petitioners argue the Commission acted arbitrarily and capriciously here because it neglected its statutory responsibility to determine the likely economic consequences of Rule 14a-11 and to connect those consequences to efficiency, competition, and capital formation.

We agree with the petitioners and hold the Commission acted arbitrarily and capriciously for having failed once again – as it did most recently in American Equity Investment Life Insurance Company and before that in Chamber of Commerce – adequately to assess the economic effects of a new rule.

The Commission predicted Rule 14a-11 would lead to "direct cost savings" for shareholders in part due to "reduced printing and postage costs" and reduced expenditures for advertising compared to those of a "traditional" proxy contest. The Commission also identified some intangible, or at least less readily quantifiable, benefits, principally that the rule "will mitigate collective action and free-rider concerns," which can discourage a shareholder from exercising his right to nominate a director in a traditional proxy contest, and "has the potential of creating the benefit of improved board performance and enhanced shareholder value." The Commission anticipated the rule would also impose costs upon companies and shareholders related to "the preparation of required disclosure, printing and mailing, and to additional solicitations" and could have "adverse effects on company and board performance," for example, by distracting management. The Commission nonetheless concluded the rule would promote the "efficiency of the economy on the whole," and the benefits of the rule would "justify the costs" of the rule.

The petitioners contend the Commission neglected both to quantify the costs companies would incur opposing shareholder nominees and to substantiate the rule's predicted benefits. They also argue the Commission failed to consider the consequences of union and state pension funds using the rule and failed properly to evaluate the frequency with which shareholders would initiate election contests.

For the foregoing reasons, we hold the Commission was arbitrary and capricious in promulgating Rule 14a-11. Accordingly, we have no occasion to address the petitioners' First Amendment challenge to the rule. The petition is granted and the rule is hereby

Vacated.

PART D CORPORATE DISSOLUTION AND TERMINATION

IN RE RADOM & NEIDORFF, INC.

COURT OF APPEALS OF NEW YORK (DESMOND, J.)
119 N.E.2D 563 (1954)

Radom & Neidorff, Inc., the proposed dissolution of which is before us here, is a domestic corporation which has for many years, conducted, with great success, the business of lithographing or printing musical compositions. For some thirty years prior to February 18, 1950, Henry Neidorff, now deceased, husband of respondent Anna Neidorff, and David Radom, brother-in-law of Neidorff and brother of Mrs. Neidorff, were the sole stockholders, each holding eighty shares. Henry Neidorff's will made his wife his executrix and bequeathed her the stock, so that, ever since his death, petitioner-appellant David Radom and Anna Neidorff, brother and sister, have been the sole and equal stockholders. Although brother and sister, they were unfriendly before Neidorff's death and their estrangement continues. On July 17, 1950, five months after Neidorff's death, Radom brought this proceeding, praying that the corporation be dissolved under section 103 of the General Corporation Law.

That statute, like others in article 9 of the General Corporation Law, describes the situations in which dissolution may be petitioned for, but, as we shall show later, it does not mandate the granting of the relief in every such case.

The petition here stated to the court that the corporation is solvent and its operations successful, but that, since Henry Neidorff's death, his widow (respondent here) has refused to co-operate with petitioner as president, and that she refuses to sign his salary checks, leaving him without salary, although he has the sole burden of running the business. It was alleged, too, that, because of 'unresolved disagreements' between petitioner and respondent, election of any directors, at a stockholders' meeting held for that purpose in June, 1950, had proved impossible. A schedule attached to the petition showed corporate assets consisting of machinery and supplies worth about $9,500, cash about $82,000, and no indebtedness except about $17,000 owed to petitioner (plus his salary claim). Mrs. Neidorff's answering papers alleged that, while her husband was alive, the two owners had each drawn about $25,000 per year from the corporation, that, shortly after her husband's death, petitioner had asked her to allow him alone to sign all checks, which request she refused, that he had then offered her $75,000 for her stock, and, on her rejection thereof, had threatened to have the corporation dissolved and to buy it in at a low price or, if she should be the purchaser, that he would start a competing business. She further alleged that she has not, since her husband's death, interfered with Radom's conduct of the business and has signed all corporate checks sent her by him except checks for his own salary which, she says, she declined to sign because of a stockholder's derivative suit brought by her against Radom, and still pending, charging him with enriching himself at this corporation's expense.

Because of other litigation now concluded, to which Mrs. Neidorff was not a party, but which had to do with a contest as to the ownership of the Radom stock, respondent's answering papers in this dissolution proceeding were not filed until three years after the petition was entered. From the answering papers it appears, without dispute, that for those three years, the corporation's profits before taxes had totaled about $242,000, or an annual average of about $71,000, on a gross annual business of about $250,000, and that the corporation had, in 1953, about $300,000 on deposit in banks. There are many other accusations and counteraccusations in these wordy papers, but the only material facts are undisputed: first, that these two equal stockholders dislike and distrust each other; second, that, despite the feuding and backbiting, there is no stalemate or impasse as to corporate policies; third, that the corporation is not sick but flourishing; fourth, that dissolution is not necessary for the corporation or for either stockholders; and, fifth, that petitioner, though he is in an uncomfortable and disagreeable situation for which he may or may not be at fault, has no grievance cognizable by a court except as to the nonpayment of his salary, hardly a ground for dissolving the corporation.

Special Term held that these papers showed a basic and irreconcilable conflict between the two stockholders requiring dissolution, for the protection of both of them, if the petition's allegations should be proven. An order for a reference was, accordingly, made, but respondent appealed therefrom, and no hearings were held by the Referee. The Appellate Division reversed the order and dismissed the petition, pointing out, among other things, that not only have the corporation's activities not been paralyzed but that its profits have increased and its assets trebled during the pendency of this proceeding, that the failure of petitioner to receive his salary did not frustrate the corporate business and was remediable by means other than dissolution. The dismissal of the proceeding was "without prejudice, however, to the bringing of another proceeding should deadlock in fact arise in the selection of a board of directors, at a meeting of stockholders to be duly called, or if other deadlock should occur threatening impairment or in fact impairing the economic operations of the corporation." Petitioner then appealed to this court.

It is worthy of passing mention, at least, that respondent has, in her papers, formally offered, and repeated the offer on the argument of the appeal before us, "to have the third director named by the American Arbitration Association, any Bar Association or any recognized and respected public body."

Clearly, the dismissal of this petition was within the discretion of the Appellate Division. There is no absolute right to dissolution under such circumstances. Even when majority stockholders file a petition because of internal corporate conflicts, the order is granted only when the competing interests "are so discordant as to prevent efficient management" and the "object of its corporate existence cannot be attained." The prime inquiry is, always, as to necessity for dissolution, that is, whether judicially imposed death "will be beneficial to the stockholders or

155

members and not injurious to the public." Taking everything in the petition as true, this was not such a case, and so there was no need for a reference, or for the taking of proof, under sections 106 and 113 of the General Corporation Law.

The order should be affirmed, with costs.

FULD, J. (dissenting).
Section 103 of the General Corporation Law, insofar as here relevant, permits a petition for dissolution of a corporation by the holders of one half of the shares of stock entitled to vote for directors "if the votes of its stockholders are so divided that they cannot elect a board of directors". That is the precise situation in the case before us, for the petition explicitly recites that petitioner Radom and respondent Neidorff "are hopelessly deadlocked with respect to the management and operation of the corporation" and that serious disputes have developed between them with the result that "the votes of the two stockholders are so divided that they cannot elect a Board of Directors."

For upwards of thirty years, petitioner Radom and Henry Neidorff, respondent's husband, shared equally in the ownership and management of Radom & Neidorff, Inc. Through all that time, their relationship was harmonious as well as profitable. Neidorff died in 1950, at which time respondent, through inheritance, acquired her present 50% stock interest in the business. Since then, all has been discord and conflict. The parties, brother and sister, are at complete loggerheads; they have been unable to elect a board of directors; dividends have neither been declared nor distributed, although the corporation has earned profits; debts of the corporation have gone unpaid, although the corporation is solvent; petitioner, who since Neidorff's death has been the sole manager of the business, has not received a penny of his salary amounting to $25,000 a year because respondent has refused to sign any corporate check to his order. More, petitioner's business judgment and integrity, never before questioned, have been directly attacked in the stockholder's derivative suit, instituted by respondent, charging that he has falsified the corporation's records, converted its assets and otherwise enriched himself at its expense. Negotiations looking to the purchase by one stockholder of the other's interest were begun in an effort to end the impasse but they, too, have failed.

In very truth, as petitioner states in his papers, "a corporation of this type, with only two stockholders in it cannot continue to operate with incessant litigation and feuding between the two stockholders, and with differences as fundamental and wholly irreconcilable as are those of Mrs. Neidorff and myself. Settlement of these differences cannot be effected, while continuance on the present basis is impossible, so that there is no alternative to judicial dissolution." Indeed, petitioner avers, in view of the unceasing discord and the fact that he has had to work without salary and advance his own money to the corporation, he does not, whether or not dissolution be granted, "propose to continue to labor in and operate this business."

It is, then, undisputed and indisputable that the stockholders are not able to elect a board of directors. In addition, it is manifest, on the facts alleged, that the Supreme Court could find that the stockholders are hopelessly deadlocked vis-à-vis the management of the corporation; that the corporation cannot long continue to function effectively or profitably under such conditions; that petitioner's resignation as president and manager which he contemplates will be highly detrimental to the interests of both corporation and stockholders and cannot help but result in substantial loss; and that petitioner is not responsible for the deadlock that exists.

Respondent, however, suggests that, in view of the fact that petitioner is managing the business profitably, he should continue to do so, defend against the stockholder's suit which she brought attacking his honor and integrity and himself start an action for the compensation denied him for more than three years. But, it seems self-evident, more and further litigation would only aggravate, not cure, the underlying deadlock of which petitioner complains. And, if he were to bring the suggested suit for salary due him, the question arises, whom should he sue, and who is to defend?[5] The mere proposal that petitioner embark on a series of actions against the corporation, of which he is president and half owner, indicates the extent of the present impasse, as well as the futility of perpetuating it.

Although respondent relies on the fact that the corporation is now solvent and operating at a profit, it is manifest that, if petitioner carries out his plan to resign as president and quits the business, there may be irreparable loss, not alone to him and respondent, as the owners of the corporation, but also to the corporation's creditors. Quite apart from that, however, the sole issue under section 103 is whether there is a deadlock as to the management of the corporation, not whether business is being conducted at a profit or loss. Whether the petition should or should not be entertained surely cannot be made to turn on proof that the corporation is on the verge of ruin or insolvency.

Insolvency may be a predicate for dissolution, but not under section 103. By virtue of other provisions of Article 9 of the General Corporation Law sections 101 and 102 directors and stockholders may seek dissolution, when the corporation is insolvent, in order to prevent further loss to the owners and creditors. Section 103, however which bears the title, "Petitions in case of deadlock" was designed to serve a far different purpose. As amended in 1944, upon the recommendation of the Law Revision Commission, that section provides for dissolution "if the votes of its stockholders are so divided that they cannot elect a board of directors." Nothing in the statute itself or in its legislative history suggests that a "Petition in case of deadlock" must wait until the corporation's profits have dried up and financial reverses set in. Had the commission or the legislature intended to incorporate such a qualification into section 103, it could readily have done so. The only test envisaged by the commission, however, was that which the legislature enacted, and a court may not import any other.

The order of the Appellate Division should be reversed and that at Special Term affirmed.

---

5   In this connection, it is, perhaps, of some moment that, according to petitioner, he is the sole officer and director of the corporation.

PART E CORPORATION ACCOUNTING AND FINANCE

BEGINNERS' GUIDE TO FINANCIAL STATEMENTS

U.S. SECURITIES AND EXCHANGE COMMISSION, 2015

There are four main financial statements. They are: (1) balance sheets; (2) income statements; (3) cash flow statements; and (4) statements of shareholders' equity. Balance sheets show what a company owns and what it owes at a fixed point in time. Income statements show how much money a company made and spent over a period of time. Cash flow statements show the exchange of money between a company and the outside world also over a period of time. The fourth financial statement, called a "statement of shareholders' equity," shows changes in the interests of the company's shareholders over time.

BALANCE SHEETS

A balance sheet provides detailed information about a company's assets, liabilities and shareholders' equity.

Assets are things that a company owns that have value. This typically means they can either be sold or used by the company to make products or provide services that can be sold. Assets include physical property, such as plants, trucks, equipment and inventory. It also includes things that can't be touched but nevertheless exist and have value, such as trademarks and patents. And cash itself is an asset. So are investments a company makes.

Liabilities are amounts of money that a company owes to others. This can include all kinds of obligations, like money borrowed from a bank to launch a new product, rent for use of a building, money owed to suppliers for materials, payroll a company owes to its employees, environmental cleanup costs, or taxes owed to the government. Liabilities also include obligations to provide goods or services to customers in the future.

Shareholders' equity is sometimes called capital or net worth. It's the money that would be left if a company sold all of its assets and paid off all of its liabilities. This leftover money belongs to the shareholders, or the owners, of the company.

The following formula summarizes what a balance sheet shows:

$$\text{ASSETS} = \text{LIABILITIES} + \text{SHAREHOLDERS' EQUITY}$$

A company's assets have to equal, or "balance," the sum of its liabilities and shareholders' equity.

A company's balance sheet is set up like the basic accounting equation shown above. On the left side of the balance sheet, companies list their assets. On the right side, they list their liabilities and shareholders' equity. Sometimes balance sheets show assets at the top, followed by liabilities, with shareholders' equity at the bottom.

Assets are generally listed based on how quickly they will be converted into cash. Current assets are things a company expects to convert to cash within one year. A good example is inventory. Most companies expect to sell their inventory for cash within one year. Noncurrent assets are things a company does not expect to convert to cash within one year or that would take longer than one year to sell. Noncurrent assets include fixed assets. Fixed assets are those assets used to operate the business but that are not available for sale, such as trucks, office furniture and other property.

Liabilities are generally listed based on their due dates. Liabilities are said to be either current or long-term. Current liabilities are obligations a company expects to pay off within the year. Long-term liabilities are obligations due more than one year away.

Shareholders' equity is the amount owners invested in the company's stock plus or minus the company's earnings or losses since inception. Sometimes companies distribute earnings, instead of retaining them. These distributions are called dividends.

A balance sheet shows a snapshot of a company's assets, liabilities and shareholders' equity at the end of the reporting period. It does not show the flows into and out of the accounts during the period.

INCOME STATEMENTS

An income statement is a report that shows how much revenue a company earned over a specific time period (usually for a year or some portion of a year). An income statement also shows the costs and expenses associated with earning that revenue. The literal "bottom line" of the statement usually shows the company's net earnings or losses. This tells you how much the company earned or lost over the period.

Income statements also report earnings per share (or "EPS"). This calculation tells you how much money shareholders would receive if the company decided to distribute all of the net earnings for the period. (Companies almost never distribute all of their earnings. Usually they reinvest them in the business.)

To understand how income statements are set up, think of them as a set of stairs. You start at the top with the total amount of sales made during the accounting period. Then you go down, one step at a time. At each step, you make a deduction for certain costs or other operating expenses associated with earning the revenue. At the bottom of the stairs, after deducting all of the expenses, you learn how much the company actually earned or lost during the accounting period. People often call this "the bottom line."

At the top of the income statement is the total amount of money brought in from sales of products or services. This top line is often referred to as gross revenues or sales. It's called "gross" because expenses have not been deducted from it yet. So the number is "gross" or unrefined.

The next line is money the company doesn't expect to collect on certain sales. This could be due, for example, to sales discounts or merchandise returns.

When you subtract the returns and allowances from the gross revenues, you arrive at the company's net revenues. It's called "net" because, if you can imagine a net, these revenues are left in the net after the deductions for returns and allowances have come out.

Moving down the stairs from the net revenue line, there are several lines that represent various kinds of operating expenses. Although these lines can be reported in various orders, the next line after net revenues typically shows the costs of the sales. This number tells you the amount of money the company spent to produce the goods or services it sold during the accounting period.

The next line subtracts the costs of sales from the net revenues to arrive at a subtotal called "gross profit" or sometimes "gross margin." It's considered "gross" because there are certain expenses that haven't been deducted from it yet.

The next section deals with operating expenses. These are expenses that go toward supporting a company's operations for a given period—for example, salaries of administrative personnel and costs of researching new products. Marketing expenses are another example. Operating expenses are different from "costs of sales," which were deducted above, because operating expenses cannot be linked directly to the production of the products or services being sold.

Depreciation is also deducted from gross profit. Depreciation takes into account the wear and tear on some assets, such as machinery, tools and furniture, which are used over the long term. Companies spread the cost of these assets over the periods they are used. This process of spreading these costs is called depreciation or amortization. The "charge" for using these assets during the period is a fraction of the original cost of the assets.

After all operating expenses are deducted from gross profit, you arrive at operating profit before interest and income tax expenses. This is often called "income from operations."

Next companies must account for interest income and interest expense. Interest income is the money companies make from keeping their cash in interest-bearing savings accounts, money market funds and the like. On the other hand, interest expense is the money companies paid in interest for money they borrow. Some income statements show interest income and interest expense separately. Some income statements combine the two numbers. The interest income and expense are then added or subtracted from the operating profits to arrive at operating profit before income tax.

Finally, income tax is deducted and you arrive at the bottom line: net profit or net losses. (Net profit is also called net income or net earnings.) This tells you how much the company actually earned or lost during the accounting period. Did the company make a profit or did it lose money?

CASH FLOW STATEMENTS

Cash flow statements report a company's inflows and outflows of cash. This is important because a company needs to have enough cash on hand to pay its expenses and purchase assets. While an income statement can tell you whether a company made a profit, a cash flow statement can tell you whether the company generated cash.

A cash flow statement shows changes over time rather than absolute dollar amounts at a point in time. It uses and reorders the information from a company's balance sheet and income statement.

The bottom line of the cash flow statement shows the net increase or decrease in cash for the period. Generally, cash flow statements are divided into three main parts. Each part reviews the cash flow from one of three types of activities: (1) operating activities; (2) investing activities; and (3) financing activities.

Operating Activities

The first part of a cash flow statement analyzes a company's cash flow from net income or losses. For most companies, this section of the cash flow statement reconciles the net income (as shown on the income statement) to the actual cash the company received from or used in its operating activities. To do this, it adjusts net income for any non-cash items (such as adding back depreciation expenses) and adjusts for any cash that was used or provided by other operating assets and liabilities.

Investing Activities

The second part of a cash flow statement shows the cash flow from all investing activities, which generally include purchases or sales of long-term assets, such as property, plant and equipment, as well as investment securities. If a company buys a piece of machinery, the cash flow statement would reflect this activity as a cash outflow from investing activities because it used cash. If the company decided to sell off some investments from an investment portfolio, the proceeds from the sales would show up as a cash inflow from investing activities because it provided cash.

Financing Activities

The third part of a cash flow statement shows the cash flow from all financing activities. Typical sources of cash flow include cash raised by selling stocks and bonds or borrowing from banks. Likewise, paying back a bank loan would show up as a use of cash flow.

READ THE FOOTNOTES

A horse called "Read The Footnotes" ran in the 2004 Kentucky Derby. He finished seventh, but if he had won, it would have been a victory for financial literacy proponents everywhere. It's so important to *read the footnotes*. The footnotes to financial statements are packed with information. Here are some of the highlights:

- <u>Significant accounting policies and practices</u>—Companies are required to disclose the accounting policies that are most important to the portrayal of the company's financial condition and results. These often require management's most difficult, subjective or complex judgments.
- <u>Income taxes</u>—The footnotes provide detailed information about the company's current and deferred income taxes. The information is broken down by level—federal, state, local and/or foreign, and the main items that affect the company's effective tax rate are described-.
- <u>Pension plans and other retirement programs</u>—The footnotes discuss the company's pension plans and other retirement or post-employment benefit programs. The notes contain specific information about the assets and costs of these programs, and indicate whether and by how much the plans are over- or under-funded.
- <u>Stock options</u>—The notes also contain information about stock options granted to officers and employees, including the method of accounting for stock-based compensation and the effect of the method on reported results.

READ THE MD&A

You can find a narrative explanation of a company's financial performance in a section of the quarterly or annual report entitled, "Management's Discussion and Analysis of Financial Condition and Results of Operations." MD&A is *management's* opportunity to provide investors with its view of the financial performance and condition of the company. It's management's opportunity to tell investors what the financial statements show and do not show, as well as important trends and risks that have shaped the past or are reasonably likely to shape the company's future.

The SEC's rules governing MD&A require disclosure about trends, events or uncertainties known to management that would have a material impact on reported financial information. The purpose of MD&A is to provide investors with information that the company's management believes to be necessary to an understanding of its financial condition, changes in financial condition and results of operations. It is intended to help investors to see the company through the eyes of management. It is also intended to provide context for the financial statements and information about the company's earnings and cash flows.

M.G. BANCORPORATION, INC. V. LEBEAU

SUPREME COURT OF DELAWARE (HOLLAND, J.)
737 A.2D 513 (1999)

This appeal is taken by Respondents-appellants, M.G. Bancorporation, Inc., and Southwest Bancorp, Inc., Delaware corporations, from a final judgment of the Court of Chancery. The proceeding arises from a cash-out merger of the minority shareholders of MGB on November 17, 1993. MGB was merged into Southwest, which owned over 91% of the outstanding shares of MGB's common stock, pursuant to 8 Del.C. § 253. The Petitioners-appellees were the record owners of 18,151 shares of MGB common stock as of the date of the Merger. The Merger consideration was $41 per share.

The Petitioners initiated an appraisal proceeding, in accordance with 8 Del. C. § 262, to determine the fair value of MGB's common stock. Following a three-day trial, the Court of Chancery concluded that the fair value of MGB's common stock as of the Merger date was $85 per share. The Respondents were ordered to pay that sum, together with interest, compounded monthly, at the rate of 8% from November 17, 1993.

This Court affirms that portion of the judgment by the Court of Chancery that awarded the Petitioners $85 per share. That portion of the judgment that awarded compound interest to the Petitioners, however, is remanded for further consideration.

The Petitioners are shareholders who owned 18,151 shares of common stock of MGB before the Merger. The Respondents are Southwest and its subsidiary, MGB. Before the Merger, MGB was a Delaware-chartered bank holding company headquartered in Worth, Illinois. MGB had two operating Illinois-chartered bank subsidiaries, Mount Greenwood Bank and Worth Bancorp, Inc. Both banks served customers in the southwestern Chicago metropolitan area. MGB owned 100% of Mount Greenwood and 75.5% of WBC.

Before the Merger, Southwest owned 91.68% of MGB's common shares. On November 17, 1993, MGB was merged into Southwest in a "short form" merger under 8 Del. C. § 253. Because the Merger was accomplished unilaterally, neither MGB's board of directors nor its minority shareholders were legally required to, or did, vote on the transaction.

Southwest engaged Alex Sheshunoff & Co. Investment Bankers to determine the "fair market value" of MGB's minority shares for the purpose of setting the Merger price. Sheshunoff determined that the fair market value of MGB's minority shares was $41 per share as of June 30, 1993. Accordingly, MGB's minority shareholders were offered $41 per share in cash as the Merger consideration. The Petitioners rejected that offer, electing instead to pursue their statutory rights, and this appraisal proceeding was commenced.

A stockholders class action based on breach of fiduciary duty was also filed challenging the Merger. On July 5, 1995, the Court of Chancery issued a decision in that companion class action, holding that Sheshunoff had not performed its appraisal in a legally proper manner. The basis for the Court of Chancery's conclusion was that Sheshunoff had determined only the "fair market value" of MGB's minority shares, as opposed to valuing MGB in its entirety as a going concern and then determining the fair value of the minority shares as a pro rata percentage of that value.

At the December 1996 trial, the Petitioners' expert witness was David Clarke. He testified that as of the Merger date the fair value of MGB common stock was $58,514,000, or $85 per share. In arriving at that conclusion, Clarke used three distinct methodologies to value MGB's two operating bank subsidiaries: the comparative publicly-traded company approach, yielding a $76.24 to $77.50 per share value; the discounted cash flow method, yielding a $73.96 to $72.23 per share value; and, the comparative acquisitions approach, yielding an $85 per share value.

In performing his analysis, Clarke added a control premium to the values of the two subsidiaries to reflect the value of MGB's controlling interest in those subsidiaries. He then added the value of MGB's remaining assets to his valuations of the two subsidiaries. Clarke arrived at an overall fair value of $85 per share for MGB.

The Respondents relied upon the expert testimony of Robert Reilly at trial. He testified that, as of the Merger date, the fair value of MGB common stock was $41.90 per share. Reilly arrived at that conclusion by performing two separate valuations: the discounted cash flow method and a "capital market" analysis. Reilly did not add any control premium to the values of MGB's two subsidiaries, because he determined that a control premium was inappropriate in valuing a holding company such as MGB.

The Court of Chancery concluded that $85 per share was the fair value of MGB's stock on the date of the merger.

The Respondents contend that the Court of Chancery erred by rejecting certain valuation opinions of both parties' experts. The seminal case on this Court's jurisprudence in an appraisal proceeding provides guidance on the admission of expert testimony. Proof of value can be

difference in opinion of what the stock was valued @

established by any techniques or methods that are generally acceptable in the financial community and otherwise admissible in court, subject only to our interpretation of 8 Del. C. § 262(h).

The qualifications of the Respondents' expert witness, Reilly, were undisputed at trial. The parties were in sharp disagreement, however, about whether Reilly's "capital market" approach was "generally accepted" within the financial community for valuing banks and bank holding companies. Reilly's capital market analysis used a number of pricing multiples related to the market value of invested capital ("MVIC"). Reilly computed the ratios of MVIC to: earnings before interest and taxes ("EBIT"); earnings before interest, depreciation and taxes ("EBIDT"); debt free net income ("DFNI"); debt free cash flow ("DFCF"); interest incomes; and total book value of invested capital ("TBVIC").

The Petitioners' expert, Clarke, testified that Reilly's capital market approach was not generally accepted in the financial community for valuing banks and bank holding companies. According to Clarke, the financial community focuses upon the ratio of price to book value and price to earnings for purposes of valuing banks and bank holding companies. The Court of Chancery concluded that the Respondents had failed to establish that Reilly's capital market methodology is generally accepted by the financial community for purposes of valuing bank holding companies, as distinguished from other types of enterprises.

The Court of Chancery also determined that Reilly's capital market valuation approach included a built-in minority discount. The Court of Chancery noted that the valuation literature, including a treatise co-authored by Reilly himself, supported that conclusion. The Court of Chancery concluded that because Reilly's capital market method resulted in a minority valuation, even if it had concluded that Reilly's capital market approach was an otherwise acceptable method of valuing a bank holding company, the use of Reilly's capital market approach is improper in a statutory appraisal proceeding.

Delaware Rule of Evidence 702, like its federal counterpart, "establishes a standard of evidentiary reliability." Delaware Rule of Evidence 702 "requires a valid connection to the pertinent inquiry as a precondition to admissibility." When the "factual basis, data, principles, methods, or their application" in an expert's opinion are challenged, the trial judge must decide if the expert's testimony "has a reliable basis in the knowledge and experience of the relevant discipline."

The record reflects that the Court of Chancery rejected Reilly's capital market approach for two independent and alternative reasons. First, it concluded that the Respondents had failed to establish that Reilly's capital market approach is generally accepted in the financial community for valuing banks and/or bank holding companies. Second, it concluded that Reilly's capital market approach contained an inherent minority discount that made its use legally impermissible in a statutory appraisal proceeding. Both of those conclusions are fully supported by the record evidence that was before the Court of Chancery and the prior holdings of this Court construing Section 262.

Both parties' experts also gave valuation opinions using the same discounted cash flow methodology. The qualifications of each parties' expert witness were accepted by the Court of Chancery. The propriety of using a discounted cash flow analysis in a statutory appraisal action was also acknowledged. The discounted cash flow methodology has been relied upon frequently by parties and the Court of Chancery in other statutory appraisal proceedings.

Although Reilly and Clarke used the same discounted cash flow methodology, each applied different assumptions. The Court of Chancery determined, for example, that "the difference between Clarke's 12% discount rate and Reilly's 18% discount rate [was] attributable primarily to their different estimates of MGB's cost of equity capital, and their different assumptions of the company specific risks confronting MGB at the time of the merger." The Court of Chancery disagreed with certain of the other assumptions applied by both of the parties' experts. The Court of Chancery ultimately concluded that it could not rely on the DCF valuation opinion of either parties' expert.

The Respondents submit the *only* significant concern raised by the Court of Chancery with respect to Clarke's DCF analysis involved his use of a 12% discount rate, i.e., it incorporated a 1% small stock premium based on a 1996 study that may contain post-merger data. The Respondents contend that particular error could have been corrected through a mathematical adjustment, i.e., the addition of a 5.2% small stock factor based on a 1992 study (which Clarke had used in several other bank appraisals) results in a 15% discount rate. The Respondents have calculated that the substitution of the 15% discount rate for Clarke's 12% rate produces a fair value for MGB of $57 per share. The Respondents argue the Court of Chancery erred by rejecting their adjusted Clarke discounted cash flow valuation of $57 as a reliable indication of fair value.

Having accepted the qualifications of both parties' experts and the propriety of using a discounted cash flow model in this statutory appraisal proceeding, the Court of Chancery was not required to adopt any one expert's methodology or calculations *in toto*. Similarly, by recognizing the discounted cash flow model as *one* proper valuation technique, the Court of Chancery was not *required* to use that methodology to make its own independent valuation calculation by either adapting or blending the factual assumptions of the parties' experts. The ultimate selection of a valuation framework is within the Court of Chancery's discretion.

The Respondents contend that the Court of Chancery failed to discharge its statutory obligation to function as an independent appraiser. The record does not support that argument.

In discharging its statutory mandate, the Court of Chancery has the discretion to select one of the parties' valuation models as its general framework or to fashion its own. The Court of Chancery's role as an independent appraiser does not necessitate a judicial determination that is completely separate and apart from the valuations performed by the parties' expert witnesses who testify at trial. It must, however, carefully consider whether the evidence supports the valuation conclusions advanced by the parties' respective experts. Thereafter, although not required to do so, it is entirely proper for the Court of Chancery to adopt any one expert's model, methodology, and mathematical calculations, *in toto*, if that valuation is supported by credible evidence and withstands a critical judicial analysis on the record.

In this case, the Court of Chancery carefully evaluated the valuation testimony and evidence proffered by the parties' experts. It determined that Reilly's capital market approach is legally impermissible, but even if valid, was improperly applied, thereby requiring the rejection of the values Reilly derived by that method. The Court of Chancery found that both Clarke's and Reilly's DCF analyses were improperly applied, thereby requiring the rejection of the values both experts derived by that approach.

The Court of Chancery concluded that Clarke's comparative acquisition approach was a legally valid method to value MGB and that the credible record evidence supported Clarke's $85 per share determination of MGB's fair value as of the Merger date. In making its independent appraisal valuation, the Court of Chancery could have relied entirely upon Clarke's comparative acquisitions approach. Instead, it critically tested Clarke's comparative acquisition approach by using its own judicial expertise to make corrective adjustments to Sheshunoff's legally improper valuation determination and found corroboration for Clarke's result.

The determination of value in a statutory appraisal proceeding is accorded a high level of deference on appeal. In the absence of legal error, this Court reviews appraisal valuations pursuant to the abuse of discretion standard. The Court of Chancery abuses its discretion when either its factual findings do not have record support or its valuation is not the result of an orderly and logical deductive process.

In this case, the findings of fact upon which the Court of Chancery predicated its decision are supported by the record. The analysis that preceded the Court of Chancery's valuation of MGB's shares exemplifies an orderly and logical deductive process. Consequently, the portion of the Court of Chancery's judgment that concluded that $85 per share was the fair value of MGB stock on the date of the Merger is affirmed.

[handwritten margin note: Chancery didn't abuse discretion]

Appraisal actions are highly complicated matters that the Court of Chancery is uniquely qualified to adjudicate in an equitable manner. Since *Weinberger*, this Court has eschewed choosing any one method of appraisal to the exclusion of all others. Today, we reinforce the substance of this philosophy and support methods that allow the Court of Chancery to perform its statutory role as appraiser, based on a solid foundation of record evidence, independent of the positions of the parties.

Section 262(h) provides that the Court of Chancery "shall appraise the shares, determining their fair value exclusive of any element of value arising from the accomplishment or expectation of the merger or consolidation together with a *fair rate of interest*, if any, to be paid upon the amount determined to be the fair value." Section 262(h) permits an award of compound interest at the discretion of the Court of Chancery. Such an award, however, is the exception rather than the rule.

We have concluded that we must remand this matter to the Court of Chancery for an elaboration upon its decision to award compound interest, on the basis of the record established in this case.

The portion of the Court of Chancery's judgment that appraised the fair value of the Petitioners' stock at $85 per share is affirmed. The portion of the judgment that awarded compound interest is remanded for further proceedings in accordance with this opinion. Jurisdiction is retained only with regard to the issue of awarding compound interest.

DELAWARE GENERAL CORPORATION LAW

SECTION 151. CLASSES AND SERIES OF STOCK; REDEMPTION; RIGHTS

(a) Every corporation may issue 1 or more classes of stock or 1 or more series of stock within any class thereof, any or all of which classes may be of stock with par value or stock without par value and which classes or series may have such voting powers, full or limited, or no voting powers, and such designations, preferences and relative, participating, optional or other special rights, and qualifications, limitations or restrictions thereof, as shall be stated and expressed in the certificate of incorporation or of any amendment thereto, or in the resolution or resolutions providing for the issue of such stock adopted by the board of directors pursuant to authority expressly vested in it by the provisions of its certificate of incorporation. Any of the voting powers, designations, preferences, rights and qualifications, limitations or restrictions of any such class or series of stock may be made dependent upon facts ascertainable outside the certificate of incorporation or of any amendment thereto, or outside the resolution or resolutions providing for the issue of such stock adopted by the board of directors pursuant to authority expressly vested in it by its certificate of incorporation, provided that the manner in which such facts shall operate upon the voting powers, designations, preferences, rights and qualifications, limitations or restrictions of such class or series of stock is clearly and expressly set forth in the certificate of incorporation or in the resolution or resolutions providing for the issue of such stock adopted by the board of directors. The term "facts," as used in this subsection, includes, but is not limited to, the occurrence of any event, including a determination or action by any person or body, including the corporation. The power to increase or decrease or otherwise adjust the capital stock as provided in this chapter shall apply to all or any such classes of stock.

(b) Any stock of any class or series may be made subject to redemption by the corporation at its option or at the option of the holders of such stock or upon the happening of a specified event; provided however, that immediately following any such redemption the corporation shall have outstanding 1 or more shares of 1 or more classes or series of stock, which share, or shares together, shall have full voting powers.

Any stock which may be made redeemable under this section may be redeemed for cash, property or rights, including securities of the same or another corporation, at such time or times, price or prices, or rate or rates, and with such adjustments, as shall be stated in the certificate of incorporation or in the resolution or resolutions providing for the issue of such stock adopted by the board of directors pursuant to subsection (a) of this section.

(c) The holders of preferred or special stock of any class or of any series thereof shall be entitled to receive dividends at such rates, on such conditions and at such times as shall be stated in the certificate of incorporation or in the resolution or resolutions providing for the issue of such stock adopted by the board of directors as hereinabove provided, payable in preference to, or in such relation to, the dividends payable on any other class or classes or of any other series of stock, and cumulative or noncumulative as shall be so stated and expressed. When dividends upon the preferred and special stocks, if any, to the extent of the preference to which such stocks are entitled, shall have been paid or declared and set apart for payment, a dividend on the remaining class or classes or series of stock may then be paid out of the remaining assets of the corporation available for dividends as elsewhere in this chapter provided.

(d) The holders of the preferred or special stock of any class or of any series thereof shall be entitled to such rights upon the dissolution of, or upon any distribution of the assets of, the corporation as shall be stated in the certificate of incorporation or in the resolution or resolutions providing for the issue of such stock adopted by the board of directors as hereinabove provided.

(e) Any stock of any class or of any series thereof may be made convertible into, or exchangeable for, at the option of either the holder or the corporation or upon the happening of a specified event, shares of any other class or classes or any other series of the same or any other class or classes of stock of the corporation, at such price or prices or at such rate or rates of exchange and with such adjustments as shall be stated in the certificate of incorporation or in the resolution or resolutions providing for the issue of such stock adopted by the board of directors as hereinabove provided.

SECTION 170(a). DIVIDENDS; PAYMENT

The directors of every corporation, subject to any restrictions contained in its certificate of incorporation, may declare and pay dividends upon the shares of its capital stock either:

(1) Out of its surplus, as defined in and computed in accordance with §§ 154 and 244 of this title; or

(2) In case there shall be no such surplus, out of its net profits for the fiscal year in which the dividend is declared and/or the preceding fiscal year.

TORRES V. SPEISER

APPELLATE DIVISION OF THE SUPREME COURT OF THE STATE
OF NEW YORK, FIRST DEPARTMENT (WILLIAMS, J.)
701 N.Y.S.2D 361 (2000)

There is no merit to plaintiff's argument that the sale of his stock is invalid under Business Corporation Law § 504 because the price of the stock was less than its par value and such defect could not be cured by the individual defendant's promises of future consideration. While section 504 prohibits an initial issuance of stock in a new corporation for less than par value or before the full purchase price is paid, it has no bearing on a re-sale of issued shares among shareholders, as occurred here. We have considered plaintiffs' other arguments and find them unpersuasive.

Motion for a default judgment and for other related relief denied.

STOKES V. CONTINENTAL TRUST CO. OF THE CITY OF NEW YORK

COURT OF APPEALS OF NEW YORK (VANN, J.)
78 N.E. 1090 (1906)

This action was brought by a stockholder to compel his corporation to issue to him at par such a proportion of an increase made in its capital stock as the number of shares held by him before such increase bore to the number of all the shares originally issued, and in case such additional shares could not be delivered to him for his damages in the premises.

The defendant is a domestic banking corporation in the city of New York, organized in 1890, with a capital stock of $500,000, consisting of 5,000 shares of the par value of $100 each. The plaintiff was one of the original stockholders and still owns all the stock issued to him at the date of organization, together with enough more acquired since to make 221 shares in all. On the 29th of January, 1902, the defendant had a surplus of $1,048,450.94, which made the book value of the stock at that time $209.69 per share. On the 2nd of January, 1902, Blair & Company, a strong and influential firm of private bankers in the city of New York, made the following proposition to the defendant:

> If your stockholders at the special meeting to be called for January 29th, 1902, vote to increase your capital stock from $500,000 to $1,000,000 you may deliver

the additional stock to us as soon as issued at $450 per share ($100 par value) for ourselves and our associates, it being understood that we may nominate ten of the 21 trustees to be elected at the adjourned annual meeting of stockholders.

The directors of the defendant promptly met and duly authorized a special meeting of the stockholders to be called to meet on January 29th, 1902, for the purpose of voting upon the proposed increase of stock and the acceptance of the offer to purchase the same. Upon due notice a meeting of the stockholders was held accordingly, more than a majority attending either in person or by proxy. A resolution to increase the stock was adopted by the vote of 4,197 shares, all that were cast. Thereupon the plaintiff demanded from the defendant the right to subscribe for 221 shares of the new stock at par, and offered to pay immediately for the same, which demand was refused. A resolution directing a sale to Blair & Company at $450 a share was then adopted by a vote of 3,596 shares to 241. The plaintiff voted for the first resolution but against the last, and before the adoption of the latter he protested against the proposed sale of his proportionate share of the stock and again demanded the right to subscribe and pay for the same, but the demand was refused.

On the 30th of January, 1902, the stock was increased, and on the same day was sold to Blair & Company at the price named. Although the plaintiff formally renewed his demand for 221 shares of the new stock at par and tendered payment therefor, it was refused upon the ground that the stock had already been issued to Blair & Company. Owing in part to the offer of Blair & Company, which had become known to the public, the market price of the stock had increased from $450 a share in September, 1901, to $550 in January, 1902, and at the time of the trial, in April, 1904, it was worth $700 per share.

Prior to the special meeting of the stockholders, by authority of the board of directors a circular letter was sent to each stockholder, including the plaintiff, giving notice of the proposition made by Blair & Company and recommending that it be accepted. Thereupon the plaintiff notified the defendant that he wished to subscribe for his proportionate share of the new stock, if issued, and at no time did he waive his right to subscribe for the same. Before the special meeting, he had not been definitely notified by the defendant that he could not receive his proportionate part of the increase, but was informed that his proposition would "be taken under consideration."

After finding these facts in substance, the trial court found, as conclusions of law, that the plaintiff had the right to subscribe for such proportion of the increase, as his holdings bore to all the stock before the increase was made; that the stockholders, directors and officers of the defendant had no power to deprive him of that right, and that he was entitled to recover the difference between the market value of 221 shares on the 30th of January, 1902, and the par value thereof, or the sum of $99,450, together with interest from said date. The judgment entered accordingly was reversed by the Appellate Division, and the plaintiff appealed to this court, giving the usual stipulation for judgment absolute in case the order of reversal should be affirmed.

The question presented for decision is whether according to the facts found the plaintiff had the legal right to subscribe for and take the same number of shares of the new stock that he held of the old? The subject is not regulated by statute and the question presented has never been directly passed upon by this court, and only to a limited extent has it been considered by courts in this state.

If the right claimed by the plaintiff was a right of property belonging to him as a stockholder he could not be deprived of it by the joint action of the other stockholders and of all the directors and officers of the corporation. What is the nature of the right acquired by a stockholder through the ownership of shares of stock? What rights can he assert against the will of a majority of the stockholders and all the officers and directors? While he does not own and cannot dispose of any specific property of the corporation, yet he and his associates own the corporation itself, its charter, franchises and all rights conferred thereby, including the right to increase the stock. He has an inherent right to his proportionate share of any dividend declared, or of any surplus arising upon dissolution, and he can prevent waste or misappropriation of the property of the corporation by those in control. Finally, he has the right to vote for directors and upon all propositions subject by law to the control of the stockholders, and this is his supreme right and main protection. Stockholders have no direct voice in transacting the corporate business, but through their right to vote they can select those to whom the law entrusts the power of management and control.

A corporation is somewhat like a partnership, if one were possible, conducted wholly by agents where the copartners have power to appoint the agents, but are not responsible for their acts. The power to manage its affairs resides in the directors, who are its agents, but the power to elect directors resides in the stockholders. This right to vote for directors and upon propositions to increase the stock or mortgage the assets, is about all the power the stockholder has. So long as the management is honest, within the corporate powers and involves no waste, the stockholders cannot interfere, even if the administration is feeble and unsatisfactory, but must correct such evils through their power to elect other directors. Hence, the power of the individual stockholder to vote in proportion to the number of his shares, is vital and cannot be cut off or curtailed by the action of all the other stockholders even with the co-operation of the directors and officers.

In the case before us the new stock came into existence through the exercise of a right belonging wholly to the stockholders. As the right to increase the stock belonged to them, the stock when increased belonged to them also, as it was issued for money and not for property or for some purpose other than the sale thereof for money. By the increase of stock the voting power of the plaintiff was reduced one-half, and while he consented to the increase he did not consent to the disposition of the new stock by a sale thereof to Blair & Company at less than its market value, nor by sale to any person in any way except by an allotment to the stockholders. The plaintiff had power, before the increase of stock, to vote on 221 shares of stock, out of a total of 5,000, at any meeting held by the stockholders for any purpose. By the action of the majority, taken against his will and protest, he now has only one-half the voting power that he had before, because the number of shares has been doubled while he still owns but 221. This touches him as a stockholder in such a way as to deprive him of a right of property. Blair & Company acquired virtual control, while he and the other stockholders lost it. We are not discussing equities, but legal rights, for this is an action at law, and the plaintiff was deprived of a strictly legal right. If the result gives him an advantage over other stockholders, it is because he stood upon his legal rights, while they did not. The question is what were his legal rights, not what his profit may be under the sale to Blair & Company, but what it might have been if the new stock had been issued to him in proportion to his holding of the old. The other stockholders could give their property to Blair & Company, but they could not give his.

We are thus led to lay down the rule that a stockholder has an inherent right to a proportionate share of new stock issued for money only and not to purchase property for the purposes of the corporation or to effect a consolidation, and while he can waive that right, he cannot be deprived of it without his consent except when the stock is issued at a fixed price not less than par and he is given the right to take at that price in proportion to his holding, or in some other equitable way that will enable him to protect his interest by acting on his own judgment and using his own resources. This rule is just to all and tends to prevent the tyranny of majorities which needs restraint, as well as virtual attempts to blackmail by small minorities which should be prevented.

The learned trial court, however, did not measure the damages according to law. The plaintiff was not entitled to the difference between the par value of the new stock and the market value thereof, for the stockholders had the right to fix the price at which the stock should be sold. They fixed the price at $450 a share, and for the failure of the defendant to offer the plaintiff his share at that price we hold it liable in damages. His actual loss, therefore, is $100 per share, or the difference between $450, the price that he would have been obliged to pay had he been permitted to purchase, and the market value on the day of sale, which was $550. This conclusion requires a reversal of the judgment rendered by the Appellate Division and a modification of that rendered by the trial court.

The order appealed from should be reversed and the judgment of the trial court modified by reducing the damages from the sum of $99,450, with interest from January 30th, 1902, to the sum of $22,100, with interest from that date, and by striking out the extra allowance of costs, and as thus modified the judgment of the trial court is affirmed, without costs in this court or in the Appellate Division to either party.

173

KATZOWITZ V. SIDLER

COURT OF APPEALS OF NEW YORK (KEATING, J.)
249 N.E.2D 359 (1969)

Isador Katzowitz is a director and stockholder of a close corporation. Two other persons, Jacob Sidler and Max Lasker, own the remaining securities and, with Katzowitz, comprise Sulburn Holding Corp.'s board of directors. Sulburn was organized in 1955 to supply propane gas to three other corporations controlled by these men. Sulburn's certificate of incorporation authorized it to issue 1,000 shares of no par value stock for which the incorporators established a $100 selling price. Katzowitz, Sidler and Lasker each invested $500 and received five shares of the corporation's stock.

The three men had been jointly engaged in several corporate ventures for more than 25 years. In this period they had always been equal partners and received identical compensation from the corporations they controlled. Though all the corporations controlled by these three men prospered, disenchantment with their inter-personal relationship flared into the open in 1956. At this time, Sidler and Lasker joined forces to oust Katzowitz from any role in managing the corporations. They first voted to replace Katzowitz as a director of Sullivan County Gas Company with the corporation's private counsel. Notice of directors' meetings was then caused to be sent out by Lasker and Sidler for Burnwell Gas Corporation. Sidler and Lasker advised Katzowitz that they intended to vote for a new board of directors. Katzowitz at this time held the position of manager of the Burnwell facility.

Katzowitz sought a temporary injunction to prevent the meeting until his rights could be judicially determined. A temporary injunction was granted to maintain the status quo until trial. The order was affirmed by the Appellate Division.

Before the issue could be tried, the three men entered into a stipulation in 1959 whereby Katzowitz withdrew from active participation in the day-to-day operations of the business. The agreement provided that he would remain on the boards of all the corporations, and each board would be limited to three members composed of the three stockholders or their designees. Katzowitz was to receive the same compensation and other fringe benefits which the controlled corporations paid Lasker and Sidler. The stipulation also provided that Katzowitz, Sidler and Lasker were "equal stockholders and each of said parties now owns the same number of shares of stock in each of the defendant corporations and that such shares of stock shall continue to be in full force and effect and unaffected by this stipulation, except as hereby otherwise expressly provided." The stipulation contained no other provision affecting equal stock interests.

The business relationship established by the stipulation was fully complied with. Sidler and Lasker, however, were still interested in disassociating themselves from Katzowitz and purchased his interest in one of the gas distribution corporations and approached him with regard to the purchase of his interest in another.

In December of 1961 Sulburn was indebted to each stockholder to the extent of $2,500 for fees and commissions earned up until September, 1961. Instead of paying this debt, Sidler and Lasker wanted Sulburn to loan the money to another corporation which all three men controlled. Sidler and Lasker called a meeting of the board of directors to propose that additional securities be offered at $100 per share to substitute for the money owed to the directors. The notice of meeting for October 30, 1961 had on its agenda "a proposition that the corporation issue common stock of its unissued common capital stock, the total par value which shall equal the total sum of the fees and commissions now owing by the corporation to its directors." Katzowitz made it quite clear at the meeting that he would not invest any additional funds in Sulburn in order for it to make a loan to this other corporation. The only resolution passed at the meeting was that the corporation would pay the sum of $2,500 to each director.

With full knowledge that Katzowitz expected to be paid his fees and commissions and that he did not want to participate in any new stock issuance, the other two directors called a special meeting of the board on December 1, 1961. The only item on the agenda for this special meeting was the issuance of 75 shares of the corporation's common stock at $100 per share. The offer was to be made to stockholders in "accordance with their respective preemptive rights for the purpose of acquiring additional working capital." The amount to be raised was the exact amount owed by the corporation to its shareholders. The offering price for the securities was 1/18 the book value of the stock. Only Sidler and Lasker attended the special board meeting. They approved the issuance of the 75 shares.

Notice was mailed to each stockholder that they had the right to purchase 25 shares of the corporation's stock at $100 a share. The offer was to expire on December 27, 1961. Failure to act by that date was stated to constitute a waiver. At about the same time Katzowitz received the notice, he received a check for $2,500 from the corporation for his fees and commissions. Katzowitz did not exercise his option to buy the additional shares. Sidler and Lasker purchased their full complement, 25 shares each. This purchase by Sidler and Lasker caused an immediate dilution of the book value of the outstanding securities.

On August 25, 1962 the principal asset of Sulburn, a tractor trailer truck, was destroyed. On August 31, 1962 the directors unanimously voted to dissolve the corporation. Upon dissolution, Sidler and Lasker each received $18,885.52 but Katzowitz only received $3,147.59.

The plaintiff instituted a declaratory judgment action to establish his right to the proportional interest in the assets of Sulburn in liquidation less the $5,000 which Sidler and Lasker used to purchase their shares in December, 1961.

Special Term (Westchester County) found the book value of the corporation's securities on the day the stock was offered at $100 to be worth $1,800. The court also found that "the individual defendants decided that in lieu of taking that sum in cash (the commissions and fees due the stockholders), they preferred to add to their investment by having the corporate defendant make available and offer each stockholder an additional twenty-five shares of unissued stock." The court reasoned that Katzowitz waived his right to purchase the stock or object to its sale to Lasker and Sidler by failing to exercise his pre-emptive right and found his protest at the time of dissolution untimely.

On the substantive legal issues and findings of fact, the Appellate Division was in agreement with Special Term. The majority agreed that the book value of the corporation's stock at the time of the stock offering was $1,800. The Appellate Division reasoned, however, that showing a disparity between book value and offering price was insufficient without also showing fraud or overreaching. Disparity in price by itself was not enough to prove fraud. The Appellate Division also found that the plaintiff had waived his right to object to his recovery in dissolution by failing to either exercise his pre-emptive rights or take steps to prevent the sale of the stock.

The concept of pre-emptive rights was fashioned by the judiciary to safeguard two distinct interests of stockholders—the right to protection against dilution of their equity in the corporation and protection against dilution of their proportionate voting control. After early decisions, legislation fixed the right enunciated with respect to proportionate voting but left to the judiciary the role of protecting existing shareholders from the dilution of their equity.

It is clear that directors of a corporation have no discretion in the choice of those to whom the earnings and assets of the corporation should be distributed. Directors, being fiduciaries of the corporation, must, in issuing new stock, treat existing shareholders fairly. Though there is very little statutory control over the price which a corporation must receive for new shares the power to determine price must be exercised for the benefit of the corporation and in the interest of all the stockholders.

Issuing stock for less than fair value can injure existing shareholders by diluting their interest in the corporation's surplus, in current and future earnings and in the assets upon liquidation. Normally, a stockholder is protected from the loss of his equity from dilution, even though the stock is being offered at less than fair value, because the shareholder receives rights which he may either exercise or sell. If he exercises, he has protected his interest and, if not, he can sell the rights, thereby compensating himself for the dilution of his remaining shares in the equity of the corporation.

When new shares are issued, however, at prices far below fair value in a close corporation or a corporation with only a limited market for its shares, existing stockholders, who do not want to invest or do not have the capacity to invest additional funds, can have their equity interest in the corporation diluted to the vanishing point.

The protection afforded by stock rights is illusory in close corporations. Even if a buyer could be found for the rights, they would have to be sold at an inadequate price because of the nature of a close corporation. Outsiders are normally discouraged from acquiring minority interests after a close corporation has been organized. Certainly a stockholder in a close corporation is at a total loss to safeguard his equity from dilution if no rights are offered and he does not want to invest additional funds.

Though it is difficult to determine fair value for a corporation's securities and courts are therefore reluctant to get into the thicket, when the issuing price is shown to be markedly below book value in a close corporation and when the remaining shareholder-directors benefit from the issuance, a case for judicial relief has been established. In that instance, the corporation's directors must show that the issuing price falls within some range which can be justified on the basis of valid business reasons. If no such showing is made by the directors, there is no reason for the judiciary to abdicate its function to a majority of the board or stockholders who have not seen fit to come forward and justify the propriety of diverting property from the corporation and allow the issuance of securities to become an oppressive device permitting the dilution of the equity of dissident stockholders.

The defendant directors here make no claim that the price set was a fair one. No business justification is offered to sustain it. Admittedly, the stock was sold at less than book value. The defendants simply contend that, as long as all stockholders were given an equal opportunity to purchase additional shares, no stockholder can complain simply because the offering dilutes his interest in the corporation.

The defendants' argument is fallacious. The corollary of a stockholder's right to maintain his proportionate equity in a corporation by purchasing additional shares is the right not to purchase additional shares without being confronted with dilution of his existing equity if no valid business justification exists for the dilution.

A stockholder's right not to purchase is seriously undermined if the stock offered is worth substantially more than the offering price. Any purchase at this price dilutes his interest and impairs the value of his original holding. "A corporation is not permitted to sell its stock for a legally inadequate price at least where there is objection. Plaintiff has a right to insist upon compliance with the law whether or not he cares to exercise his option. He cannot block a sale for a fair price merely because he disagrees with the wisdom of the plan but he can insist that the sale price be fixed accordance with legal requirements." (Judicial review in this area is limited to whether under all the circumstances, including the disparity between issuing price of the stock and its true value, the nature of the corporation, the business necessity for establishing an offering price at a certain amount to facilitate raising new capital, and the ability of stockholders to sell rights, the additional offering of securities should be condemned because the directors in establishing the sale price did not fix it with reference to financial considerations with respect to the ready disposition of securities.

Here the obvious disparity in selling price and book value was calculated to force the dissident stockholder into investing additional sums. No valid business justification was advanced for the disparity in price, and the only beneficiaries of the disparity were the two director-stockholders who were eager to have additional capital in the business.

Sidler; Lasher tried to force Katzowitz's hand

It is no answer to Katzowitz' action that he was also given a chance to purchase additional shares at this bargain rate. The price was not so much a bargain as it was a tactic, conscious or unconscious on the part of the directors, to place Katzowitz in a compromising situation. The price was so fixed to make the failure to invest costly. However, Katzowitz at the time might not have been aware of the dilution because no notice of the effect of the issuance of the new shares on the already outstanding shares was disclosed. In addition, since the stipulation entitled Katzowitz to the same compensation as Sidler and Lasker, the disparity in equity interest caused by their purchase of additional securities in 1961 did not affect stockholder income from Sulburn and, therefore, Katzowitz possibly was not aware of the effect of the stock issuance on his interest in the corporation until dissolution.

No reason exists at this time to permit Sidler and Lasker to benefit from their course of conduct. Katzowitz' delay in commencing the action did not prejudice the defendants. By permitting the defendants to recover their additional investment in Sulburn before the remaining assets of Sulburn are distributed to the stockholders upon dissolution, all the stockholders will be treated equitably. Katzowitz, therefore, should receive his aliquot share of the assets of Sulburn less the amount invested by Sidler and Lasker for their purchase of stock on December 27, 1961.

Accordingly, the order of the Appellate Division should be reversed, with costs, and judgment granted in favor of the plaintiff against the individual defendants.

KLANG V. SMITH'S FOOD & DRUG CENTERS, INC.

SUPREME COURT OF DELAWARE (VEASEY, C.J.)
702 A.2D 150 (1997)

This appeal calls into question the actions of a corporate board in carrying out a merger and self-tender offer. Plaintiff in this purported class action alleges that a corporation's repurchase of shares violated the statutory prohibition against the impairment of capital. Plaintiff also claims that the directors violated their fiduciary duty of candor by failing to disclose material facts prior to seeking stockholder approval of the transactions in question.

No corporation may repurchase or redeem its own shares except out of "surplus," as statutorily defined, or except as expressly authorized by provisions of the statute not relevant here. Balance sheets are not, however, conclusive indicators of surplus or a lack thereof. Corporations may revalue assets to show surplus, but perfection in that process is not required. Directors have reasonable latitude to depart from the balance sheet to calculate surplus, so long as they evaluate assets and liabilities in good faith, on the basis of acceptable data, by methods that they reasonably believe reflect present values, and arrive at a determination of the surplus that is not so far off the mark as to constitute actual or constructive fraud.

We hold that, on this record, the Court of Chancery was correct in finding that there was no impairment of capital and there were no disclosure violations. Accordingly, we affirm.

Smith's Food & Drug Centers, Inc. is a Delaware corporation that owns and operates a chain of supermarkets in the Southwestern United States. Slightly more than three years ago, Jeffrey P. Smith, SFD's Chief Executive Officer, began to entertain suitors with an interest in acquiring SFD. At the time, and until the transactions at issue, Mr. Smith and his family held common and preferred stock constituting 62.1% voting control of SFD. Plaintiff and the class he purports to represent are holders of common stock in SFD.

On January 29, 1996, SFD entered into an agreement with The Yucaipa Companies, a California partnership also active in the supermarket industry. Under the agreement, the following would take place:

1. Smitty's Supermarkets, Inc., a wholly-owned subsidiary of Yucaipa that operated a supermarket chain in Arizona, was to merge into Cactus Acquisition, Inc., a subsidiary of SFD, in exchange for which SFD would deliver to Yucaipa slightly over 3 million newly-issued shares of SFD common stock;
2. SFD was to undertake a recapitalization, in the course of which SFD would assume a sizable amount of new debt, retire old debt, and offer to repurchase up to fifty percent of its outstanding shares (other than those issued to Yucaipa) for $36 per share; and
3. SFD was to repurchase 3 million shares of preferred stock from Jeffrey Smith and his family.

SFD hired the investment firm of Houlihan Lokey Howard & Zukin ("Houlihan") to examine the transactions and render a solvency opinion. Houlihan eventually issued a report to the SFD Board replete with assurances that the transactions would not endanger SFD's solvency, and would not impair SFD's capital in violation of 8 *Del. C.* § 160. On May 17, 1996, in reliance on the Houlihan opinion, SFD's Board determined that there existed sufficient surplus to consummate the transactions, and enacted a resolution proclaiming as much. On May 23, 1996, SFD's stockholders voted to approve the transactions, which closed on that day. The self-tender offer was over-subscribed, so SFD repurchased fully fifty percent of its shares at the offering price of $36 per share.

A corporation may not repurchase its shares if, in so doing, it would cause an impairment of capital, unless expressly authorized by Section 160. A repurchase impairs capital if the funds used in the repurchase exceed the amount of the corporation's "surplus," defined by 8 *Del. C.* § 154 to mean the excess of net assets over the par value of the corporation's issued stock.

Plaintiff asked the Court of Chancery to rescind the transactions in question as violative of Section 160. As we understand it, plaintiff contends that SFD's balance sheets constitute conclusive evidence of capital impairment. He argues that the negative net worth that appeared on SFD's books following the repurchase compels us to find a violation of Section 160.

In an April 25, 1996 proxy statement, the SFD Board released a pro forma balance sheet showing that the merger and self-tender offer would result in a deficit to surplus on SFD's books of more than $100 million. A balance sheet the SFD Board issued shortly after the transactions confirmed this result. Plaintiff asks us to adopt an interpretation of 8 *Del. C.* § 160 whereby balance-sheet net worth is controlling for purposes of determining compliance with the statute. Defendants do not dispute that SFD's books showed a negative net worth in the wake of its transactions with Yucaipa, but argue that corporations should have the presumptive right to revalue assets and liabilities to comply with Section 160.

Plaintiff advances an erroneous interpretation of Section 160. We understand that the books of a corporation do not necessarily reflect the current values of its assets and liabilities. Among other factors, unrealized appreciation or depreciation can render book numbers inaccurate. It is unrealistic to hold that a corporation is bound by its balance sheets for purposes of determining compliance with Section 160. Accordingly, we adhere to the principles of *Morris v. Standard Gas & Electric Co.* allowing corporations to revalue properly its assets and liabilities to show a surplus and thus conform to the statute.

It is helpful to recall the purpose behind Section 160. The General Assembly enacted the statute to prevent boards from draining corporations of assets to the detriment of creditors and the long-term health of the corporation. That a corporation has not yet realized or reflected on its balance sheet the appreciation of assets is irrelevant to this concern. Regardless of what a balance sheet that has not been updated may show, an actual, though unrealized, appreciation reflects real economic value that the corporation may borrow against or that creditors may claim or levy upon. Allowing corporations to revalue assets and liabilities to reflect current realities complies with the statute and serves well the policies behind this statute.

The record contains, in the form of the Houlihan opinion, substantial evidence that the transactions complied with Section 160. Plaintiff has provided no reason to distrust Houlihan's analysis. In cases alleging impairment of capital under Section 160, the trial court may defer to the board's measurement of surplus unless a plaintiff can show that the directors "failed to fulfill their duty to evaluate the assets on the basis of acceptable data and by standards which they are entitled to believe reasonably reflect present values." In the absence of bad faith or fraud on the part of the board, courts will not "substitute our concepts of wisdom for that of the directors." Here, plaintiff does not argue that the SFD Board acted in bad faith. Nor has he met his burden of showing that the methods and data that underlay the board's analysis are unreliable or that its determination of surplus is so far off the mark as to constitute actual or constructive fraud. Therefore, we defer to the board's determination of surplus, and hold that SFD's self-tender offer did not violate 8 *Del. C.* § 160.

The judgment of the Court of Chancery is affirmed.

EQUITY-LINKED INVESTORS, L.P. V. ADAMS

COURT OF CHANCERY OF DELAWARE, NEW CASTLE (ALLEN, C.)
705 A.2D 1040 (1997)

The case now under consideration involves a conflict between the financial interests of the holders of a convertible preferred stock with a liquidation preference, and the interests of the common stock. The conflict arises because the company, Genta Incorporated, is on the lip of insolvency and in liquidation it would probably be worth substantially less than the $30 million liquidation preference of the preferred stock. Thus, if the liquidation preference of the preferred were treated as a liability of Genta, the firm would certainly be insolvent now. Yet Genta, a bio- pharmaceutical company that has never made a profit, does have several promising technologies in research and there is some ground to think that the value of products that might be developed from those technologies could be very great. Were that to occur, naturally, a large part of the "upside" gain would accrue to the benefit of the common stock, in equity the residual owners of the firm's net cash flows. (Of course, whatever the source of funds that would enable a nearly insolvent company to achieve that result would also negotiate for a share of those future gains—which is what this case is about). But since the current net worth of the company would be put at risk in such an effort—or more accurately would continue at risk—if Genta continues to try to develop these opportunities, any loss that may eventuate will in effect fall, not on the common stock, but on the preferred stock.

As the story sketched below shows, the Genta board sought actively to find a means to continue the firm in operation so that some chance to develop commercial products from its promising technologies could be achieved. It publicly announced its interest in finding new sources of capital. Contemporaneously, the holders of the preferred stock, relatively few institutional investors, were seeking a means to cut their losses, which meant, in effect, liquidating Genta and distributing most or all of its assets to the preferred. The contractual rights of the preferred stock did not, however, give the holders the necessary legal power to force this course of action on the corporation. Negotiations held between Genta's management and representatives of the preferred stock with respect to the rights of the preferred came to an unproductive and somewhat unpleasant end in January 1997.

Shortly thereafter, Genta announced that a third party source of additional capital had been located and that an agreement had been reached that would enable the corporation to pursue its business plan for a further period. The evidence indicates that at the time set for the closing of that transaction, Genta had available sufficient cash to cover its operations for only one additional week. A Petition in Bankruptcy had been prepared by counsel.

This suit by a lead holder of the preferred stock followed the announcement of the loan transaction. Plaintiff is Equity-Linked Investors, L.P., one of the institutional investors that holds Genta's Series A preferred stock. The suit challenges the transaction in which Genta borrowed on a secured basis some $3,000,000 and received other significant consideration from Paramount Capital Asset Management, Inc., a manager of the Aries Fund, in exchange for a note, warrants exercisable into half of Genta's outstanding stock, and other consideration. The suit seeks an injunction or other equitable relief against this transaction.

While from a realistic or finance perspective, the heart of the matter is the conflict between the interests of the institutional investors that own the preferred stock and the economic interests of the common stock, *from a legal perspective*, the case has been presented as one on behalf of the common stock, or more correctly on behalf of all holders of equity securities. The legal theory of the case, as it was tried, was that the Aries transaction was a "change of corporate control" transaction that placed upon Genta special obligations—"Revlon duties"—which the directors failed to satisfy.

While the facts out of which this dispute arises indisputably entail the imposition by the board of (or continuation of) economic risks upon the preferred stock which the holders of the preferred did not want, and while this board action was taken for the benefit largely of the common stock, those facts do not constitute a breach of duty. While the board in these circumstances could have made a different business judgment, in my opinion, it violated no duty owed to the preferred in not doing so. The special protections offered to the preferred are contractual in nature. The corporation is, of course, required to respect those legal rights. But, aside from the insolvency point just alluded to, generally it will be the duty of the board, where discretionary judgment is to be exercised, to prefer the interests of common stock—as the good faith judgment of the board sees them to be—to the interests created by the special rights, preferences, etc., of preferred stock, where there is a conflict. The facts of this case do not involve any violation by the board of any special right or privilege of the Series A preferred stock, nor of any residual right of the preferred as owners of equity.

As I have said, that is, I think, the heart of the matter. It is my opinion that the Genta board fully satisfied its obligations of good faith and attention with respect to the Aries transaction. The directors of Genta did not, therefore, breach a fiduciary duty owed to the corporation or any of its equity security holders. I conclude that with respect to this transaction, the board was independent; it was motivated throughout by a good faith attempt to maximize long-term corporate value; and that the board and senior management were appropriately informed of alternatives available *to implement the business plan that the directors sought to achieve*. Moreover, if reviewed under a reasonableness criterion, I conclude that the board acted in an entirely reasonable way to achieve its goal and that its goal, although obviously one that reasonable minds could disagree about—was not one that was impermissible.

Judgment will be granted for defendants and against plaintiff. Each party to bear its own costs.

CHAPTER 7:

CORPORATE FIDUCIARY DUTIES

INTRODUCTION

As you are by now well acquainted, corporate law can be quite formalistic in its approach, providing simple rules that seem to prefer form over substance. But attorneys are clever folk, and they often treat rigidity in the law as an opportunity for manipulation. Moreover, it is quite impossible for policymakers to anticipate the endless ways in which shrewd lawyers can take advantage of an unyielding architecture. The more rigid the system, the greater the opportunity for evading its strictures. Thus, it has been essential to the success of corporate law that it develop a mechanism for guarding against abusive practices. Fairness can only exist if the rules are honored in their spirit as well as in their letter.

With this concern in mind, corporate law judges and policymakers have attempted to ameliorate the myriad opportunities for abuse by adopting an overarching golden rule. Following Judge Cardozo's blueprint in Meinhard v. Salmon, corporate law borrowed the concept of fiduciary duties and imported them into the business realm. Although specific rules may allow for manipulation, a manager's fiduciary responsibilities require her to maneuver through them in a manner that serves the preferences of the entire corporation (and its shareholders) rather than act on the basis of her selfish interests.

Note that for those who would criticize our system of corporate influence—and for those who would defend it—it is in the realm of fiduciary duties that the war is waged. The underlying challenge lies in the balance between discretion and accountability. As Berle and Means warned, parties exercising control over a corporation's affairs must be held accountable for their lack of due care and loyalty. However, for the delegation of authority from owner to manager to be meaningful (and, indeed, useful), there must be an accompanying grant of managerial discretion. Without a doubt, someone must watch the watchers—but not too closely, lest they are reduced to mere puppets. For reformers, the system offers too little accountability; for defenders, too little discretion. The outcome of the battle hinges upon where on this continuum the pendulum comes to rest.

Unlike partnership fiduciary duties, which are generally described as being of a single whole, corporate law fiduciary duties have been sliced and diced into a sort of holy trinity—the duties of care, loyalty, and good faith. Corporate fiduciary duties also differ from those applying to partnerships with regard to the identity of the persons to whom they relate. In a partnership, each partner has powers of management, so each must exercise those powers in accordance with their fiduciary responsibilities. In most corporations, by contrast, control is exercised by officers and directors rather than shareholders, so it is they who are generally assigned fiduciary status.

Shareholders do have fiduciary duties in the context of small businesses, however, where the limited number of owners poses a risk that minority shareholders will suffer "oppression." This scheme is the subject of Part A. Part B then explicates the directors' duty of care, while Parts C and D examine in turn the directors' duties of loyalty and good faith. Regarding each topic, the cases in this chapter are uniformly well known and influential in their own right. These are not merely examples chosen from a myriad of similar decisions. Rather, these cases made the law what it is today.

In Part E, we take a brief pause from our study of state corporation law and examine the federal regulation of fiduciary conduct. In the wake of the simultaneous crashes of the dotcom and telecom industries in 2001, Congress adopted the Sarbanes-Oxley Act. Critics have claimed that this statute goes further than previous federal incursions into corporate regulation by imposing affirmative duties of care and loyalty at the national level. At the same time, it is important to remember that large companies whose stock is traded on a national exchange must abide by the rules of that exchange. We therefore briefly analyze both Sarbanes-Oxley and the corporate governance rules of the New York Stock Exchange.

At the end of this chapter, you will understand the overarching framework that attempts to keep corporate managers (and sometimes shareholders) honest. These doctrines may be of greatest interest to litigators, as planners will invariably advise their clients that it is safest to follow the rules as they were intended. Thus, the question of what duties are owed by corporate managers is often one that is resolved in front of a jury.

SHAREHOLDER FIDUCIARY DUTIES PART A

DONAHUE V. RODD ELECTROTYPE CO. OF NEW ENGLAND, INC.

SUPREME JUDICIAL COURT OF MASSACHUSETTS (TAURO, C.J.)
328 N.E.2D 505 (1975)

The plaintiff, Euphemia Donahue, a minority stockholder in the Rodd Electrotype Company of New England, Inc., a Massachusetts corporation, brings this suit against the directors of Rodd Electrotype, Charles H. Rodd, Frederick I. Rodd and Mr. Harold E. Magnuson, against Harry C. Rodd, a former director, officer, and controlling stockholder of Rodd Electrotype and against Rodd Electrotype (hereinafter called defendants). The plaintiff seeks to rescind Rodd Electrotype's purchase of Harry Rodd's shares in Rodd Electrotype and to compel Harry Rodd "to repay to the corporation the purchase price of said shares, $36,000, together with interest from the date of purchase." The plaintiff alleges that the defendants caused the corporation to purchase the shares in violation of their fiduciary duty to her, a minority stockholder of Rodd Electrotype.[1]

The trial judge, after hearing oral testimony, dismissed the plaintiff's bill on the merits. He found that the purchase was without prejudice to the plaintiff and implicitly found that the transaction had been carried out in good faith and with inherent fairness.

The evidence may be summarized as follows: In 1935, the defendant, Harry C. Rodd, began his employment with Rodd Electrotype, then styled the Royal Electrotype Company of New England, Inc. At that time, the company was a wholly-owned subsidiary of a Pennsylvania corporation, the Royal Electrotype Company.

In 1936, the plaintiff's husband, Joseph Donahue (now deceased), was hired by Royal of New England as a "finisher" of electrotype plates. Although he ultimately achieved the positions of plant superintendent (1946) and corporate vice president (1955), Donahue never participated in the "management" aspect of the business.

In the years preceding 1955, the parent company made available shares of the common stock in its subsidiary, Royal of New England. Harry Rodd took advantage of the opportunities and acquired 200 shares. Donahue, at the suggestion of Rodd, who hoped to interest Donahue in the

---

1   In form, the plaintiff's bill of complaint presents, at least in part, a derivative action, brought on behalf of the corporation, and, in the words of the bill, "on behalf of . . . (the) stockholders" of Rodd Electrotype. Yet the plaintiff's bill, in substance, was one seeking redress because of alleged breaches of the fiduciary duty owed to her, a minority stockholder, by the controlling stockholders. We treat that bill of complaint (as have the parties) as presenting a proper cause of suit in the personal right of the plaintiff.

business, eventually obtained fifty shares. The parent company at all times retained 725 of the 1,000 outstanding shares.

In 1955, Royal of New England purchased all 725 of its shares owned by its parent company. A substantial portion of Royal of New England's cash expenditures was loaned to the company by Harry Rodd, who mortgaged his house to obtain some of the necessary funds. The stock purchases left Harry Rodd in control of Royal of New England. His 200 shares gave him a dominant eighty per cent interest. Joseph Donahue, at this time, was the only minority stockholder.

From 1959 to 1967, Harry Rodd pursued what may fairly be termed a gift program by which he distributed the majority of his shares equally among his two sons and his daughter. Each child received thirty-nine shares. In May 1970, Harry Rodd was seventy-seven years old. His sons wished him to retire. They authorized Rodd Electrotype's president to execute an agreement between Harry Rodd and the company in which the company would purchase forty-five shares for $800 a share ($36,000). Harry Rodd completed divestiture of his stock in the following year, transferring his remaining shares to his children in equal proportion.

A few weeks after the sale, the Donahues, acting through their attorney, offered their shares to the corporation on the same terms given to Harry Rodd. The company's clerk replied by letter that the corporation would not purchase the shares and was not in a financial position to do so.

In her argument before this court, the plaintiff has characterized the corporate purchase of Harry Rodd's shares as an unlawful distribution of corporate assets to controlling stockholders. She urges that the distribution constitutes a breach of the fiduciary duty owed by the Rodds, as controlling stockholders, to her, a minority stockholder in the enterprise, because the Rodds failed to accord her an equal opportunity to sell her shares to the corporation. The defendants reply that the stock purchase was within the powers of the corporation and met the requirements of good faith and inherent fairness imposed on a fiduciary in his dealings with the corporation. They assert that there is no right to equal opportunity in corporate stock purchases for the corporate treasury. For the reasons hereinafter noted, we agree with the plaintiff and reverse the decree of the Superior Court. However, we limit the applicability of our holding to "close corporations," as hereinafter defined. Whether the holding should apply to other corporations is left for decision in another case, on a proper record.

In previous opinions, we have alluded to the distinctive nature of the close corporation, but have never defined precisely what is meant by a close corporation. There is no single, generally accepted definition. Some commentators emphasize an "integration of ownership and management," in which the stockholders occupy most management positions. Others focus on the number of stockholders and the nature of the market for the stock. In this view, close corporations have few stockholders; there is little market for corporate stock. The Supreme Court of Illinois adopted this latter view in *Galler v. Galler*: "For our purposes, a close corporation is one in which the stock is held in a few hands, or in a few families, and wherein it is not at all, or only rarely, dealt in by buying or selling." We accept aspects of both definitions. We deem a close corporation to the typified by: (1) a small number of stockholders; (2) no ready market for the corporate stock; and (3) substantial majority stockholder participation in the management, direction and operations of the corporation.

As thus defined, the close corporation bears striking resemblance to a partnership. Commentators and courts have noted that the close corporation is often little more than an "incorporated" or "chartered" partnership.[2] The stockholders "clothe" their partnership "with the benefits peculiar to a corporation, limited liability, perpetuity and the like." In essence, though, the enterprise remains one in which ownership is limited to the original parties or transferees of their stock to whom the other stockholders have agreed, in which ownership and management are in the same hands, and in which the owners are quite dependent on one another for the success of the enterprise. Many close corporations are "really partnerships, between two or three people who contribute their capital, skills, experience and labor." Just as in a partnership, the relationship among the stockholders must be one of trust, confidence and absolute loyalty if the enterprise is to succeed. Close corporations with substantial assets and with more numerous stockholders are no different from smaller close corporations in this regard. All participants rely on the fidelity and abilities of those stockholders who hold office. Disloyalty and self-seeking conduct on the part of any stockholder will engender bickering, corporate stalemates, and, perhaps, efforts to achieve dissolution.

Although the corporate form provides the above-mentioned advantages for the stockholders (limited liability, perpetuity, and so forth), it also supplies an opportunity for the majority stockholders to oppress or disadvantage minority stockholders. The minority is vulnerable to a variety of oppressive devices, termed "freezeouts," which the majority may employ. An authoritative study of such "freeze-outs" enumerates some of the possibilities: "The squeezers (those who employ the freeze-out techniques) may refuse to declare dividends; they may drain off the corporation's earnings in the form of exorbitant salaries and bonuses to the majority shareholder-officers and perhaps to their relatives, or in the form of high rent by the corporation for property leased from majority shareholders; they may deprive minority shareholders of corporate offices and of employment by the company; they may cause the corporation to sell its assets at an inadequate price to the majority shareholders." In particular, the power of the board of directors, controlled by the majority, to declare or withhold dividends and to deny the minority employment is easily converted to a device to disadvantage minority stockholders.

The minority can, of course, initiate suit against the majority and their directors. Self-serving conduct by directors is proscribed by the director's fiduciary obligation to the corporation. However, in practice, the plaintiff will find difficulty in challenging dividend or employment

---

2   The United States Internal Revenue Code gives substantial recognition to the fact that close corporations are often merely incorporated partnerships. The so called Subchapter S enables "small business corporations," defined by the statute, to make an election which generally exempts the corporation from taxation and causes inclusion of the corporation's undistributed, as well as distributed, taxable income in the gross income of the stockholders for the year. This is essentially the manner in which partnership earnings are taxed.

policies. Such policies are considered to be within the judgment of the directors. This court has said: "The courts prefer not to interfere with the sound financial management of the corporation by its directors, but declare as general rule that the declaration of dividends rests within the sound discretion of the directors, refusing to interfere with their determination unless a plain abuse of discretion is made to appear." Judicial reluctance to interfere combines with the difficulty of proof when the standard is "plain abuse of discretion" or bad faith to limit the possibilities for relief. Although contractual provisions in an "agreement of association and articles of organization" or in by-laws have justified decrees in this jurisdiction ordering dividend declarations, generally, plaintiffs who seek judicial assistance against corporate dividend or employment policies do not prevail.

Thus, when these types of "freeze-outs" are attempted by the majority stockholders, the minority stockholders, cut off from all corporation-related revenues, must either suffer their losses or seek a buyer for their shares. Many minority stockholders will be unwilling or unable to wait for an alteration in majority policy. Typically, the minority stockholder in a close corporation has a substantial percentage of his personal assets invested in the corporation. The stockholder may have anticipated that his salary from his position with the corporation would be his livelihood. Thus, he cannot afford to wait passively. He must liquidate his investment in the close corporation in order to reinvest the funds in income-producing enterprises.

At this point, the true plight of the minority stockholder in a close corporation becomes manifest. He cannot easily reclaim his capital. In a large public corporation, the oppressed or dissident minority stockholder could sell his stock in order to extricate some of his invested capital. By definition, this market is not available for shares in the close corporation. In a partnership, a partner who feels abused by his fellow partners may cause dissolution by his "express will at any time" and recover his share of partnership assets and accumulated profits. If dissolution results in a breach of the partnership articles, the culpable partner will be liable in damages. By contrast, the stockholder in the close corporation or "incorporated partnership" may achieve dissolution and recovery of his share of the enterprise assets only by compliance with the rigorous terms of the applicable chapter of the General Laws. "The dissolution of a corporation which is a creature of the Legislature is primarily a legislative function, and the only authority courts have to deal with this subject is the power conferred upon them by the Legislature." To secure dissolution of the ordinary close corporation subject to G.L. c. 156B, the stockholder, in the absence of corporate deadlock, must own at least fifty per cent of the shares or have the advantage of a favorable provision in the articles of organization. The minority stockholder, by definition lacking fifty per cent of the corporate shares, can never "authorize" the corporation to file a petition for dissolution under G.L. c. 156B, § 99(a), by his own vote. He will seldom have at his disposal the requisite favorable provision in the articles of organization.

Thus, in a close corporation, the minority stockholders may be trapped in a disadvantageous situation. No outsider would knowingly assume the position of the disadvantaged minority. The outsider would have the same difficulties. To cut losses, the minority stockholder may be compelled to deal with the majority. This is the capstone of the majority plan. Majority "freeze-out" schemes which withhold dividends are designed to compel the minority to relinquish stock at inadequate prices. When the minority stockholder agrees to sell out at less than fair value, the majority has won.

Because of the fundamental resemblance of the close corporation to the partnership, the trust and confidence which are essential to this scale and manner of enterprise, and the inherent danger to minority interests in the close corporation, we hold that stockholders[3] in the close corporation owe one another substantially the same fiduciary duty in the operation of the enterprise[4] that partners owe to one another. In our previous decisions, we have defined the standard of duty owed by partners to one another as the "utmost good faith and loyalty." Stockholders in close corporations must discharge their management and stockholder responsibilities in conformity with this strict good faith standard. They may not act out of avarice, expediency or self-interest in derogation of their duty of loyalty to the other stockholders and to the corporation.

We contrast this strict good faith standard with the somewhat less stringent standard of fiduciary duty to which directors and stockholders[5] of all corporations must adhere in the discharge of their corporate responsibilities. Corporate directors are held to a good faith and inherent fairness standard of conduct and are not "permitted to serve two masters whose interests are antagonistic." "Their paramount duty is to the corporation, and their personal pecuniary interests are subordinate to that duty."

The more rigorous duty of partners and participants in a joint adventure, here extended to stockholders in a close corporation, was described by then Chief Judge Cardozo of the New York Court of Appeals in Meinhard v. Salmon: "Joint adventurers, like copartners, owe to one another, while the enterprise continues, the duty of the finest loyalty. Many forms of conduct permissible in a workaday world for those acting at arm's length, are forbidden to those bound by fiduciary ties. Not honesty alone, but the punctilio of an honor the most sensitive, is then the standard of behavior."

Under settled Massachusetts law, a domestic corporation, unless forbidden by statute, has the power to purchase its own shares. An agreement to reacquire stock "is enforceable, subject, at least, to the limitations that the purchase must be made in good faith and without prejudice to creditors and stockholders." When the corporation reacquiring its own stock is a close corporation, the purchase is subject to the additional requirement, in the light of our holding in this opinion, that the stockholders, who, as directors or controlling stockholders, caused the

---

3   We do not limit our holding to majority stockholders. In the close corporation, the minority may do equal damage through unscrupulous and improper "sharp dealings" with an unsuspecting majority.

4   We stress that the strict fiduciary duty which we apply to stockholders in a close corporation in this opinion governs only their actions relative to the operations of the enterprise and the effects of that operation on the rights and investments of other stockholders. We express no opinion as to the standard of duty applicable to transactions in the shares of the close corporation when the corporation is not a party to the transaction.

5   The rule set out in many jurisdictions is: "The majority has the right to control; but when it does so, it occupies a fiduciary relation toward the minority, as much so as the corporation itself or its officers and directors."

corporation to enter into the stock purchase agreement, must have acted with the utmost good faith and loyalty to the other stockholders.

To meet this test, if the stockholder whose shares were purchased was a member of the controlling group, the controlling stockholders must cause the corporation to offer each stockholder an equal opportunity to sell a ratable number of his shares to the corporation at an identical price. Purchase by the corporation confers substantial benefits on the members of the controlling group whose shares were purchased. These benefits are not available to the minority stockholders if the corporation does not also offer them an opportunity to sell their shares. The controlling group may not, consistent with its strict duty to the minority, utilize its control of the corporation to obtain special advantages and disproportionate benefit from its share ownership.

The purchase also distributes corporate assets to the stockholder whose shares were purchased. Unless an equal opportunity is given to all stockholders, the purchase of shares from a member of the controlling group operates as a preferential distribution of assets. In exchange for his shares, he receives a percentage of the contributed capital and accumulated profits of the enterprise. The funds he so receives are available for his personal use. The other stockholders benefit from no such access to corporate property and cannot withdraw their shares of the corporate profits and capital in this manner unless the controlling group acquiesces. Although the purchase price for the controlling stockholder's shares may seem fair to the corporation and other stockholders under the tests established in the prior case law the controlling stockholder whose stock has been purchased has still received a relative advantage over his fellow stockholders, inconsistent with his strict fiduciary duty—an opportunity to turn corporate funds to personal use.

The rule of equal opportunity in stock purchases by close corporations provides equal access to these benefits for all stockholders. We hold that, in any case in which the controlling stockholders have exercised their power over the corporation to deny the minority such equal opportunity, the minority shall be entitled to appropriate relief.

We turn now to the application of the learning set forth above to the facts of the instant case.

The strict standard of duty is plainly applicable to the stockholders in Rodd Electrotype. Rodd Electrotype is a close corporation. Members of the Rodd and Donahue families are the sole owners of the corporation's stock. In actual numbers, the corporation, immediately prior to the corporate purchase of Harry Rodd's shares, had six stockholders. The shares have not been traded, and no market for them seems to exist. Harry Rodd, Charles Rodd, Frederick Rodd, William G. Mason (Phyllis Mason's husband), and the plaintiff's husband all worked for the corporation. The Rodds have retained the paramount management positions.

Through their control of these management positions and of the majority of the Rodd Electrotype stock, the Rodds effectively controlled the corporation. In testing the stock purchase from Harry Rodd against the applicable strict fiduciary standard, we treat the Rodd family as a single controlling group. We reject the defendants' contention that the Rodd family cannot be treated as a unit for this purpose. From the evidence, it is clear that the Rodd family was a close-knit one with a strong community of interest.

Moreover, a strong motive of interest requires that the Rodds be considered a controlling group. When Charles Rodd and Frederick Rodd were called on to represent the corporation in its dealings with their father, they must have known that further advancement within the corporation and benefits would follow their father's retirement and the purchase of his stock.

On its face, then, the purchase of Harry Rodd's shares by the corporation is a breach of the duty which the controlling stockholders, the Rodds, owed to the minority stockholders, the plaintiff and her son. The purchase distributed a portion of the corporate assets to Harry Rodd, a member of the controlling group, in exchange for his shares. The plaintiff and her son were not offered an equal opportunity to sell their shares to the corporation. In fact, their efforts to obtain an equal opportunity were rebuffed by the corporate representative. As the trial judge found, they did not, in any manner, ratify the transaction with Harry Rodd.

Because of the foregoing, we hold that the plaintiff is entitled to relief. Two forms of suitable relief are set out hereinafter. The judge below is to enter an appropriate judgment. The judgment may require Harry Rodd to remit $36,000 with interest at the legal rate from July 15, 1970, to Rodd Electrotype in exchange for forty-five shares of Rodd Electrotype treasury stock. This, in substance, is the specific relief requested in the plaintiff's bill of complaint. Interest is manifestly appropriate. A stockholder, who, in violation of his fiduciary duty to the other stockholders, has obtained assets from his corporation and has had those assets available for his own use, must pay for that use. In the alternative, the judgment may require Rodd Electrotype to purchase all of the plaintiff's shares for $36,000 without interest. In the circumstances of this case, we view this as the equal opportunity which the plaintiff should have received. Harry Rodd's retention of thirty-six shares, which were to be sold and given to his children within a year of the Rodd Electrotype purchase, cannot disguise the fact that the corporation acquired one hundred per cent of that portion of his holdings (forty-five shares) which he did not intend his children to own. The plaintiff is entitled to have one hundred per cent of her forty-five shares similarly purchased.

So ordered.

WILKINS, J. (concurring).

I agree with much of what the Chief Justice says in support of granting relief to the plaintiff. However, I do not join in any implication that the rule concerning a close corporation's purchase of a controlling stockholder's shares applies to all operations of the corporation as they affect minority stockholders. That broader issue, which is apt to arise in connection with salaries and dividend policy, is not involved in this case. The analogy to partnerships may not be a complete one.

BUSINESS ASSOCIATIONS

WILKES V. SPRINGSIDE NURSING HOME, INC.

SUPREME JUDICIAL COURT OF MASSACHUSETTS (HENNESSEY, C.J.)
353 N.E.2D 657 (1976)

On August 5, 1971, the plaintiff (Wilkes) filed a bill in equity for declaratory judgment in the Probate Court for Berkshire County, naming as defendants T. Edward Quinn, Leon L. Riche, the First Agricultural National Bank of Berkshire County and Frank Sutherland MacShane as executors under the will of Lawrence R. Connor, and the Springside Nursing Home, Inc. Wilkes alleged that he, Quinn, Riche and Dr. Hubert A. Pipkin entered into a partnership agreement in 1951, prior to the incorporation of Springside, which agreement was breached in 1967 when Wilkes's salary was terminated and he was voted out as an officer and director of the corporation. Wilkes sought, among other forms of relief, damages in the amount of the salary he would have received had he continued as a director and officer of Springside subsequent to March, 1967.

A judgment was entered dismissing Wilkes's action on the merits. We granted direct appellate review. On appeal, Wilkes argued in the alternative that (1) he should recover damages for breach of the alleged partnership agreement; and (2) he should recover damages because the defendants, as majority stockholders in Springside, breached their fiduciary duty to him as a minority stockholder by their action in February and March, 1967.

We conclude that the master's findings were warranted by the evidence and that his report was properly confirmed. However, we reverse so much of the judgment as dismisses Wilkes's complaint and order the entry of a judgment substantially granting the relief sought by Wilkes under the second alternative set forth above.

In 1951 Wilkes acquired an option to purchase a building and lot located on the corner of Springside Avenue and North Street in Pittsfield, Massachusetts, the building having previously housed the Hillcrest Hospital. Though Wilkes was principally engaged in the roofing and siding business, he had gained a reputation locally for profitable dealings in real estate. Riche, an acquaintance of Wilkes, learned of the option, and interested Quinn (who was known to Wilkes through membership on the draft board in Pittsfield) and Pipkin (an acquaintance of both Wilkes and Riche) in joining Wilkes in his investment. The four men met and decided to participate jointly in the purchase of the building and lot as a real estate investment which, they believed, had good profit potential on resale or rental.

The parties later determined that the property would have its greatest potential for profit if it were operated by them as a nursing home. Wilkes consulted his attorney, who advised him that if the four men were to operate the contemplated nursing home as planned, they would be partners and would be liable for any debts incurred by the partnership and by each other. On the attorney's suggestion, and after consultation among themselves, ownership of the property was vested in Springside, a corporation organized under Massachusetts law.

Each of the four men invested $1,000 and subscribed to ten shares of $100 par value stock in Springside. At the time of incorporation it was understood by all of the parties that each would be a director of Springside and each would participate actively in the management and decision making involved in operating the corporation.[6] It was, further, the understanding and intention of all the parties that, corporate resources permitting, each would receive money from the corporation in equal amounts as long as each assumed an active and ongoing responsibility for carrying a portion of the burdens necessary to operate the business.

The work involved in establishing and operating a nursing home was roughly apportioned, and each of the four men undertook his respective tasks. Initially, Riche was elected president of Springside, Wilkes was elected treasurer, and Quinn was elected clerk. Each of the four was listed in the articles of organization as a director of the corporation.

At some time in 1952, it became apparent that the operational income and cash flow from the business were sufficient to permit the four stockholders to draw money from the corporation on a regular basis. Each of the four original parties initially received $35 a week from the corporation. As time went on the weekly return to each was increased until, in 1955, it totalled $100.

In 1959, after a long illness, Pipkin sold his shares in the corporation to Connor, who was known to Wilkes, Riche and Quinn through past transactions with Springside in his capacity as president of the First Agricultural National Bank of Berkshire County. Connor received a weekly stipend from the corporation equal to that received by Wilkes, Riche and Quinn. He was elected a director of the corporation but never held any other office. He was assigned no specific area of responsibility in the operation of the nursing home but did participate in business discussions and decisions as a director and served additionally as financial adviser to the corporation.

In 1965 the stockholders decided to sell a portion of the corporate property to Quinn who, in addition to being a stockholder in Springside, possessed an interest in another corporation which desired to operate a rest home on the property. Wilkes was successful in prevailing on the other stockholders of Springside to procure a higher sale price for the property than Quinn apparently anticipated paying or desired to pay. After the sale was consummated, the relationship between Quinn and Wilkes began to deteriorate.

The bad blood between Quinn and Wilkes affected the attitudes of both Riche and Connor. As a consequence of the strained relations among the parties, Wilkes, in January of 1967, gave notice of his intention to sell his shares for an amount based on an appraisal of their value. In February of 1967 a directors' meeting was held and the board exercised its right to establish the

---

6   Wilkes testified before the master that, when the corporate officers were elected, all four men "were guaranteed directorships." Riche's understanding of the parties' intentions was that they all wanted to play a part in the management of the corporation and wanted to have some "say" in the risks involved; that, to this end, they all would be directors; and that "unless you (were) a director and officer you could not participate in the decisions of (the) enterprise."

salaries of its officers and employees.[7] A schedule of payments was established whereby Quinn was to receive a substantial weekly increase and Riche and Connor were to continue receiving $100 a week. Wilkes, however, was left off the list of those to whom a salary was to be paid. The directors also set the annual meeting of the stockholders for March, 1967.

At the annual meeting in March, Wilkes was not reelected as a director, nor was he reelected as an officer of the corporation. He was further informed that neither his services nor his presence at the nursing home was wanted by his associates.

The meetings of the directors and stockholders in early 1967, the master found, were used as a vehicle to force Wilkes out of active participation in the management and operation of the corporation and to cut off all corporate payments to him. Though the board of directors had the power to dismiss any officers or employees for misconduct or neglect of duties, there was no indication in the minutes of the board of directors' meeting of February, 1967, that the failure to establish a salary for Wilkes was based on either ground. The severance of Wilkes from the payroll resulted not from misconduct or neglect of duties, but because of the personal desire of Quinn, Riche and Connor to prevent him from continuing to receive money from the corporation. Despite a continuing deterioration in his personal relationship with his associates, Wilkes had consistently endeavored to carry on his responsibilities to the corporation in the same satisfactory manner and with the same degree of competence he had previously shown. Wilkes was at all times willing to carry on his responsibilities and participation if permitted so to do and provided that he receive his weekly stipend.

We turn to Wilkes's claim for damages based on a breach of the fiduciary duty owed to him by the other participants in this venture. In light of the theory underlying this claim, we do not consider it vital to our approach to this case whether the claim is governed by partnership law or the law applicable to business corporations. This is so because, as all the parties agree, Springside was at all times relevant to this action, a close corporation as we have recently defined such an entity in *Donahue v. Rodd Electrotype Co. of New England, Inc.*

In *Donahue*, we held that "stockholders in the close corporation owe one another substantially the same fiduciary duty in the operation of the enterprise that partners owe to one another." As determined in previous decisions of this court, the standard of duty owed by partners to one another is one of "utmost good faith and loyalty." Thus, we concluded in *Donahue*, with regard to "their actions relative to the operations of the enterprise and the effects of that operation on the rights and investments of other stockholders," "(s)tockholders in close corporations must discharge their management and stockholder responsibilities in conformity with this strict good faith standard. They may not act out of avarice, expediency or self-interest in derogation of their duty of loyalty to the other stockholders and to the corporation."

---

7 The by-laws of the corporation provided that the directors, subject to the approval of the stockholders, had the power to fix the salaries of all officers and employees. This power, however, up until February 1967, had not been exercised formally; all payments made to the four participants in the venture had resulted from the informal but unanimous approval of all the parties concerned.

In the *Donahue* case we recognized that one peculiar aspect of close corporations was the opportunity afforded to majority stockholders to oppress, disadvantage or "freeze out" minority stockholders. In *Donahue* itself, for example, the majority refused the minority an equal opportunity to sell a ratable number of shares to the corporation at the same price available to the majority. The net result of this refusal, we said, was that the minority could be forced to "sell out at less than fair value" since there is by definition no ready market for minority stock in a close corporation.

"Freeze outs," however, may be accomplished by the use of other devices. One such device which has proved to be particularly effective in accomplishing the purpose of the majority is to deprive minority stockholders of corporate offices and of employment with the corporation. This "freeze-out" technique has been successful because courts fairly consistently have been disinclined to interfere in those facets of internal corporate operations, such as the selection and retention or dismissal of officers, directors and employees, which essentially involve management decisions subject to the principle of majority control. As one authoritative source has said, "(M)any courts apparently feel that there is a legitimate sphere in which the controlling (directors or) shareholders can act in their own interest even if the minority suffers."

The denial of employment to the minority at the hands of the majority is especially pernicious in some instances. A guaranty of employment with the corporation may have been one of the "basic reason(s) why a minority owner has invested capital in the firm."

The minority stockholder typically depends on his salary as the principal return on his investment, since the "earnings of a close corporation are distributed in major part in salaries, bonuses and retirement benefits."[8] Other noneconomic interests of the minority stockholder are likewise injuriously affected by barring him from corporate office. Such action severely restricts his participation in the management of the enterprise, and he is relegated to enjoying those benefits incident to his status as a stockholder. In sum, by terminating a minority stockholder's employment or by severing him from a position as an officer or director, the majority effectively frustrate the minority stockholder's purposes in entering on the corporate venture and also deny him an equal return on his investment.

The *Donahue* decision acknowledged, as a "natural outgrowth" of the case law of this Commonwealth, a strict obligation on the part of majority stockholders in a close corporation to deal with the minority with the utmost good faith and loyalty. On its face, this strict standard is applicable in the instant case. The distinction between the majority action in *Donahue* and the majority action in this case is more one of form than of substance. Nevertheless, we are concerned that untempered application of the strict good faith standard enunciated in *Donahue* to cases such as the one before us will result in the imposition of limitations on legitimate action by the controlling group in a close corporation which will unduly hamper its effectiveness in managing the corporation in the best interests of all concerned. The majority, concededly, have

---

8 We note here that the master found that Springside never declared or paid a dividend to its stockholders.

certain rights to what has been termed "selfish ownership" in the corporation which should be balanced against the concept of their fiduciary obligation to the minority.

Therefore, when minority stockholders in a close corporation bring suit against the majority alleging a breach of the strict good faith duty owed to them by the majority, we must carefully analyze the action taken by the controlling stockholders in the individual case. It must be asked whether the controlling group can demonstrate a legitimate business purpose for its action. In asking this question, we acknowledge the fact that the controlling group in a close corporation must have some room to maneuver in establishing the business policy of the corporation. It must have a large measure of discretion, for example, in declaring or withholding dividends, deciding whether to merge or consolidate, establishing the salaries of corporate officers, dismissing directors with or without cause, and hiring and firing corporate employees.

When an asserted business purpose for their action is advanced by the majority, however, we think it is open to minority stockholders to demonstrate that the same legitimate objective could have been achieved through an alternative course of action less harmful to the minority's interest. If called on to settle a dispute, our courts must weigh the legitimate business purpose, if any, against the practicability of a less harmful alternative.

Applying this approach to the instant case it is apparent that the majority stockholders in Springside have not shown a legitimate business purpose for severing Wilkes from the payroll of the corporation or for refusing to reelect him as a salaried officer and director. The master's subsidiary findings relating to the purpose of the meetings of the directors and stockholders in February and March, 1967, are supported by the evidence. There was no showing of misconduct on Wilkes's part as a director, officer or employee of the corporation which would lead us to approve the majority action as a legitimate response to the disruptive nature of an undesirable individual bent on injuring or destroying the corporation. On the contrary, it appears that Wilkes had always accomplished his assigned share of the duties competently, and that he had never indicated an unwillingness to continue to do so.

It is an inescapable conclusion from all the evidence that the action of the majority stockholders here was a designed "freeze out" for which no legitimate business purpose has been suggested. Furthermore, we may infer that a design to pressure Wilkes into selling his shares to the corporation at a price below their value well may have been at the heart of the majority's plan.[9]

In the context of this case, several factors bear directly on the duty owed to Wilkes by his associates. At a minimum, the duty of utmost good faith and loyalty would demand that the majority consider that their action was in disregard of a long-standing policy of the stockholders that each would be a director of the corporation and that employment with the corporation would go hand in hand with stock ownership; that Wilkes was one of the four originators of the nursing home venture;

---

9   This inference arises from the fact that Connor, acting on behalf of the three controlling stockholders, offered to purchase Wilkes's shares for a price Connor admittedly would not have accepted for his own shares.

and that Wilkes, like the others, had invested his capital and time for more than fifteen years with the expectation that he would continue to participate in corporate decisions. Most important is the plain fact that the cutting off of Wilkes's salary, together with the fact that the corporation never declared a dividend assured that Wilkes would receive no return at all from the corporation.

So ordered.

NIXON V. BLACKWELL

SUPREME COURT OF DELAWARE (VEASEY, C.J.)
626 A.2D 1366 (1993)

In this action we review a decision of the Court of Chancery holding that the defendant directors of a closely-held corporation breached their fiduciary duties to the plaintiffs by maintaining a discriminatory policy that unfairly favors employee stockholders over plaintiffs. The Vice Chancellor found that the directors treated the plaintiffs unfairly by establishing an employee stock ownership plan and by purchasing key man life insurance policies to provide liquidity for defendants and other corporate employees to enable them to sell their stock while providing no comparable liquidity for minority stockholders. We conclude that the Court of Chancery applied erroneous legal standards. Accordingly, we REVERSE and REMAND.

Plaintiffs are 14 minority stockholders of Class B, non-voting, stock of E.C. Barton & Co. The individual defendants are the members of the board of directors. The Corporation is also a defendant. Plaintiffs collectively own only Class B stock, and own no Class A stock. Their total holdings comprise approximately 25 percent of all the common stock outstanding as of the end of fiscal year 1989.

At all relevant times, the Board consisted of ten individuals who either are currently employed, or were once employed, by the Corporation. At the time this suit was filed, these directors collectively owned approximately 47.5 percent of all the outstanding Class A shares. The remaining Class A shares were held by certain other present and former employees of the Corporation.

In November 1975 the Corporation established an Employee Stock Option Plan designed to hold Class B non-voting stock for the benefit of eligible employees of the Corporation. The ESOP is a tax-qualified profit-sharing plan whereby employees of the Corporation are allocated a share of the assets held by the plan in proportion to their annual compensation, subject to certain vesting requirements. The ESOP is funded by annual cash contributions from the Corporation. Under the plan, terminating and retiring employees are entitled to receive their interest in the ESOP by taking Class B stock or cash in lieu of stock. It appears from the record that most terminating employees and retirees elect to receive cash in lieu of stock. The Corporation commissions an annual appraisal of the Corporation to determine the value of its stock for ESOP purposes. Thus, the ESOP provides employee Class B stockholders with a substantial measure of liquidity not available to non-employee stockholders. The Corporation had the option of repurchasing Class A stock from the employees upon their retirement or death. The estates of the employee stockholders did not have a corresponding right to put the stock to the Corporation.

Defendants contend that the trial court erred in not applying the business judgment rule. Since the defendants benefited from the ESOP and could have benefited from the key man life insurance beyond that which benefited other stockholders generally, the defendants are on both sides of the transaction. For that reason, we agree with the trial court that the entire fairness test applies to this aspect of the case. Accordingly, defendants have the burden of showing the entire fairness of those transactions.

The trial court in this case, however, appears to have adopted the novel legal principle that Class B stockholders had a right to "liquidity" equal to that which the court found to be available to the defendants. It is well established in our jurisprudence that stockholders need not always be treated equally for all purposes. To hold that fairness necessarily requires precise equality is to beg the question:

Many scholars, though few courts, conclude that one aspect of fiduciary duty is the equal treatment of investors. Their argument takes the following form: fiduciary principles require fair conduct; equal treatment is fair conduct; hence, fiduciary principles require equal treatment. The conclusion does not follow. The argument depends on an equivalence between *equal* and *fair* treatment. To say that fiduciary principles require equal treatment is to beg the question whether investors would contract for equal or even equivalent treatment.

This holding of the trial court overlooks the significant facts that the minority stockholders were not: (a) employees of the Corporation; (b) entitled to share in an ESOP; (c) qualified for key man insurance; or (d) protected by specific provisions in the certificate of incorporation, by-laws, or a stockholders' agreement.

There is support in this record for the fact that the ESOP is a corporate benefit and was established, at least in part, to benefit the Corporation. Generally speaking, the creation of ESOPs is a normal corporate practice and is generally thought to benefit the corporation. The same is true generally with respect to key man insurance programs. If such corporate practices were necessarily to require equal treatment for non-employee stockholders, that would be a matter for legislative determination in Delaware. There is no such legislation to that effect. If we were to adopt such a rule, our decision would border on judicial legislation.

Accordingly, we hold that the Vice Chancellor erred as a matter of law in concluding that the liquidity afforded to the employee stockholders by the ESOP and the key man insurance required substantially equal treatment for the non-employee stockholders.

We hold on this record that defendants have met their burden of establishing the entire fairness of their dealings with the non-employee Class B stockholders, and are entitled to judgment. The record is sufficient to conclude that plaintiffs' claim that the defendant directors have maintained a discriminatory policy of favoring Class A employee stockholders over Class B non-employee stockholders is without merit. The directors have followed a consistent policy originally established by Mr. Barton, the founder of the Corporation, whose intent from the formation of the Corporation was to use the Class A stock as the vehicle for the Corporation's continuity through employee management and ownership.

We wish to address one further matter which was raised at oral argument before this Court: Whether there should be any special, judicially-created rules to "protect" minority stockholders of closely-held Delaware corporations.

The case at bar points up the basic dilemma of minority stockholders in receiving fair value for their stock as to which there is no market and no market valuation. It is not difficult to be sympathetic, in the abstract, to a stockholder who finds himself or herself in that position. A stockholder who bargains for stock in a closely-held corporation and who pays for those shares (unlike the plaintiffs in this case who acquired their stock through gift) can make a business judgment whether to buy into such a minority position, and if so on what terms. One could bargain for definitive provisions of self-ordering permitted to a Delaware corporation through the certificate of incorporation or by-laws by reason of the provisions in 8 Del.C. §§ 102, 109, and 141(a). Moreover, in addition to such mechanisms, a stockholder intending to buy into a minority position in a Delaware corporation may enter into definitive stockholder agreements, and such agreements may provide for elaborate earnings tests, buy-out provisions, voting trusts, or other voting agreements.

The tools of good corporate practice are designed to give a purchasing minority stockholder the opportunity to bargain for protection before parting with consideration. It would do violence to normal corporate practice and our corporation law to fashion an ad hoc ruling which would result in a court-imposed stockholder buy-out for which the parties had not contracted.

In 1967, when the Delaware General Corporation Law was significantly revised, a new subchapter XIV entitled "Close Corporations; Special Provisions," became a part of that law for the first time. Subchapter XIV is a narrowly constructed statute which applies only to a corporation which is designated as a "close corporation" in its certificate of incorporation, and which fulfills other requirements, including a limitation to 30 on the number of stockholders, that all classes of stock have to have at least one restriction on transfer, and that there be no "public offering." Accordingly, subchapter XIV applies only to "close corporations," as defined in section 342. "Unless a corporation elects to become a close corporation under this subchapter in the manner prescribed in this subchapter, it shall be subject in all respects to this chapter, except this subchapter." The corporation before the Court in this matter, is not a "close corporation." Therefore it is not governed by the provisions of subchapter XIV.

One cannot read into the situation presented in the case at bar any special relief for the minority stockholders in this closely-held, but not statutory "close corporation" because the provisions of subchapter XIV relating to close corporations and other statutory schemes preempt the field in their respective areas. It would run counter to the spirit of the doctrine of independent legal significance, and would be inappropriate judicial legislation for this Court to fashion a special judicially-created rule for minority investors when the entity does not fall within those statutes, or when there are no negotiated special provisions in the certificate of incorporation, by-laws, or stockholder agreements. The entire fairness test, correctly applied and articulated, is the proper judicial approach.

We hold that the Court of Chancery correctly determined that the entire fairness test is applicable in reviewing the actions of the defendants in establishing and implementing the ESOP and the key man life insurance program. The Vice Chancellor erred, however, as a matter of law in concluding on this record that the defendants had not carried their burden of showing entire fairness. The trial court erroneously undertook to create a novel theory of corporation law and erroneously failed to set forth and apply articulable standards for determining fairness. Moreover, certain findings of fact by the trial court were not the product of an orderly and deductive reasoning process.

In a case such as this where the business judgment rule is not applicable and the entire fairness test is applicable, the imposition of the latter test is not, alone, outcome-determinative. The doctrine of entire fairness does not lend itself to bright line precision or rigid doctrine. Yet it does not necessarily require equality, it cannot be a matter of total subjectivity on the part of the trial court, and it cannot result in a random pattern of ad hoc determinations which could do violence to the stability of our corporation law.

Accordingly, we REVERSE the judgment of the Court of Chancery and REMAND the matter for proceedings not inconsistent with this opinion.

DIRECTOR DUTY OF CARE PART B

LITWIN V. ALLEN

NEW YORK SUPREME COURT (SHIENTAG, J.)
25 N.Y.S.2D 667 (1940)

These actions, consolidated for purposes of trial, are derivative stockholders' actions brought on behalf of persons owning 36 shares of the stock of Guaranty Trust Company of New York out of 900,000 shares outstanding. The defendants are directors and the estates of deceased directors of Guaranty Trust Company of New York and its wholly owned subsidiary, now in liquidation, Guaranty Company of New York, together with members of the banking firm of J. P. Morgan & Co.

The main transactions attacked in this case took place in October, 1930. There had been a crash in the stock market in October, 1929. In April, 1930, there was an upswing in the market. Shortly thereafter there began a slow but steady decline until October, 1930, when there was another severe break. The real significance of what was taking place was, generally speaking, missed at the time, but is plain in the retrospect. Forces were at work which for the most part were unforeseeable. Men who were judging conditions in October, 1930, by what had been the course and the experience of past panics thought that the bottom had been reached and that the worst of the depression was over; that any change would be for the better and that recovery might reasonably be envisaged for the near future. Experience turned out to be fallacious and judgment proved to be erroneous; but that did not become apparent until some time in 1931. In order to judge the transactions complained of, therefore, we must not only hold an inquest on the past but, what is much more difficult, we must attempt to take ourselves back to the time when the events here questioned occurred and try to put ourselves in the position of those who engaged in them.

This transaction involves the participation by the Trust Company or Guaranty Company or both, to the extent of $3,000,000, in a purchase of Missouri Pacific Convertible debentures on October 16, 1930, through the firm of J. P. Morgan & Co. at par, with an option to the seller, Alleghany Corporation to repurchase them at the same price at any time within six months.

In the fall of 1930, the question of putting Alleghany Corporation in funds to the extent of $10,500,000 was first broached. Alleghany had purchased certain terminal properties in Kansas City and St. Joseph, Missouri, and the balance of the purchase price, amounting to slightly in excess of $10,000,000 and interest, had to be paid by October 16. Alleghany needed money to make this payment. Because of the borrowing limitation in Alleghany's charter (which limitation had been reached or exceeded in October 1930) Alleghany was unable to borrow the money. To overcome this borrowing limitation and solely to enable Alleghany to consummate the purchase of the terminal properties, discussions were commenced concerning the means whereby the necessary money could be raised. It is important that this circumstance be constantly kept in mind, in order that the purpose and pattern of the transaction as it did take place be fully understood.

Not being able to make a loan, the way that Alleghany could raise the necessary funds was by sale of some of the securities that it held. Among them was a large block of about $23,500,000 of Missouri Pacific convertible 5 1/2% debentures. These were unsecured and subordinate to other Missouri Pacific bond issues. They were convertible into common stock at the rate of ten shares for each $1,000 bond.

The Van Sweringens suggested that $10,000,000 of these bonds be sold to J. P. Morgan & Co. for cash at par, the latter to give an option to Alleghany to buy them back within six months for the price paid. If the transaction were carried through on that basis, namely, a sale by Alleghany with an option to them to repurchase at the same price, the same purpose would be accomplished, for Alleghany at any rate, as if a loan had been made.

There is no evidence in this case of any improper influence or domination of the directors or officers of the Trust Company or of the Guaranty Company by J. P. Morgan & Co. Moreover, there is no evidence to indicate that any of the defendants' officers or directors acted in bad faith or profited or attempted to profit or gain personally by reason of any phase of this transaction.

If the transaction was a subterfuge for a loan, as the plaintiffs claim, then it clearly was improper because the essential and most elementary requirement of a loan was lacking; no one obligated himself to repay it. I reject this contention. The transaction was not a subterfuge for a loan; it was a substitute for a loan, and should be viewed on that basis. The fact that a transaction, from the point of view of the party receiving the funds, answers substantially all the requirements of a loan, does not make it a loan in law.

Directors are not in the position of trustees of an express trust who, regardless of good faith, are personally liable for losses arising from an infraction of their trust deed. If liability is to be imposed on these directors it should rest on a more solid foundation. I find liability in this transaction because the entire arrangement was so improvident, so risky, so unusual and unnecessary as to be contrary to fundamental conceptions of prudent banking practice. A bank director when appointed or elected takes oath that he will, so far as the duty devolves on him "diligently and honestly administer the affairs of the bank or trust company." The oath merely adds solemnity to the obligation which the law itself imposes. Honesty alone does not suffice; the honesty of the directors in this case is unquestioned. But there must be more than honesty—there must be diligence, and that means care and prudence, as well. This transaction, it has been said, was unusual; it was

directors didn't exercise care, diligence, or prudence in entering this deal unique, yet there is nothing in the record to indicate that the advice of counsel was sought. It is not surprising that a precedent cannot be found dealing with such a situation.

What sound reason is there for a bank, desiring to make an investment, short term or otherwise, to buy securities under an arrangement whereby any appreciation will inure to the benefit of the seller and any loss will be borne by the bank? The five and one-half point differential is no answer. It does not meet the fundamental objection that whatever loss there is would have to be borne by the Bank and whatever gain would go to the customer. There is more here than a question of business judgment as to which men might well differ. The directors plainly failed in this instance to bestow the care which the situation demanded. Unless we are to do away entirely with the doctrine that directors of a bank are liable for negligence in administering its affairs liability should be imposed in connection with this transaction.

This transaction was so improvident, so dangerous, so unusual and so contrary to ordinary prudent banking practice as to subject the directors who approved it to liability in a derivative stockholders' action.

SMITH V. VAN GORKOM

SUPREME COURT OF DELAWARE (HORSEY, J.)
488 A.2D 858 (1985)

This appeal from the Court of Chancery involves a class action brought by shareholders of the defendant Trans Union Corporation against the defendant members of the Board of Directors of Trans Union.

Trans Union was a publicly-traded, diversified holding company, the principal earnings of which were generated by its railcar leasing business. During the period here involved, the Company had a cash flow of hundreds of millions of dollars annually. However, the Company had difficulty in generating sufficient taxable income to offset increasingly large investment tax credits.

Van Gorkom, a certified public accountant and lawyer, had been an officer of Trans Union for 24 years, its Chief Executive Officer for more than 17 years, and Chairman of its Board for 2 years. It is noteworthy in this connection that he was then approaching 65 years of age and mandatory retirement.

Van Gorkom decided to meet with Jay A. Pritzker, a well-known corporate takeover specialist and a social acquaintance. However, rather than approaching Pritzker simply to determine his interest in acquiring Trans Union, Van Gorkom assembled a proposed per share price for sale of the Company and a financing structure by which to accomplish the sale. Van Gorkom did so without consulting either his Board or any members of Senior Management except one: Carl Peterson, Trans Union's Controller.

Having thus chosen the $55 figure, based solely on the availability of a leveraged buy-out, Van Gorkom multiplied the price per share by the number of shares outstanding to reach a total value of the Company of $690 million.

Van Gorkom arranged a meeting with Pritzker at the latter's home on Saturday, September 13, 1980. Van Gorkom prefaced his presentation by stating to Pritzker: "Now as far as you are concerned, I can, I think, show how you can pay a substantial premium over the present stock price and pay off most of the loan in the first five years. If you could pay $55 for this Company, here is a way in which I think it can be financed."

Van Gorkom then reviewed with Pritzker his calculations based upon his proposed price of $55 per share. However, Van Gorkom stated that to be sure that $55 was the best price obtainable, Trans Union should be free to accept any better offer. Pritzker demurred, stating that his organization would serve as a "stalking horse" for an "auction contest" only if Trans Union would permit Pritzker to buy 1,750,000 shares of Trans Union treasury stock at market price which Pritzker could then sell to any higher bidder.

Pritzker instructed his attorney, a merger and acquisition specialist, to begin drafting merger documents. At this point, Pritzker insisted that the Trans Union Board act on his merger proposal within the next three days.

On Friday, September 19, Van Gorkom called a special meeting of the Trans Union Board for noon the following day. He also called a meeting of the Company's Senior Management to convene at 11:00 a.m., prior to the meeting of the Board. No one was told the purpose of the meetings. Van Gorkom did not invite Trans Union's investment banker, Salomon Brothers or its Chicago-based partner, to attend.

Senior Management's reaction to the Pritzker proposal was completely negative. Nevertheless, Van Gorkom proceeded to the Board meeting as scheduled without further delay.

Van Gorkom began the Special Meeting of the Board with a twenty-minute oral presentation. Copies of the proposed Merger Agreement were delivered too late for study before or during the meeting. He reviewed the Company's tax and depreciation problems and the efforts theretofore made to solve them. He discussed his initial meeting with Pritzker and his motivation in arranging that meeting. Van Gorkom did not disclose to the Board, however, the methodology by which he alone had arrived at the $55 figure, or the fact that he first proposed the $55 price in his negotiations with Pritzker.

Van Gorkom outlined the terms of the Pritzker offer as follows: Pritzker would pay $55 in cash for all outstanding shares of Trans Union stock upon completion of which Trans Union would be merged into New T Company, a subsidiary wholly-owned by Pritzker and formed to implement the merger; for a period of 90 days, Trans Union could receive, but could not actively solicit, competing offers; the offer had to be acted on by the next evening, Sunday,

September 21; Trans Union could only furnish to competing bidders published information, and not proprietary information; the offer was subject to Pritzker obtaining the necessary financing by October 10, 1980; if the financing contingency were met or waived by Pritzker, Trans Union was required to sell to Pritzker one million newly-issued shares of Trans Union at $38 per share.

Van Gorkom took the position that putting Trans Union "up for auction" through a 90-day market test would validate a decision by the Board that $55 was a fair price. He told the Board that the "free market will have an opportunity to judge whether $55 is a fair price." Van Gorkom framed the decision before the Board not as whether $55 per share was the highest price that could be obtained, but as whether the $55 price was a fair price that the stockholders should be given the opportunity to accept or reject.

Attorney James Brennan advised the members of the Board that they might be sued if they failed to accept the offer and that a fairness opinion was not required as a matter of law.

CFO Donald Romans told the Board that, in his opinion, $55 was "in the range of a fair price," but "at the beginning of the range."

The Board meeting of September 20 lasted about two hours. Based solely upon Van Gorkom's oral presentation, Romans' oral statement, Brennan's legal advice, and their knowledge of the market history of the Company's stock, the directors approved the proposed Merger Agreement. While the Board now claims to have reserved the right to accept any better offer received after the announcement of the Pritzker agreement, it is undisputed that the Board did not reserve the right to actively solicit alternate offers.

The Merger Agreement was executed by Van Gorkom during the evening of September 20 at a formal social event that he hosted for the opening of the Chicago Lyric Opera. Neither he nor any other director read the agreement prior to its signing and delivery to Pritzker.

Van Gorkom reconvened the Board on October 8 and it authorized the employment of Salomon Brothers, its investment banker, to solicit other offers for Trans Union during the proposed "market test" period.

On January 26, Trans Union's Board met and, after a lengthy meeting, voted to proceed with the Pritzker merger. On February 10, the stockholders of Trans Union approved the Pritzker merger proposal. Of the outstanding shares, 69.9% were voted in favor of the merger; 7.25% were voted against the merger; and 22.85% were not voted.

We turn to the issue of the application of the business judgment rule to the September 20 meeting of the Board.

The Court of Chancery concluded from the evidence that the Board of Directors' approval of the Pritzker merger proposal fell within the protection of the business judgment rule. The Court found that the Board had given sufficient time and attention to the transaction, since the directors had considered the Pritzker proposal on three different occasions, on September 20, and on October 8, 1980 and finally on January 26, 1981. On that basis, the Court reasoned that the Board had acquired, over the four-month period, sufficient information to reach an informed business judgment on the cash-out merger proposal. The Court ruled:

> that given the market value of Trans Union's stock, the business acumen of the members of the board of Trans Union, the substantial premium over market offered by the Pritzkers and the ultimate effect on the merger price provided by the prospect of other bids for the stock in question, that the board of directors of Trans Union did not act recklessly or improvidently in determining on a course of action which they believed to be in the best interest of the stockholders of Trans Union.

Under Delaware law, the business judgment rule is the offspring of the fundamental principle that the business and affairs of a Delaware corporation are managed by or under its board of directors. In carrying out their managerial roles, directors are charged with an unyielding fiduciary duty to the corporation and its shareholders. The business judgment rule exists to protect and promote the full and free exercise of the managerial power granted to Delaware directors. The rule itself "is a presumption that in making a business decision, the directors of a corporation acted on an informed basis, in good faith and in the honest belief that the action taken was in the best interests of the company." Thus, the party attacking a board decision as uninformed must rebut the presumption that its business judgment was an informed one.

The determination of whether a business judgment is an informed one turns on whether the directors have informed themselves "prior to making a business decision, of all material information reasonably available to them."

Under the business judgment rule there is no protection for directors who have made "an unintelligent or unadvised judgment." A director's duty to inform himself in preparation for a decision derives from the fiduciary capacity in which he serves the corporation and its stockholders. Since a director is vested with the responsibility for the management of the affairs of the corporation, he must execute that duty with the recognition that he acts on behalf of others. Such obligation does not tolerate faithlessness or self-dealing. But fulfillment of the fiduciary function requires more than the mere absence of bad faith or fraud. Representation of the financial interests of others imposes on a director an affirmative duty to protect those interests and to proceed with a critical eye in assessing information of the type and under the circumstances present here.

Thus, a director's duty to exercise an informed business judgment is in the nature of a duty of care, as distinguished from a duty of loyalty. Here, there were no allegations of fraud, bad faith, or self-dealing, or proof thereof. Hence, it is presumed that the directors reached their business judgment in good faith, and considerations of motive are irrelevant to the issue before us.

The standard of care applicable to a director's duty of care has also been recently restated by this Court. In *Aronson*, we stated:

While the Delaware cases use a variety of terms to describe the applicable standard of care, our analysis satisfies us that under the business judgment rule director liability is predicated upon concepts of gross negligence.

We again confirm that view. We think the concept of gross negligence is also the proper standard for determining whether a business judgment reached by a board of directors was an informed one.

In the specific context of a proposed merger of domestic corporations, a director has a duty, along with his fellow directors, to act in an informed and deliberate manner in determining whether to approve an agreement of merger before submitting the proposal to the stockholders. Certainly in the merger context, a director may not abdicate that duty by leaving to the shareholders alone the decision to approve or disapprove the agreement.

The issue of whether the directors reached an informed decision to "sell" the Company on September 20, 1980 must be determined only upon the basis of the information then reasonably available to the directors and relevant to their decision to accept the Pritzker merger proposal.

On the record before us, we must conclude that the Board of Directors did not reach an informed business judgment on September 20, 1980 in voting to "sell" the Company for $55 per share pursuant to the Pritzker cash-out merger proposal. Our reasons, in summary, are as follows:

The directors (1) did not adequately inform themselves as to Van Gorkom's role in forcing the "sale" of the Company and in establishing the per share purchase price; (2) were uninformed as to the intrinsic value of the Company; and (3) given these circumstances, at a minimum, were grossly negligent in approving the "sale" of the Company upon two hours' consideration, without prior notice, and without the exigency of a crisis or emergency.

As has been noted, the Board based its September 20 decision to approve the cash-out merger primarily on Van Gorkom's representations. None of the directors, other than Van Gorkom and Chelberg, had any prior knowledge that the purpose of the meeting was to propose a cash-out merger of Trans Union. No members of Senior Management were present, other than Chelberg, Romans and Peterson; and the latter two had only learned of the proposed sale an hour earlier. Both general counsel Moore and former general counsel Browder attended the meeting, but were equally uninformed as to the purpose of the meeting and the documents to be acted upon.

Without any documents before them concerning the proposed transaction, the members of the Board were required to rely entirely upon Van Gorkom's 20-minute oral presentation of the proposal. No written summary of the terms of the merger was presented; the directors were given no documentation to support the adequacy of $55 price per share for sale of the Company; and the Board had before it nothing more than Van Gorkom's statement of his understanding of the substance of an agreement which he admittedly had never read, nor which any member of the Board had ever seen.

207

1. A substantial premium may provide one reason to recommend a merger, but in the absence of other sound valuation information, the fact of a premium alone does not provide an adequate basis upon which to assess the fairness of an offering price. Here, the judgment reached as to the adequacy of the premium was based on a comparison between the historically depressed Trans Union market price and the amount of the Pritzker offer. Using market price as a basis for concluding that the premium adequately reflected the true value of the Company was a clearly faulty, indeed fallacious, premise, as the defendants' own evidence demonstrates.

The record is clear that before September 20, Van Gorkom and other members of Trans Union's Board knew that the market had consistently undervalued the worth of Trans Union's stock, despite steady increases in the Company's operating income in the seven years preceding the merger. The Board related this occurrence in large part to Trans Union's inability to use its tax credits as previously noted. Van Gorkom testified that he did not believe the market price accurately reflected Trans Union's true worth; and several of the directors testified that, as a general rule, most chief executives think that the market undervalues their companies' stock. Yet, on September 20, Trans Union's Board apparently believed that the market stock price accurately reflected the value of the Company for the purpose of determining the adequacy of the premium for its sale.

The parties do not dispute that a publicly-traded stock price is solely a measure of the value of a minority position and, thus, market price represents only the value of a single share. Nevertheless, on September 20, the Board assessed the adequacy of the premium over market, offered by Pritzker, solely by comparing it with Trans Union's current and historical stock price.

Indeed, as of September 20, the Board had no other information on which to base a determination of the intrinsic value of Trans Union as a going concern. As of September 20, the Board had made no evaluation of the Company designed to value the entire enterprise, nor had the Board ever previously considered selling the Company or consenting to a buy-out merger. Thus, the adequacy of a premium is indeterminate unless it is assessed in terms of other competent and sound valuation information that reflects the value of the particular business.

Despite the foregoing facts and circumstances, there was no call by the Board, either on September 20 or thereafter, for any valuation study or documentation of the $55 price per share as a measure of the fair value of the Company in a cash-out context. It is undisputed that the major asset of Trans Union was its cash flow. Yet, at no time did the Board call for a valuation study taking into account that highly significant element of the Company's assets.

The Board rested on Romans' elicited response that the $55 figure was within a "fair price range" within the context of a leveraged buy-out. No director sought any further information from Romans. No director asked him why he put $55 at the bottom of his range. No director asked Romans for any details as to his study, the reason why it had been undertaken or its depth. No director asked to see the study; and no director asked Romans whether Trans Union's finance department could do a fairness study within the remaining 36-hour period available under the Pritzker offer.

The record also establishes that the Board accepted without scrutiny Van Gorkom's representation as to the fairness of the $55 price per share for sale of the Company—a subject that the Board had never previously considered. The Board thereby failed to discover that Van Gorkom had suggested the $55 price to Pritzker and, most crucially, that Van Gorkom had arrived at the $55 figure based on calculations designed solely to determine the feasibility of a leveraged buy-out.[10] No questions were raised either as to the tax implications of a cash-out merger or how the price for the one million share option granted Pritzker was calculated.

We do not say that the Board of Directors was not entitled to give some credence to Van Gorkom's representation that $55 was an adequate or fair price. Under § 141(e), the directors were entitled to rely upon their chairman's opinion of value and adequacy, provided that such opinion was reached on a sound basis. Here, the issue is whether the directors informed themselves as to all information that was reasonably available to them. Had they done so, they would have learned of the source and derivation of the $55 price and could not reasonably have relied thereupon in good faith.

None of the directors, Management or outside, were investment bankers or financial analysts. Yet the Board did not consider recessing the meeting until a later hour that day (or requesting an extension of Pritzker's Sunday evening deadline) to give it time to elicit more information as to the sufficiency of the offer, either from inside Management (in particular Romans) or from Trans Union's own investment banker, Salomon Brothers, whose Chicago specialist in merger and acquisitions was known to the Board and familiar with Trans Union's affairs.

Thus, the record compels the conclusion that on September 20 the Board lacked valuation information adequate to reach an informed business judgment as to the fairness of $55 per share for sale of the Company.

2. This brings us to the post-September 20 "market test" upon which the defendants ultimately rely to confirm the reasonableness of their September 20 decision to accept the Pritzker proposal. In this connection, the directors present a two-part argument: (a) that by making a "market test" of Pritzker's $55 per share offer a condition of their September 20 decision to accept his offer, they cannot be found to have acted impulsively or in an uninformed manner on September 20; and (b) that the adequacy of the $17 premium for sale of the Company was conclusively established over the following 90 to 120 days by the most reliable evidence available—the marketplace. Thus, the defendants impliedly contend that the "market test" eliminated

---

10   As of September 20 the directors did not know: that Van Gorkom had arrived at the $55 figure alone, and subjectively, as the figure to be used by Controller Peterson in creating a feasible structure for a leveraged buy-out by a prospective purchaser; that Van Gorkom had not sought advice, information or assistance from either inside or outside Trans Union directors as to the value of the Company as an entity or the fair price per share for 100% of its stock; that Van Gorkom had not consulted with the Company's investment bankers or other financial analysts; that Van Gorkom had not consulted with or confided in any officer or director of the Company except Chelberg; and that Van Gorkom had deliberately chosen to ignore the advice and opinion of the members of his Senior Management group regarding the adequacy of the $55 price.

the need for the Board to perform any other form of fairness test either on September 20, or thereafter.

Again, the facts of record do not support the defendants' argument. There is no evidence that a public auction was in fact permitted to occur.

Van Gorkom states that the Agreement as submitted incorporated the ingredients for a market test by authorizing Trans Union to receive competing offers over the next 90-day period. However, he concedes that the Agreement barred Trans Union from actively soliciting such offers and from furnishing to interested parties any information about the Company other than that already in the public domain.

3. The directors' unfounded reliance on both the premium and the market test as the basis for accepting the Pritzker proposal undermines the defendants' remaining contention that the Board's collective experience and sophistication was a sufficient basis for finding that it reached its September 20 decision with informed, reasonable deliberation.[11] In *Gimbel v. Signal Companies, Inc.*, the Court of Chancery preliminarily enjoined a board's sale of stock of its wholly-owned subsidiary for an alleged grossly inadequate price. It did so based on a finding that the business judgment rule had been pierced for failure of management to give its board "the opportunity to make a reasonable and reasoned decision." The Court there reached this result notwithstanding the board's sophistication and experience; the company's need of immediate cash; and the board's need to act promptly due to the impact of an energy crisis on the value of the underlying assets being sold—all of its subsidiary's oil and gas interests. The Court found those factors denoting competence to be outweighed by evidence of gross negligence; that management in effect sprang the deal on the board by negotiating the asset sale without informing the board; that the buyer intended to "force a quick decision" by the board; that the board meeting was called on only one-and-a-half days' notice; that its outside directors were not notified of the meeting's purpose; that during a meeting spanning "a couple of hours" a sale of assets worth $480 million was approved; and that the Board failed to obtain a *current* appraisal of its oil and gas interests. The analogy of *Signal* to the case at bar is significant.

The defendants ultimately rely on the stockholder vote of February 10 for exoneration. The defendants contend that the stockholders' "overwhelming" vote approving the Pritzker Merger

---

11   Trans Union's five "inside" directors had backgrounds in law and accounting, 116 years of collective employment by the Company and 68 years of combined experience on its Board. Trans Union's five "outside" directors included four chief executives of major corporations and an economist who was a former dean of a major school of business and chancellor of a university. The "outside" directors had 78 years of combined experience as chief executive officers of major corporations and 50 years of cumulative experience as directors of Trans Union. Thus, defendants argue that the Board was eminently qualified to reach an informed judgment on the proposed "sale" of Trans Union notwithstanding their lack of any advance notice of the proposal, the shortness of their deliberation, and their determination not to consult with their investment banker or to obtain a fairness opinion.

Agreement had the legal effect of curing any failure of the Board to reach an informed business judgment in its approval of the merger.

Applying this standard to the record before us, we find that Trans Union's stockholders were not fully informed of all facts material to their vote on the Pritzker Merger and that the Trial Court's ruling to the contrary is clearly erroneous.

To summarize: we hold that the directors of Trans Union breached their fiduciary duty to their stockholders (1) by their failure to inform themselves of all information reasonably available to them and relevant to their decision to recommend the Pritzker merger; and (2) by their failure to disclose all material information such as a reasonable stockholder would consider important in deciding whether to approve the Pritzker offer.

We hold, therefore, that the Trial Court committed reversible error in applying the business judgment rule in favor of the director defendants in this case.

On remand, the Court of Chancery shall conduct an evidentiary hearing to determine the fair value of the shares represented by the plaintiffs' class, based on the intrinsic value of Trans Union on September 20, 1980. Such valuation shall be made in accordance with *Weinberger v. UOP, Inc.* Thereafter, an award of damages may be entered to the extent that the fair value of Trans Union exceeds $55 per share.

REVERSED and REMANDED for proceedings consistent herewith.

McNEILLY, J. (dissenting).

Trans Union's Board of Directors consisted of ten men, five of whom were "inside" directors and five of whom were "outside" directors. The "inside" directors were Van Gorkom, Chelberg, Bonser, William B. Browder, Senior Vice-President-Law, and Thomas P. O'Boyle, Senior Vice-President-Administration. At the time the merger was proposed the inside five directors had collectively been employed by the Company for 116 years and had 68 years of combined experience as directors. The "outside" directors were A.W. Wallis, William B. Johnson, Joseph B. Lanterman, Graham J. Morgan and Robert W. Reneker. With the exception of Wallis, these were all chief executive officers of Chicago based corporations that were at least as large as Trans Union. The five "outside" directors had 78 years of combined experience as chief executive officers, and 53 years cumulative service as Trans Union directors.

The inside directors wear their badge of expertise in the corporate affairs of Trans Union on their sleeves. But what about the outsiders? Dr. Wallis is or was an economist and math statistician, a professor of economics at Yale University, dean of the graduate school of business at the University of Chicago, and Chancellor of the University of Rochester. Dr. Wallis had been on the Board of Trans Union since 1962. He also was on the Board of Bausch & Lomb, Kodak, Metropolitan Life Insurance Company, Standard Oil and others.

William B. Johnson is a University of Pennsylvania law graduate, President of Railway Express until 1966, Chairman and Chief Executive of I.C. Industries Holding Company, and member of Trans Union's Board since 1968.

Joseph Lanterman, a Certified Public Accountant, is or was President and Chief Executive of American Steel, on the Board of International Harvester, Peoples Energy, Illinois Bell Telephone, Harris Bank and Trust Company, Kemper Insurance Company and a director of Trans Union for four years.

Graham Morgan is a chemist, was Chairman and Chief Executive Officer of U.S. Gypsum, and in the 17 and 18 years prior to the Trans Union transaction had been involved in 31 or 32 corporate takeovers.

Robert Reneker attended University of Chicago and Harvard Business Schools. He was President and Chief Executive of Swift and Company, director of Trans Union since 1971, and member of the Boards of seven other corporations including U.S. Gypsum and the Chicago Tribune.

Directors of this caliber are not ordinarily taken in by a "fast shuffle". I submit they were not taken into this multi-million dollar corporate transaction without being fully informed and aware of the state of the art as it pertained to the entire corporate panoroma of Trans Union. True, even directors such as these, with their business acumen, interest and expertise, can go astray. I do not believe that to be the case here. These men knew Trans Union like the back of their hands and were more than well qualified to make on the spot informed business judgments concerning the affairs of Trans Union including a 100% sale of the corporation. Lest we forget, the corporate world of then and now operates on what is so aptly referred to as "the fast track". These men were at the time an integral part of that world, all professional business men, not intellectual figureheads.

At the time of the September 20, 1980 meeting the Board was acutely aware of Trans Union and its prospects. The problems created by accumulated investment tax credits and accelerated depreciation were discussed repeatedly at Board meetings, and all of the directors understood the problem thoroughly. Moreover, at the July, 1980 Board meeting the directors had reviewed Trans Union's newly prepared five-year forecast, and at the August, 1980 meeting Van Gorkom presented the results of a comprehensive study of Trans Union made by The Boston Consulting Group. This study was prepared over an 18 month period and consisted of a detailed analysis of all Trans Union subsidiaries, including competitiveness, profitability, cash throw-off, cash consumption, technical competence and future prospects for contribution to Trans Union's combined net income.

Following the October 8 board meeting of Trans Union, the investment banking firm of Salomon Brothers was retained by the corporation to search for better offers than that of the Pritzkers, Salomon Brothers being charged with the responsibility of doing "whatever possible to see if there is a superior bid in the marketplace over a bid that is on the table for Trans Union".

In undertaking such project, it was agreed that Salomon Brothers would be paid the amount of $500,000 to cover its expenses as well as a fee equal to ⅜ths of 1% of the aggregate fair market value of the consideration to be received by the company in the case of a merger or the like, which meant that in the event Salomon Brothers should find a buyer willing to pay a price of $56.00 a share instead of $55.00, such firm would receive a fee of roughly $2,650,000 plus disbursements.

I have no quarrel with the majority's analysis of the business judgment rule. It is the application of that rule to these facts which is wrong. An overview of the entire record, rather than the limited view of bits and pieces which the majority has exploded like popcorn, convinces me that the directors made an informed business judgment which was buttressed by their test of the market.

These directors were acutely aware of the historical problems facing Trans Union which were caused by the tax laws. They had discussed these problems *ad nauseam*. In fact, within two months of the September 20 meeting the board had reviewed and discussed an outside study of the company done by The Boston Consulting Group and an internal five year forecast prepared by management.

DELAWARE GENERAL CORPORATION LAW

SECTION 102(b). CONTENTS OF CERTIFICATE OF INCORPORATION

In addition to the matters required to be set forth in the certificate of incorporation by subsection (a) of this section, the certificate of incorporation may also contain any or all of the following matters:

(7) A provision eliminating or limiting the personal liability of a director to the corporation or its stockholders for monetary damages for breach of fiduciary duty as a director, provided that such provision shall not eliminate or limit the liability of a director: (i) For any breach of the director's duty of loyalty to the corporation or its stockholders; (ii) for acts or omissions not in good faith or which involve intentional misconduct or a knowing violation of law; (iii) under § 174 of this title; or (iv) for any transaction from which the director derived an improper personal benefit. No such provision shall eliminate or limit the liability of a director for any act or omission occurring prior to the date when such provision becomes effective. All references in this paragraph to a director shall also be deemed to refer to such other person or persons, if any, who, pursuant to a provision of the certificate of incorporation in accordance with § 141(a) of this title, exercise or perform any of the powers or duties otherwise conferred or imposed upon the board of directors by this title.

[handwritten margin note: corps. may waive their directors' liability for breaching the duty of care, but not the duty of loyalty or good faith]

IN RE CAREMARK INTERNATIONAL INC. DERIVATIVE LITIGATION

COURT OF CHANCERY OF DELAWARE (ALLEN, J.)
698 A.2D 959 (1996)

[handwritten margin note: Shareholders suing board for breaching fiduciary duty of care]

Pending is a motion pursuant to Chancery Rule 23.1 to approve as fair and reasonable a proposed settlement of a consolidated derivative action on behalf of Caremark International, Inc. The suit involves claims that the members of Caremark's board of directors breached their fiduciary duty of care to Caremark in connection with alleged violations by Caremark employees of federal and state laws and regulations applicable to health care providers. As a result of the alleged violations, Caremark was subject to an extensive four year investigation by the United States Department of Health and Human Services and the Department of Justice. In 1994 Caremark was charged in an indictment with multiple felonies. It thereafter entered into a number of agreements with the Department of Justice and others. Those agreements included a plea agreement in which Caremark pleaded guilty to a single felony of mail fraud and agreed to pay civil and criminal fines. Subsequently, Caremark agreed to make reimbursements to various private and public parties. In all, the payments that Caremark has been required to make total approximately $250 million.

This suit was filed in 1994, purporting to seek on behalf of the company recovery of these losses from the individual defendants who constitute the board of directors of Caremark. The parties now propose that it be settled and, after notice to Caremark shareholders, a hearing on the fairness of the proposal was held on August 16, 1996.

The ultimate issue then is whether the proposed settlement appears to be fair to the corporation and its absent shareholders.

Legally, evaluation of the central claim made entails consideration of the legal standard governing a board of directors' obligation to supervise or monitor corporate performance. For the reasons set forth below I conclude, in light of the discovery record, that there is a very low probability that it would be determined that the directors of Caremark breached any duty to appropriately monitor and supervise the enterprise. Indeed the record tends to show an active consideration by Caremark management and its Board of the Caremark structures and programs that ultimately led to the company's indictment and to the large financial losses incurred in the settlement of those claims. It does not tend to show knowing or intentional violation of law. Neither the fact that the Board, although advised by lawyers and accountants, did not accurately predict the severe consequences to the company that would ultimately follow from the deployment by the company of the strategies and practices that ultimately led to this liability, nor the scale of the liability, gives rise to an inference of breach of any duty imposed by corporation law upon the directors of Caremark.

Caremark, a Delaware corporation with its headquarters in Northbrook, Illinois, was created in November 1992 when it was spun-off from Baxter International, Inc. and became a publicly held company listed on the New York Stock Exchange. The business practices that created the problem pre-dated the spin-off. During the relevant period Caremark was involved in two main health care business segments, providing patient care and managed care services.

A substantial part of the revenues generated by Caremark's businesses is derived from third party payments, insurers, and Medicare and Medicaid reimbursement programs. The latter source of payments are subject to the terms of the Anti-Referral Payments Law which prohibits health care providers from paying any form of remuneration to induce the referral of Medicare or Medicaid patients. From its inception, Caremark entered into a variety of agreements with hospitals, physicians, and health care providers for advice and services, as well as distribution agreements with drug manufacturers, as had its predecessor prior to 1992. Specifically, Caremark did have a practice of entering into contracts for services (*e.g.*, consultation agreements and research grants) with physicians at least some of whom prescribed or recommended services or products that Caremark provided to Medicare recipients and other patients. Such contracts were not prohibited by the ARPL but they obviously raised a possibility of unlawful "kickbacks."

As early as 1989, Caremark's predecessor issued an internal "Guide to Contractual Relationships" to govern its employees in entering into contracts with physicians and hospitals. The Guide tended to be reviewed annually by lawyers and updated. Each version of the Guide stated as Caremark's and its predecessor's policy that no payments would be made in exchange for or to induce patient referrals. But what one might deem a prohibited *quid pro quo* was not always clear. Due to a scarcity of court decisions interpreting the ARPL, however, Caremark repeatedly publicly stated that there was uncertainty concerning Caremark's interpretation of the law.

In August 1991, the HHS Office of the Inspector General initiated an investigation of Caremark's predecessor. Caremark's predecessor was served with a subpoena requiring the production of documents, including contracts between Caremark's predecessor and physicians (Quality Service Agreements). Under the QSAs, Caremark's predecessor appears to have paid physicians fees for monitoring patients under Caremark's predecessor's care, including Medicare and Medicaid recipients. Sometimes apparently those monitoring patients were referring physicians, which raised ARPL concerns.

During the relevant period, Caremark had approximately 7,000 employees and ninety branch operations. It had a decentralized management structure. By May 1991, however, Caremark asserts that it had begun making attempts to centralize its management structure in order to increase supervision over its branch operations.

The first action taken by management, as a result of the initiation of the OIG investigation, was an announcement that as of October 1, 1991, Caremark's predecessor would no longer pay management fees to physicians for services to Medicare and Medicaid patients. Despite this decision, Caremark asserts that its management, pursuant to advice, did not believe that such payments were illegal under the existing laws and regulations.

During this period, Caremark's Board took several additional steps consistent with an effort to assure compliance with company policies concerning the ARPL and the contractual forms in the Guide. In April 1992, Caremark published a fourth revised version of its Guide apparently designed to assure that its agreements either complied with the ARPL and regulations or excluded Medicare and Medicaid patients altogether. In addition, in September 1992, Caremark instituted a policy requiring its regional officers, Zone Presidents, to approve each contractual relationship entered into by Caremark with a physician.

Although there is evidence that inside and outside counsel had advised Caremark's directors that their contracts were in accord with the law, Caremark recognized that some uncertainty respecting the correct interpretation of the law existed. In its 1992 annual report, Caremark disclosed the ongoing government investigations, acknowledged that if penalties were imposed on the company they could have a material adverse effect on Caremark's business, and stated that no assurance could be given that its interpretation of the ARPL would prevail if challenged.

Throughout the period of the government investigations, Caremark had an internal audit plan designed to assure compliance with business and ethics policies. In addition, Caremark employed Price Waterhouse as its outside auditor. On February 8, 1993, the Ethics Committee of Caremark's Board received and reviewed an outside auditors report by Price Waterhouse which concluded that there were no material weaknesses in Caremark's control structure. Despite the positive findings of Price Waterhouse, however, on April 20, 1993, the Audit & Ethics Committee adopted a new internal audit charter requiring a comprehensive review of compliance policies and the compilation of an employee ethics handbook concerning such policies.

The Board appears to have been informed about this project and other efforts to assure compliance with the law. For example, Caremark's management reported to the Board that Caremark's sales force was receiving an ongoing education regarding the ARPL and the proper use of Caremark's form contracts which had been approved by in-house counsel. On July 27, 1993, the new ethics manual, expressly prohibiting payments in exchange for referrals and requiring employees to report all illegal conduct to a toll free confidential ethics hotline, was approved and allegedly disseminated.[12] The record suggests that Caremark continued these policies in subsequent years, causing employees to be given revised versions of the ethics manual and requiring them to participate in training sessions concerning compliance with the law.

---

12   Prior to the distribution of the new ethics manual, on March 12, 1993, Caremark's president had sent a letter to all senior, district, and branch managers restating Caremark's policies that no physician be paid for referrals, that the standard contract forms in the Guide were not to be modified, and that deviation from such policies would result in the immediate termination of employment.

On August 4, 1994, a federal grand jury in Minnesota issued a 47 page indictment charging Caremark, two of its officers (not the firm's chief officer), an individual who had been a sales employee of Genentech, Inc., and David R. Brown, a physician practicing in Minneapolis, with violating the ARPL over a lengthy period. According to the indictment, over $1.1 million had been paid to Brown to induce him to distribute Protropin, a human growth hormone drug marketed by Caremark.

In reaction to the Minnesota indictment and the subsequent filing of this and other derivative actions in 1994, the Board met and was informed by management that the investigation had resulted in an indictment; Caremark denied any wrongdoing relating to the indictment and believed that the OIG investigation would have a favorable outcome. Management reiterated the grounds for its view that the contracts were in compliance with law.

Subsequently, five stockholder derivative actions were filed in this court and consolidated into this action.

On September 21, 1994, a federal grand jury in Columbus, Ohio issued another indictment alleging that an Ohio physician had defrauded the Medicare program by requesting and receiving $134,600 in exchange for referrals of patients whose medical costs were in part reimbursed by Medicare in violation of the ARPL. Although unidentified at that time, Caremark was the health care provider who allegedly made such payments.

The complaint charges the director defendants with breach of their duty of attention or care in connection with the on-going operation of the corporation's business. The claim is that the directors allowed a situation to develop and continue which exposed the corporation to enormous legal liability and that in so doing they violated a duty to be active monitors of corporate performance. The complaint thus does not charge either director self-dealing or the more difficult loyalty-type problems arising from cases of suspect director motivation, such as entrenchment or sale of control contexts. The theory here advanced is possibly the most difficult theory in corporation law upon which a plaintiff might hope to win a judgment.

Director liability for a breach of the duty to exercise appropriate attention may, in theory, arise in two distinct contexts. First, such liability may be said to follow *from a board decision* that results in a loss because that decision was ill advised or "negligent". Second, liability to the corporation for a loss may be said to arise from an *unconsidered failure of the board to act* in circumstances in which due attention would, arguably, have prevented the loss. The first class of cases will typically be subject to review under the director-protective business judgment rule, assuming the decision made was the product of *a process* that was *either* deliberately considered in good faith or was otherwise rational. What should be understood, but may not widely be understood by courts or commentators who are not often required to face such questions, is that compliance with a director's duty of care can never appropriately be judicially determined by reference to *the content of the board decision* that leads to a corporate loss, apart from consideration of the good faith *or* rationality of the process employed. That is, whether a judge or jury *directors just need to act in good faith even if they make substantively bad decisions*

considering the matter after the fact, believes a decision substantively wrong, or degrees of wrong extending through "stupid" to "egregious" or "irrational", provides no ground for director liability, so long as the court determines that the process employed was either rational or employed in *a good faith* effort to advance corporate interests. To employ a different rule—one that permitted an "objective" evaluation of the decision—would expose directors to substantive second guessing by ill-equipped judges or juries, which would, in the long-run, be injurious to investor interests. Thus, the business judgment rule is process oriented and informed by a deep respect for all *good faith* board decisions.

Indeed, one wonders on what moral basis might shareholders attack a *good faith* business decision of a director as "unreasonable" or "irrational". Where a director *in fact exercises a good faith effort to be informed and to exercise appropriate judgment,* he or she should be deemed to satisfy fully the duty of attention. If the shareholders thought themselves entitled to some other quality of judgment than such a director produces in the good faith exercise of the powers of office, then the shareholders should have elected other directors.

The second class of cases in which director liability for inattention is theoretically possible entail circumstances in which a loss eventuates not from a decision but, from unconsidered inaction. Most of the decisions that a corporation, acting through its human agents, makes are, of course, not the subject of director attention. Legally, the board itself will be required only to authorize the most significant corporate acts or transactions: mergers, changes in capital structure, fundamental changes in business, appointment and compensation of the CEO, etc. As the facts of this case graphically demonstrate, ordinary business decisions that are made by officers and employees deeper in the interior of the organization can, however, vitally affect the welfare of the corporation and its ability to achieve its various strategic and financial goals. If this case did not prove the point itself, recent business history would. Recall for example the displacement of senior management and much of the board of Salomon, Inc.; the replacement of senior management of Kidder, Peabody following the discovery of large trading losses resulting from phantom trades by a highly compensated trader; or the extensive financial loss and reputational injury suffered by Prudential Insurance as a result of its junior officers misrepresentations in connection with the distribution of limited partnership interests. Financial and organizational disasters such as these raise the question, what is the board's responsibility with respect to the organization and monitoring of the enterprise to assure that the corporation functions within the law to achieve its purposes?

Modernly this question has been given special importance by an increasing tendency, especially under federal law, to employ the criminal law to assure corporate compliance with external legal requirements, including environmental, financial, employee and product safety as well as assorted other health and safety regulations. In 1991, pursuant to the Sentencing Reform Act of 1984, the United States Sentencing Commission adopted Organizational Sentencing Guidelines which impact importantly on the prospective effect these criminal sanctions might

218

have on business corporations. The Guidelines set forth a uniform sentencing structure for organizations to be sentenced for violation of federal criminal statutes and provide for penalties that equal or often massively exceed those previously imposed on corporations. The Guidelines offer powerful incentives for corporations today to have in place compliance programs to detect violations of law, promptly to report violations to appropriate public officials when discovered, and to take prompt, voluntary remedial efforts.

It would, in my opinion, be a mistake to conclude that corporate boards may satisfy their obligation to be reasonably informed concerning the corporation, without assuring themselves that information and reporting systems exist in the organization that are reasonably designed to provide to senior management and to the board itself timely, accurate information sufficient to allow management and the board, each within its scope, to reach informed judgments concerning both the corporation's compliance with law and its business performance.

Obviously the level of detail that is appropriate for such an information system is a question of business judgment. And obviously too, no rationally designed information and reporting system will remove the possibility that the corporation will violate laws or regulations, or that senior officers or directors may nevertheless sometimes be misled or otherwise fail reasonably to detect acts material to the corporation's compliance with the law. But it is important that the board exercise a good faith judgment that the corporation's information and reporting system is in concept and design adequate to assure the board that appropriate information will come to its attention in a timely manner as a matter of ordinary operations, so that it may satisfy its responsibility.

Thus, I am of the view that a director's obligation includes a duty to attempt in good faith to assure that a corporate information and reporting system, which the board concludes is adequate, exists, and that failure to do so under some circumstances may, in theory at least, render a director liable for losses caused by non-compliance with applicable legal standards. I now turn to an analysis of the claims asserted with this concept of the directors duty of care, as a duty satisfied in part by assurance of adequate information flows to the board, in mind.

In order to show that the Caremark directors breached their duty of care by failing adequately to control Caremark's employees, plaintiffs would have to show either (1) that the directors knew or (2) should have known that violations of law were occurring and, in either event, (3) that the directors took no steps in a good faith effort to prevent or remedy that situation, and (4) that such failure proximately resulted in the losses complained of, although under *Cede & Co. v. Technicolor, Inc.* this last element may be thought to constitute an affirmative defense.

Concerning the possibility that the Caremark directors knew of violations of law, none of the documents submitted for review, nor any of the deposition transcripts appear to provide evidence of it. Certainly the Board understood that the company had entered into a variety of contracts with physicians, researchers, and health care providers and it was understood that some of these contracts were with persons who had prescribed treatments that Caremark participated

219

in providing. The board was informed that the company's reimbursement for patient care was frequently from government funded sources and that such services were subject to the ARPL. But the Board appears to have been informed by experts that the company's practices while contestable, were lawful. There is no evidence that reliance on such reports was not reasonable. Thus, this case presents no occasion to apply a principle to the effect that knowingly causing the corporation to violate a criminal statute constitutes a breach of a director's fiduciary duty. It is not clear that the Board knew the detail found, for example, in the indictments arising from the Company's payments. But, of course, the duty to act in good faith to be informed cannot be thought to require directors to possess detailed information about all aspects of the operation of the enterprise. Such a requirement would simply be inconsistent with the scale and scope of efficient organization size in this technological age.

Since it does appear that the Board was to some extent unaware of the activities that led to liability, I turn to a consideration of the other potential avenue to director liability that the pleadings take: director inattention or "negligence". Generally where a claim of directorial liability for corporate loss is predicated upon ignorance of liability creating activities within the corporation, as in *Graham* or in this case, in my opinion only a sustained or systematic failure of the board to exercise oversight—such as an utter failure to attempt to assure a reasonable information and reporting system exists—will establish the lack of good faith that is a necessary condition to liability. Such a test of liability—lack of good faith as evidenced by sustained or systematic failure of a director to exercise reasonable oversight—is quite high. But, a demanding test of liability in the oversight context is probably beneficial to corporate shareholders as a class, as it is in the board decision context, since it makes board service by qualified persons more likely, while continuing to act as a stimulus to *good faith performance of duty* by such directors.

Here the record supplies essentially no evidence that the director defendants were guilty of a sustained failure to exercise their oversight function. To the contrary, insofar as I am able to tell on this record, the corporation's information systems appear to have represented a good faith attempt to be informed of relevant facts. If the directors did not know the specifics of the activities that lead to the indictments, they cannot be faulted.

The liability that eventuated in this instance was huge. But the fact that it resulted from a violation of criminal law alone does not create a breach of fiduciary duty by directors. The record at this stage does not support the conclusion that the defendants either lacked good faith in the exercise of their monitoring responsibilities or conscientiously permitted a known violation of law by the corporation to occur. The claims asserted against them must be viewed at this stage as extremely weak.

The proposed settlement provides very modest benefits. Under the settlement agreement, plaintiffs have been given express assurances that Caremark will have a more centralized, active supervisory system in the future. Specifically, the settlement mandates duties to be performed by the newly named Compliance and Ethics Committee on an ongoing basis and increases the responsibility for monitoring compliance with the law at the lower levels of management. In adopting the resolutions required under the settlement, Caremark has further clarified its policies concerning the prohibition of providing remuneration for referrals. These appear to be positive consequences of the settlement of the claims brought by the plaintiffs, even if they are not highly significant. Nonetheless, given the weakness of the plaintiffs' claims the proposed settlement appears to be an adequate, reasonable, and beneficial outcome for all of the parties. Thus, the proposed settlement will be approved.

[handwritten: Shareholders didn't lose alot, weren't gaining alot, so it's fine]

CINERAMA, INC. V. TECHNICOLOR, INC.

SUPREME COURT OF DELAWARE (HOLLAND, J.)
663 A.2D 1156 (1993)

Today's opinion completes a trilogy of decisions by this Court. The case involves claims by the plaintiff-appellant, Cinerama, Inc., against the directors of Technicolor, Inc. and others. The issues presented relate to the sale of Technicolor to MacAndrews & Forbes Group, Inc. in a two-stage tender offer/merger transaction for $23 per share in cash. Cinerama was at all times the owner of 201,200 shares of the common stock of Technicolor, representing 4.405 percent of the total shares outstanding.

In January 1986, Cinerama filed a personal liability action in the Court of Chancery against Technicolor, seven of the nine members of the Technicolor board of directors at the time of the merger, MAF, Macanfor and Ronald O. Perelman. Perelman was MAF's board chairman and controlling shareholder. Cinerama's personal liability action alleged fraud, breach of fiduciary duty and unfair dealing. It included a claim for rescissory damages and other relief.

The business judgment rule "operates as *both a procedural guide* for litigants *and a substantive rule of law.*" As a *procedural* guide the business judgment presumption is a *rule of evidence* that places the initial burden of proof on the plaintiff. In *Cede II*, this Court described the rule's evidentiary, or procedural, operation as follows:

[handwritten: Business judgment rule gives procedural & substantive guidance]

> If a shareholder plaintiff fails to meet this evidentiary burden, the business judgment rule attaches to protect corporate officers and directors and the decisions they make, and our courts will not second-guess these business judgments. If the rule is rebutted, the burden shifts to the defendant directors, the proponents of the challenged transaction, to prove to the trier of fact the "entire fairness" of the transaction to the shareholder plaintiff.

[handwritten: Procedural = initial BoP on Π]

[handwritten: 221 Shareholder]

Burden shifting does not create *per se* liability on the part of the directors. Rather, it "is a procedure by which Delaware courts of equity determine under what standard of review director liability is to be judged." In remanding this case for review under the entire fairness standard, this Court expressly acknowledged that its holding in *Cede II* did *not* establish liability.

Where, as in this case, the presumption of the business judgment rule has been rebutted, the board of directors' action is examined under the entire fairness standard. This Court has described the dual aspects of entire fairness, as follows:

> The concept of fairness has two basic aspects: fair dealing and fair price. The former embraces questions of when the transaction was timed, how it was initiated, structured, negotiated, disclosed to the directors, and how the approvals of the directors and the stockholders were obtained. The latter aspect of fairness relates to the economic and financial considerations of the proposed merger, including all relevant factors: assets, market value, earnings, future prospects, and any other elements that affect the intrinsic or inherent value of a company's stock. However, the test for fairness is not a bifurcated one as between fair dealing and price. All aspects of the issue must be examined as a whole since the question is one of entire fairness.

Thus, the entire fairness standard requires the board of directors to establish "to the *court's* satisfaction that the transaction was the product of both fair dealing *and* fair price." In this case, because the contested action is the sale of a company, the "fair price" aspect of an entire fairness analysis requires the board of directors to demonstrate "that the price offered was the highest value reasonably available under the circumstances."

Because the decision that the *procedural* presumption of the business judgment rule has been rebutted does not establish *substantive* liability under the entire fairness standard, such a ruling does not necessarily present an insurmountable obstacle for a board of directors to overcome. Thus, an initial judicial determination that a given breach of a board's fiduciary duties has rebutted the presumption of the business judgment rule does not preclude a subsequent judicial determination that the board action was entirely fair, and is, therefore, not outcome-determinative *per se*. To avoid substantive liability, *notwithstanding* the quantum of adverse evidence that has defeated the business judgment rule's protective procedural presumption, the board will have to demonstrate entire fairness by presenting evidence of the cumulative manner by which it otherwise discharged all of its fiduciary duties.

222

DIRECTOR DUTY OF LOYALTY PART C

LEWIS GENERAL TIRES, INC. V. LEWIS

UNITED STATES COURT OF APPEALS, SECOND CIRCUIT (KEARSE, J.)
629 F.2D 764 (1980)

This case arises out of an intra-family dispute over the management of two closely-held affiliated corporations. Plaintiff Donald E. Lewis, a shareholder of S.L. & E., Inc., appeals from judgments entered against him in the United States District Court for the Western District of New York, Harold P. Burke, Judge, after a bench trial of his derivative claim against directors of SLE, and of a claim asserted against him by the other corporation, Lewis General Tires, Inc., which intervened in the suit. The defendants Alan E. Lewis, Leon E. Lewis, and Richard E. Lewis, are the brothers of Donald; they were, at pertinent times herein, directors of SLE and officers, directors and shareholders of LGT. Donald charged that his brothers had wasted the assets of SLE by causing SLE to lease business premises to LGT from 1966 to 1972 at an unreasonably low rental. LGT was permitted to intervene in the action, and filed a complaint seeking specific performance of an agreement by Donald to sell his SLE stock to LGT in 1972. The district court held that Donald had failed to prove waste by the defendant directors, and entered judgment in their favor. The court also awarded attorneys' fees to the defendant directors and to SLE, and granted LGT specific performance of Donald's agreement to sell his SLE stock.

On appeal, Donald argues that the district court improperly allocated to him the burden of proving his claims of waste, and that since defendants failed to prove that the transactions in question were fair and reasonable, he was entitled to judgment. Donald also argues that the awards of attorneys' fees were improper. We agree with each of these contentions, and therefore reverse and remand.

For many years Leon Lewis, Sr., the father of Donald and the defendant directors, was the principal shareholder of SLE and LGT. LGT, formed in 1933, operated a tire dealership in Rochester, New York. SLE, formed in 1943, owned the land and complex of buildings at 260 East Avenue in Rochester. This property was SLE's only significant asset. Prior to 1956 LGT occupied SLE's premises without benefit of a lease; the rent paid was initially $200 per month, and had increased over the years to $800 per month by 1956, when additional parcels were added. On February 28, 1956, SLE granted LGT a 10-year lease on the newly expanded property, for a rent of $1200 per month, or $14,400 per year. Under the terms of the lease, SLE was responsible for payment of real estate taxes on the Property, while all other current expenses were to be borne by the tenant, LGT.

In 1962, Leon Lewis, Sr., transferred his SLE stock, 90 shares in all, to his six children (defendants Richard, Alan and Leon, Jr., plaintiff Donald, and two daughters, Margaret and Carol), giving 15 shares to each. At that time Richard, Alan and Leon, Jr., were already shareholders, officers and directors of LGT. Contemporaneously with their receipt of SLE stock, all six of the children entered into a "shareholders' agreement" with LGT, under which each child who was not a shareholder of LGT on June 1, 1972 would be required to sell his or her SLE shares to LGT, within 30 days of that date, at a price equal to the book value of the SLE stock as of June 1, 1972.

LGT's lease on the SLE property expired on February 28, 1966. At that time the directors of SLE were Richard, Alan, Leon, Jr., Leon, Sr., and Henry Etsberger; these five were also the directors of LGT. In 1966 Alan owned 44% of LGT, Richard owned 30%, Leon, Jr., owned 19%, and Leon, Sr., owned 7%. From 1967 to 1972 Richard owned 61% of LGT and Leon, Jr., owned the remaining 39%. When the lease expired in 1966, no new lease was entered into. LGT nonetheless continued to occupy the property and to pay SLE at the old rate, $14,400 per year. According to the defendants' testimony at trial, there was never any thought or discussion among the SLE directors of entering into a new lease or of increasing the rent. Richard testified: "We never gave consideration to a new lease." From all that appears, the defendant directors viewed SLE as existing purely for the benefit of LGT. Richard testified, for example, that although real estate taxes rose sharply during the period 1966–1971, from approximately $7,800 to more than $11,000, to be paid by SLE out of its constant $14,400 rental income, raising the rent was never mentioned. He testified that SLE was "only a shell to protect the operating company [LGT]." When this suit was commenced there had not been a formal meeting of either the shareholders or the directors of SLE since 1962. Richard, Alan and Leon, Jr., had largely ignored SLE's separate corporate existence and disregarded the fact that SLE had shareholders who were not shareholders of LGT and who therefore could not profit from actions that used SLE solely for the benefit of LGT.

Neither Donald nor his sisters ever owned LGT stock. As the June 1972 date approached for the required sale of their SLE stock to LGT, Donald apparently came to believe that SLE's book value was lower than it should have been. He sought SLE financial information from Richard, who had been president of SLE since 1967. Richard refused to provide information. Donald therefore refused to sell his SLE shares in 1972, and commenced this shareholders' derivative action in the district court in August 1973, basing jurisdiction on diversity of citizenship. The sole claim raised in the complaint was that the defendant directors had wasted the assets of SLE by "grossly undercharging" LGT for the latter's occupancy and use of the Property.

There ensued an eight-day bench trial, at which plaintiff sought to prove, by the testimony of several expert witnesses, that the fair rental value of the Property was greater than the $14,400 per year that SLE had been paid by LGT.

224

The district court subsequently filed lengthy and detailed findings of fact and conclusions of law. On this basis, the court held that Donald had failed to establish the rental value of the Property during the period at issue, and that defendants were therefore entitled to judgment on the derivative claims. Implicit in the district court's ruling, granting judgment for defendants upon plaintiff's failure to prove waste, was a determination that plaintiff bore the burden of proof on that issue.

Turning first to the question of burden of proof, we conclude that the district court erred in placing upon plaintiff the burden of proving waste. Because the directors of SLE were also officers, directors and/or shareholders of LGT, the burden was on the defendant directors to demonstrate that the transactions between SLE and LGT were fair and reasonable.

Under normal circumstances the directors of a corporation may determine, in the exercise of their business judgment, what contracts the corporation will enter into and what consideration is adequate, without review of the merits of their decisions by the courts. The business judgment rule places a heavy burden on shareholders who would attack corporate transactions. But the business judgment rule presupposes that the directors have no conflict of interest. When a shareholder attacks a transaction in which the directors have an interest other than as directors of the corporation, the directors may not escape review of the merits of the transaction. At common law such a transaction was voidable unless shown by its proponent to be fair, and reasonable to the corporation. BCL section 713, in both its current and its prior versions, carries forward this common law principle, and provides special rules for scrutiny of a transaction between the corporation and an entity in which its directors are directors or officers or have a substantial financial interest.

The current version of section 713, which became effective on September 1, 1971, and governs at least so much of the dealing between SLE and LGT as occurred after that date, expressly provides that a contract between a corporation and an entity in which its directors are interested may be set aside unless the proponent of the contract "shall establish affirmatively that the contract or transaction was fair and reasonable as to the corporation at the time it was approved by the board." Thus when the transaction is challenged in a derivative action against the interested directors, they have the burden of proving that the transaction was fair and reasonable to the corporation.

During the entire period 1966–1972, Richard, Alan and Leon, Jr., were directors of both SLE and LGT; there were no SLE directors who were not also directors of LGT. Richard, Alan and Leon, Jr., were all shareholders of LGT in 1966, and from 1967 to 1972 Richard and Leon, Jr., were the sole shareholders of LGT. Under BCL section 713, therefore, Richard, Alan and Leon, Jr., had the burden of proving that $14,400 was a fair and reasonable annual rent for the SLE property for the period February 28, 1966 through June 1, 1972.

Our review of the record convinces us that defendants failed to carry their burden.

225

Quite clearly Richard, Alan and Leon, Jr., had made no effort to determine contemporaneously what rental would be fair during the years 1966-1972. Their view was that the rent should simply cover expenses and that SLE existed for the benefit of LGT.

We conclude, therefore, that defendants failed to prove that the rental paid by LGT to SLE for the years 1966-1972 was fair and reasonable. Thus, Donald is not required to sell his SLE shares to LGT without such upward adjustment in the June 1, 1972, book value of SLE as may be necessary to reflect the amount by which the fair rental value of the Property exceeded $14,400 in any of the years 1966–1972.

SINCLAIR OIL CORP. V. LEVIEN

SUPREME COURT OF DELAWARE (WOLCOTT, C.J.)
280 A.2D 717 (1971)

This is an appeal by the defendant, Sinclair Oil Corporation, from an order of the Court of Chancery in a derivative action requiring Sinclair to account for damages sustained by its subsidiary, Sinclair Venezuelan Oil Company, organized by Sinclair for the purpose of operating in Venezuela, as a result of dividends paid by Sinven, the denial to Sinven of industrial development, and a breach of contract between Sinclair's wholly-owned subsidiary, Sinclair International Oil Company, and Sinven.

Sinclair, operating primarily as a holding company, is in the business of exploring for oil and of producing and marketing crude oil and oil products. At all times relevant to this litigation, it owned about 97% Of Sinven's stock. The plaintiff owns about 3000 of 120,000 publicly held shares of Sinven. Sinven, incorporated in 1922, has been engaged in petroleum operations primarily in Venezuela and since 1959 has operated exclusively in Venezuela.

Sinclair nominates all members of Sinven's board of directors. The Chancellor found as a fact that the directors were not independent of Sinclair. Almost without exception, they were officers, directors, or employees of corporations in the Sinclair complex. By reason of Sinclair's domination, it is clear that Sinclair owed Sinven a fiduciary duty. Sinclair concedes this.

The Chancellor held that because of Sinclair's fiduciary duty and its control over Sinven, its relationship with Sinven must meet the test of intrinsic fairness. The standard of intrinsic fairness involves both a high degree of fairness and a shift in the burden of proof. Under this standard the burden is on Sinclair to prove, subject to careful judicial scrutiny, that its transactions with Sinven were objectively fair.

Sinclair argues that the transactions between it and Sinven should be tested, not by the test of intrinsic fairness with the accompanying shift of the burden of proof, but by the business

226

judgment rule under which a court will not interfere with the judgment of a board of directors unless there is a showing of gross and palpable overreaching. A board of directors enjoys a presumption of sound business judgment, and its decisions will not be disturbed if they can be attributed to any rational business purpose. A court under such circumstances will not substitute its own notions of what is or is not sound business judgment.

We think, however, that Sinclair's argument in this respect is misconceived. When the situation involves a parent and a subsidiary, with the parent controlling the transaction and fixing the terms, the test of intrinsic fairness, with its resulting shifting of the burden of proof, is applied. The basic situation for the application of the rule is the one in which the parent has received a benefit to the exclusion and at the expense of the subsidiary.

A parent does indeed owe a fiduciary duty to its subsidiary when there are parent-subsidiary dealings. However, this alone will not evoke the intrinsic fairness standard. This standard will be applied only when the fiduciary duty is accompanied by self-dealing—the situation when a parent is on both sides of a transaction with its subsidiary. Self-dealing occurs when the parent, by virtue of its domination of the subsidiary, causes the subsidiary to act in such a way that the parent receives something from the subsidiary to the exclusion of, and detriment to, the minority stockholders of the subsidiary.

We turn now to the facts. The plaintiff argues that, from 1960 through 1966, Sinclair caused Sinven to pay out such excessive dividends that the industrial development of Sinven was effectively prevented, and it became in reality a corporation in dissolution.

From 1960 through 1966, Sinven paid out $108,000,000 in dividends ($38,000,000 in excess of Sinven's earnings during the same period). The Chancellor held that Sinclair caused these dividends to be paid during a period when it had a need for large amounts of cash. Although the dividends paid exceeded earnings, the plaintiff concedes that the payments were made in compliance with 8 Del.C. section 170, authorizing payment of dividends out of surplus or net profits. However, the plaintiff attacks these dividends on the ground that they resulted from an improper motive—Sinclair's need for cash. The Chancellor, applying the intrinsic fairness standard, held that Sinclair did not sustain its burden of proving that these dividends were intrinsically fair to the minority stockholders of Sinven.

Since it is admitted that the dividends were paid in strict compliance with 8 Del. C. section 170, the alleged excessiveness of the payments alone would not state a cause of action. Nevertheless, compliance with the applicable statute may not, under all circumstances, justify all dividend payments. If a plaintiff can meet his burden of proving that a dividend cannot be grounded on any reasonable business objective, then the courts can and will interfere with the board's decision to pay the dividend.

We do not accept the argument that the intrinsic fairness test can never be applied to a dividend declaration by a dominated board, although a dividend declaration by a dominated board will not inevitably demand the application of the intrinsic fairness standard. If such

227

a dividend is in essence self-dealing by the parent, then the intrinsic fairness standard is the proper standard. For example, suppose a parent dominates a subsidiary and its board of directors. The subsidiary has outstanding two classes of stock, X and Y. Class X is owned by the parent and Class Y is owned by minority stockholders of the subsidiary. If the subsidiary, at the direction of the parent, declares a dividend on its Class X stock only, this might well be self-dealing by the parent. It would be receiving something from the subsidiary to the exclusion of and detrimental to its minority stockholders. This self-dealing, coupled with the parent's fiduciary duty, would make intrinsic fairness the proper standard by which to evaluate the dividend payments.

Consequently it must be determined whether the dividend payments by Sinven were, in essence, self-dealing by Sinclair. The dividends resulted in great sums of money being transferred from Sinven to Sinclair. However, a proportionate share of this money was received by the minority shareholders of Sinven. Sinclair received nothing from Sinven to the exclusion of its minority stockholders. As such, these dividends were not self-dealing. We hold therefore that the Chancellor erred in applying the intrinsic fairness test as to these dividend payments. The business judgment standard should have been applied.

We conclude that the facts demonstrate that the dividend payments complied with the business judgment standard and with 8 Del. C. section 170. The motives for causing the declaration of dividends are immaterial unless the plaintiff can show that the dividend payments resulted from improper motives and amounted to waste. The plaintiff contends only that the dividend payments drained Sinven of cash to such an extent that it was prevented from expanding.

The plaintiff proved no business opportunities which came to Sinven independently and which Sinclair either took to itself or denied to Sinven. As a matter of fact, with two minor exceptions which resulted in losses, all of Sinven's operations have been conducted in Venezuela, and Sinclair had a policy of exploiting its oil properties located in different countries by subsidiaries located in the particular countries.

From 1960 to 1966 Sinclair purchased or developed oil fields in Alaska, Canada, Paraguay, and other places around the world. The plaintiff contends that these were all opportunities which could have been taken by Sinven. The Chancellor concluded that Sinclair had not proved that its denial of expansion opportunities to Sinven was intrinsically fair. He based this conclusion on the following findings of fact. Sinclair made no real effort to expand Sinven. The excessive dividends paid by Sinven resulted in so great a cash drain as to effectively deny to Sinven any ability to expand. During this same period Sinclair actively pursued a company-wide policy of developing through its subsidiaries new sources of revenue, but Sinven was not permitted to participate and was confined in its activities to Venezuela.

However, the plaintiff could point to no opportunities which came to Sinven. Therefore, Sinclair usurped no business opportunity belonging to Sinven. Since Sinclair received nothing from Sinven to the exclusion of and detriment to Sinven's minority stockholders, there was no self-dealing. Therefore, business judgment is the proper standard by which to evaluate Sinclair's expansion policies.

Since there is no proof of self-dealing on the part of Sinclair, it follows that the expansion policy of Sinclair and the methods used to achieve the desired result must, as far as Sinclair's treatment of Sinven is concerned, be tested by the standards of the business judgment rule. Accordingly, Sinclair's decision, absent fraud or gross overreaching, to achieve expansion through the medium of its subsidiaries, other than Sinven, must be upheld.

Even if Sinclair was wrong in developing these opportunities as it did, the question arises, with which subsidiaries should these opportunities have been shared? No evidence indicates a unique need or ability of Sinven to develop these opportunities. The decision of which subsidiaries would be used to implement Sinclair's expansion policy was one of business judgment with which a court will not interfere absent a showing of gross and palpable overreaching. No such showing has been made here.

Next, Sinclair argues that the Chancellor committed error when he held it liable to Sinven for breach of contract.

In 1961 Sinclair created Sinclair International Oil Company, a wholly owned subsidiary used for the purpose of coordinating all of Sinclair's foreign operations. All crude purchases by Sinclair were made thereafter through International.

On September 28, 1961, Sinclair caused Sinven to contract with International whereby Sinven agreed to sell all of its crude oil and refined products to International at specified prices. The contract provided for minimum and maximum quantities and prices. The plaintiff contends that Sinclair caused this contract to be breached in two respects. Although the contract called for payment on receipt, International's payments lagged as much as 30 days after receipt. Also, the contract required International to purchase at least a fixed minimum amount of crude and refined products from Sinven. International did not comply with this requirement.

Clearly, Sinclair's act of contracting with its dominated subsidiary was self-dealing. Under the contract Sinclair received the products produced by Sinven, and of course the minority shareholders of Sinven were not able to share in the receipt of these products. If the contract was breached, then Sinclair received these products to the detriment of Sinven's minority shareholders. We agree with the Chancellor's finding that the contract was breached by Sinclair, both as to the time of payments and the amounts purchased.

Although a parent need not bind itself by a contract with its dominated subsidiary, Sinclair chose to operate in this manner. As Sinclair has received the benefits of this contract, so must it comply with the contractual duties.

Under the intrinsic fairness standard, Sinclair must prove that its causing Sinven not to enforce the contract was intrinsically fair to the minority shareholders of Sinven. Sinclair has failed to meet this burden. Late payments were clearly breaches for which Sinven should have sought and received adequate damages. As to the quantities purchased, Sinclair argues that it purchased all the products produced by Sinven. This, however, does not satisfy the standard of intrinsic fairness. Sinclair has failed to prove that Sinven could not possibly have produced or someway have obtained the contract minimums. As such, Sinclair must account on this claim.

We will therefore reverse that part of the Chancellor's order that requires Sinclair to account to Sinven for damages sustained as a result of dividends paid between 1960 and 1966, and by reason of the denial to Sinven of expansion during that period. We will affirm the remaining portion of that order and remand the cause for further proceedings.

reverse on 2 issues! affirm on 1 (breach)

ZAHN V. TRANSAMERICA CORP.

CIRCUIT COURT OF APPEALS, THIRD CIRCUIT (BIGGS, J.)
162 F.2D 36 (1947)

Zahn, a holder of Class A common stock of Axton-Fisher Tobacco Company, a corporation of Kentucky, sued Transamerica Corporation, a Delaware company, on his own behalf and on behalf of all stockholders similarly situated, in the District Court of the United States for the District of Delaware. His complaint as amended asserts that Transamerica caused Axton-Fisher to redeem its Class A stock at $80.80 per share on July 1, 1943, instead of permitting the Class A stockholders to participate in the assets on the liquidation of their company in June, 1944. He alleges in brief that if the Class A stockholders had been allowed to participate in the assets on liquidation of Axton-Fisher and had received their respective shares of the assets, he and the other Class A stockholders would have received $240 per share instead of $80.80.

Prior to April 30, 1943, Axton-Fisher had authorized and outstanding three classes of stock, designated respectively as preferred stock, Class A stock and Class B stock. Each share of preferred stock had a par value of $100 and was entitled to cumulative dividends at the rate of $6 per annum and possessed a liquidation value of $105 plus accrued dividends. The Class A stock, specifically described in the charter as a "common" stock, was entitled to an annual cumulative dividend of $3.20 per share. If further funds were made available by action of the board of directors by way of dividends, the Class A stock and the Class B stock were entitled to share equally therein. Upon liquidation of the company and the payment of the sums required by the preferred stock, the Class A stock was entitled to share with the Class B stock in the distribution of the remaining assets, but the Class A stock was entitled to receive twice as much per share as the Class B stock.

Each share of Class A stock was convertible at the option of the shareholder into one share of Class B stock. All or any of the shares of Class A stock were callable by the corporation at any quarterly dividend date upon sixty days' notice to the shareholders, at $60 per share with accrued

forced stockholders to liquidate early, so they lost $$$

dividends. The voting rights were vested in the Class B stock but if there were four successive defaults in the payment of quarterly dividends, the class or classes of stock as to which such defaults occurred gained voting rights equal share for share with the Class B stock. By reason of this provision the Class A stock had possessed equal voting rights with the Class B stock since on or about January 1, 1937.

On or about May 16, 1941, Transamerica purchased 80,160 shares of Axton-Fisher's Class B common stock. This was about 71.5% of the outstanding Class B stock and about 46.7% of the total voting stocks of Axton-Fisher. By August 15, 1942, Transamerica owned 5,332 shares of Class A stock and 82,610 shares of Class B stock. By March 31, 1943, the amount of Class A stock of Axton-Fisher owned by Transamerica had grown to 30,168 shares or about 66 2/3% of the total amount of this stock outstanding, and the amount of Class B stock owned by Transamerica had increased to 90,768 shares or about 80% of the total outstanding. Additional shares of Class B stock were acquired by Transamerica after April 30, 1943, and Transamerica converted the Class A stock owned by it into Class B stock so that on or about the end of May, 1944 Transamerica owned virtually all of the outstanding Class B stock of Axton-Fisher. Since May 16, 1941, Transamerica had control of and had dominated the management, directorate, financial policies, business and affairs of Axton-Fisher. Since the date last stated Transamerica had elected a majority of the board of directors of Axton-Fisher. These individuals are in large part officers or agents of Transamerica.

In the fall of 1942 and in the spring of 1943 Axton-Fisher possessed as its principal asset leaf tobacco which had cost it about $6,361,981. This asset was carried on Axton-Fisher's books in that amount. The value of leaf tobacco had risen sharply and, to quote the words of the complaint, "unbeknown to the public holders of Class A common stock of Axton-Fisher, but known to Transamerica, the market value of the tobacco had, in March and April of 1943, attained the huge sum of about $20,000,000."

The complaint then alleges the gist of the plaintiff's grievance, viz., that Transamerica, knowing of the great value of the tobacco which Axton-Fisher possessed, conceived a plan to appropriate the value of the tobacco to itself by redeeming the Class A stock at the price of $60 a share plus accrued dividends, the redemption being made to appear as if "incident to the continuance of the business of Axton-Fisher as a going concern," and thereafter, the redemption of the Class A stock being completed, to liquidate Axton-Fisher; that this would result, after the disbursal of the sum required to be paid to the preferred stock, in Transamerica gaining for itself most of the value of the warehouse tobacco. The complaint further alleges that in pursuit of this plan Transamerica, by a resolution of the Board of Directors of Axton-Fisher on April 30, 1943, called the Class A stock at $60 and, selling a large part of the tobacco to Phillip-Morris Company, Ltd., Inc., together with substantially all of the other assets of Axton-Fisher, thereafter liquidated Axton-Fisher, paid off the preferred stock and pocketed the balance of the proceeds of the sale. Warehouse receipts representing the remainder of the tobacco were distributed to the Class B stockholders.

Assuming as we must that the allegations of the complaint are true, it will be observed that agents or representatives of Transamerica constituted Axton-Fisher's board of directors at the times of the happening of the events complained of, and that Transamerica was Axton-Fisher's principal and controlling stockholder at such times.

The circumstances of the case at bar are *sui generis* and we can find no Kentucky decision squarely on point. In our opinion, however, the law of Kentucky imposes upon the directors of a corporation or upon those who are in charge of its affairs by virtue of majority stock ownership or otherwise the same fiduciary relationship in respect to the corporation and to its stockholders as is imposed generally by the laws of Kentucky's sister states or which was imposed by federal law prior to *Erie R. Co. v. Tompkins*.

The tenor of the federal decisions in respect to the general fiduciary duty of those in control of a corporation is unmistakable. The Supreme Court in *Southern Pacific Co. v. Bogert* said: "The rule of corporation law and of equity invoked is well settled and has been often applied. The majority has the right to control; but when it does so, it occupies a fiduciary relation toward the minority, as much so as the corporation itself or its officers and directors."

It is appropriate to emphasize at this point that the right to call the Class A stock for redemption was confided by the charter of Axton-Fisher to the directors and not to the stockholders of that corporation. We must also re-emphasize the statement of the court in *Haldeman v. Haldeman*, and its reiteration in *Kirwan v. Parkway Distillery*, that there is a radical difference when a stockholder is voting strictly as a stockholder and when voting as a director; that when voting as a stockholder he may have the legal right to vote with a view of his own benefits and to represent himself only; but that when he votes as a director he represents all the stockholders in the capacity of a trustee for them and cannot use his office as a director for his personal benefit at the expense of the stockholders.

Two theories are presented on one of which the case at bar must be decided: One, vigorously asserted by Transamerica and based on its interpretation of the decision in the *Taylor* case, is that the board of directors of Axton-Fisher, whether or not dominated by Transamerica, the principal Class B stockholder, at any time and for any purpose, might call the Class A stock for redemption; the other, asserted with equal vigor by Zahn, is that the board of directors of Axton-Fisher as fiduciaries were not entitled to favor Transamerica, the Class B stockholder, by employing the redemption provisions of the charter for its benefit.

We must of course treat the decision of the Court of Appeals of Kentucky in the *Taylor* case as evidence of what is the law of Kentucky. The Court took the position on that record that the directors at any time might call the Class A stock for redemption and that the redemption provision of the charter was written as much for the benefit of the Class B as for the Class A stock. It is argued by Transamerica very persuasively that what the Court of Appeals of Kentucky held was that when the Class A stock received its allocation of $60 a share plus accrued dividends it received its full due and that the directors had the right at any time to eliminate Class A stock from the corporate setup for the benefit of the Class B stock. It does not appear from the opinion of the Court of Appeals of Kentucky whether or not the subsequent liquidation of Axton-Fisher was brought to the attention of the Court. But it is clear from the pleading that the subsequent liquidation was not an issue in the case. We think that it is the settled law of Kentucky that directors may not declare or withhold the declaration of dividends for the purpose of personal profit or, by analogy, take any corporate action for such a purpose.

The difficulty in accepting Transamerica's contentions in the case at bar is that the directors of Axton-Fisher, if the allegations of the complaint be accepted as true, were the instruments of Transamerica, were directors voting in favor of their special interest, that of Transamerica, could not and did not exercise an independent judgment in calling the Class A stock, but made the call for the purpose of profiting their true principal, Transamerica. In short a puppet-puppeteer relationship existed between the directors of Axton-Fisher and Transamerica.

The act of the board of directors in calling the Class A stock, an act which could have been legally consummated by a disinterested board of directors, was here effected at the direction of the principal Class B stockholder in order to profit it. Such a call is voidable in equity at the instance of a stockholder injured thereby. It must be pointed out that under the allegations of the complaint there was no reason for the redemption of the Class A stock to be followed by the liquidation of Axton-Fisher except to enable the Class B stock to profit at the expense of the Class A stock. As has been hereinbefore stated the function of the call was confided to the board of directors by the charter and was not vested by the charter in the stockholders of any class. It was the intention of the framers of Axton-Fisher's charter to require the board of directors to act disinterestedly if that body called the Class A stock, and to make the call with a due regard for its fiduciary obligations. If the allegations of the complaint be proved, it follows that the directors of Axton-Fisher, the instruments of Transamerica, have been derelict in that duty. Liability which flows from the dereliction must be imposed upon Transamerica which, under the allegations of the complaint, constituted the board of Axton-Fisher and controlled it.

In our opinion, if the allegations of the complaint be proved, Zahn may maintain his cause of action to recover from Transamerica the value of the stock retained by him as that shall be represented by its aliquot share of the proceeds of Axton-Fisher on dissolution.

The judgment will be reversed.

233

DELAWARE GENERAL CORPORATION LAW

SECTION 144(a). INTERESTED DIRECTORS; QUORUM

No contract or transaction between a corporation and 1 or more of its directors or officers, or between a corporation and any other corporation, partnership, association, or other organization in which 1 or more if its directors or officers, are directors or officers, or have a financial interest, shall be void or voidable solely for this reason, or solely because the director or officer is present at or participates in the meeting of the board or committee which authorizes the contract or transaction, or solely because any such director's or officer's votes are counted for such purpose if:

(1) The material facts as to the director's or officer's relationship or interest and as to the contract or transaction are disclosed or are known to the board of directors or the committee, and the board or committee in good faith authorizes the contract or transaction by the affirmative vote of a majority of disinterested directors, even though the disinterested directors be less than a quorum; or

(2) The material facts as to the director's or officer's relationship or interest and as to the contract or transaction are disclosed or are known to the stockholders entitled to vote thereon, and the contract or transaction is specifically approved in good faith by vote of the stockholders; or

(3) The contract or transaction is fair as to the corporation as of the time it is authorized, approved or ratified, by the board of directors, a committee or the stockholders.

COOKIES FOOD PRODUCTS, INC. V. LAKES WAREHOUSE DISTRIBUTING, INC.

SUPREME COURT OF IOWA (NEUMAN, J.)
430 N.W.2D 447 (1988)

This is a shareholders' derivative suit brought by the minority shareholders of a closely held Iowa corporation specializing in barbeque sauce, Cookies Food Products, Inc. The target of the lawsuit is the majority shareholder, Duane "Speed" Herrig and two of his family-owned corporations, Lakes Warehouse Distributing, Inc. and Speed's Automotive Co., Inc. Plaintiffs alleged that Herrig, by acquiring control of Cookies and executing self-dealing contracts, breached his fiduciary duty to the company and fraudulently misappropriated and converted corporate funds. Plaintiffs sought actual and punitive damages. Trial to the court resulted in a verdict for the defendants, the district court finding that Herrig's actions benefited, rather than harmed, Cookies. We affirm.

L.D. Cook of Storm Lake, Iowa, founded Cookies in 1975 to produce and distribute his original barbeque sauce. Searching for a plant site in a community that would provide financial backing, Cook met with business leaders in seventeen Iowa communities, outlining his plans to build a growth-oriented company. He selected Wall Lake, Iowa, persuading thirty-five members of that community, including Herrig and the plaintiffs, to purchase Cookies stock. All of the investors hoped Cookies would improve the local job market and tax base. The record reveals that it has done just that.

Early sales of the product, however, were dismal. After the first year's operation, Cookies was in dire financial straits. At that time, Herrig was one of thirty-five shareholders and held only two hundred shares. He was also the owner of an auto parts business, Speed's Automotive, and Lakes Warehouse Distributing, Inc., a company that distributed auto parts from Speed's. Cookies' board of directors approached Herrig with the idea of distributing the company's products. It authorized Herrig to purchase Cookies' sauce for twenty percent under wholesale price, which he could then resell at full wholesale price. Under this arrangement, Herrig began to market and distribute the sauce to his auto parts customers and to grocery outlets from Lakes' trucks as they traversed the regular delivery routes for Speed's Automotive.

In May 1977, Cookies formalized this arrangement by executing an exclusive distribution agreement with Lakes. Pursuant to this agreement, Cookies was responsible only for preparing the product; Lakes, for its part, assumed all costs of warehousing, marketing, sales, delivery, promotion, and advertising. Cookies retained the right to fix the sales price of its products and agreed to pay Lakes thirty percent of its gross sales for these services.

Cookies' sales have soared under the exclusive distributorship contract with Lakes. Gross sales in 1976, the year prior to the agreement, totaled only $20,000, less than half of Cookies' expenses that year. In 1977, however, sales jumped five-fold, then doubled in 1978, and have continued to show phenomenal growth every year thereafter. By 1985, when this suit was commenced, annual sales reached $2,400,000.

In 1981, L.D. Cook, the majority shareholder up to this time, decided to sell his interest in Cookies. He first offered the directors an opportunity to buy his stock, but the board declined to purchase any of his 8100 shares. Herrig then offered Cook and all other shareholders $10 per share for their stock, which was twice the original price. Because of the overwhelming response to these offers, Herrig had purchased enough Cookies stock by January 1982 to become the majority shareholder. His investment of $140,000 represented fifty-three percent of the 28,700 outstanding shares. Other shareholders had invested a total of $67,500 for the remaining forty-seven percent.

Shortly after Herrig acquired majority control he replaced four of the five members of the Cookies' board with members he selected. This restructuring of authority, following on the heels

Herrig installs his own board

of an unsuccessful attempt by certain stockholders to prevent Herrig from acquiring majority status, solidified a division of opinion within the shareholder ranks. Subsequent changes made in the corporation under Herrig's leadership formed the basis for this lawsuit.

First, under Herrig's leadership, Cookies' board has extended the term of the exclusive distributorship agreement with Lakes and expanded the scope of services for which it compensates Herrig and his companies. In April 1982, when a sales increase of twenty-five percent over the previous year required Cookies to seek additional short-term storage for the peak summer season, the board accepted Herrig's proposal to compensate Lakes at the "going rate" for use of its nearby storage facilities.

Second, Herrig moved from his role as director and distributor to take on an additional role in product development. This created a dispute over a royalty Herrig began to receive. Herrig's role in product development began in 1982 when Cookies diversified its product line to include taco sauce. Herrig developed the recipe because he recognized that taco sauce, while requiring many of the same ingredients needed in barbeque sauce, is less expensive to produce. Further, since consumer demand for taco sauce is more consistent throughout the year than the demand for barbeque sauce, this new product line proved to be a profitable method for increasing year-round utilization of production facilities and staff.

Third, since 1982 Cookies' board has twice approved additional compensation for Herrig. In January 1983, the board authorized payment of a $1000 per month "consultant fee" in lieu of salary, because accelerated sales required Herrig to spend extra time managing the company. Averaging eighty-hour work weeks, Herrig devoted approximately fifteen percent of his time to Cookies and eighty percent to Lakes business. In August, 1983, the board authorized another increase in Herrig's compensation. As a direct result of this action, by 1986 Cookies regularly shipped products to several states throughout the country.

As we have previously noted, however, Cookies' growth and success has not pleased all its shareholders. The discontent is motivated by two factors that have effectively precluded shareholders from sharing in Cookies' financial success: the fact that Cookies is a closely held corporation, and the fact that it has not paid dividends. Because Cookies' stock is not publicly traded, shareholders have no ready access to buyers for their stock at current values that reflect the company's success. Without dividends, the shareholders have no ready method of realizing a return on their investment in the company. This is not to say that Cookies has improperly refused to pay dividends. The evidence reveals that Cookies would have violated the terms of its loan with the Small Business Administration had it declared dividends before repaying that debt. That SBA loan was not repaid until the month before the plaintiffs filed this action.

Unsatisfied with the status quo, a group of minority shareholders commenced this equitable action in 1985. Based on the facts we have detailed, the plaintiffs claimed that the sums paid Herrig and his companies have grossly exceeded the value of the services rendered, thereby

236

substantially reducing corporate profits and shareholder equity. Through the exclusive distributorship agreements, taco sauce royalty, warehousing fees, and consultant fee, plaintiffs claimed that Herrig breached his fiduciary duties to the corporation and its shareholders because he allegedly negotiated for these arrangements without fully disclosing the benefit he would gain.

Having heard the evidence presented on these claims at trial, the district court concluded that Herrig had breached no duties owed to Cookies or to its minority shareholders.

Herrig, as an officer and director of Cookies, owes a fiduciary duty to the company and its shareholders. Herrig concedes that Iowa law imposed the same fiduciary responsibilities based on his status as majority stockholder.

Conversely, before acquiring majority control in February 1982, Herrig owed no fidicuary duty to Cookies or plaintiffs. Therefore, Herrig's conduct is subject to scrutiny only from the time he began to exercise control of Cookies.

The legislature enacted section 496A.34, quoted here in pertinent part, that establishes three sets of circumstances under which a director may engage in self-dealing without clearly violating the duty of loyalty:

> No contract or other transaction between a corporation and one or more of its directors or any other corporation, firm, association or entity in which one or more of its directors are directors or officers or are financially interested, shall be either void or voidable because of such relationship or interest ... if any of the following occur:
>
> 1. The fact of such relationship or interest is disclosed or known to the board of directors or committee which authorizes, approves, or ratifies the contract or transaction ... without counting the votes ... of such interested director.
> 2. The fact of such relationship or interest is disclosed or known to the shareholders entitled to vote [on the transaction] and they authorize ... such contract or transaction by vote or written consent.
> 3. The contract or transaction is fair and reasonable to the corporation.

Some commentators have supported the view that satisfaction of any *one* of the foregoing statutory alternatives, in and of itself, would prove that a director has fully met the duty of loyalty. We are obliged, however, to interpret statutes in conformity with the common law wherever statutory language does not directly negate it. Because the common law and section 496A.34 require directors to show "good faith, honesty, and fairness" in self-dealing, we are persuaded that satisfaction of any one of these three alternatives under the statute would merely preclude us from rendering the transaction void or voidable *outright* solely on the basis "of such director's relationship or interest." To the contrary, we are convinced that the legislature did not intend by this statute to enable a court, in a shareholder's derivative suit, to rubber stamp *any* transaction to which a board of directors or the shareholders of a corporation have consented. Such an interpretation would invite those who stand to gain from such transactions to engage in improprieties to obtain consent. We thus require directors who engage in self-dealing to establish the additional element that they have acted in good faith, honesty, and fairness.

Given an instance of alleged director enrichment at corporate expense, the burden to establish fairness resting on the director requires not only a showing of "fair price" but also a showing of the fairness of the bargain to the interests of the corporation.

Applying such reasoning to the record before us, however, we cannot agree with appellants' assertion that Herrig's services were either unfairly priced or inconsistent with Cookies corporate interest.

There can be no serious dispute that the four agreements in issue—for exclusive distributorship, taco sauce royalty, warehousing, and consulting fees—have all benefited Cookies, as demonstrated by its financial success. Even if we assume Cookies could have procured similar services from other vendors at lower costs, we are not convinced that Herrig's fees were therefore unreasonable or exorbitant.

With regard to the board of directors, the record before us aptly demonstrates that all members of Cookies' board were well aware of Herrig's dual ownership in Lakes and Speed's. We are unaware of any authority supporting plaintiffs' contention that Herrig was obligated to disclose to Cookies' board or shareholders the extent of his profits resulting from these distribution and warehousing agreements; nevertheless, the exclusive distribution agreement with Lakes authorized the board to ascertain that information had it so desired. Appellants cannot reasonably claim that Herrig owed Cookies a duty to render such services at no profit to himself or his companies. Having found that the compensation he received from these agreements was fair and reasonable, we are convinced that Herrig furnished sufficient pertinent information to Cookies' board to enable it to make prudent decisions concerning the contracts.

AFFIRMED.

SCHULTZ, J. (dissenting).

My quarrel with the majority opinion is not with its interpretation of the law, but with its application of the law to the facts. I would reverse the trial court's holding.

The majority opinion correctly stated the common law and statutory principles. When there is self-dealing by a majority stockholder which is challenged, the majority stockholder has the burden to establish that they have acted in good faith, honesty and fairness. This burden of fairness requires not just a showing of profitability, but also a showing of the fairness of the bargain to the interest of the corporation. I would hold that Herrig failed to sustain his burden.

Much of Herrig's evidence concerned the tremendous success of the company. I believe that the trial court and the majority opinion have been so enthralled by the success of the company that they have failed to examine whether these matters of self-dealing were fair to the stockholders.

While much credit is due to Herrig for the success of the company, this does not mean that these transactions were fair to the company.

I believe that Herrig failed on his burden of proof by what he did not show. He did not produce evidence of the local going rate for distribution contracts or storage fees outside of a very limited amount of self-serving testimony. He simply did not show the fair market value of his services or expense for freight, advertising and storage cost. He did not show that his taco sauce royalty was fair. This was his burden. He cannot succeed on it by merely showing the success of the company.

In summary, I believe the majority was dazzled by the tales of Herrig's efforts and Cookies' success in these difficult economic times. In the process, however, it is forgotten that Herrig owes a fiduciary duty to the corporation to deal fairly and reasonably with it in his self-dealing transactions.

BROZ V. CELLULAR INFORMATION SYSTEMS, INC.

SUPREME COURT OF DELWARE (VEASEY, C.J.)
673 A.2D 148 (1996)

Robert F. Broz is the President and sole stockholder of RFB Cellular, Inc., a Delaware corporation engaged in the business of providing cellular telephone service in the Midwestern United States. At the time of the conduct at issue in this appeal, Broz was also a member of the board of directors of plaintiff below-appellee, Cellular Information Systems, Inc. CIS is a publicly held Delaware corporation and a competitor of RFBC.

RFBC owns and operates an FCC license area, known as the Michigan-4 Rural Service Area Cellular License. The license entitles RFBC to provide cellular telephone service to a portion of rural Michigan. Although Broz' efforts have been devoted primarily to the business operations of RFBC, he also served as an outside director of CIS at the time of the events at issue in this case. CIS was at all times fully aware of Broz' relationship with RFBC and the obligations incumbent upon him by virtue of that relationship.

In April of 1994, Mackinac Cellular Corp. sought to divest itself of Michigan-2, the license area immediately adjacent to Michigan-4. To this end, Mackinac contacted Daniels & Associates and arranged for the brokerage firm to seek potential purchasers for Michigan-2. In compiling a list of prospects, Daniels included RFBC as a likely candidate.

Michigan-2 was not, however, offered to CIS. Apparently, Daniels did not consider CIS to be a viable purchaser for Michigan-2 in light of CIS' recent financial difficulties. The record shows that, at the time Michigan-2 was offered to Broz, CIS had recently emerged from lengthy and contentious Chapter 11 proceedings. Pursuant to the Chapter 11 Plan of Reorganization, CIS

239

entered into a loan agreement that substantially impaired the company's ability to undertake new acquisitions or to incur new debt. In fact, CIS would have been unable to purchase Michigan-2 without the approval of its creditors.

The CIS reorganization resulted from the failure of CIS' rather ambitious plans for expansion. From 1989 onward, CIS had embarked on a series of cellular license acquisitions. In 1992, however, CIS' financing failed, necessitating the liquidation of the company's holdings and reduction of the company's total indebtedness. During the period from early 1992 until the time of CIS' emergence from bankruptcy in 1994, CIS divested itself of some fifteen separate cellular license systems. CIS contracted to sell four additional license areas on May 27, 1994, leaving CIS with only five remaining license areas, all of which were outside of the Midwest.

On June 13, 1994, following a meeting of the CIS board, Broz spoke with CIS' Chief Executive Officer, Richard Treibick, concerning his interest in acquiring Michigan-2. Treibick communicated to Broz that CIS was not interested in Michigan-2. Treibick further stated that he had been made aware of the Michigan-2 opportunity prior to the conversation with Broz, and that any offer to acquire Michigan-2 was rejected. After the commencement of the PriCellular tender offer, in August of 1994, Broz contacted another CIS director, Peter Schiff, to discuss the possible acquisition of Michigan-2 by RFBC. Schiff, like Treibick, indicated that CIS had neither the wherewithal nor the inclination to purchase Michigan-2. In late September of 1994, Broz also contacted Stanley Bloch, a director and counsel for CIS, to request that Bloch represent RFBC in its dealings with Mackinac. Bloch agreed to represent RFBC, and, like Schiff and Treibick, expressed his belief that CIS was not at all interested in the transaction. Ultimately, all the CIS directors testified at trial that, had Broz inquired at that time, they each would have expressed the opinion that CIS was not interested in Michigan-2.[13]

On June 28, 1994, following various overtures from PriCellular concerning an acquisition of CIS, six CIS directors entered into agreements with PriCellular to sell their shares in CIS at a price of $2.00 per share. These agreements were contingent upon, *inter alia*, the consummation of a PriCellular tender offer for all CIS shares at the same price. Pursuant to their agreements with PriCellular, the CIS directors also entered into a "standstill" agreement which prevented the directors from engaging in any transaction outside the regular course of CIS' business or incurring any new liabilities until the close of the PriCellular tender offer. On August 2, 1994, PriCellular commenced a tender offer for all outstanding shares of CIS at $2.00 per share. The PriCellular tender offer mirrored the standstill agreements entered into by the CIS directors.

---

13 We assume arguendo that informal contacts and individual opinions of board members are not a substitute for a formal process of presenting an opportunity to a board of directors. Nevertheless, in our view such a formal process was not necessary under the circumstances of this case in order for Broz to avoid liability. These contacts with individual board members do, however, tend to show that Broz was not acting surreptitiously or in bad faith.

PriCellular's tender offer was originally scheduled to close on September 16, 1994. At the time the tender offer was launched, however, the source of the $106,000,000 in financing required to consummate the transaction was still in doubt. Financing difficulties ultimately caused PriCellular to delay the closing date of the tender offer from September 16, 1994 until November 9, 1994.

During this time period, PriCellular also began negotiations with Mackinac to arrange an option for the purchase of Michigan-2. CIS was fully aware that PriCellular and Broz were bidding for Michigan-2 and did not interpose CIS in this bidding war.

In late September of 1994, PriCellular reached agreement with Mackinac on an option to purchase Michigan-2. The agreement provided that Mackinac was free to sell Michigan-2 to any party who was willing to exceed the exercise price of the Mackinac-PriCellular option contract by at least $500,000. On November 14, 1994, Broz agreed to pay Mackinac $7.2 million for the Michigan-2 license, thereby meeting the terms of the option agreement. An asset purchase agreement was thereafter executed by Mackinac and RFBC.

Nine days later, on November 23, 1994, PriCellular completed its financing and closed its tender offer for CIS. Prior to that point, PriCellular owned no equity interest in CIS.

The doctrine of corporate opportunity represents but one species of the broad fiduciary duties assumed by a corporate director or officer. A corporate fiduciary agrees to place the interests of the corporation before his or her own in appropriate circumstances. In light of the diverse and often competing obligations faced by directors and officers, however, the corporate opportunity doctrine arose as a means of defining the parameters of fiduciary duty in instances of potential conflict. The classic statement of the doctrine is derived from the venerable case of *Guth v. Loft, Inc.* In *Guth*, this Court held that:

> if there is presented to a corporate officer or director a business opportunity which the corporation is financially able to undertake, is, from its nature, in the line of the corporation's business and is of practical advantage to it, is one in which the corporation has an interest or a reasonable expectancy, and, by embracing the opportunity, the self-interest of the officer or director will be brought into conflict with that of the corporation, the law will not permit him to seize the opportunity for himself.

We note at the outset that Broz became aware of the Michigan-2 opportunity in his individual and not his corporate capacity. As the Court of Chancery found, "Broz did not misuse proprietary information that came to him in a corporate capacity nor did he otherwise use any power he might have over the governance of the corporation to advance his own interests." This fact is not the subject of serious dispute. In fact, it is clear from the record that Mackinac did not consider CIS a viable candidate for the acquisition of Michigan-2. Accordingly, Mackinac did not offer the property to CIS. In this factual posture, many of the fundamental concerns undergirding the law of corporate opportunity are not present (*e.g.*, misappropriation of the corporation's proprietary information). The burden imposed upon Broz to show adherence to his fiduciary duties to CIS is thus lessened to some extent. Nevertheless, this fact is not dispositive. The determination of whether a particular fiduciary has usurped a corporate opportunity necessitates a careful examination of the circumstances, giving due credence to the factors enunciated in *Guth* and subsequent cases.

We turn now to an analysis of the factors relied on by the trial court. First, we find that CIS was not financially capable of exploiting the Michigan-2 opportunity. Although the Court of Chancery concluded otherwise, we hold that this finding was not supported by the evidence. The record shows that CIS was in a precarious financial position at the time Mackinac presented the Michigan-2 opportunity to Broz.

Second, while it may be said with some certainty that the Michigan-2 opportunity was within CIS' line of business, it is not equally clear that CIS had a cognizable interest or expectancy in the license. Under the third factor laid down by this Court in *Guth*, for an opportunity to be deemed to belong to the fiduciary's corporation, the corporation must have an interest or expectancy in that opportunity. As this Court stated in *Johnston v. Greene*, "For the corporation to have an actual or expectant interest in any specific property, there must be some tie between that property and the nature of the corporate business." Despite the fact that the nature of the Michigan-2 opportunity was historically close to the core operations of CIS, changes were in process. At the time the opportunity was presented, CIS was actively engaged in the process of divesting its cellular license holdings. CIS' articulated business plan did not involve any new acquisitions. Further, as indicated by the testimony of the entire CIS board, the Michigan-2 license would not have been of interest to CIS even absent CIS' financial difficulties and CIS' then current desire to liquidate its cellular license holdings. Thus, CIS had no interest or expectancy in the Michigan-2 opportunity.

Finally, the corporate opportunity doctrine is implicated only in cases where the fiduciary's seizure of an opportunity results in a conflict between the fiduciary's duties to the corporation and the self-interest of the director as actualized by the exploitation of the opportunity. In the instant case, Broz' interest in acquiring and profiting from Michigan-2 created no duties that were inimicable to his obligations to CIS. Broz, at all times relevant to the instant appeal, was the sole party in interest in RFBC, a competitor of CIS. CIS was fully aware of Broz' potentially conflicting duties. Broz, however, comported himself in a manner that was wholly in accord with his obligations to CIS. Broz took care not to usurp any opportunity which CIS was willing and able to pursue. Broz sought only to compete with an outside entity, PriCellular, for acquisition of an opportunity which both sought to possess. Broz was not obligated to refrain from competition with PriCellular.

In reaching our conclusion on this point, we note that certainty and predictability are values to be promoted in our corporation law. Broz, as an active participant in the cellular telephone industry, was entitled to proceed in his own economic interest in the absence of any countervailing duty. The right of a director or officer to engage in business affairs outside of his or her fiduciary capacity would be illusory if these individuals were required to consider every potential, future occurrence in determining whether a particular business strategy would implicate fiduciary duty concerns. In order for a director to engage meaningfully in business unrelated to his or her corporate role, the director must be allowed to make decisions based on the situation as it exists at the time a given opportunity is presented. Absent such a rule, the corporate fiduciary would be constrained to refrain from exploiting any opportunity for fear of liability based on the occurrence of subsequent events. This state of affairs would unduly restrict officers and directors and would be antithetical to certainty in corporation law.

The corporate opportunity doctrine represents a judicially crafted effort to harmonize the competing demands placed on corporate fiduciaries in a modern business environment. The doctrine seeks to reduce the possibility of conflict between a director's duties to the corporation and interests unrelated to that role. In the instant case, Broz adhered to his obligations to CIS. We hold that the Court of Chancery erred as a matter of law in concluding that Broz had a duty formally to present the Michigan-2 opportunity to the CIS board. We also hold that the trial court erred in its application of the corporate opportunity doctrine under the unusual facts of this case, where CIS had no interest or financial ability to acquire the opportunity, but the impending acquisition of CIS by PriCellular would or could have caused a change in those circumstances.

Therefore, we hold that Broz did not breach his fiduciary duties to CIS. Accordingly, we REVERSE the judgment of the Court of Chancery holding that Broz diverted a corporate opportunity properly belonging to CIS and imposing a constructive trust.

DIRECTOR DUTY OF GOOD FAITH PART D

IN RE THE WALT DISNEY CO. DERIVATIVE LITIGATION

SUPREME COURT OF DELAWARE (JACOBS, J.)
906 A.2D 27 (2006)

In August 1995, Michael Ovitz and The Walt Disney Company entered into an employment agreement under which Ovitz would serve as President of Disney for five years. In December 1996, only fourteen months after he commenced employment, Ovitz was terminated without cause, resulting in a severance payout to Ovitz valued at approximately $130 million. [Ovitz = former president of Disney]

In January 1997, several Disney shareholders brought derivative actions in the Court of Chancery, on behalf of Disney, against Ovitz and the directors of Disney who served at the time *shareholder derivative suit against Ovitz + directors*

of the events complained of. The plaintiffs claimed that the $130 million severance payout was the product of fiduciary duty and contractual breaches by Ovitz, and breaches of fiduciary duty by the Disney defendants, and a waste of assets. After the disposition of several pretrial motions and an appeal to this Court, the case was tried before the Chancellor over 37 days between October 20, 2004 and January 19, 2005. In August 2005, the Chancellor handed down a well-crafted 174 page Opinion and Order, determining that "the director defendants did not breach their fiduciary duties or commit waste." The Court entered judgment in favor of all defendants on all claims alleged in the amended complaint.

affirming for Ds

The plaintiffs have appealed from that judgment, claiming that the Court of Chancery committed multitudinous errors. We conclude, for the reasons that follow, that the Chancellor's factual findings and legal rulings were correct and not erroneous in any respect. Accordingly, the judgment entered by the Court of Chancery will be affirmed.

In 1994 Disney lost in a tragic helicopter crash its President and Chief Operating Officer, Frank Wells, who together with Michael Eisner, Disney's Chairman and Chief Executive Officer, had enjoyed remarkable success at the Company's helm. Eisner temporarily assumed Disney's presidency, but only three months later, heart disease required Eisner to undergo quadruple bypass surgery. Those two events persuaded Eisner and Disney's board of directors that the time had come to identify a successor to Eisner.

Eisner picks Ovitz to succeed him - seemingly informal procedures

Eisner's prime candidate for the position was Michael Ovitz, who was the leading partner and one of the founders of Creative Artists Agency, the premier talent agency whose business model had reshaped the entire industry. By 1995, CAA had 550 employees and a roster of about 1400 of Hollywood's top actors, directors, writers, and musicians. That roster generated about $150 million in annual revenues and an annual income of over $20 million for Ovitz, who was regarded as one of the most powerful figures in Hollywood.

Eisner and Ovitz had enjoyed a social and professional relationship that spanned nearly 25 years.

On August 14, Eisner and Ovitz signed a letter agreement, which outlined the basic terms of Ovitz's employment, and stated that the agreement (which would ultimately be embodied in a formal contract) was subject to approval by Disney's compensation committee and board of directors. Eisner contacted each of the board members by phone to inform them of the impending new hire, and to explain his friendship with Ovitz and Ovitz's qualifications.

stock goes up when Ovitz announced

That same day, a press release made the news of Ovitz's hiring public. The reaction was extremely positive: Disney was applauded for the decision, and Disney's stock price rose 4.4% in a single day, thereby increasing Disney's market capitalization by over $1 billion.

On September 26, 1995, the Disney compensation committee (which consisted of Messrs. Russell, Watson, Poitier and Lozano) met for one hour to consider, among other agenda items, the proposed terms of the Ovitz Employment Agreement. A term sheet was distributed at the meeting, although a draft of the OEA was not. The topics discussed were historical comparables, such as Eisner's and Wells' option grants, and also the factors that Russell, Watson and Crystal had considered in setting the size of the option grants and the termination provisions of the contract. Watson testified that he provided the compensation committee with the spreadsheet analysis that he had performed in August, and discussed his findings with the committee. The committee voted unanimously to approve the OEA terms, subject to "reasonable further negotiations within the framework of the terms and conditions" described in the OEA.

Ovitz's tenure as President of the Walt Disney Company officially began on October 1, 1995, the date that the OEA was executed. When Ovitz took office, the initial reaction was optimistic, and Ovitz did make some positive contributions while serving as President of the Company. By the fall of 1996, however, it had become clear that Ovitz was "a poor fit with his fellow executives." By then the Disney directors were discussing that the disconnect between Ovitz and the Company was likely irreparable and that Ovitz would have to be terminated.

The Court of Chancery identified three competing theories as to why Ovitz did not succeed:

> First, plaintiffs argue that Ovitz failed to follow Eisner's directives, especially in regard to acquisitions, and that generally, Ovitz did very little. Second, Ovitz contends Eisner's micromanaging prevented Ovitz from having the authority necessary to make the changes that Ovitz thought were appropriate. In addition, Ovitz believes he was not given enough time for his efforts to bear fruit. Third, the remaining defendants simply posit that Ovitz failed to transition from a private to a public company, from the "sell side to the buy side," and otherwise did not adapt to the Company culture or fit in with other executives. In the end, however, it makes no difference why Ovitz was not as successful as his reputation would have led many to expect, so long as he was not grossly negligent or malfeasant.

Ovitz's relationship with the Disney executives did continue to deteriorate through September 1996. In mid-September, Litvack, with Eisner's approval, told Ovitz that he was not working out at Disney and that he should start looking for a graceful exit from Disney and a new job. Litvack reported this conversation to Eisner, who sent Litvack back to Ovitz to make it clear that Eisner no longer wanted Ovitz at Disney and that Ovitz should seriously consider other opportunities, including one then developing at Sony. Ovitz responded by telling Litvack that he was not leaving and that if Eisner wanted him to leave Disney, Eisner could tell him that to his face.

During this period Eisner was also working with Litvack to explore whether they could terminate Ovitz under the OEA for cause. If so, Disney would not owe Ovitz a no-fault termination payment. From the very beginning, Litvack advised Eisner that he did not believe there was cause to terminate Ovitz under the OEA. Litvack's advice never changed.

The Disney board next met on November 25. By then the board knew Ovitz was going to be fired, yet the only action recorded in the minutes concerning Ovitz was his re-nomination to a new three-year term on the board.

After returning from a Thanksgiving trip, Ovitz met with Eisner on December 3, to discuss his termination. Ovitz asked for several concessions, all of which Eisner ultimately rejected. Eisner told Ovitz that all he would receive was what he had contracted for in the OEA.

On December 11, Eisner met with Ovitz to agree on the wording of a press release to announce the termination, and to inform Ovitz that he would not receive any of the additional items that he requested. By that time it had already been decided that Ovitz would be terminated without cause and that he would receive his contractual payment, but nothing more. Eisner and Ovitz agreed that neither Ovitz nor Disney would disparage each other in the press, and that the separation was to be undertaken with dignity and respect for both sides. After his December 11 meeting with Eisner, Ovitz never returned to Disney.

A December 27, 1996 letter from Litvack to Ovitz, which Ovitz signed, memorialized the termination, accelerated Ovitz's departure date from January 31, 1997 to December 31, 1996, and informed Ovitz that he would receive roughly $38 million in cash and that the first tranche of three million options would vest immediately. By the terms of that letter agreement, Ovitz's tenure as an executive and a director of Disney officially ended on December 27, 1996. Shortly thereafter, Disney paid Ovitz what was owed under the OEA minus a holdback of $1 million pending final settlement of Ovitz's accounts. One month after Disney paid Ovitz, the plaintiffs filed this action.

Cause of action

The appellants' claims of error are that the Disney defendants breached their fiduciary duties to act with due care and in good faith by approving the OEA, and specifically, its no-fault termination provisions. It is notable that the appellants do *not* contend that the Disney defendants are directly liable as a consequence of those fiduciary duty breaches. Rather, appellants' core argument is indirect, *i.e.*, that those breaches of fiduciary duty deprive the Disney defendants of the protection of business judgment review, and require them to shoulder the burden of establishing that their acts were entirely fair to Disney. That burden, the appellants contend, the Disney defendants failed to carry. The appellants claim that by ruling that the Disney defendants did not breach their fiduciary duty to act with due care or in good faith, the Court of Chancery committed reversible error in numerous respects.

The Court of Chancery held that the business judgment rule presumptions protected the decisions of the compensation committee and the remaining Disney directors, not only because they had acted with due care but also because they had not acted in bad faith. That latter ruling, the appellants claim, was reversible error because the Chancellor formulated and then applied an incorrect definition of bad faith.

In its Opinion the Court of Chancery defined bad faith as follows:

> Upon long and careful consideration, I am of the opinion that the concept of *intentional dereliction of duty, a conscious disregard for one's responsibilities,* is an appropriate (although not the only) standard for determining whether fiduciaries have acted in good faith. Deliberate indifference and inaction *in the face of a duty to act* is, in my mind, conduct that is clearly disloyal to the corporation. It is the epitome of faithless conduct.

This case is one in which the duty to act in good faith has played a prominent role, yet to date is not a well-developed area of our corporate fiduciary law. Although the good faith concept has recently been the subject of considerable scholarly writing, which includes articles focused on this specific case, the duty to act in good faith is, up to this point relatively uncharted. Because of the increased recognition of the importance of good faith, some conceptual guidance to the corporate community may be helpful. For that reason we proceed to address the merits of the appellants' second argument.

The precise question is whether the Chancellor's articulated standard for bad faith corporate fiduciary conduct-intentional dereliction of duty, a conscious disregard for one's responsibilities-is legally correct. In approaching that question, we note that the Chancellor characterized that definition as *"an* appropriate *(although not the only)* standard for determining whether fiduciaries have acted in good faith." That observation is accurate and helpful, because as a matter of simple logic, at least three different categories of fiduciary behavior are candidates for the "bad faith" pejorative label.

The first category involves so-called "subjective bad faith," that is, fiduciary conduct motivated by an actual intent to do harm. That such conduct constitutes classic, quintessential bad faith is a proposition so well accepted in the liturgy of fiduciary law that it borders on axiomatic. We need not dwell further on this category, because no such conduct is claimed to have occurred, or did occur, in this case.

The second category of conduct, which is at the opposite end of the spectrum, involves lack of due care—that is, fiduciary action taken solely by reason of gross negligence and without any malevolent intent. In this case, appellants assert claims of gross negligence to establish breaches not only of director due care but also of the directors' duty to act in good faith. Although the Chancellor found, and we agree, that the appellants failed to establish gross negligence, to afford guidance we address the issue of whether gross negligence (including a failure to inform one's self of available material facts), without more, can also constitute bad faith. The answer is clearly no.

From a broad philosophical standpoint, that question is more complex than would appear, if only because (as the Chancellor and others have observed) "issues of good faith are (to a certain degree) inseparably and necessarily intertwined with the duties of care and loyalty." But, in the pragmatic, conduct-regulating legal realm which calls for more precise conceptual line drawing, the answer is that grossly negligent conduct, without more, does not and cannot constitute a breach of the fiduciary duty to act in good faith. The conduct that is the subject of due care may overlap with the conduct that comes within the rubric of good faith in a psychological sense, but from a legal standpoint those duties are and must remain quite distinct. Both our legislative history and our common law jurisprudence distinguish sharply between the duties to exercise due care and to act in good faith, and highly significant consequences flow from that distinction.

The Delaware General Assembly has addressed the distinction between bad faith and a failure to exercise due care (*i.e.*, gross negligence) in two separate contexts. The first is Section 102(b)(7) of the DGCL, which authorizes Delaware corporations, by a provision in the certificate of incorporation, to exculpate their directors from monetary damage liability for a breach of the duty of care. That exculpatory provision affords significant protection to directors of Delaware corporations. The statute carves out several exceptions, however, including most relevantly, "for acts or omissions not in good faith." Thus, a corporation can exculpate its directors from monetary liability for a breach of the duty of care, but not for conduct that is not in good faith. To adopt a definition of bad faith that would cause a violation of the duty of care automatically to become an act or omission "not in good faith." would eviscerate the protections accorded to directors by the General Assembly's adoption of Section 102(b)(7).

A second legislative recognition of the distinction between fiduciary conduct that is grossly negligent and conduct that is not in good faith, is Delaware's indemnification statute, found at 8 Del. C. § 145. To oversimplify, subsections (a) and (b) of that statute permit a corporation to indemnify (*inter alia*) any person who is or was a director, officer, employee or agent of the corporation against expenses (including attorneys' fees), judgments, fines and amounts paid in settlement of specified actions, suits or proceedings, where (among other things): (i) that person is, was, or is threatened to be made a party to that action, suit or proceeding, and (ii) that person "acted in good faith and in a manner the person reasonably believed to be in or not opposed to the best interests of the corporation." Thus, under Delaware statutory law a director or officer of a corporation can be indemnified for liability (and litigation expenses) incurred by reason of a violation of the duty of care, but not for a violation of the duty to act in good faith.

Section 145, Like Section 102(b)(7), evidences the intent of the Delaware General Assembly to afford significant protections to directors (and, in the case of Section 145, other fiduciaries) of Delaware corporations. To adopt a definition that conflates the duty of care with the duty to act in good faith by making a violation of the former an automatic violation of the latter, would nullify those legislative protections and defeat the General Assembly's intent. There is no basis in policy, precedent or common sense that would justify dismantling the distinction between gross negligence and bad faith.

That leaves the third category of fiduciary conduct, which falls in between the first two categories of (1) conduct motivated by subjective bad intent and (2) conduct resulting from gross negligence. This third category is what the Chancellor's definition of bad faith—intentional dereliction of duty, a conscious disregard for one's responsibilities—is intended to capture. The question is whether such misconduct is properly treated as a non-exculpable, non-indemnifiable violation of the fiduciary duty to act in good faith. In our view it must be, for at least two reasons.

First, the universe of fiduciary misconduct is not limited to either disloyalty in the classic sense (*i.e.*, preferring the adverse self-interest of the fiduciary or of a related person to the interest of the corporation) or gross negligence. Cases have arisen where corporate directors have no conflicting self-interest in a decision, yet engage in misconduct that is more culpable than simple inattention or failure to be informed of all facts material to the decision. To protect the interests of the corporation and its shareholders, fiduciary conduct of this kind, which does not involve disloyalty (as traditionally defined) but is qualitatively more culpable than gross negligence, should be proscribed. A vehicle is needed to address such violations doctrinally, and that doctrinal vehicle is the duty to act in good faith. The Chancellor implicitly so recognized in his Opinion, where he identified different examples of bad faith as follows:

The good faith required of a corporate fiduciary includes not simply the duties of care and loyalty, in the narrow sense that I have discussed them above, but all actions required by a true faithfulness and devotion to the interests of the corporation and its shareholders. A failure to act in good faith may be shown, for instance, where the fiduciary intentionally acts with a purpose other than that of advancing the best interests of the corporation, where the fiduciary acts with the intent to violate applicable positive law, or where the fiduciary intentionally fails to act in the face of a known duty to act, demonstrating a conscious disregard for his duties. There may be other examples of bad faith yet to be proven or alleged, but these three are the most salient.

Those articulated examples of bad faith are not new to our jurisprudence. Indeed, they echo pronouncements our courts have made throughout the decades.

Second, the legislature has also recognized this intermediate category of fiduciary misconduct, which ranks between conduct involving subjective bad faith and gross negligence. Section 102(b)(7)(ii) of the DGCL expressly denies money damage exculpation for "acts or omissions not in good faith or which involve intentional misconduct or a knowing violation of law." By its very terms that provision distinguishes between "intentional misconduct" and a "knowing violation of law" (both examples of subjective bad faith) on the one hand, and "acts ... not in good faith," on the other. Because the statute exculpates directors only for conduct amounting to gross negligence, the statutory denial of exculpation for "acts ... not in good faith" must encompass the intermediate category of misconduct captured by the Chancellor's definition of bad faith.

For these reasons, we uphold the Court of Chancery's definition as a legally appropriate, although not the exclusive, definition of fiduciary bad faith. We need go no further. To engage in an effort to craft (in the Court's words) "a definitive and categorical definition of the universe of acts that would constitute bad faith" would be unwise and is unnecessary to dispose of the issues presented on this appeal.

For the reasons stated above, the judgment of the Court of Chancery is affirmed.

STONE V. RITTER

SUPREME COURT OF DELAWARE (HOLLAND, J.)
911 A.2D 362 (2006)

This is an appeal from a final judgment of the Court of Chancery dismissing a derivative complaint against fifteen present and former directors of AmSouth Bancorporation, a Delaware corporation.

The Court of Chancery characterized the allegations in the derivative complaint as a "classic *Caremark* claim," a claim that derives its name from *In re Caremark Int'l Deriv. Litig.* In *Caremark*, the Court of Chancery recognized that: "Generally where a claim of directorial liability for corporate loss is predicated upon ignorance of liability creating activities within the corporation only a sustained or systematic failure of the board to exercise oversight—such as an utter failure to attempt to assure a reasonable information and reporting system exists—will establish the lack of good faith that is a necessary condition to liability."

This derivative action is brought on AmSouth's behalf by William and Sandra Stone, who allege that they owned AmSouth common stock "at all relevant times." The nominal defendant, AmSouth, is a Delaware corporation with its principal executive offices in Birmingham, Alabama. During the relevant period, AmSouth's wholly-owned subsidiary, AmSouth Bank, operated about 600 commercial banking branches in six states throughout the southeastern United States and employed more than 11,600 people.

In 2004, AmSouth and AmSouth Bank paid $40 million in fines and $10 million in civil penalties to resolve government and regulatory investigations pertaining principally to the failure by bank employees to file "Suspicious Activity Reports", as required by the federal Bank Secrecy Act and various anti-money-laundering regulations. No fines or penalties were imposed on AmSouth's directors, and no other regulatory action was taken against them.

The *Caremark* standard for so-called "oversight" liability draws heavily upon the concept of director failure to act in good faith. That is consistent with the definition(s) of bad faith recently approved by this Court in its recent *Disney* decision, where we held that a failure to act in good faith requires conduct that is qualitatively different from, and more culpable than, the conduct giving rise to a violation of the fiduciary duty of care (i.e., gross negligence). In *Disney*, we identified the following examples of conduct that would establish a failure to act in good faith:

> A failure to act in good faith may be shown, for instance, where the fiduciary intentionally acts with a purpose other than that of advancing the best interests of the corporation, where the fiduciary acts with the intent to violate applicable positive law, or where the fiduciary intentionally fails to act in the face of a known duty to act, demonstrating a conscious disregard for his duties. There may be other

examples of bad faith yet to be proven or alleged, but these three are the most salient.

The third of these examples describes, and is fully consistent with, the lack of good faith conduct that the *Caremark* court held was a "necessary condition" for director oversight liability, i.e., "a sustained or systematic failure of the board to exercise oversight—such as an utter failure to attempt to assure a reasonable information and reporting system exists." Indeed, our opinion in *Disney* cited *Caremark* with approval for that proposition. Accordingly, the Court of Chancery applied the correct standard in assessing whether demand was excused in this case where failure to exercise oversight was the basis or theory of the plaintiffs' claim for relief.

It is important, in this context, to clarify a doctrinal issue that is critical to understanding fiduciary liability under *Caremark* as we construe that case. The phraseology used in *Caremark* and that we employ here—describing the lack of good faith as a "necessary condition to liability"—is deliberate. The purpose of that formulation is to communicate that a failure to act in good faith is not conduct that results, *ipso facto*, in the direct imposition of fiduciary liability. The failure to act in good faith may result in liability because the requirement to act in good faith "is a subsidiary element," i.e., a condition, "of the fundamental duty of loyalty." It follows that because a showing of bad faith conduct, in the sense described in *Disney* and *Caremark*, is essential to establish director oversight liability, the fiduciary duty violated by that conduct is the duty of loyalty.

This view of a failure to act in good faith results in two additional doctrinal consequences. First, although good faith may be described colloquially as part of a "triad" of fiduciary duties that includes the duties of care and loyalty, the obligation to act in good faith does not establish an independent fiduciary duty that stands on the same footing as the duties of care and loyalty. Only the latter two duties, where violated, may directly result in liability, whereas a failure to act in good faith may do so, but indirectly. The second doctrinal consequence is that the fiduciary duty of loyalty is not limited to cases involving a financial or other cognizable fiduciary conflict of interest. It also encompasses cases where the fiduciary fails to act in good faith. As the Court of Chancery aptly put it in *Guttman*, "A director cannot act loyally towards the corporation unless she acts in the good faith belief that her actions are in the corporation's best interest."

We hold that *Caremark* articulates the necessary conditions predicate for director oversight liability: (a) the directors utterly failed to implement any reporting or information system or controls; *or* (b) having implemented such a system or controls, consciously failed to monitor or oversee its operations thus disabling themselves from being informed of risks or problems requiring their attention. In either case, imposition of liability requires a showing that the directors knew that they were not discharging their fiduciary obligations. Where directors fail to act in the face of a known duty to act, thereby demonstrating a conscious disregard for their responsibilities, they breach their duty of loyalty by failing to discharge that fiduciary obligation in good faith.

For the plaintiffs' derivative complaint to withstand a motion to dismiss, "only a sustained or systematic failure of the board to exercise oversight—such as an utter failure to attempt to assure a reasonable information and reporting system exists—will establish the lack of good faith that is a necessary condition to liability." As the *Caremark* decision noted:

> Such a test of liability—lack of good faith as evidenced by sustained or systematic failure of a dirctor to exercise reasonable oversight—is quite high. But, a demanding test of liability in the oversight context is probably beneficial to corporate shareholders as a class, as it is in the board decision context, since it makes board service by qualified persons more likely, while continuing to act as a stimulus to *good faith performance of duty* by such directors.

The KPMG Report—which the plaintiffs explicitly incorporated by reference into their derivative complaint—refutes the assertion that the directors "never took the necessary steps to ensure that a reasonable BSA compliance and reporting system existed." KPMG's findings reflect that the Board received and approved relevant policies and procedures, delegated to certain employees and departments the responsibility for filing SARs and monitoring compliance, and exercised oversight by relying on periodic reports from them. Although there ultimately may have been failures by employees to report deficiencies to the Board, there is no basis for an oversight claim seeking to hold the directors personally liable for such failures by the employees.

With the benefit of hindsight, the plaintiffs' complaint seeks to equate a bad outcome with bad faith. The lacuna in the plaintiffs' argument is a failure to recognize that the directors' good faith exercise of oversight responsibility may not invariably prevent employees from violating criminal laws, or from causing the corporation to incur significant financial liability, or both, as occurred in *Graham, Caremark* and this very case. In the absence of red flags, good faith in the context of oversight must be measured by the directors' actions "to assure a reasonable information and reporting system exists" and not by second-guessing after the occurrence of employee conduct that results in an unintended adverse outcome. Accordingly, we hold that the Court of Chancery properly applied *Caremark* and dismissed the plaintiffs' derivative complaint.

The judgment of the Court of Chancery is affirmed.

FEDERAL FIDUCIARY DUTIES PART E

SARBANES-OXLEY ACT OF 2002

SECTION 302(a). CORPORATE RESPONSIBILITY FOR FINANCIAL REPORTS.

REGULATIONS REQUIRED. The Commission shall, by rule, require, for each company filing periodic reports under section 13(a) or 15(d) of the Securities Exchange Act of 1934, that the principal executive officer or officers and the principal financial officer or officers, or persons performing similar functions, certify in each annual or quarterly report filed or submitted under either such section of such Act that

(1) the signing officer has reviewed the report;

(2) based on the officer's knowledge, the report does not contain any untrue statement of a material fact or omit to state a material fact necessary in order to make the statements made, in light of the circumstances under which such statements were made, not misleading;

(3) based on such officer's knowledge, the financial statements, and other financial information included in the report, fairly present in all material respects the financial condition and results of operations of the issuer as of, and for, the periods presented in the report;

(4) the signing officers

(a) are responsible for establishing and maintaining internal controls;

(b) have designed such internal controls to ensure that material information relating to the issuer and its consolidated subsidiaries is made known to such officers by others within those entities, particularly during the period in which the periodic reports are being prepared;

(c) have evaluated the effectiveness of the issuer's internal controls as of a date within 90 days prior to the report; and

(d) have presented in the report their conclusions about the effectiveness of their internal controls based on their evaluation as of that date;

(5) the signing officers have disclosed to the issuer's auditors and the audit committee of the board of directors (or persons fulfilling the equivalent function)

(a) all significant deficiencies in the design or operation of internal controls which could adversely affect the issuer's ability to record, process, summarize, and report financial data and have identified for the issuer's auditors any material weaknesses in internal controls; and

(b) any fraud, whether or not material, that involves management or other employees who have a significant role in the issuer's internal controls; and

(6) the signing officers have indicated in the report whether or not there were significant changes in internal controls or in other factors that could significantly affect internal controls

253

subsequent to the date of their evaluation, including any corrective actions with regard to significant deficiencies and material weaknesses.

SECTION 304(a). FORFEITURE OF CERTAIN BONUSES AND PROFITS.

ADDITIONAL COMPENSATION PRIOR TO NONCOMPLIANCE WITH COMMISSION FINANCIAL REPORTING REQUIREMENTS. If an issuer is required to prepare an accounting restatement due to the material noncompliance of the issuer, as a result of misconduct, with any financial reporting requirement under the securities laws, the chief executive officer and chief financial officer of the issuer shall reimburse the issuer for

(1) any bonus or other incentive-based or equity-based compensation received by that person from the issuer during the 12-month period following the first public issuance or filing with the Commission (whichever first occurs) of the financial document embodying such financial reporting requirement; and

(2) any profits realized from the sale of securities of the issuer during that 12-month period.

SECTION 402(a). ENHANCED CONFLICT OF INTEREST PROVISIONS.

PROHIBITION ON PERSONAL LOANS TO EXECUTIVES. Section 13 of the Securities Exchange Act of 1934 is amended by adding at the end the following:

"(k) PROHIBITION ON PERSONAL LOANS TO EXECUTIVES.

(1) IN GENERAL. It shall be unlawful for any issuer (as defined in section 2 of the Sarbanes-Oxley Act of 2002), directly or indirectly, including through any subsidiary, to extend or maintain credit, to arrange for the extension of credit, or to renew an extension of credit, in the form of a personal loan to or for any director or executive officer (or equivalent thereof) of that issuer. An extension of credit maintained by the issuer on the date of enactment of this subsection shall not be subject to the provisions of this subsection, provided that there is no material modification to any term of any such extension of credit or any renewal of any such extension of credit on or after that date of enactment."

SECTION 404. MANAGEMENT ASSESSMENT OF INTERNAL CONTROLS.

(a) RULES REQUIRED. The Commission shall prescribe rules requiring each annual report required by section 13(a) or 15(d) of the Securities Exchange Act of 1934 (15 U.S.C. 78m or 78o(d)) to contain an internal control report, which shall

(1) state the responsibility of management for establishing and maintaining an adequate internal control structure and procedures for financial reporting; and

(2) contain an assessment, as of the end of the most recent fiscal year of the issuer, of the effectiveness of the internal control structure and procedures of the issuer for financial reporting.

(b) INTERNAL CONTROL EVALUATION AND REPORTING. With respect to the internal control assessment required by subsection (a), each registered public accounting firm that prepares or issues the audit report for the issuer shall attest to, and report on, the assessment made by the management of the issuer. An attestation made under this subsection shall be made in accordance with standards for attestation engagements issued or adopted by the Board. Any such attestation shall not be the subject of a separate engagement.

SECTION 406(a). CODE OF ETHICS FOR SENIOR FINANCIAL OFFICERS.

CODE OF ETHICS DISCLOSURE. The Commission shall issue rules to require each issuer, together with periodic reports required pursuant to section 13(a) or 15(d) of the Securities Exchange Act of 1934, to disclose whether or not, and if not, the reason therefor, such issuer has adopted a code of ethics for senior financial officers, applicable to its principal financial officer and comptroller or principal accounting officer, or persons performing similar functions.

SECTION 906(a). CORPORATE RESPONSIBILITY FOR FINANCIAL REPORTS.

IN GENERAL. Chapter 63 of title 18, United States Code, is amended by inserting after section 1349, as created by this Act, the following:

"§1350. Failure of corporate officers to certify financial reports

(a) CERTIFICATION OF PERIODIC FINANCIAL REPORTS. Each periodic report containing financial statements filed by an issuer with the Securities Exchange Commission pursuant to section 13(a) or 15(d) of the Securities Exchange Act of 1934 shall be accompanied by a written statement by the chief executive officer and chief financial officer (or equivalent thereof) of the issuer.

(b) CONTENT. The statement required under subsection (a) shall certify that the periodic report containing the financial statements fully complies with the requirements of section 13(a) or 15(d) of the Securities Exchange Act pf 1934 and that information contained in the periodic report fairly presents, in all material respects, the financial condition and results of operations of the issuer.

(c) CRIMINAL PENALTIES. Whoever

(1) certifies any statement as set forth in subsections (a) and (b) of this section knowing that the periodic report accompanying the statement does not comport with all the

requirements set forth in this section shall be fined not more than $1,000,000 or imprisoned not more than 10 years, or both; or

(2) willfully certifies any statement as set forth in sub-sections (a) and (b) of this section knowing that the periodic report accompanying the statement does not comport with all the requirements set forth in this section shall be fined not more than $5,000,000, or imprisoned not more than 20 years, or both."

NEW YORK STOCK EXCHANGE LISTED COMPANY MANUAL

301.00. INTRODUCTION

Investors expect that if a company's shares are listed on the New York Stock Exchange, the company has complied with specified financial standards and disclosure policies developed and administered by the Exchange. In addition, consistent with the Exchange's long-standing commitment to encourage high standards of corporate democracy, every listed company is expected to follow certain practices aimed at maintaining appropriate standards of corporate responsibility, integrity and accountability to shareholders.

303A.01. INDEPENDENT DIRECTORS

Listed companies must have a majority of independent directors.

303A.02(a). INDEPENDENCE TESTS

In order to tighten the definition of "independent director" for purposes of these standards:

(i) No director qualifies as "independent" unless the board of directors affirmatively determines that the director has no material relationship with the listed company (either directly or as a partner, shareholder or officer of an organization that has a relationship with the company).

(ii) In addition, in affirmatively determining the independence of any director who will serve on the compensation committee of the listed company's board of directors, the board of directors must consider all factors specifically relevant to determining whether a director has a relationship to the listed company which is material to that director's ability to be independent from management in connection with the duties of a compensation committee member, including, but not limited to:

(a) the source of compensation of such director, including any consulting, advisory or other compensatory fee paid by the listed company to such director; and

(b) whether such director is affiliated with the listed company, a subsidiary of the listed company or an affiliate of a subsidiary of the listed company.

303A.04(a). NOMINATING/CORPORATE GOVERNANCE COMMITTEE

Listed companies must have a nominating/corporate governance committee composed entirely of independent directors.

303A.05(a). COMPENSATION COMMITTEE

Listed companies must have a compensation committee composed entirely of independent directors.

303A.06. AUDIT COMMITTEE

Listed companies must have an audit committee that satisfies the requirements of Rule 10A-3 under the Exchange Act.

303A.07(a). AUDIT COMMITTEE ADDITIONAL REQUIREMENTS

The audit committee must have a minimum of three members. All audit committee members must satisfy the requirements for independence set out in Section 303A.02 and, in the absence of an applicable exemption, Rule 10A-3(b)(1).

303A.10. CODE OF BUSINESS CONDUCT AND ETHICS

Listed companies must adopt and disclose a code of business conduct and ethics for directors, officers and employees, and promptly disclose any waivers of the code for directors or executive officers.

303A.12. CERTIFICATION REQUIREMENTS

(a) Each listed company CEO must certify to the NYSE each year that he or she is not aware of any violation by the listed company of NYSE corporate governance listing standards, qualifying the certification to the extent necessary.

(b) Each listed company CEO must promptly notify the NYSE in writing after any executive officer of the listed company becomes aware of any non-compliance with any applicable provisions of this Section 303A.

(c) Each listed company must submit an executed Written Affirmation annually to the NYSE. In addition, each listed company must submit an interim Written Affirmation as and when required by the interim Written Affirmation form specified by the NYSE.

CHAPTER 8:

CORPORATE PERSONAL LIABILITY

INTRODUCTION

Limited liability is, for many, the hallmark of the corporate form. By placing a veil between the corporation and its shareholders, the law protects investors from excessive loss, thereby enabling them to bear greater risk. In contrast to the unlimited liability faced by partners, corporate shareholders cannot lose more than they venture. It is therefore safe for them to place a comparatively modest bet on a novel industry because they are not gambling with the entirety of their wealth. The resulting opportunity to diversify their investments has enabled entrepreneurs to raise capital in small amounts from large numbers of non-experts—to, in effect, tap the vast savings of the upper middle class. In this way, limited liability has enabled corporations to accumulate the kinds of capital that no single investor, however wealthy, could have borne alone.

Having acknowledged the benefits of limited liability, we must also recognize its limits. When corporations fail to play by the rules, their managers and owners need to be held accountable. Parts A and B of this chapter explore two mechanisms for holding investors liable for the debts of their corporations—piercing the corporate veil and equitable subordination.

As you consider the cases in this chapter, notice the degree to which the concept of limited liability flows from the underlying architecture of the corporate system. The issue is not one of fairness or justice but of structure and form. Then notice how quickly limited liability is discarded when investors fail to respect the imaginary construct that the law calls a corporation. Consider, too, the larger public policy issues at stake.

In Part C, we change course and examine the complex rules that govern lawsuits against managers for breaches of their fiduciary duties. Lawsuits can be either direct or derivative. In a direct suit, the plaintiff is the injured party and is entitled to receive any damages that the court awards. In a derivative suit, the plaintiff-shareholder is actually suing in the name of the corporation. It is the entity as a whole, not the particular shareholder, who was allegedly wronged by the managers' lack of care or loyalty. Moreover, as the injured party, it is the corporation, not the plaintiff-shareholder, that is entitled to receive any damages.

Needless to say, this is an awkward system fraught with peril. On the one hand, it does not seem wise to trust managers to sue themselves when they misbehave. On the other hand, entrusting the reins of the corporation to a random shareholder seems equally imprudent. After all, the plaintiff-shareholder was not elected in any democratic manner, may or may not have any appropriate expertise, and may or may not have the best interests of the corporate enterprise in mind. In response to these tensions, Delaware courts have fashioned a complex set of what amounts to rules of civil procedure that govern the conduct of derivative actions.

Finally, Part D examines the concept of indemnification. To what extent may (or must) corporations reimburse their officers and directors for liabilities they incur while acting in such capacities? The answer to this question has important implications for the degree of accountability actually faced by managers.

At the end of this chapter, you will understand the procedures for bringing direct lawsuits against corporate shareholders as well as derivative lawsuits against corporate managers. You will also understand how to use this knowledge to protect your corporate clients by structuring their affairs so as to minimize the likelihood that liability will ever extend beyond the corporate veil.

PART A PIERCING THE CORPORATE VEIL

WALKOVSZKY V. CARLTON

COURT OF APPEALS OF NEW YORK (FULD, J.)
223 N.E.2D 6 (1966)

This case involves what appears to be a rather common practice in the taxicab industry of vesting the ownership of a taxi fleet in many corporations, each owning only one or two cabs.

The complaint alleges that the plaintiff was severely injured four years ago in New York City when he was run down by a taxicab owned by the defendant Seon Cab Corporation and

260

negligently operated at the time by the defendant Marchese. The individual defendant, Carlton, is claimed to be a stockholder of 10 corporations, including Seon, each of which has but two cabs registered in its name, and it is implied that only the minimum automobile liability insurance required by law (in the amount of $10,000) is carried on any one cab. Although seemingly independent of one another, these corporations are alleged to be "operated as a single entity, unit and enterprise" with regard to financing, supplies, repairs, employees and garaging, and all are named as defendants. The plaintiff asserts that he is also entitled to hold their stockholders personally liable for the damages sought because the multiple corporate structure constitutes an unlawful attempt "to defraud members of the general public" who might be injured by the cabs.

The defendant Carlton has moved to dismiss the complaint on the ground that as to him it "fails to state a cause of action". The court at Special Term granted the motion but the Appellate Division, by a divided vote, reversed, holding that a valid cause of action was sufficiently stated. The defendant Carlton appeals to us, from the nonfinal order, by leave of the Appellate Division on a certified question.

The law permits the incorporation of a business for the very purpose of enabling its proprietors to escape personal liability but, manifestly, the privilege is not without its limits. Broadly speaking, the courts will disregard the corporate form, or, to use accepted terminology, "pierce the corporate veil," whenever necessary "to prevent fraud or to achieve equity." In determining whether liability should be extended to reach assets beyond those belonging to the corporation, we are guided, as Judge Cardozo noted, by "general rules of agency." In other words, whenever anyone uses control of the corporation to further his own rather than the corporation's business, he will be liable for the corporation's acts "upon the principle of *respondeat superior* applicable even where the agent is a natural person." Such liability, moreover, extends not only to the corporation's commercial dealings but to its negligent acts as well.

In the case before us, the plaintiff has explicitly alleged that none of the corporations "had a separate existence of their own" and, as indicated above, all are named as defendants. However, it is one thing to assert that a corporation is a fragment of a larger corporate combine which actually conducts the business. It is quite another to claim that the corporation is a "dummy" for its individual stockholders who are in reality carrying on the business in their personal capacities for purely personal rather than corporate ends. Either circumstance would justify treating the corporation as an agent and piercing the corporate veil to reach the principal but a different result would follow in each case. In the first, only a larger *corporate* entity would be held financially responsible while, in the other, the stockholder would be personally liable. Either the stockholder is conducting the business in his individual capacity or he is not. If he is, he will be liable; if he is not, then, it does not matter—Insofar as his personal liability is concerned—that the enterprise is actually being carried on by a larger "enterprise entity".

Reading the complaint in this case most favorably and liberally, we do not believe that there can be gathered from its averments the allegations required to spell out a valid cause of action against the defendant Carlton.

The individual defendant is charged with having "organized, managed, dominated and controlled" a fragmented corporate entity but there are no allegations that he was conducting business in his individual capacity. Had the taxicab fleet been owned by a single corporation, it would be readily apparent that the plaintiff would face formidable barriers in attempting to establish personal liability on the part of the corporation's stockholders. The fact that the fleet ownership has been deliberately split up among many corporations does not ease the plaintiff's burden in that respect. The corporate form may not be disregarded merely because the assets of the corporation, together with the mandatory insurance coverage of the vehicle which struck the plaintiff, are insufficient to assure him the recovery sought. If Carlton were to be held individually liable on those facts alone, the decision would apply equally to the thousands of cabs which are owned by their individual drivers who conduct their businesses through corporations organized pursuant to section 401 of the Business Corporation Law and carry the minimum insurance required by subdivision 1 (par. [a]) of section 370 of the Vehicle and Traffic Law. These taxi owner-operators are entitled to form such corporations, and we agree with the court at Special Term that, if the insurance coverage required by statute "is inadequate for the protection of the public, the remedy lies not with the courts but with the Legislature." It may very well be sound policy to require that certain corporations must take out liability insurance which will afford adequate compensation to their potential tort victims. However, the responsibility for imposing conditions on the privilege of incorporation has been committed by the Constitution to the Legislature and it may not be fairly implied, from any statute, that the Legislature intended, without the slightest discussion or debate, to require of taxi corporations that they carry automobile liability insurance over and above that mandated by the Vehicle and Traffic Law.

This is not to say that it is impossible for the plaintiff to state a valid cause of action against the defendant Carlton. However, the simple fact is that the plaintiff has just not done so here. While the complaint alleges that the separate corporations were undercapitalized and that their assets have been intermingled, it is barren of any "sufficiently particularized statements" that the defendant Carlton and his associates are actually doing business in their individual capacities, shuttling their personal funds in and out of the corporations "without regard to formality and to suit their immediate convenience." Such a "perversion of the privilege to do business in a corporate form" would justify imposing personal liability on the individual stockholders. Nothing of the sort has in fact been charged, and it cannot reasonably or logically be inferred from the happenstance that the business of Seon Cab Corporation may actually be carried on by a larger corporate entity composed of many corporations which, under general principles of agency, would be liable to each other's creditors in contract and in tort.

In point of fact, the principle relied upon in the complaint to sustain the imposition of personal liability is not agency but fraud. Such a cause of action cannot withstand analysis. If it is not fraudulent for the owner-operator of a single cab corporation to take out only the minimum required liability insurance, the enterprise does not become either illicit or fraudulent merely because it consists of many such corporations. The plaintiff's injuries are the same regardless of whether the cab which strikes him is owned by a single corporation or part of a fleet with ownership fragmented among many corporations. Whatever rights he may be able to assert against parties other than the registered owner of the vehicle come into being not because he has been defrauded but because, under the principle of *respondeat superior*, he is entitled to hold the whole enterprise responsible for the acts of its agents.

In sum, then, the complaint falls short of adequately stating a cause of action against the defendant Carlton in his individual capacity.

KEATING, J. (dissenting).
The defendant Carlton, the shareholder here sought to be held for the negligence of the driver of a taxicab, was a principal shareholder and organizer of the defendant corporation which owned the taxicab. The corporation was one of 10 organized by the defendant, each containing two cabs and each cab having the "minimum liability" insurance coverage mandated by section 370 of the Vehicle and Traffic Law. The sole assets of these operating corporations are the vehicles themselves and they are apparently subject to mortgages.

From their inception these corporations were intentionally undercapitalized for the purpose of avoiding responsibility for acts which were bound to arise as a result of the operation of a large taxi fleet having cars out on the street 24 hours a day and engaged in public transportation. And during the course of the corporations' existence all income was continually drained out of the corporations for the same purpose.

The issue presented by this action is whether the policy of this State, which affords those desiring to engage in a business enterprise the privilege of limited liability through the use of the corporate device, is so strong that it will permit that privilege to continue no matter how much it is abused, no matter how irresponsibly the corporation is operated, no matter what the cost to the public. I do not believe that it is.

Justice Roger Traynor, speaking for the Supreme Court of California, outlined the applicable law in this area. "The figurative terminology 'alter ego' and 'disregard of the corporate entity' ", he wrote, "is generally used to refer to the various situations that are an abuse of the corporate privilege. The equitable owners of a corporation, for example, are personally liable when they treat the assets of the corporation as their own and add or withdraw capital from the corporation at will; when they hold themselves out as being personally liable for the debts of the corporation; *or when they provide inadequate capitalization and actively participate in the conduct of corporate affairs*".

The defendant Carlton claims that, because the minimum amount of insurance required by the statute was obtained, the corporate veil cannot and should not be pierced despite the fact that the assets of the corporation which owned the cab were "trifling compared with the business to be done and the risks of loss" which were certain to be encountered. I do not agree.

The Legislature in requiring minimum liability insurance of $10,000, no doubt, intended to provide at least some small fund for recovery against those individuals and corporations who just did not have and were not able to raise or accumulate assets sufficient to satisfy the claims of those who were injured as a result of their negligence. It certainly could not have intended to shield those individuals who organized corporations, with the specific intent of avoiding responsibility to the public, where the operation of the corporate enterprise yielded profits sufficient to purchase additional insurance. Moreover, it is reasonable to assume that the Legislature believed that those individuals and corporations having substantial assets would take out insurance far in excess of the minimum in order to protect those assets from depletion. Given the costs of hospital care and treatment and the nature of injuries sustained in auto collisions, it would be unreasonable to assume that the Legislature believed that the minimum provided in the statute would in and of itself be sufficient to recompense "innocent victims of motor vehicle accidents for the injury and financial loss inflicted upon them".

The defendant contends that a decision holding him personally liable would discourage people from engaging in corporate enterprise.

What I would merely hold is that a participating shareholder of a corporation vested with a public interest, organized with capital insufficient to meet liabilities which are certain to arise in the ordinary course of the corporation's business, may be held personally responsible for such liabilities. Where corporate income is not sufficient to cover the cost of insurance premiums above the statutory minimum or where initially adequate finances dwindle under the pressure of competition, bad times or extraordinary and unexpected liability, obviously the shareholder will not be held liable.

The only types of corporate enterprises that will be discouraged as a result of a decision allowing the individual shareholder to be sued will be those such as the one in question, designed solely to abuse the corporate privilege at the expense of the public interest.

For these reasons I would vote to affirm the order of the Appellate Division.

SEA-LAND SERVICES, INC. V. THE PEPPER SOURCE

UNITED STATES COURT OF APPEALS, SEVENTH CIRCUIT (BAUER, C.J.)
941 F.2D 519 (1991)

This spicy case finds its origin in several shipments of Jamaican sweet peppers. Appellee Sea-Land Services, Inc., an ocean carrier, shipped the peppers on behalf of The Pepper Source, one of the appellants here. PS then stiffed Sea-Land on the freight bill, which was rather substantial. Sea-Land filed a federal diversity action for the money it was owed. On December 2, 1987, the district court entered a default judgment in favor of Sea-Land and against PS in the amount of $86,767.70. But PS was nowhere to be found; it had been "dissolved" in mid-1987 for failure to pay the annual state franchise tax. Worse yet for Sea-Land, even had it not been dissolved, PS apparently had no assets. With the well empty, Sea-Land could not recover its judgment against PS. Hence the instant lawsuit.

In June 1988, Sea-Land brought this action against Gerald J. Marchese and five business entities he owns: PS, Caribe Crown, Inc., Jamar Corp., Salescaster Distributors, Inc., and Marchese Fegan Associates.[1] Marchese also was named individually. Sea-Land sought by this suit to pierce PS's corporate veil and render Marchese personally liable for the judgment owed to Sea-Land, and then "reverse pierce" Marchese's other corporations so that they, too, would be on the hook for the $87,000. Thus, Sea-Land alleged in its complaint that all of these corporations "are alter egos of each other and hide behind the veils of alleged separate corporate existence for the purpose of defrauding plaintiff and other creditors." Not only are the corporations alter egos of each other, alleged Sea-Land, but also they are alter egos of Marchese, who should be held individually liable for the judgment because he created and manipulated these corporations and their assets for his own personal uses. (Hot on the heels of the filing of Sea-Land's complaint, PS took the necessary steps to be reinstated as a corporation in Illinois.)

In an order dated June 22, 1990, the court discussed and applied the test for corporate veil-piercing explicated in *Van Dorn Co. v. Future Chemical and Oil Corp.* Analyzing Illinois law, we held in *Van Dorn* that a corporate entity will be disregarded and the veil of limited liability pierced when two requirements are met:

> First, there must be such unity of interest and ownership that the separate personalities of the corporation and the individual or other corporation no longer exist; and second, circumstances must be such that adherence to the fiction of separate corporate existence would sanction a fraud or promote injustice.

The court concluded that both halves and all features of the test had been satisfied, and, therefore, entered judgment in favor of Sea-Land and against PS, Caribe Crown, Jamar, Salescaster, Tie-Net, and Marchese individually. These defendants were held jointly liable for Sea-Land's $87,000 judgment, as well as for post-judgment interest under Illinois law. From that judgment Marchese and the other defendants brought a timely appeal.

---

1   This last defendant is a partnership. Because Sea-Land served only one partner—Marchese—the district court did not consider or enter judgment on Sea-Land's claims against this entity. Thus, for all practical purposes, the entity of Marchese Fegan Associates is out of this case, and henceforth our references to "the defendants" do not include this entity.

Because this is an appeal from a grant of summary judgment, our review is *de novo*. Thus, our task is to examine the evidence for ourselves, apply the same standard as the district court (namely, the *Van Dorn* test), and determine whether there is no genuine issue of material fact and whether Sea-Land is entitled to judgment as a matter of law.

The first and most striking feature that emerges from our examination of the record is that these corporate defendants are, indeed, little but Marchese's playthings. Marchese is the sole shareholder of PS, Caribe Crown, Jamar, and Salescaster. He is one of the two shareholders of Tie-Net. Except for Tie-Net, none of the corporations ever held a single corporate meeting. (At the handful of Tie-Net meetings held by Marchese and Andre, no minutes were taken.) During his deposition, Marchese did not remember any of these corporations ever passing articles of incorporation, bylaws, or other agreements. As for physical facilities, Marchese runs all of these corporations (including Tie-Net) out of the same, single office, with the same phone line, the same expense accounts, and the like. And how he does "run" the expense accounts! When he fancies to, Marchese "borrows" substantial sums of money from these corporations—interest free, of course. The corporations also "borrow" money from each other when need be, which left at least PS completely out of capital when the Sea-Land bills came due. What's more, Marchese has used the bank accounts of these corporations to pay all kinds of personal expenses, including alimony and child support payments to his ex-wife, education expenses for his children, maintenance of his personal automobiles, health care for his pet—the list goes on and on. Marchese did not even have a personal bank account! (With "corporate" accounts like these, who needs one?)

In sum, we agree with the district court that their can be no doubt that the "shared control/unity of interest and ownership" part of the *Van Dorn* test is met in this case: corporate records and formalities have not been maintained; funds and assets have been commingled with abandon; PS, the offending corporation, and perhaps others have been undercapitalized; and corporate assets have been moved and tapped and "borrowed" without regard to their source. Thus, Sea-Land is entitled to judgment on these points.

The second part of the *Van Dorn* test is more problematic, however. "Unity of interest and ownership" is not enough; Sea-Land also must show that honoring the separate corporate existences of the defendants "would sanction a fraud or promote injustice." This last phrase truly is disjunctive:

Although an intent to defraud creditors would surely play a part if established, the Illinois test does not require proof of such intent. Once the first element of the test is established, *either* the sanctioning of a fraud (intentional wrongdoing) or the promotion of injustice, will satisfy the second element.

Seizing on this, Sea-Land has abandoned the language in its two complaints that make repeated references to "fraud" by Marchese, and has chosen not to attempt to *prove* that PS and Marchese intended to defraud it—which would be quite difficult on summary judgment. Instead, Sea-Land has argued that honoring the defendants' separate identities would "promote injustice."

But what, exactly, does "promote injustice" mean, and how does one establish it on summary judgment? These are the critical, troublesome questions in this case. To start with, as the above passage from *Van Dorn* makes clear, "promote injustice" means something less than an affirmative showing of fraud—but how much less? In its one-sentence treatment of this point, the district court held that it was enough that "Sea-Land would be denied a judicially-imposed recovery." Sea-Land defends this reasoning on appeal, arguing that "permitting the appellants to hide behind the shield of limited liability would clearly serve as an injustice against appellee" because it would "impermissibly deny appellee satisfaction." But that cannot be what is meant by "promote injustice." The prospect of an unsatisfied judgment looms in every veil-piercing action; why else would a plaintiff bring such an action? Thus, if an unsatisfied judgment is enough for the "promote injustice" feature of the test, then *every* plaintiff will pass on that score, and *Van Dorn* collapses into a one-step "unity of interest and ownership" test.

Because we cannot abide such a result, we will undertake our own review of Illinois cases to determine how the "promote injustice" feature of the veil-piercing inquiry has been interpreted. In *Pederson*, a recent case from the Illinois court of appeals, the court offered the following summary: "Some element of unfairness, something akin to fraud or deception or the existence of a compelling public interest must be present in order to disregard the corporate fiction."

Gromer, Wittenstrom & Meyer, P.C. v. Strom was another unfortunately complicated case in which our issue was addressed. Basically, three individuals, W, M, and S, were partners. All three signed a note agreeing to be jointly and severally liable for a debt owed to a bank. S left the partnership and it dissolved. W & M then formed a new corporation, W & M Co., of which they were the sole shareholders. W & M Co. paid off the bank and became the assignee of the note, and then promptly sued S for collection on the note. Putting to one side the rather abstruse procedural posture of the case, suffice it to say that W & M Co. won at the trial level and appealed. On appeal, S claimed that the court should pierce the corporate veil and recognize W & M Co. for what it really was—his former partners and cosigners on the note; the reason being that cosigners cannot payoff a note and then take judgment on the note against another cosigner. The appellate court agreed and vacated the judgment:

> We believe that these facts and arguments sufficiently indicate that to recognize W & M Co. as an entity separate from its shareholders would be to sanction an injustice. Where such an injustice would result and there is such unity of interest between the corporation and the individual shareholders that the separate personalities no longer exist, the corporate veil must be pierced.

In *B. Kreisman & Co. v. First Arlington Nat'l Bank of Arlington Heights*, the appellate court reversed the trial court's refusal to pierce the veil. Defendant corporation stiffed plaintiff for the bill on some restaurant equipment, so plaintiff sued for a mechanics lien. Plaintiff won at trial, but the trial court would not pierce the defendant corporation's veil and also hold liable the individual who was the "dominant force" controlling the defendant corporation. Noting that the equipment, though never paid for, was used by the defendant corporation for several years, the appellate court stated, "Under these circumstances we believe the corporate veil should be pierced to require the 'dominant individual' to be personally liable; to say otherwise would promote an injustice and permit her to be unjustly enriched at plaintiff's expense."

Federal district courts sitting in Illinois also have on occasion discussed what kind of "injustice" suffices under the second half of the *Van Dorn* test. *In re Conticommodity Services, Inc., Securities Litigation* involved a complex, multidistrict litigation that ultimately had little to do with veil-piercing. At one point in its opinion, however, the district court considered whether a trial was necessary on the claim that a parent corporation should be pierced to satisfy a liability of one of its subsidiaries. The court concluded that the issue should go to trial, because "it may be an injustice" to allow the parent to avoid the sub's liabilities when the parent closed down the sub and left it with insufficient funds to satisfy its liabilities, and those liabilities were caused in part by a practice of the sub mandated by the parent.

Finally, *Van Dorn* itself is somewhat instructive. In that case, we affirmed the district court's decision to pierce the corporate veil of one corporation ("Future") to get at the assets held by another ("Sovereign of Illinois") for the benefit of a creditor who had shipped Future some packing cans ("Milton"). As to the second half of the test, we stated as follows:

> Eventually Future was stripped of its assets and rendered insolvent to the prejudice of Milton, its only creditor, while Sovereign of Illinois received the benefits of the Milton can shipments. The record supported the trial court's finding that such a result was unjust and warranted piercing the corporate veil between Future and Sovereign of Illinois to hold Sovereign of Illinois liable for the price of the cans.

Further, it is clear from various other passages in the opinion that the district court concluded, and the evidence showed, that Roth, the individual who controlled both Future and Sovereign of Illinois, intentionally manipulated the corporations so that Future assumed the liabilities but held no assets, while other corporations received the assets but not the liabilities.

Generalizing from these cases, we see that the courts that properly have pierced corporate veils to avoid "promoting injustice" have found that, unless it did so, some "wrong" beyond a creditor's inability to collect would result: the common sense rules of adverse possession would be undermined; former partners would be permitted to skirt the legal rules concerning monetary obligations; a party would be unjustly enriched; a parent corporation that caused a sub's liabilities and its inability to pay for them would escape those liabilities; or an intentional scheme to squirrel assets into a liability-free corporation while heaping liabilities upon an asset-free corporation would be successful. Sea–Land, although it alleged in its complaint the kind of intentional asset- and liability-shifting found in *Van Dorn*, has yet to come forward with evidence akin to the "wrongs" found in these cases. Apparently, it believed, as did the district court, that its unsatisfied judgment was enough. That belief was in error, and the entry of summary judgment premature. We, therefore, reverse the judgment and remand the case to the district court.

On remand, the court should require that Sea–Land produce, if it desires summary judgment, evidence and argument that would establish the kind of additional "wrong" present in the above cases. For example, perhaps Sea–Land could establish that Marchese, like Roth in *Van Dorn*, used these corporate facades to avoid its responsibilities to creditors; or that PS, Marchese, or one of the other corporations will be "unjustly enriched" unless liability is shared by all. Of course, Sea–Land is not required fully to prove intent to defraud, which it probably could not do on summary judgment anyway. But it is required to show the kind of injustice to merit the evocation of the court's essentially equitable power to prevent "injustice." It may well be that, after more of such evidence is adduced, no genuine issue of fact exists to prevent Sea–Land from reaching Marchese's other pet corporations for PS's debt. Or it may be that only a finder of fact will be able to determine whether fraud or "injustice" is involved here. In any event, the record as it currently stands is insufficient to uphold the entry of summary judgment.

REVERSED and REMANDED with instructions.

IN RE: SILICONE GEL BREAST IMPLANTS PRODUCTS LIABILITY LITIGATION

UNITED STATES DISTRICT COURT, NORTHERN
DISTRICT, ALABAMA (POINTER, C.J.)
867 F.SUPP. 1447 (1995)

Under submission after appropriate discovery, extensive briefing, and oral argument is the motion for summary judgment filed by defendant Bristol-Myers Squibb Co. Bristol is the sole shareholder of Medical Engineering Corporation, a major supplier of breast implants, but has never itself manufactured or distributed breast implants. Bristol asserts that the evidence is insufficient for the plaintiffs' claims to proceed against it, whether through piercing the corporate veil or under a theory of direct liability. For the reasons stated below, the court concludes that Bristol is not entitled to summary judgment.

[handwritten margin note: applying P. the CV against parent corp liable for subsidiary's conduct]

[handwritten note: MEC = subsidiary of Bristol-Meyers Squibb]

For purposes of Bristol's summary judgment motion, the court treats the following facts as established, either because they are not in genuine dispute or because they are supported by evidence viewed in the light most favorable to the plaintiffs.

MEC was incorporated in Wisconsin in 1969, with its principal place of business in Racine. It was an independent, privately-held corporation manufacturing a variety of medical and plastic surgery devices, including breast implants.

In 1982, after an extensive due diligence review that included information regarding capsular contracture, rupture, and gel bleed, Bristol, a Delaware corporation, purchased MEC's stock for $28 million through a series of mergers and corporate reorganizations. Bristol created a wholly-owned subsidiary, Lakeside Engineering, Inc., a Delaware corporation, which created MEC Acquisition Corporation, a Wisconsin corporation. After MEC merged into MEC Acquisition (extinguishing MEC Acquisition), it then merged into Lakeside, and the surviving corporation changed its name to Medical Engineering Corporation. Since this series of transactions in 1982, MEC, a Delaware corporation with a principal place of business in Racine, Wisconsin, has been a wholly-owned subsidiary of Bristol, operated by Bristol as part of its Health Care Group.

In 1988 Bristol expanded its breast implant business by purchasing from the Cooper Companies two other breast-implant manufacturers, Natural Y Surgical Specialties, Inc. and Aesthetech Corporation. Though executed in the name of MEC and the Cooper Companies, the purchase was negotiated between Bristol and the Cooper Companies, and the purchase price of $8.7 million was paid from a Bristol account (though charged to MEC). The due diligence review, which indicated potential hazards and possible liability relating to polyurethane-coated breast implants, was conducted jointly by MEC and Bristol.

Documents reflect that MEC has had, at least in form, a board of three directors, generally consisting of the Bristol Vice President then serving as President of Bristol's Health Care Group, another Bristol executive, and MEC's president. Bristol's Health Care Group President, who reported to Bristol's president or chairman, could not be outvoted by the other two MEC board members. Several of the former MEC presidents did not recall that MEC had a board, let alone that they were members; and one of these stated that he did not attend, call, or receive notice of board meetings in his five years of service because he had a designated Bristol officer to contact. The few resolutions that were adopted by MEC's board were apparently prepared by Bristol officials.

MEC prepared "significant event" reports for Bristol's Corporate Policy Committee. These reports included information on breast implant production, such as publicity, testing, expenses, lawsuit settlements, and backorders caused by sterilization difficulties. Neither Bristol managers nor MEC Presidents recall any orders or recommendations being issued by Bristol as a result of these reviews. Bristol also required MEC to prepare and submit a five-year plan for its review.

MEC submitted budgets for approval by Bristol's senior management. For this submission, MEC filled out a series of standard Bristol forms that included information on projected sales, profits and losses, cash flow, balance sheets, and capital requirements. Bristol had the authority to modify this budget, though it rarely, if ever, actually did so.

Cash received by MEC was transferred to an account maintained by Bristol. This money was credited to MEC, but the interest earned was credited to Bristol. Bristol was MEC's banker, providing such loans as it determined MEC needed. Bristol required MEC to obtain its approval for capital appropriations, though most, if not all, of these requests were approved.

Bristol set the employment policies and wage scales that applied to MEC's employees. Before hiring a top executive or negotiating the salary, MEC was required to seek Bristol's approval. Before hiring a vice president of MEC, MEC's president and his superior at Bristol interviewed the candidate. Key executive employees were rated on the Bristol schedule. Bristol set a target for salary increases below the key executive level and approved those for employees above that level. Key executives of MEC received stock options for Bristol stock. MEC employees could participate in Bristol's pension and savings plans.

Bristol provided various services to MEC. Zimmer International, another Bristol subsidiary, distributed MEC breast implants but did not receive any benefit for doing so. Bristol's corporate development group assisted MEC in seeking out new product lines. Bristol's scientific experts researched the hazards of breast implants and polyurethane foam. Bristol provided funds for MEC to conduct sales contests. Bristol funded tests on breast implants. Another Bristol subsidiary, ConvaTec, assisted MEC in developing its premarket approval application (PMAA) regarding breast implants for the FDA. In addition to this assistance, Bristol hired an outside laboratory to verify ConvaTec's analysis. Bristol also conducted post-market surveillance at the request of the FDA.

Some of Bristol's in-house counsel acted as MEC attorneys. These attorneys advised MEC on virtually every aspect of its business including budgets, price increases, new product development, package inserts, liability, compliance with FDA regulations, and negotiated settlements with individuals claiming damages from breast implants. They also developed the system for handling complaints about MEC products. They reviewed all breast implant promotional materials and responses to allegations of harm and liability.

Bristol's Technical Evaluation and Service Department performed auditing and review functions for MEC once or twice a year. They performed all Good Manufacturing Practices audits at MEC. These audits were designed to ensure consistent quality of MEC's products. Bristol expected MEC to comply with any manufacturing deficiencies TESD found. A number of the conditions listed as needing corrective action regarded breast implants. TESD also audited MEC's sterilization and lab companies.

Bristol's public relations department issued statements regarding the allegations of TDA production and cancer in rats implanted with polyurethane implants. Bristol's corporate communication department prepared question and answer scripts for MEC employees for use in responding to questions about breast implant safety. Bristol's public affairs department developed a strategic plan to address concerns about the MEME implant and to respond to questions and concerns about the safety of breast implants in general. Bristol's press releases consistently represented that Bristol was researching breast implant safety. For example, in a release dated July 9, 1991, Bristol stated that tests underway would "confirm the well-established safety profile of polyurethane-coated breast implants" and that Bristol completed testing which showed that earlier findings concerning the production of TDA from the breakdown of polyurethane were the result of inappropriate testing conditions. In a statement dated July 24, 1991, Bristol represented that numerous other studies were being undertaken to assure the public and the FDA of the safety of polyurethane-coated breast implants.

Bristol's name and logo were contained in the package inserts and promotional products regarding breast implants, apparently as a marketing tool to increase confidence in the product. Bristol's name was used in all sales and promotional communications with physicians.

MEC posted a profit every year between 1983 and 1990. Total sales increased from approximately $14 million in 1983 to $65 million in 1990. Bristol never received dividends from MEC. Bristol prepared consolidated federal income tax returns but MEC prepared its own Wisconsin tax forms. Bristol also purchased insurance for MEC under its policy. This insurance has a face value of over $2 billion.

Bristol's executive vice president suspended MEC's sales of polyurethane-coated breast implants on April 17, 1991, and determined not to submit a PMAA for the implants to the FDA. MEC ceased its breast implant business in 1991 and later that year MEC ceased all operations by selling its urology division. This sale could not have occurred without Bristol's approval, and proceeds from the sale were turned over to Bristol, which then executed a low-interest demand note for $57,518,888 payable to MEC. MEC's only assets at this time are this demand note and its indemnity insurance.

The various theories of recovery made by plaintiffs against Bristol can be generally divided between those involving "corporate control" and those asserting direct liability. The corporate control claims deal with piercing the corporate veil to abrogate limited liability and hold Bristol responsible for actions of MEC. The direct liability theories include strict products liability, negligence, negligent failure to warn, negligence per se for not complying with FDA regulations, misrepresentation, fraud, and participation.

The potential for abuse of the corporate form is greatest when, as here, the corporation is owned by a single shareholder. The evaluation of corporate control claims cannot, however, disregard the fact that, no different from other stockholders, a parent corporation is expected—indeed, required—to exert some control over its subsidiary. Limited liability is the rule, not the exception. However, when a corporation is so controlled as to be the alter ego or mere instrumentality of its stockholder, the corporate form may be disregarded in the interests of justice.

The totality of circumstances must be evaluated in determining whether a subsidiary may be found to be the alter ego or mere instrumentality of the parent corporation. Although the standards are not identical in each state, all jurisdictions require a showing of substantial domination. Among the factors to be considered are whether:

- the parent and the subsidiary have common directors or officers
- the parent and the subsidiary have common business departments
- the parent and the subsidiary file consolidated financial statements and tax returns
- the parent finances the subsidiary
- the parent caused the incorporation of the subsidiary
- the subsidiary operates with grossly inadequate capital
- the parent pays the salaries and other expenses of the subsidiary
- the subsidiary receives no business except that given to it by the parent
- the parent uses the subsidiary's property as its own
- the daily operations of the two corporations are not kept separate
- the subsidiary does not observe the basic corporate formalities, such as keeping separate books and records and holding shareholder and board meetings.

The fact-finder at a trial could find that the evidence supports the conclusion that many of these factors have been proven: two of MEC's three directors were Bristol directors; MEC was part of Bristol's Health Care group and used Bristol's legal, auditing, and communications departments; MEC and Bristol filed consolidated federal tax returns and Bristol prepared consolidated financial reports; Bristol operated as MEC's finance company, providing loans for the purchase of Aesthetech and Natural Y, receiving interest on MEC's funds, and requiring MEC to make requests for capital appropriations; Bristol effectively used MEC's resources as its own by obtaining interest on MEC's money and requiring MEC to make requests for capital appropriations to obtain its own funds; some members of MEC's board were not aware that MEC had a board of directors, let alone that they were members; and the senior Bristol member of MEC's board could not be out-voted by the other two directors. These facts, even apart from evidence that might establish some of the other factors listed above, would provide significant support for a finding at trial that MEC is Bristol's alter ego.

There is, however, evidence precluding summary judgment even in jurisdictions that require a finding of fraud, inequity, or injustice. This conclusion is not based merely on the evidence that, even accepting Bristol's contentions regarding the amount of insurance available to MEC, MEC may have insufficient funds to satisfy the potential risks of responding to, and defending against, the numerous existing and potential claims of the plaintiffs. Equally significant is the fact that Bristol permitted its name to appear on breast implant advertisements, packages, and product inserts to improve sales by giving the product additional credibility. Combined with the evidence of potentially insufficient assets, this fact would support a finding that it would be inequitable and unjust to allow Bristol now to avoid liability to those induced to believe Bristol was vouching for this product.

Because the evidence available at a trial could support—if not, under some state laws, perhaps mandate—a finding that the corporate veil should be pierced, Bristol is not entitled through summary judgment to dismissal of the claims against it.

There is an additional reason why Bristol is not entitled to summary judgment. Under the law in most jurisdictions, it may also be subject to liability under at least one of the direct liability claims made by plaintiffs; namely, the theory of negligent undertaking pursuant to Restatement (Second) of Torts § 324A.

Under this theory, frequently applied in connection with safety inspections by insurers or with third-party repairs to equipment or premises, a duty that would not otherwise have existed can arise when an individual or company nevertheless undertakes to perform some action. The potential liability for failure to use reasonable care in such circumstances extends to persons who may reasonably be expected to suffer harm from that negligence. Doctrinally, a cause of action under § 324A does not involve an assertion of derivative liability but one of direct liability, since it is based on the actions of defendant itself. The existence of a parent-subsidiary relationship, while not required, is obviously no defense to such a claim.

By allowing its name to be placed on breast implant packages and product inserts, Bristol held itself out as supporting the product, apparently to increase confidence in the product and to increase sales. Bristol also issued press releases stating that polyurethane-coated breast implants were safe. Having engaged in this type of marketing, it cannot now deny its potential responsibility under § 324A.

Plaintiffs have asserted various other direct liability claims against Bristol in addition to those under § 324A. Having concluded that, because of genuine disputes relating to corporate control issues and relating to potential liability under § 324A, Bristol is not entitled to summary judgment, the court declines to address such alternative causes of action.

For the reasons stated in the accompanying opinion, defendant Bristol-Myers Squibb's Motion for summary judgment is hereby DENIED.

KAYCEE LAND AND LIVESTOCK V. FLAHIVE

SUPREME COURT OF WYOMING (KITE, J.)
46 P.3D 323 (2002)

This matter comes before this court as a question certified to us by the district court for resolution under W.R.A.P. 11. The certified question seeks resolution of whether, in the absence of fraud, the entity veil of a limited liability company (LLC) can be pierced in the same manner as that of a corporation. We answer the certified question in the affirmative.

The question we have agreed to answer is phrased as follows:

> In the absence of fraud, is a claim to pierce the Limited Liability entity veil or disregard the Limited Liability Company entity in the same manner as a court would pierce a corporate veil or disregard a corporate shield, an available remedy against a Wyoming Limited Liability Company under Wyoming's Limited Liability Company Act.

In a W.R.A.P. 11 certification of a question of law, we rely entirely upon the factual determinations made in the trial court. The district court submitted the following statement of facts in its order certifying the question of law:

1. Flahive Oil & Gas is a Wyoming Limited Liability Company with no assets at this time.
2. Kaycee Land and Livestock entered into a contract with Flahive Oil & Gas LLC allowing Flahive Oil & Gas to use the surface of its real property.
3. Roger Flahive is and was the managing member of Flahive Oil & Gas at all relevant times.
4. Kaycee Land and Livestock alleges that Flahive Oil & Gas caused environmental contamination to its real property located in Johnson County, Wyoming.
5. Kaycee Land and Livestock seeks to pierce the LLC veil and disregard the L[L]C entity of Flahive Oil & Gas Limited Liability Company and hold Roger Flahive individually liable for the contamination.
6. There is no allegation of fraud.

The question presented is limited to whether, in the absence of fraud, the remedy of piercing the veil is available against a company formed under the Wyoming Limited Liability Company Act. To answer this question, we must first examine the development of the doctrine within Wyoming's corporate context. As a general rule, a corporation is a separate entity distinct from the individuals comprising it. Wyoming statutes governing corporations do not address the circumstances under which the veil can be pierced. However, since 1932, this court has espoused the concept that a corporation's legal entity will be disregarded whenever the recognition thereof in a particular case will lead to injustice. In *Miles v. CEC Homes, Inc.*, this court summarized the circumstances under which the corporate veil would be pierced pursuant to Wyoming law:

> Before a corporation's acts and obligations can be legally recognized as those of a particular person, and vice versa, it must be made to appear that the corporation is not only influenced and governed by that person, but that there is such a unity of interest and ownership that the individuality, or separateness, of such person and

corporation has ceased, and that the facts are such that an adherence to the fiction of the separate existence of the corporation would, under the particular circumstances, sanction a fraud or promote injustice.

Wyoming courts, as well as courts across the country, have typically utilized a fact driven inquiry to determine whether circumstances justify a decision to pierce a corporate veil. This case comes to us as a certified question in the abstract with little factual context, and we are asked to broadly pronounce that there are no circumstances under which this court will look through a failed attempt to create a separate LLC entity and prevent injustice. We simply cannot reach that conclusion and believe it is improvident for this court to prohibit this remedy from applying to any unforeseen circumstance that may exist in the future.

We have long recognized that piercing the corporate veil is an equitable doctrine. The concept of piercing the corporate veil is a judicially created remedy for situations where corporations have not been operated as separate entities as contemplated by statute and, therefore, are not entitled to be treated as such. The determination of whether the doctrine applies centers on whether there is an element of injustice, fundamental unfairness, or inequity. The concept developed through common law and is absent from the statutes governing corporate organization.

We note that Wyoming was the first state to enact LLC statutes. Many years passed before the Internal Revenue Service's approval of taxation of LLCs as partnerships led to other states adopting LLC legislation and the broad usage of this form for business organizations. Wyoming's statute is very short and establishes only minimal requirements for creating and operating LLCs. It seems highly unlikely that the Wyoming legislature gave any consideration to whether the common-law doctrine of piercing the veil should apply to the liability limitation granted by that fledgling statute. It is true that some other states have adopted specific legislation extending the doctrine to LLCs while Wyoming has not. However, that situation seems more attributable to the fact that Wyoming was a pioneer in the LLC arena and states which adopted LLC statutes much later had the benefit of years of practical experience during which this issue was likely raised.

With the dearth of legislative consideration on this issue in Wyoming, we are left to determine whether applying the well established common law to LLCs somehow runs counter to what the legislature would have intended had it considered the issue. In that regard, it is instructive that: "Every state that has enacted LLC piercing legislation has chosen to follow corporate law standards and not develop a separate LLC standard." Statutes which create corporations and LLCs have the same basic purpose—to limit the liability of individual investors with a corresponding benefit to economic development. Statutes created the legal fiction of the corporation being a completely separate entity which could act independently from individual persons. If the corporation were created and operated in conformance with the statutory requirements, the law would treat it as a separate entity and shelter the individual shareholders from any liability caused by corporate action, thereby encouraging investment. However, courts throughout the country have consistently recognized certain unjust circumstances can arise if immunity from liability shelters those who have failed to operate a corporation as a separate entity. Consequently, when corporations fail to follow the statutorily mandated formalities, co-mingle funds, or ignore the restrictions in their articles of incorporation regarding separate treatment of corporate property, the courts deem it appropriate to disregard the separate identity and do not permit shareholders to be sheltered from liability to third parties for damages caused by the corporations' acts.

We can discern no reason, in either law or policy, to treat LLCs differently than we treat corporations. If the members and officers of an LLC fail to treat it as a separate entity as contemplated by statute, they should not enjoy immunity from individual liability for the LLC's acts that cause damage to third parties. Most, if not all, of the expert LLC commentators have concluded the doctrine of piercing the veil should apply to LLCs. It also appears that most courts faced with a similar situation—LLC statutes which are silent and facts which suggest the LLC veil should be pierced—have had little trouble concluding the common law should be applied and the factors weighed accordingly.

Certainly, the various factors which would justify piercing an LLC veil would not be identical to the corporate situation for the obvious reason that many of the organizational formalities applicable to corporations do not apply to LLCs. The LLC's operation is intended to be much more flexible than a corporation's. Factors relevant to determining when to pierce the corporate veil have developed over time in a multitude of cases. It would be inadvisable in this case, which lacks a complete factual context, to attempt to articulate all the possible factors to be applied to LLCs in Wyoming in the future. For guidance, we direct attention to commentators who have opined on the appropriate factors to be applied in the LLC context.

The certified question presents an interesting internal inconsistency. It begins, "In the absence of fraud," thereby presenting the assumption that a court may pierce an LLC's veil in a case of fraud. Thus, the certified question assumes that, when fraud is found, the courts are able to disregard the LLC entity despite the statutory framework which supposedly precludes such a result. Either the courts continue to possess the equitable power to take such action or they do not. Certainly, nothing in the statutes suggests the legislature gave such careful consideration and delineated the specific circumstances under which the courts can act in this arena. If the assumption is correct, individual LLC members can be held personally liable for damages to innocent third parties when the LLC has committed fraud. Yet, when the LLC has caused damage and has inadequate capitalization, co-mingled funds, diverted assets, or used the LLC as a mere shell, individual members are immune from liability. Legislative silence cannot be stretched to condone such an illogical result.

In *Amfac Mechanical Supply Co.*, this court clarified that a showing of fraud or an intent to defraud is not necessary to disregard a corporate entity. We clearly stated: "Fraud is, of course, a matter of concern in suits to disregard corporate fictions, but it is not a prerequisite to such a result." Other courts have echoed this view: "Liability on the basis of fraud, however, does not encompass the entire spectrum of cases in which the veil was pierced in the interest of equity." Thus, even absent fraud, courts have the power to impose liability on corporate shareholders. This same logic should naturally be extended to the LLC context. We have made clear that: "Each case involving the disregard of the separate entity doctrine must be governed by the special facts of that case." Determinations of fact are within the trier of fact's province. The district court must complete a fact intensive inquiry and exercise its equitable powers to determine whether piercing the veil is appropriate under the circumstances presented in this case.

No reason exists in law or equity for treating an LLC differently than a corporation is treated when considering whether to disregard the legal entity. We conclude the equitable remedy of piercing the veil is an available remedy under the Wyoming Limited Liability Company Act.

[handwritten margin note: facts here to warrant -remanded PTV]

PART B EQUITABLE SUBORDINATION

COSTELLO V. FAZIO

UNITED STATES COURT OF APPEALS, NINTH CIRCUIT (HAMLEY, C.J.)
256 F.2D 903 (1958)

Creditors' claims against the bankrupt estate of Leonard Plumbing and Heating Supply, Inc., were filed by J. A. Fazio and Lawrence C. Ambrose. The trustee in bankruptcy objected to these claims, and moved for an order subordinating them to the claims of general unsecured creditors. The referee in bankruptcy denied the motion, and his action was sustained by the district court. The trustee appeals.

The following facts are not in dispute: A partnership known as "Leonard Plumbing and Heating Supply Co." was organized in October, 1948. The three partners, Fazio, Ambrose, and B. T. Leonard, made initial capital contributions to the business aggregating $44,806.40. The capital contributions of the three partners, as they were recorded on the company books in September 1952, totaled $51,620.78, distributed as follows: Fazio, $43,169.61; Ambrose, $6,451.17; and Leonard, $2,000.

In the fall of that year, it was decided to incorporate the business. In contemplation of this step, Fazio and Ambrose, on September 15, 1952, withdrew all but $2,000 apiece of their capital contributions to the business. This was accomplished by the issuance to them, on that date, of partnership promissory notes in the sum of $41,169.61 and $4,451.17, respectively. These were demand notes, no interest being specified. The capital contribution to the partnership business then stood at $6,000, or $2,000 for each partner.

The closing balance sheet of the partnership showed current assets to be $160,791.87 and current liabilities at $162,162.22. There were also fixed assets in the sum of $6,482.90, and other assets in the sum of $887.45. The partnership had cash on hand in the sum of $66.66, and an overdraft at the bank in the amount of $3,422.78.

Of the current assets, $41,357.76, representing "Accounts receivable—Trade," was assigned to American Trust Co., to secure $50,000 of its $59,000 in notes payable. Both before and after the incorporation, the business had a $75,000 line of credit with American Trust Co., secured by accounts receivable and the personal guaranty of the three partners and stockholders, and their marital communities.

The net sales of the partnership during its last year of operations were $389,543.72, as compared to net sales of $665,747.55 in the preceding year. A net loss of $22,521.34 was experienced during this last year, as compared to a net profit of $40,935.12 in the year ending September 30, 1951.

Based on the reduced capitalization of the partnership, the corporation was capitalized for six hundred shares of no par value common stock valued at ten dollars per share. Two hundred shares were issued to each of the three partners in consideration of the transfer to the corporation of their interests in the partnership. Fazio became president, and Ambrose, secretary-treasurer of the new corporation. Both were directors. The corporation assumed all liabilities of the partnership, including the notes to Fazio and Ambrose.

In June 1954, after suffering continued losses, the corporation made an assignment to the San Francisco Board of Trade for the benefit of creditors. On October 8, 1954, it filed a voluntary petition in bankruptcy. At this time, the corporation was not indebted to any creditors whose obligations were incurred by the pre-existing partnership, saving the promissory notes issued to Fazio and Ambrose.

Fazio filed a claim against the estate in the sum of $34,147.55, based on the promissory note given to him when the capital of the partnership was reduced. Ambrose filed a similar claim in the sum of $7,871.17. The discrepancy between these amounts and the amounts of the promissory notes is due to certain setoffs and transfers not here in issue.

In asking that these claims be subordinated to the claims of general unsecured creditors, the trustee averred that the amounts in question represent a portion of the capital investment in the partnership. It was alleged that the transfer of this sum from the partnership capital account to an account entitled 'Loans from Copartners,' effectuated a scheme and plan to place copartners in the same class as unsecured creditors. The trustee further alleged, with respect to each claimant:

If said claimant is permitted to share in the assets of said bankrupt now in the hands of the trustee, in the same parity with general unsecured creditors, he will receive a portion of the capital invested which should be used to satisfy the claims of creditors before any capital investment can be returned to the owners and stockholders of said bankrupt.

William B. Logan, a business analyst and consultant called by the trustee, expressed the view that $6,000 was inadequate capitalization for this company. John S. Curran, a business analyst, also called by the trustee, expressed the view that the corporation needed at least as much capital as the partnership required prior to the reduction of capital.

Robert H. Laborde, Jr., a certified public accountant, has handled the accounting problems of the partnership and corporation. He was called by the trustee as an adverse witness, pursuant to the Bankruptcy Act. Laborde readily conceded that the transaction whereby Fazio and Ambrose obtained promissory notes from the partnership was for the purpose of transferring a capital account into a loan or debt account. He stated that this was done in contemplation of the formation of the corporation, and with knowledge that the partnership was losing money.

The prime reason for incorporating the business was to protect the personal interest of Fazio, who had made the greatest capital contribution to the business. In this connection, it was pointed out that the "liabilities on the business as a partnership were pretty heavy." There was apparently also a tax angle. Laborde testified that it was contemplated that the notes would be paid out of the profits of the business. He agreed that, if promissory notes had not been issued, the profits would have been distributed only as dividends, and that as such they would have been taxable.

In the year immediately preceding incorporation, net sales aggregated $390,000. In order to handle such a turnover, the partners apparently found that capital in excess of $50,000 was necessary. They actually had $51,620.78 in the business at that time. Even then, the business was only "two jumps ahead of the wolf." A net loss of $22,000 was sustained in that year; there was only $66.66 in the bank; and there was an overdraft of $3,422.78.

Yet, despite this precarious financial condition, Fazio and Ambrose withdrew $45,620.78 of the partnership capital—more than eighty-eight percent of the total capital. The $6,000 capital left in the business was only one-sixty-fifth of the last annual net sales. All this is revealed by the books of the company.

We therefore hold that the factual conclusion of the referee, that the corporation was adequately capitalized at the time of its organization, is clearly erroneous.

The best evidence of this is what happened to the business after incorporation, and what will happen to its creditors if the reduction in capital is allowed to stand. The likelihood that business failure would result from such undercapitalization should have been apparent to anyone who knew the company's financial and business history and who had access to its balance sheet and profit and loss statements.

Accordingly, we hold that the factual conclusion, that the claimants, in withdrawing capital, did not act for their own personal or private benefit and to the detriment of the corporation and creditors, is clearly erroneous.

Recasting the facts in the light of what is said above, the question which appellant presents is this:

> Where, in connection with the incorporation of a partnership, and for their own personal and private benefit, two partners who are to become officers, directors, and controlling stockholders of the corporation, convert the bulk of their capital contributions into loans, taking promissory notes, thereby leaving the partnership and succeeding corporation grossly undercapitalized, to the detriment of the corporation and its creditors, should their claims against the estate of the subsequently bankrupted corporation be subordinated to the claims of the general unsecured creditors?

The question almost answers itself.

In allowing and disallowing claims, courts of bankruptcy apply the rules and principles of equity jurisprudence. Where the claim is found to be inequitable, it may be set aside or subordinated to the claims of other creditors. As stated in *Taylor v. Standard Gas Co.*, the question to be determined when the plan or transaction which gives rise to a claim is challenged as inequitable is "whether, within the bounds of reason and fairness, such a plan can be justified."

Where, as here, the claims are filed by persons standing in a fiduciary relationship to the corporation, another test which equity will apply is "whether or not under all the circumstances the transaction carries the earmarks of an arm's length bargain."

Under either of these tests, the transaction here in question stands condemned.

Appellees argue that more must be shown than mere undercapitalization if the claims are to be subordinated. Much more than mere undercapitalization was shown here. Persons serving in a fiduciary relationship to the corporation actually withdrew capital already committed to the business, in the face of recent adverse financial experience. They stripped the business of eighty-eight per cent of its stated capital at a time when it had a minus working capital and had suffered substantial business losses. This was done for personal gain, under circumstances which charge them with knowledge that the corporation and its creditors would be endangered. Taking advantage of their fiduciary position, they thus sought to gain equality of treatment with general creditors.

The fact that the withdrawal of capital occurred prior to incorporation is immaterial. This transaction occurred in contemplation of incorporation. The participants then occupied a fiduciary relationship to the partnership; and expected to become controlling stockholders, directors, and officers of the corporation. This plan was effectuated, and they were serving in those fiduciary capacities when the corporation assumed the liabilities of the partnership, including the notes here in question.

Nor is the fact that the business, after being stripped of necessary capital, was able to survive long enough to have a turnover of creditors a mitigating circumstance. The inequitable conduct of appellees consisted not in acting to the detriment of creditors then known, but in acting to the detriment of present or future creditors, whoever they may be.

Reversed and remanded for further proceedings not inconsistent with this opinion.

PART C SHAREHOLDER DERIVATIVE SUITS

GALL V. EXXON CORP.

UNITED STATES DISTRICT COURT, SOUTHERN DISTRICT,
NEW YORK (CARTER, J.)
418 F.SUPP. 508 (1976)

Defendants have moved for summary judgment dismissing plaintiff's complaint on the grounds that the Special Committee on Litigation, acting as the Board of Directors of Exxon Corporation, has determined in the good faith exercise of its sound business judgment that it is contrary to the interests of Exxon to institute suit on the basis of any matters raised in plaintiff's complaint. Defendants' motion is hereby denied without prejudice to its renewal after plaintiff has conducted relevant discovery.

On September 24, 1975, Exxon's Board of Directors unanimously resolved to establish a Special Committee on Litigation, composed of Exxon directors Jack F. Bennett, Richard P. Dobson and Edward G. Harness,[2] and refer to the Special Committee for the determination of Exxon's action the matters raised in this and several other pending actions relating to the Italian expenditures.

On January 23, 1976, after an investigation of approximately four months, including interviews with over 100 witnesses, the Special Committee issued the "Determination and Report

---

2 According to the affidavits submitted, each of the members of the Special Committee has confirmed that he has not been in any way connected or involved with the matters relating to the Italian expenditures referred to in this action or in the other related actions and none has been named as a defendant in any of the pending actions. Indeed, none of the members of the Committee was elected to the Exxon Board until long after the Italian expenditures complained of were terminated and Exxon had taken steps to ensure that such expenditures would not be resumed.

of the Special Committee on Litigation", an 82-page document summarizing the Committee's findings and recommendations.

The matters complained of by plaintiff center around the activities of Dr. Vincenzo Cazzaniga who was President and Managing Director of Esso Italiana, a wholly-owned subsidiary of Exxon Corporation. Exxon's investigation revealed that in 1964 and 1965, and again in 1971 Cazzaniga secretly (and apparently without authorization by Exxon) entered into certain side agreements in the name of Esso Italiana in connection with a transaction between Esso International (another Exxon subsidiary) and SNAM, a gas pipeline subsidiary of the Italian State petroleum company, ENI. In 1971, presumably pursuant to these side agreements, Cazzaniga made several unauthorized payments out of the funds of Esso Italiana to SNAM. The payments were in excess of $10 million.

Exxon's investigation further revealed that during the period 1963-72, Cazzaniga had made other unauthorized payments of approximately $19 million. The $10 million of unauthorized payments to SNAM and approximately $19 million of other unauthorized payments were largely made from approximately forty secret bank accounts not recorded on the books of Esso Italiana, and known only to Cazzaniga and, in part, his personal assistants. There also flowed through these secret bank accounts approximately $13.5 million purportedly expended with respect to authorized political contributions but which the investigation revealed had been recycled into the secret accounts.

The investigation also revealed that political contributions by Esso Italiana to various Italian political parties during the nine-year period from 1963 through 1971 totaled $27.9 million.

Of this amount, $13.5 million were recycled into one or more of the 40 secret bank accounts. All political contributions by Esso Italiana were ended in 1972.

It is clear that several of the Exxon directors named as defendants in this suit were aware of the existence of the political payments in Italy prior to their termination in 1972.

It is likely that the subject of political contributions was mentioned to the Audit Committee of the Exxon Board at its October, 1970, meeting. The Audit Committee at that time included defendants W. H. Franklin and E. G. Collado. The Report indicates that there was only a passing reference to the subject of political contributions in terms which did not suggest unlawfulness. There has been no report that the subject of political contributions was mentioned to the members of the Audit Committee at any other time prior to 1972.

Finally, the Report mentions that several directors were aware prior to 1972 of the existence of political contributions in Italy, but were unaware again, prior to the disclosures of 1972 of the off-the-books bank accounts maintained by Cazzaniga, or of the Special Budget format initiated in 1968. In this category is C. C. Garvin, Jr., who later became Chairman and Chief Executive Officer of Exxon. Garvin was informed about the existence of political contributions in Italy some time in the latter half of 1969 by the Controller, Mays. At the time, Garvin was serving for a brief period as Contact Director for Europe. Garvin's recollection is that Mays told him the budget was too large but that it was being reduced or phased out by Esso Europe and that Paust had said that the contributions were legal.

Finally, D. M. Cox claims that some time during the several years prior to September, 1967, while he was a Vice President for natural gas of Esso Europe, he became aware through some conversation with Thompson that political contributions were being made in Italy.

Apart from those discussed above, the remainder of the directors (both past and present) were apparently unaware that political contributions were being made at least until the Exxon investigation in 1972. The subject of political payments never came before the Board prior to the disclosures of 1972, nor did the subject come before any committee of the Board prior to 1972 except before the Audit Committee in October, 1970, discussed above.

After careful review, analysis and investigation, and with the advice and concurrence of Special Counsel, the Special Committee unanimously determined on January 23, 1976, that it would be contrary to the interests of Exxon and its shareholders for Exxon, or anyone on its behalf, to institute or maintain a legal action against any present or former Exxon director or officer.[3] The Committee further resolved to direct and authorize the proper officers of Exxon and its General Counsel to oppose and seek dismissal of all shareholder derivative actions relating to payments made by or on behalf of Esso Italiana S.p.A., which had been filed against any present or former Exxon director or officer.

There is no question that the rights sought to be vindicated in this lawsuit are those of Exxon and not those of the plaintiff suing derivatively on the corporation's behalf. Since it is the interests of the corporation which are at stake, it is the responsibility of the directors of the corporation to determine, in the first instance, whether an action should be brought on the corporation's behalf. It follows that the decision of corporate directors whether or not to assert a cause of action held by the corporation rests within the sound business judgment of the management.

This principle, which has come to be known as the business judgment rule, was articulated by Mr. Justice Brandeis speaking for a unanimous Court in *United Copper Securities Co. v. Amalgamated Copper Co.* In that case the directors of a corporation chose not to bring an antitrust action against a third party. Mr. Justice Brandeis said:

> Whether or not a corporation shall seek to enforce in the courts a cause of action for damages is, like other business questions, ordinarily a matter of internal management, and is left to the discretion of the directors, in the absence of instruction by vote of the stockholders. Courts interfere seldom to control such discretion intra vires the corporation, except where the directors are guilty of misconduct

---

3 Among the factors cited by the Special Committee in reaching its decision were the unfavorable prospects for success of the litigation, the cost of conducting the litigation, interruption of corporate business affairs and the undermining of personnel morale.

equivalent to a breach of trust, or where they stand in a dual relation which prevents an unprejudiced exercise of judgment.

It is clear that absent allegations of fraud, collusion, self-interest, dishonesty or other misconduct of a breach of trust nature, and absent allegations that the business judgment exercised was grossly unsound, the court should not at the instigation of a single shareholder interfere with the judgment of the corporate officers.

Even assuming that the political payments in Italy were illegal where made, the business judgment rule is nonetheless applicable. The decision not to bring suit with regard to past conduct which may have been illegal is not itself a violation of law and does not result in the continuation of the alleged violation of law. Rather, it is a decision by the directors of the corporation that pursuit of a cause of action based on acts already consummated is not in the best interest of the corporation. Such a determination, like any other business decision, must be made by the corporate directors in the exercise of their sound business judgment.

In recent months, the legality and morality of foreign political contributions, bribes and other payments by American corporations has been widely debated. The issue before me for decision, however, is not whether the payments made by Esso Italiana to Italian political parties and other unauthorized payments were proper or improper. Were the court to frame the issue in this way, it would necessarily involve itself in the business decisions of every corporation, and be required to mediate between the judgment of the directors and the judgment of the shareholders with regard to particular corporate actions. As Mr. Justice Brandeis said in his concurring opinion in *Ashwander v. Tennessee Valley Authority*, "if a stockholder could compel the officers to enforce every legal right, courts instead of chosen officers, would be the arbiters of the corporation's fate." Rather, the issue is whether the Special Committee, acting as Exxon's Board of Directors and in the sound exercise of their business judgment, may determine that a suit against any present or former director or officer would be contrary to the best interests of the corporation.

Plaintiff also calls into question the disinterestedness and bona fides of the Special Committee, suggesting that the members of the Special Committee may have been personally involved in the transactions in question, or, at the least, interested in the alleged wrongdoing "in a way calculated to impair their exercise of business judgment on behalf of the corporation."

With the foregoing in mind, I am constrained to conclude that it is premature at this stage of the lawsuit to grant summary judgment. Plaintiff must be given an opportunity to test the bona fides and independence of the Special Committee through discovery and, if necessary, at a plenary hearing. Issues of intent, motivation, and good faith are particularly inappropriate for summary disposition.

Accordingly, defendants' motion for summary judgment is hereby denied without prejudice to its renewal after plaintiff has conducted relevant discovery.

ZAPATA CORP. V. MALDONADO

SUPREME COURT OF DELAWARE (QUILLEN, J.)
430 A.2D 779 (1981)

This is an interlocutory appeal from an order entered on April 9, 1980, by the Court of Chancery denying appellant-defendant Zapata Corporation's alternative motions to dismiss the complaint or for summary judgment. The issue to be addressed has reached this Court by way of a rather convoluted path.

In June, 1975, William Maldonado, a stockholder of Zapata, instituted a derivative action in the Court of Chancery on behalf of Zapata against ten officers and/or directors of Zapata, alleging, essentially, breaches of fiduciary duty. Maldonado did not first demand that the board bring this action, stating instead such demand's futility because all directors were named as defendants and allegedly participated in the acts specified. In June, 1977, Maldonado commenced an action in the United States District Court for the Southern District of New York against the same defendants, save one, alleging federal security law violations as well as the same common law claims made previously in the Court of Chancery.

By June, 1979, four of the defendant-directors were no longer on the board, and the remaining directors appointed two new outside directors to the board. The board then created an "Independent Investigation Committee", composed solely of the two new directors, to investigate Maldonado's actions, as well as a similar derivative action then pending in Texas, and to determine whether the corporation should continue any or all of the litigation. The Committee's determination was stated to be "final, not subject to review by the Board of Directors and in all respects binding upon the Corporation."

Following an investigation, the Committee concluded, in September, 1979, that each action should "be dismissed forthwith as their continued maintenance is inimical to the Company's best interests." Consequently, Zapata moved for dismissal or summary judgment in the three derivative actions. On January 24, 1980, the District Court for the Southern District of New York granted Zapata's motion for summary judgment, holding, under its interpretation of Delaware law, that the Committee had the authority, under the "business judgment" rule, to require the termination of the derivative action. Maldonado appealed that decision to the Second Circuit Court of Appeals.

On March 18, 1980, the Court of Chancery, in a reported opinion, the basis for the order of April 9, 1980, denied Zapata's motions, holding that Delaware law does not sanction this means of dismissal. More specifically, it held that the "business judgment" rule is not a grant of authority

286

to dismiss derivative actions and that a stockholder has an individual right to maintain derivative actions in certain instances.

The "business judgment" rule is a judicial creation that presumes propriety, under certain circumstances, in a board's decision. Viewed defensively, it does not create authority. In this sense the "business judgment" rule is not relevant in corporate decision making until after a decision is made. It is generally used as a defense to an attack on the decision's soundness. The board's managerial decision making power, however, comes from § 141(a). The judicial creation and legislative grant are related because the "business judgment" rule evolved to give recognition and deference to directors' business expertise when exercising their managerial power under § 141(a).

In the case before us, although the corporation's decision to move to dismiss or for summary judgment was, literally, a decision resulting from an exercise of the directors' (as delegated to the Committee) business judgment, the question of "business judgment", in a defensive sense, would not become relevant until and unless the decision to seek termination of the derivative lawsuit was attacked as improper. This question was not reached by the Vice Chancellor because he determined that the stockholder had an individual right to maintain this derivative action.

Thus, the focus in this case is on the power to speak for the corporation as to whether the lawsuit should be continued or terminated.

Accordingly, we turn first to the Court of Chancery's conclusions concerning the right of a plaintiff stockholder in a derivative action. We find that its determination that a stockholder, once demand is made and refused, possesses an independent, individual right to continue a derivative suit for breaches of fiduciary duty over objection by the corporation, as an absolute rule, is erroneous.

Moreover, *McKee v. Rogers* stated "as a general rule" that "a stockholder cannot be permitted to invade the discretionary field committed to the judgment of the directors and sue in the corporation's behalf when the managing body refuses. This rule is a well settled one."

The *McKee* rule, of course, should not be read so broadly that the board's refusal will be determinative in every instance. Board members, owing a well-established fiduciary duty to the corporation, will not be allowed to cause a derivative suit to be dismissed when it would be a breach of their fiduciary duty. Generally disputes pertaining to control of the suit arise in two contexts.

Consistent with the purpose of requiring a demand, a board decision to cause a derivative suit to be dismissed as detrimental to the company, after demand has been made and refused, will be respected unless it was wrongful.[4] A claim of a wrongful decision not to sue is thus the first

---

4   In other words, when stockholders, after making demand and having their suit rejected, attack the board's decision as improper, the board's decision falls under the "business judgment" rule and will be respected if the requirements of the rule are met. That situation should be distinguished from the instant case, where demand was not made, and the power of the board to seek a dismissal, due to disqualification, presents a threshold issue. For examples of what has been held to be a wrongful decision not to sue. We recognize that the two contexts can overlap in practice.

exception and the first context of dispute. Absent a wrongful refusal, the stockholder in such a situation simply lacks legal managerial power.

But it cannot be implied that, absent a wrongful board refusal, a stockholder can never have an individual right to initiate an action. For, as is stated in *McKee*, a "well settled" exception exists to the general rule:

> A stockholder may sue in equity in his derivative right to assert a cause of action in behalf of the corporation, without prior demand upon the directors to sue, when it is apparent that a demand would be futile, that the officers are under an influence that sterilizes discretion and could not be proper persons to conduct the litigation.

These comments in *McKee* make obvious sense. A demand, when required and refused (if not wrongful), terminates a stockholder's legal ability to initiate a derivative action. But where demand is properly excused, the stockholder does possess the ability to initiate the action on his corporation's behalf.

We see no inherent reason why the "two phases" of a derivative suit, the stockholder's suit to compel the corporation to sue and the corporation's suit, should automatically result in the placement in the hands of the litigating stockholder sole control of the corporate right throughout the litigation. To the contrary, it seems to us that such an inflexible rule would recognize the interest of one person or group to the exclusion of all others within the corporate entity.

The question to be decided becomes: When, if at all, should an authorized board committee be permitted to cause litigation, properly initiated by a derivative stockholder in his own right, to be dismissed? Even when demand is excusable, circumstances may arise when continuation of the litigation would not be in the corporation's best interests. Our inquiry is whether, under such circumstances, there is a permissible procedure under § 141(a) by which a corporation can rid itself of detrimental litigation. If there is not, a single stockholder in an extreme case might control the destiny of the entire corporation. This concern was bluntly expressed by the Ninth Circuit: "To allow one shareholder to incapacitate an entire board of directors merely by leveling charges against them gives too much leverage to dissident shareholders." But, when examining the means, including the committee mechanism examined in this case, potentials for abuse must be recognized. This takes us to the second and third aspects of the issue on appeal.

The corporate power inquiry then focuses on whether the board, tainted by the self-interest of a majority of its members, can legally delegate its authority to a committee of two disinterested directors. We find our statute clearly requires an affirmative answer to this question. As has been noted, under an express provision of the statute, § 141(c), a committee can exercise all of the authority of the board to the extent provided in the resolution of the board.

We do not think that the interest taint of the board majority is *per se* a legal bar to the delegation of the board's power to an independent committee composed of disinterested board members. The committee can properly act for the corporation to move to dismiss derivative litigation that is believed to be detrimental to the corporation's best interest.

Our focus now switches to the Court of Chancery which is faced with a stockholder assertion that a derivative suit, properly instituted, should continue for the benefit of the corporation and a corporate assertion, properly made by a board committee acting that the same derivative suit should be dismissed as inimical to the best interests of the corporation.

At the risk of stating the obvious, the problem is relatively simple. If, on the one hand, corporations can consistently wrest bona fide derivative actions away from well-meaning derivative plaintiffs through the use of the committee mechanism, the derivative suit will lose much, if not all, of its generally-recognized effectiveness. If, on the other hand, corporations are unable to rid themselves of meritless or harmful litigation, the derivative action, created to benefit the corporation, will produce the opposite, unintended result. It thus appears desirable to us to find a balancing point where bona fide stockholder power to bring corporate causes of action cannot be unfairly trampled on by the board of directors, but the corporation can rid itself of detrimental litigation.

As we noted, the question has been treated by other courts as one of the "business judgment" of the board committee. If a "committee, composed of independent and disinterested directors, conducted a proper review of the matters before it, considered a variety of factors and reached, in good faith, a business judgment that the action was not in the best interest of the corporation," the action must be dismissed. The issues become solely independence, good faith, and reasonable investigation. The ultimate conclusion of the committee, under that view, is not subject to judicial review.

We are not satisfied, however, that acceptance of the "business judgment" rationale at this stage of derivative litigation is a proper balancing point. While we admit an analogy with a normal case respecting board judgment, it seems to us that there is sufficient risk in the realities of a situation like the one presented in this case to justify caution beyond adherence to the theory of business judgment.

The context here is a suit against directors where demand on the board is excused. We think some tribute must be paid to the fact that the lawsuit was properly initiated. It is not a board refusal case.

Notwithstanding our conviction that Delaware law entrusts the corporate power to a properly authorized committee, we must be mindful that directors are passing judgment on fellow directors in the same corporation and fellow directors, in this instance, who designated them to serve both as directors and committee members. The question naturally arises whether a "there but for the grace of God go I" empathy might not play a role. And the further question arises whether inquiry as to independence, good faith and reasonable investigation is sufficient safeguard against abuse, perhaps subconscious abuse.

There is some analogy to a settlement in that there is a request to terminate litigation without a judicial determination of the merits.

After an objective and thorough investigation of a derivative suit, an independent committee may cause its corporation to file a pretrial motion to dismiss in the Court of Chancery. The basis of the motion is the best interests of the corporation, as determined by the committee. The motion should include a thorough written record of the investigation and its findings and recommendations. Under appropriate Court supervision, akin to proceedings on summary judgment, each side should have an opportunity to make a record on the motion. As to the limited issues presented by the motion noted below, the moving party should be prepared to meet the normal burden under Rule 56 that there is no genuine issue as to any material fact and that the moving party is entitled to dismiss as a matter of law. The Court should apply a two-step test to the motion.

First, the Court should inquire into the independence and good faith of the committee and the bases supporting its conclusions. Limited discovery may be ordered to facilitate such inquiries. The corporation should have the burden of proving independence, good faith and a reasonable investigation, rather than presuming independence, good faith and reasonableness. If the Court determines either that the committee is not independent or has not shown reasonable bases for its conclusions, or, if the Court is not satisfied for other reasons relating to the process, including but not limited to the good faith of the committee, the Court shall deny the corporation's motion. If, however, the Court is satisfied under Rule 56 standards that the committee was independent and showed reasonable bases for good faith findings and recommendations, the Court may proceed, in its discretion, to the next step.

The second step provides, we believe, the essential key in striking the balance between legitimate corporate claims as expressed in a derivative stockholder suit and a corporation's best interests as expressed by an independent investigating committee. The Court should determine, applying its own independent business judgment, whether the motion should be granted. This means, of course, that instances could arise where a committee can establish its independence and sound bases for its good faith decisions and still have the corporation's motion denied. The second step is intended to thwart instances where corporate actions meet the criteria of step one, but the result does not appear to satisfy its spirit, or where corporate actions would simply prematurely terminate a stockholder grievance deserving of further consideration in the corporation's interest. The Court of Chancery of course must carefully consider and weigh how compelling the corporate interest in dismissal is when faced with a non-frivolous lawsuit. The Court of Chancery should, when appropriate, give special consideration to matters of law and public policy in addition to the corporation's best interests.

290

If the Court's independent business judgment is satisfied, the Court may proceed to grant the motion, subject, of course, to any equitable terms or conditions the Court finds necessary or desirable.

The interlocutory order of the Court of Chancery is reversed and the cause is remanded for further proceedings consistent with this opinion.

ARONSON V. LEWIS

SUPREME COURT OF DELAWARE (MOORE, J.)
473 A.2D 805 (1984)

When is a stockholder's demand upon a board of directors, to redress an alleged wrong to the corporation, excused as futile prior to the filing of a derivative suit? We granted this interlocutory appeal to the defendants, Meyers Parking System, Inc., a Delaware corporation, and its directors, to review the Court of Chancery's denial of their motion to dismiss this action, pursuant to Chancery Rule 23.1, for the plaintiff's failure to make such a demand or otherwise demonstrate its futility. The Vice Chancellor ruled that plaintiff's allegations raised a "reasonable inference" that the directors' action was unprotected by the business judgment rule. Thus, the board could not have impartially considered and acted upon the demand.

We cannot agree with this formulation of the concept of demand futility. In our view demand can only be excused where facts are alleged with particularity which create a reasonable doubt that the directors' action was entitled to the protections of the business judgment rule. Because the plaintiff failed to make a demand, and to allege facts with particularity indicating that such demand would be futile, we reverse the Court of Chancery and remand with instructions that plaintiff be granted leave to amend the complaint.

The issues of demand futility rest upon the allegations of the complaint. The plaintiff, Harry Lewis, is a stockholder of Meyers. The defendants are Meyers and its ten directors, some of whom are also company officers.

In 1979, Prudential Building Maintenance Corp. spun off its shares of Meyers to Prudential's stockholders. Prior thereto Meyers was a wholly owned subsidiary of Prudential. Meyers provides parking lot facilities and related services throughout the country. Its stock is actively traded over-the-counter.

This suit challenges certain transactions between Meyers and one of its directors, Leo Fink, who owns 47% of its outstanding stock. Plaintiff claims that these transactions were approved only because Fink personally selected each director and officer of Meyers.

The complaint charges that these transactions had "no valid business purpose", and were a "waste of corporate assets" because the amounts to be paid are "grossly excessive."

The complaint alleged that no demand had been made on the Meyers board because:

13. Such attempt would be futile for the following reasons:

(a) All of the directors in office are named as defendants herein and they have participated in, expressly approved and/or acquiesced in, and are personally liable for, the wrongs complained of herein.
(b) Defendant Fink, having selected each director, controls and dominates every member of the Board and every officer of Meyers.
(c) Institution of this action by present directors would require the defendant-directors to sue themselves, thereby placing the conduct of this action in hostile hands and preventing its effective prosecution.

The relief sought included the cancellation of the Meyers-Fink employment contract and an accounting by the directors, including Fink, for all damage sustained by Meyers and for all profits derived by the directors and Fink.

A cardinal precept of the General Corporation Law of the State of Delaware is that directors, rather than shareholders, manage the business and affairs of the corporation. Section 141(a) states in pertinent part:

> The *business and affairs* of a corporation organized under this chapter *shall be managed by or under the direction* of a board of directors except as may be otherwise provided in this chapter or in its certificate of incorporation.

The existence and exercise of this power carries with it certain fundamental fiduciary obligations to the corporation and its shareholders. Moreover, a stockholder is not powerless to challenge director action which results in harm to the corporation. The machinery of corporate democracy and the derivative suit are potent tools to redress the conduct of a torpid or unfaithful management. The derivative action developed in equity to enable shareholders to sue in the corporation's name where those in control of the company refused to assert a claim belonging to it. The nature of the action is two-fold. First, it is the equivalent of a suit by the shareholders to compel the corporation to sue. Second, it is a suit by the corporation, asserted by the shareholders on its behalf, against those liable to it.

By its very nature the derivative action impinges on the managerial freedom of directors. Hence, the demand requirement of Chancery Rule 23.1 exists at the threshold, first to insure that a stockholder exhausts his intracorporate remedies, and then to provide a safeguard against strike suits. Thus, by promoting this form of alternate dispute resolution, rather than immediate recourse to litigation, the demand requirement is a recognition of the fundamental precept that directors manage the business and affairs of corporations.

In our view the entire question of demand futility is inextricably bound to issues of business judgment and the standards of that doctrine's applicability. The business judgment rule is an acknowledgment of the managerial prerogatives of Delaware directors under Section 141(a). It is a presumption that in making a business decision the directors of a corporation acted on an informed basis, in good faith and in the honest belief that the action taken was in the best interests of the company. Absent an abuse of discretion, that judgment will be respected by the courts. The burden is on the party challenging the decision to establish facts rebutting the presumption.

The function of the business judgment rule is of paramount significance in the context of a derivative action. It comes into play in several ways—in addressing a demand, in the determination of demand futility, in efforts by independent disinterested directors to dismiss the action as inimical to the corporation's best interests, and generally, as a defense to the merits of the suit. However, in each of these circumstances there are certain common principles governing the application and operation of the rule.

First, its protections can only be claimed by disinterested directors whose conduct otherwise meets the tests of business judgment. From the standpoint of interest, this means that directors can neither appear on both sides of a transaction nor expect to derive any personal financial benefit from it in the sense of self-dealing, as opposed to a benefit which devolves upon the corporation or all stockholders generally. Thus, if such director interest is present, and the transaction is not approved by a majority consisting of the disinterested directors, then the business judgment rule has no application whatever in determining demand futility.

Second, to invoke the rule's protection directors have a duty to inform themselves, prior to making a business decision, of all material information reasonably available to them. Having become so informed, they must then act with requisite care in the discharge of their duties. While the Delaware cases use a variety of terms to describe the applicable standard of care, our analysis satisfies us that under the business judgment rule director liability is predicated upon concepts of gross negligence.

However, it should be noted that the business judgment rule operates only in the context of director action. Technically speaking, it has no role where directors have either abdicated their functions, or absent a conscious decision, failed to act. But it also follows that under applicable principles, a conscious decision to refrain from acting may nonetheless be a valid exercise of business judgment and enjoy the protections of the rule.

Delaware courts have addressed the issue of demand futility on several earlier occasions. The rule emerging from these decisions is that where officers and directors are under an influence which sterilizes their discretion, they cannot be considered proper persons to conduct litigation on behalf of the corporation. Thus, demand would be futile.

However, those cases cannot be taken to mean that any board approval of a challenged transaction automatically connotes "hostile interest" and "guilty participation" by directors, or some other form of sterilizing influence upon them. Were that so, the demand requirements of our law would be meaningless, leaving the clear mandate of Chancery Rule 23.1 devoid of its purpose and substance.

The trial court correctly recognized that demand futility is inextricably bound to issues of business judgment, but stated the test to be based on allegations of fact, which, if true, "show that there is a reasonable inference" the business judgment rule is not applicable for purposes of a pre-suit demand.

The problem with this formulation is the concept of reasonable inferences to be drawn against a board of directors based on allegations in a complaint. As is clear from this case, and the conclusory allegations upon which the Vice Chancellor relied, demand futility becomes virtually automatic under such a test. Bearing in mind the presumptions with which director action is cloaked, we believe that the matter must be approached in a more balanced way.

Our view is that in determining demand futility the Court of Chancery in the proper exercise of its discretion must decide whether, under the particularized facts alleged, a reasonable doubt is created that: (1) the directors are disinterested and independent and (2) the challenged transaction was otherwise the product of a valid exercise of business judgment. Hence, the Court of Chancery must make two inquiries, one into the independence and disinterestedness of the directors and the other into the substantive nature of the challenged transaction and the board's approval thereof. As to the latter inquiry the court does not assume that the transaction is a wrong to the corporation requiring corrective steps by the board. Rather, the alleged wrong is substantively reviewed against the factual background alleged in the complaint. As to the former inquiry, directorial independence and disinterestedness, the court reviews the factual allegations to decide whether they raise a reasonable doubt, as a threshold matter, that the protections of the business judgment rule are available to the board. Certainly, if this is an "interested" director transaction, such that the business judgment rule is inapplicable to the board majority approving the transaction, then the inquiry ceases. In that event futility of demand has been established by any objective or subjective standard.

However, the mere threat of personal liability for approving a questioned transaction, standing alone, is insufficient to challenge either the independence or disinterestedness of directors, although in rare cases a transaction may be so egregious on its face that board approval cannot meet the test of business judgment, and a substantial likelihood of director liability therefore exists. In sum the entire review is factual in nature. The Court of Chancery in the exercise of its sound discretion must be satisfied that a plaintiff has alleged facts with particularity which, taken as true, support a reasonable doubt that the challenged transaction was the product of a valid exercise of business judgment. Only in that context is demand excused.

test for futility

Having outlined the legal framework within which these issues are to be determined, we consider plaintiff's claims of futility here: Fink's domination and control of the directors, board approval of the Fink-Meyers employment agreement, and board hostility to the plaintiff's derivative action due to the directors' status as defendants.

Plaintiff's claim that Fink dominates and controls the Meyers' board is based on: (1) Fink's 47% ownership of Meyers' outstanding stock, and (2) that he "personally selected" each Meyers director. Plaintiff also alleges that mere approval of the employment agreement illustrates Fink's domination and control of the board. In addition, plaintiff argued on appeal that 47% stock ownership, though less than a majority, constituted control given the large number of shares outstanding, 1,245,745.

Such contentions do not support any claim under Delaware law that these directors lack independence. In *Kaplan v. Centex Corp.*, the Court of Chancery stated that "stock ownership alone, at least when it amounts to less than a majority, is not sufficient proof of domination or control". Moreover, in the demand context even proof of majority ownership of a company does not strip the directors of the presumptions of independence, and that their acts have been taken in good faith and in the best interests of the corporation. There must be coupled with the allegation of control such facts as would demonstrate that through personal or other relationships the directors are beholden to the controlling person. To date the principal decisions dealing with the issue of control or domination arose only after a full trial on the merits. Thus, they are distinguishable in the demand context unless similar particularized facts are alleged to meet the test of Chancery Rule 23.1.

The requirement of director independence inhers in the conception and rationale of the business judgment rule. The presumption of propriety that flows from an exercise of business judgment is based in part on this unyielding precept. Independence means that a director's decision is based on the corporate merits of the subject before the board rather than extraneous considerations or influences. While directors may confer, debate, and resolve their differences through compromise, or by reasonable reliance upon the expertise of their colleagues and other qualified persons, the end result, nonetheless, must be that each director has brought his or her own informed business judgment to bear with specificity upon the corporate merits of the issues without regard for or succumbing to influences which convert an otherwise valid business decision into a faithless act.

Thus, it is not enough to charge that a director was nominated by or elected at the behest of those controlling the outcome of a corporate election. That is the usual way a person becomes a corporate director. It is the care, attention and sense of individual responsibility to the performance of one's duties, not the method of election, that generally touches on independence.

We conclude that in the demand-futile context a plaintiff charging domination and control of one or more directors must allege particularized facts manifesting "a direction of corporate conduct in such a way as to comport with the wishes or interests of the corporation (or persons) doing the controlling". The shorthand shibboleth of "dominated and controlled directors" is insufficient. In recognizing that *Kaplan* was decided after trial and full discovery, we stress that the plaintiff need only allege specific facts; he need not plead evidence. Otherwise, he would be forced to make allegations which may not comport with his duties under Chancery Rule 11.

Here, plaintiff has not alleged any facts sufficient to support a claim of control. The personal-selection-of-directors allegation stands alone, unsupported. At best it is a conclusion devoid of factual support. The causal link between Fink's control and approval of the employment agreement is alluded to, but nowhere specified. The director's approval, alone, does not establish control, even in the face of Fink's 47% stock ownership. The claim that Fink is unlikely to perform any services under the agreement, because of his age, and his conflicting consultant work with Prudential, adds nothing to the control claim. Therefore, we cannot conclude that the complaint factually particularizes any circumstances of control and domination to overcome the presumption of board independence, and thus render the demand futile.

Turning to the board's approval of the Meyers-Fink employment agreement, plaintiff's argument is simple: all of the Meyers directors are named defendants, because they approved the wasteful agreement; if plaintiff prevails on the merits all the directors will be jointly and severally liable; therefore, the directors' interest in avoiding personal liability automatically and absolutely disqualifies them from passing on a shareholder's demand.

Such allegations are conclusory at best. In Delaware mere directorial approval of a transaction, absent particularized facts supporting a breach of fiduciary duty claim, or otherwise establishing the lack of independence or disinterestedness of a majority of the directors, is insufficient to excuse demand. Here, plaintiff's suit is premised on the notion that the Meyers-Fink employment agreement was a waste of corporate assets. So, the argument goes, by approving such waste the directors now face potential personal liability, thereby rendering futile any demand on them to bring suit. Unfortunately, plaintiff's claim fails in its initial premise. The complaint does not allege particularized facts indicating that the agreement is a waste of corporate assets. Indeed, the complaint as now drafted may not even state a cause of action, given the directors' broad corporate power to fix the compensation of officers.

Plaintiff's final argument is the incantation that demand is excused because the directors otherwise would have to sue themselves, thereby placing the conduct of the litigation in hostile hands and preventing its effective prosecution. This bootstrap argument has been made to and dismissed by other courts. Its acceptance would effectively abrogate Rule 23.1 and weaken the managerial power of directors. Unless facts are alleged with particularity to overcome the presumptions of independence and a proper exercise of business judgment, in which case the directors could not be expected to sue themselves, a bare claim of this sort raises no legally cognizable issue under Delaware corporate law.

In sum, we conclude that the plaintiff has failed to allege facts with particularity indicating that the Meyers directors were tainted by interest, lacked independence, or took action contrary to Meyers' best interests in order to create a reasonable doubt as to the applicability of the business judgment rule. Only in the presence of such a reasonable doubt may a demand be deemed futile. Hence, we reverse the Court of Chancery's denial of the motion to dismiss, and remand with instructions that plaintiff be granted leave to amend his complaint to bring it into compliance with Rule 23.1 based on the principles we have announced today.

INDEMNIFICATION AND PART D INSURANCE

DELAWARE GENERAL CORPORATION LAW

SECTION 145. INDEMNIFICATION OF OFFICERS, DIRECTORS, EMPLOYEES AND AGENTS; INSURANCE

(a) A corporation shall have power to indemnify any person who was or is a party or is threatened to be made a party to any threatened, pending or completed action, suit or proceeding, whether civil, criminal, administrative or investigative (other than an action by or in the right of the corporation) by reason of the fact that the person is or was a director, officer, employee or agent of the corporation, or is or was serving at the request of the corporation as a director, officer, employee or agent of another corporation, partnership, joint venture, trust or other enterprise, against expenses (including attorneys' fees), judgments, fines and amounts paid in settlement actually and reasonably incurred by the person in connection with such action, suit or proceeding if the person acted in good faith an in a manner the person reasonably believed to be in or not opposed to the best interests of the corporation, and, with respect to any criminal action or proceeding, had no reasonable cause to believe the person's conduct was unlawful.

(b) A corporation shall have power to indemnify any person who was or is a party or is threatened to be made a party to any threatened, pending or completed action or suit by or in the right of the corporation to procure a judgment in its favor by reason of the fact that the person is or was a director, officer, employee or agent of the corporation, or is or was serving at the request of the corporation as a director, officer, employee or agent of another corporation, partnership, joint venture, trust or other enterprise, against expenses (including attorneys' fees) actually and reasonably incurred by the person in connection with the defense or settlement of such action or suit if the person acted in good faith and in a manner the person reasonably believed to be in or not opposed to the best interests of the corporation and except that no indemnification shall be made in respect of any claim, issue or matter as which such person shall have been adjudged to be liable to the corporation unless and only to the extent that the Court of Chancery or the court in which such action or suit was brought shall determine upon application that, despite the adjudication of liability but in view of all the circumstances of the case, such person is fairly and reasonably entitled to indemnity for such expenses which the Court of Chancery or such other court shall deem proper.

(c) To the extent that a present or former director or officer of a corporation has been successful on the merits or otherwise in defense of any action, suit or proceeding referred to in subsections (a) and (b) of this section, or in defense of any claim, issue or matter therein, such person shall be indemnified against expenses (including attorneys' fees) actually and reasonably incurred by such person in connection therewith.

(d) Any indemnification under subsections (a) and (b) of this section (unless ordered by a court) shall be made by the corporation only as authorized in the specific case upon a determination that indemnification of the present or former director, officer, employee or agent is proper in the circumstances because the person has met the applicable standard of conduct set forth in subsections (a) and (b) of this section. Such determination shall be made, with respect to a person who is a director or officer of the corporation at the time of such determination:

(1) By a majority vote of the directors who are not parties to such action, suit or proceeding, even though less than a quorum; or

(2) By a committee of such directors designated by majority vote of such directors, even though less than a quorum; or

(3) If there are no such directors, or if such directors so direct, by independent legal counsel in a written opinion; or

(4) By the stockholders.

(e) Expenses (including attorneys' fees) incurred by an officer or director of the corporation in defending any civil, criminal, administrative or investigative action, suit or proceeding may be paid by the corporation in advance of the final disposition of such action, suit or proceeding upon receipt of an undertaking by or on behalf of such director or officer to repay such amount if it shall ultimately be determined that such person is not entitled to be indemnified by the corporation as authorized in this section. Such expenses (including attorneys' fees) incurred by former directors and officers or other employees and agents of the corporation or by persons serving at the request of the corporation as directors, officers, employees or agents of another corporation, partnership, joint venture, trust or other enterprise may be so paid upon such terms and conditions, if any, as the corporation deems appropriate.

(f) The indemnification and advancement of expenses provided by, or granted pursuant to, the other subsections of this section shall not be deemed exclusive of any other rights to which those seeking indemnification or advancement of expenses may be entitled under any bylaw, agreement, vote of stockholders or disinterested directors or otherwise, both as to action in such person's official capacity and as to action in another capacity while holding such office. A right to indemnification or to advancement of expenses arising under a provision of the certificate of incorporation or a bylaw shall not be eliminated or impaired by an amendment to the certificate of incorporation or the bylaws after the occurrence of the act or omission that is the subject of the civil, criminal, administrative or investigative action, suit or proceeding for which indemnification or advancement of expenses is sought, unless the provision in effect at the time of such act or omission explicitly authorizes such elimination or impairment after such action or omission has occurred.

(g) A corporation shall have the power to purchase and maintain insurance on behalf of any person who is or was a director, officer, employee or agent of the corporation, or is or was serving at the request of the corporation as a director, officer, employee or agent of another corporation, partnership, joint venture, trust or other enterprise against any liability asserted against such person and incurred by such person in any such capacity, or arising out of such person's status as such, whether or not the corporation would have the power to indemnify such person against such liability under this section.

WALTUCH V. CONTICOMMODITY SERVICES, INC.

UNITED STATES COURT OF APPEALS, SECOND CIRCUIT (JACOBS, J.)
88 F.3D 87 (1996)

Famed silver trader Norton Waltuch spent $2.2 million in unreimbursed legal fees to defend himself against numerous civil lawsuits and an enforcement proceeding brought by the Commodity Futures Trading Commission. In this action under Delaware law, Waltuch seeks indemnification of his legal expenses from his former employer. The district court denied any indemnity, and Waltuch appeals.

As vice-president and chief metals trader for Conticommodity Services, Inc., Waltuch traded silver for the firm's clients, as well as for his own account. In late 1979 and early 1980, the silver price spiked upward as the then-billionaire Hunt brothers and several of Waltuch's foreign clients bought huge quantities of silver futures contracts. Just as rapidly, the price fell until (on a day remembered in trading circles as "Silver Thursday") the silver market crashed. Between 1981 and 1985, angry silver speculators filed numerous lawsuits against Waltuch and Conticommodity, alleging fraud, market manipulation, and antitrust violations. All of the suits eventually settled and were dismissed with prejudice, pursuant to settlements in which Conticommodity paid over $35 million to the various suitors. Waltuch himself was dismissed from the suits with no settlement contribution. His unreimbursed legal expenses in these actions total approximately $1.2 million.

Waltuch was also the subject of an enforcement proceeding brought by the CFTC, charging him with fraud and market manipulation. The proceeding was settled, with Waltuch agreeing to a penalty that included a $100,000 fine and a six-month ban on buying or selling futures contracts from any exchange floor. Waltuch spent $1 million in unreimbursed legal fees in the CFTC proceeding.

Waltuch brought suit in the United States District Court for the Southern District of New York against Conticommodity and its parent company, Continental Grain Co., for indemnification of his unreimbursed expenses. Only two of Waltuch's claims reach us on appeal.

Waltuch first claims that Article Ninth of Conticommodity's articles of incorporation requires Conti to indemnify him for his expenses in both the private and CFTC actions. Conti responds that this claim is barred by subsection (a) of § 145 of Delaware's General Corporation Law, which permits indemnification only if the corporate officer acted "in good faith," something that Waltuch has not established. Waltuch counters that subsection (f) of the same statute permits a corporation to grant indemnification rights outside the limits of subsection (a), and that Conticommodity did so with Article Ninth (which has no stated good-faith limitation). The district court held that, notwithstanding § 145(f), Waltuch could recover under Article Ninth only if Waltuch met the "good faith" requirement of § 145(a). On the factual issue of whether Waltuch had acted "in good faith," the court denied Conti's summary judgment motion and cleared the way for trial. The parties then stipulated that they would forgo trial on the issue of Waltuch's "good faith," agree to an entry of final judgment against Waltuch on his claim under Article Ninth and § 145(f), and allow Waltuch to take an immediate appeal of the judgment to this Court. Thus, as to Waltuch's first claim, the only question left is how to interpret §§ 145(a) and 145(f), assuming Waltuch acted with less than "good faith." As we explain in part I below, we affirm the district court's judgment as to this claim and hold that § 145(f) does not permit a corporation to bypass the "good faith" requirement of § 145(a).

Waltuch's second claim is that subsection (c) of § 145 requires Conti to indemnify him because he was "successful on the merits or otherwise" in the private lawsuits. The district court ruled for Conti on this claim as well. The court explained that, even though all the suits against Waltuch were dismissed without his making any payment, he was not "successful on the merits or otherwise," because Conti's settlement payments to the plaintiffs were partially on Waltuch's behalf. For the reasons stated in part II below, we reverse this portion of the district court's ruling, and hold that Conti must indemnify Waltuch under § 145(c) for the $1.2 million in unreimbursed legal fees he spent in defending the private lawsuits.

Article Ninth, on which Waltuch bases his first claim, is categorical and contains no requirement of "good faith":

> The Corporation shall indemnify and hold harmless each of its incumbent or former directors, officers, employees and agents against expenses actually and necessarily incurred by him in connection with the defense of any action, suit or proceeding threatened, pending or completed, in which he is made a party, by reason of his serving in or having held such position or capacity, except in relation to matters as to which he shall be adjudged in such action, suit or proceeding to be liable for negligence or misconduct in the performance of duty.

Conti argues that § 145(a) of Delaware's General Corporation Law, which does contain a "good faith" requirement, fixes the outer limits of a corporation's power to indemnify; Article Ninth is thus invalid under Delaware law, says Conti, to the extent that it requires indemnification of officers who have acted in bad faith. The affirmative grant of power in § 145(a) is as follows:

> *A corporation shall have power to indemnify* any person who was or is a party or is threatened to be made a party to any threatened, pending or completed action, suit or proceeding, whether civil, criminal, administrative or investigative (other than an action by or in the right of the corporation) by reason of the fact that he is or was a director, officer, employee or agent of the corporation, or is or was serving at the request of the corporation as a director, officer, employee or agent of another corporation, partnership, joint venture, trust or other enterprise, against expenses (including attorneys' fees), judgments, fines and amounts paid in settlement actually and reasonably incurred by him in connection with such action, suit or proceeding *if he acted in good faith and in a manner he reasonably believed to be in or not opposed to the best interests of the corporation,* and, with respect to any criminal action or proceeding, had no reasonable cause to believe his conduct was unlawful.

[handwritten margin note: discretionary if corp wants to indemnify director? [if he acted in good faith]]

In order to escape the "good faith" clause of § 145(a), Waltuch argues that § 145(a) is not an *exclusive* grant of indemnification power, because § 145(f) expressly allows corporations to indemnify officers in a manner broader than that set out in § 145(a). The "nonexclusivity" language of § 145(f) provides:

> The indemnification and advancement of expenses provided by, or granted pursuant to, the other subsections of this section *shall not be deemed exclusive of any other rights* to which those seeking indemnification or advancement of expenses may be entitled under any bylaw, agreement, vote of stockholders or disinterested directors

or otherwise, both as to action in his official capacity and as to action in another capacity while holding such office.

Waltuch contends that the "nonexclusivity" language in § 145(f) is a separate grant of indemnification power, not limited by the good faith clause that governs the power granted in § 145(a). Conti on the other hand contends that § 145(f) must be limited by "public policies," one of which is that a corporation may indemnify its officers only if they act in "good faith."

No Delaware court has decided the very issue presented here; but the applicable cases tend to support the proposition that a corporation's grant of indemnification rights cannot be *inconsistent* with the substantive statutory provisions of § 145, notwithstanding § 145(f).

The "consistency" rule suggested by Delaware cases is reinforced by our reading of § 145 as a whole. Subsections (a) (indemnification for third-party actions) and (b) (similar indemnification for derivative suits) expressly grant a corporation the power to indemnify directors, officers, and others, if they "acted in good faith and in a manner reasonably believed to be in or not opposed to the best interest of the corporation." These provisions thus limit the scope of the power that they confer. They are permissive in the sense that a corporation may exercise less than its full power to grant the indemnification rights set out in these provisions. By the same token, subsection (f) permits the corporation to grant additional rights: the rights provided in the rest of § 145 "shall not be deemed exclusive of any other rights to which those seeking indemnification may be entitled." But crucially, subsection (f) merely acknowledges that one seeking indemnification may be entitled to "other rights" (of indemnification or otherwise); it does not speak in terms of corporate power, and therefore cannot be read to free a corporation from the "good faith" limit explicitly imposed in subsections (a) and (b).

When the Legislature intended a subsection of § 145 to augment the powers limited in subsection (a), it set out the additional powers expressly. Thus subsection (g) explicitly allows a corporation to circumvent the "good faith" clause of subsection (a) by purchasing a directors and officers liability insurance policy. Significantly, that subsection is framed as a grant of corporate power:

> A corporation shall have power to purchase and maintain insurance on behalf of any person who is or was a director, officer, employee or agent of the corporation against any liability asserted against him and incurred by him in any such capacity, or arising out of his status as such, *whether or not the corporation would have the power to indemnify him against such liability under this section.*

The italicized passage reflects the principle that corporations have the power under § 145 to indemnify in some situations and not in others. Since § 145(f) is neither a grant of corporate power nor a limitation on such power, subsection (g) must be referring to the limitations set out in § 145(a) and the other provisions of § 145 that describe corporate power. If § 145 (through subsection (f) or another part of the statute) gave corporations unlimited power to indemnify directors and officers, then the final clause of subsection (g) would be unnecessary: that is, its grant of "power to purchase and maintain insurance" (exercisable regardless of whether the corporation itself would have the power to indemnify the loss directly) is meaningful only because, in some insurable situations, the corporation simply lacks the power to indemnify its directors and officers directly.

We hold that Conti's Article Ninth, which would require indemnification of Waltuch even if he acted in bad faith, is inconsistent with § 145(a) and thus exceeds the scope of a Delaware corporation's power to indemnify. Since Waltuch has agreed to forgo his opportunity to prove at trial that he acted in good faith, he is not entitled to indemnification under Article Ninth for the $2.2 million he spent in connection with the private lawsuits and the CFTC proceeding. We therefore affirm the district court on this issue.

Unlike § 145(a), which grants a discretionary indemnification power, § 145(c) affirmatively *requires* corporations to indemnify its officers and directors for the "successful" defense of certain claims:

> To the extent that a director, officer, employee or agent of a corporation has been successful on the merits or otherwise in defense of any action, suit or proceeding referred to in subsections (a) and (b) of this section, or in defense of any claim, issue or matter therein, he shall be indemnified against expenses (including attorneys' fees) actually and reasonably incurred by him in connection therewith.

Waltuch argues that he was "successful on the merits or otherwise" in the private lawsuits, because they were dismissed with prejudice without any payment or assumption of liability by him. Conti argues that the claims against Waltuch were dismissed only because of Conti's $35 million settlement payments, and that this payment was contributed, in part, "on behalf of Waltuch."

The district court agreed with Conti that "the successful settlements cannot be credited to Waltuch but are attributable solely to Conti's settlement payments. It was not Waltuch who was successful, but Conti who was successful for him." The district court held that § 145(c) mandates indemnification when the director or officer "is vindicated," but that there was no vindication here:

> Vindication is also ordinarily associated with a dismissal with prejudice without any payment. However, a director or officer is not vindicated when the reason he did not have to make a settlement payment is because someone else assumed that liability. Being bailed out is not the same thing as being vindicated.

We believe that this understanding and application of the "vindication" concept is overly broad and is inconsistent with a proper interpretation of § 145(c).

303

Under the holding in *Merritt-Chapman & Scott Corp. v. Wolfson*, then, vindication, when used as a synonym for "success" under § 145(c), does not mean moral exoneration. Escape from an adverse judgment or other detriment, for whatever reason, is determinative. According to *Merritt*, the only question a court may ask is what the result was, not why it was.

Conti's contention that, because of its $35 million settlement payments, Waltuch's settlement without payment should not really count as settlement without payment, is inconsistent with the rule in *Merritt*. Here, Waltuch was sued, and the suit was dismissed without his having paid a settlement. Under the approach taken in *Merritt*, it is not our business to ask why this result was reached. Once Waltuch achieved his settlement gratis, he achieved success "on the merits or otherwise." And, as we know from *Merritt*, success is sufficient to constitute vindication (at least for the purposes of § 145(c)). Waltuch's settlement thus vindicated him.

The concept of "vindication" pressed by Conti is also inconsistent with the fact that a director or officer who is able to defeat an adversary's claim by asserting a technical defense is entitled to indemnification under § 145(c). In such cases, the indemnitee has been "successful" in the palpable sense that he has won, and the suit has been dismissed, whether or not the victory is deserved in merits terms. If a technical defense is deemed "vindication" under Delaware law, it cannot matter why Waltuch emerged unscathed, or whether Conti "bailed him out", or whether his success was deserved. Under § 145(c), mere success is vindication enough.

The judgment of the district court is affirmed in part and reversed in part. This case is remanded to the district court so that judgment may be entered in favor of Waltuch on his claim for $1,228,586.67, representing the unreimbursed expenses from the private lawsuits.

304

CHAPTER 9:

INTRODUCTION TO MERGERS & ACQUISITIONS

INTRODUCTION

Once we establish that a corporation is nothing more than a legal fiction, it becomes possible to play with the boundaries of that fiction. Corporations, in other words, may be reorganized in any number of different ways. They may be merged, consolidated, purchased, or sold. Their parts may be spun off as an in-kind dividend, or they may be transferred from one entity to another. Their boundaries can be reimagined in whatever form we can conceive. This is the realm of mergers and acquisitions, or M&A, and it constitutes a large percentage of what business lawyers actually do for their clients.

To understand how this can occur, remember that a corporation is at some level merely an agreed-upon understanding that a given set of assets and relationships should be treated as a single whole. In the same manner that we all agree to pretend that small, green pieces of cloth constitute valuable consideration—some pieces quite a bit more valuable than others—we all pretend that a specified set of assets and relationships can be summarized by the moniker "Nike" or "Citibank." Building on this logic, we can agree to change the terms of our understanding and redraw the lines that demarcate the boundaries of one or more corporations. In this manner, we can purchase or sell entire corporations or pieces thereof. Thus, when presented with the imaginary conceit of corporations ABC and XYZ, the logic of corporate law suggests that we can reimagine them as a single ABCXYZ corporation. Alternatively, we might imagine them as three corporations—AB, CX, and YZ—or as some other combination, such as BCX and AYZ. The potential this creates for planning and structuring—and restructuring—corporate firms is nearly boundless. What remains is to determine the procedures for making such reorganizations happen. That is the subject of this chapter.

One of the key lessons of M&A is that the law is again highly formalistic. Form trumps substance, meaning that the parties to a transaction may select their preferred deal structure. The courts will honor their choice, provided they satisfy the requirements of their chosen structure, and will not attempt to recharacterize the deal as something else. Thus, having a clear understanding of the pluses and minuses of each possible transaction will enable you to make the best choice from among the available options. Pay attention, then, as you study each of the basic structures, to which type of transaction seems best suited for which legal structure. Although each deal is unique, there are a number of general principles that we may deduce.

Part A provides illustrations of the three basic deal structures—asset sales, statutory mergers, and stock sales. Everything else in M&A is a variation on these three norms. When reading the cases in this section, pay particular attention to the various parties who must (or need not) approve each form of transaction. Much of the game here lies in structuring deals in a manner that disenfranchises a constituent who might not agree to the transaction if asked to vote. Equally important is the treatment of assets and liabilities. Which party, after the transaction is completed, will be liable for the corporation's debts? And what third-party approvals will be needed to make the asset transfer successful?

Part B introduces an additional layer of complexity—we play with the consideration to be paid, sometimes using cash and sometimes issuing newly minted shares of the purchasing or surviving corporation. In this manner, the parties may use the form of one deal structure to accomplish the goals of another. Part B also introduces the use of debt to perform a leveraged buyout, or LBO.

Of course, corporate reorganizations are not always consensual. Sometimes, a potential acquirer will bypass the management of the target company and instead deal directly with its shareholders. Such deals are referred to as hostile takeovers and were extremely common during the merger wave of the 1980s. In Part C, we therefore take a brief look at the rights of shareholders who vote "no" in a merger. Then, in Part D, we examine two of history's most infamous takeover battles. Although the invention of powerful anti-takeover legal maneuvers has today made hostile deals an extreme rarity, we cannot overlook their importance to the development of modern corporate law. We study them partly because they provide additional insight into the complex world of M&A and partly because much of the Delaware law regarding fiduciary duties was established in the context of the so-called hostile-takeover "wars."

In order to become proficient at the practice of M&A, we generally recommend you take both a specialty upper-level course devoted to the subject and a course on corporate taxation. Either way, at the end of this chapter, you will understand the basic contours of M&A and how to structure and execute the most common forms of corporate reorganization.

BASIC DEAL STRUCTURES PART A

majority shareholder

HOLLINGER INC. V. HOLLINGER INTERNATIONAL, INC.

COURT OF CHANCERY OF DELAWARE (STRINE, J.)
858 A.2D 342 (2004)

[handwritten margin notes: Int'l / Telegraph / Telegraph spectator / Int'l selling Telegraph to Barclays / Inc. contesting]

Hollinger Inc. (or "Inc.") seeks a preliminary injunction preventing Hollinger International, Inc. (or "International") from selling the *Telegraph* Group Ltd. (England) to Press Holdings International, an entity controlled by Frederick and David Barclay (hereinafter, the "Barclays"). The *Telegraph* Group is an indirect, wholly owned subsidiary of International and publishes the *Telegraph* newspaper and the *Spectator* magazine. The *Telegraph* newspaper is a leading one in the United Kingdom, both in terms of its circulation and its journalistic reputation.

The key question addressed in this decision is whether Inc. and the other International stockholders must be provided with the opportunity to vote on the sale of the *Telegraph* Group because that sale involves "substantially all" the assets of International within the meaning of 8 *Del. C. § 271*. The sale of the *Telegraph* followed a lengthy auction process whereby International and all of Hollinger's operating assets were widely shopped to potential bidders. As a practical matter, Inc.'s vote would be the only one that matters because although it now owns only 18% of International's total equity, it, through high-vote Class B shares, controls 68% of the voting power.

Inc. argues that a preliminary injunction should issue because it is clear that the sale of the *Telegraph* satisfies the quantitative and qualitative test used to determine whether an asset sale involves substantially all of a corporation's assets. The *Telegraph* Group is one of the most profitable parts of International and is its most prestigious asset. After its sale, International will be transformed from a respected international publishing company controlling one of the world's major newspapers to a primarily American publishing company whose most valuable remaining asset, the *Chicago Sun-Times*, is the second leading newspaper in the Second City.

In response to these arguments, International makes several points.

Initially, it contends that the sale of the *Telegraph* Group does not trigger § 271. However prestigious the Telegraph Group, International says its sale does not involve, either quantitatively or qualitatively, the sale of substantially all International's assets. Whether or not the Chicago Sun-Times is as prestigious as the Daily Telegraph, it remains a profitable newspaper in a major city. Along with a group of profitable Chicago-area community newspapers, the Chicago Sun-Times has made the "Chicago Group" International's most profitable operating segment in the last two years and its contribution to International's profits has been comparable to that of the

Telegraph Group for many years. Moreover, International retains a number of smaller newspapers in Canada and the prestigious Jerusalem Post. After the sale of the Telegraph Group, International therefore will quantitatively retain a sizable percentage of its existing assets and will qualitatively remain in the same business line. Although the Telegraph sale is admittedly a major transaction, International stresses that § 271 does not apply to every major transaction; it only applies to transactions that strike at the heart of a corporation's existence, which this transaction does not. Only by ignoring the statute's language, International argues, can this court determine that International will have sold substantially all its assets by divesting itself of the *Telegraph* Group.

In this opinion, I conclude that Inc.'s motion for a preliminary injunction motion should be denied as neither its § 271 nor its equitable claims have a reasonable probability of success.

As to the § 271 claim, I choose not to decide whether International's technical statutory defense has merit. It is common for public companies to hold all of their operating assets through indirect, wholly owned subsidiaries. International wants me to hold that a parent company board may unilaterally direct and control a process by which its indirect, wholly owned subsidiary sells assets that would, if held directly by the parent, possibly comprise substantially all of the parent's assets and by which the sale proceeds under a contract that the parent corporation itself negotiates, signs, and fully guarantees. In that circumstance, International says that § 271 would have no application unless the selling subsidiary has no corporate dignity under the strict test for veil piercing. A ruling of that kind would, as a practical matter, render § 271 an illusory check on unilateral board power at most public companies. And while that ruling would involve a rational reading of § 271, it would not represent the only possible interpretation of that statute. Because this motion can be resolved on substantive economic grounds and because the policy implications of ruling on International's technical defense are important, prudence counsels in favor of deferring a necessarily hasty decision on the interesting question presented.

Instead, I address the economic merits of Inc.'s § 271 claim and treat the *Telegraph* Group as if it were directly owned by International. An application of the governing test, which was originally articulated in *Gimbel v. Signal Cos.*, to the facts demonstrates that the *Telegraph* Group does not come close to comprising "substantially all" of International's assets. Although the *Telegraph* Group is a very important asset of International's and is likely its most valuable asset, International possesses several other important assets. Prominent among these is its so-called Chicago Group, a valuable collection of publications that, by any objective standard approaches the *Telegraph* Group in economic importance to International. In fact, earlier this year, Inc. based its decision to try to sell itself to the Barclays on advice that the Chicago Group was worth more than the *Telegraph* Group. And the record is replete with evidence indicating that the Chicago Group's recent performance in outperforming the profitability of the *Telegraph* Group was not anomalous and that many reasoned observers—including Inc.'s controlling stockholder, Conrad

Substantially all = everything

Black—believe that the Chicago Group will continue to generate EBITDA at levels akin to those of the *Telegraph* Group.

Put simply, after the *Telegraph* Group is sold, International will retain considerable assets that are capable of generating substantial free cash flow. Section 271 does not require a vote when a major asset or trophy is sold; it requires a vote only when the assets to be sold, when considered quantitatively and qualitatively, amount to "substantially all" of the corporation's assets.

Inc.'s inability to meet this economically focused test has led it to place great weight on the greater journalistic reputation of the *Telegraph* newspaper when compared to the *Sun-Times* and the social importance of that newspaper in British life. The problem with this argument is that § 271 is designed as a protection for rational owners of capital and its proper interpretation requires this court to focus on the economic importance of assets and not their aesthetic worth. The economic value of the *Telegraph's* prestige was reflected in the sales process for the *Telegraph* Group and in the cash flows projected for that Group. The Barclays' bid includes the economic value that bidders place on the *Telegraph's* social cachet and does not approach a price that puts the *Telegraph* Group close to being substantially all of International's assets. Nor does the sale of the *Telegraph* Group break any solemn promise to International stockholders. During its history, International has continually bought and sold publishing assets, and no rational investor would view the *Telegraph* Group as immune from the company's ongoing M & A activity.

BRANMAR THEATRE CO. V. BRANMAR, INC.

COURT OF CHANCERY OF DELAWARE, NEW CASTLE (SHORT, V.C.)
264 A.2D 526 (1970)

This is an action for a declaratory judgment in which plaintiff seeks to enjoin defendant from cancelling a lease agreement previously executed by the parties. Defendant, by its answer, prays the court to find that it was entitled to treat the lease agreement as terminated because of a violation of a covenant therein prohibiting assignment by the lessee. This is the decision after final hearing.

Plaintiff was incorporated under the laws of Delaware on June 7, 1967. The owners of its outstanding capital stock were the Robert Rappaport family of Cleveland, Ohio. On June 9, 1967 plaintiff and defendant entered into a lease agreement for a motion picture theatre in the Branmar Shopping Center, New Castle County, Delaware. The lease, sixteen pages in length, recites that the lessor is to erect a theatre building in the shopping center. It provides for the payment of rent by the lessee to the lessor of $27,500 per year plus a percentage of gross admissions receipts, plus five per cent of any amounts paid to the lessee by refreshment concessionaires. The percentage of admissions figure is regulated by the type of attractions in the theatre, the minimum being five per cent and the maximum ten. The lease provides for a twenty year term with an option in the lessee to renew for an additional ten years. The lessee is to provide the lessor with a loan of $60,000, payable in installments, to be used for construction. The lessee is to provide, at its cost, whatever fixtures and equipment are necessary to operate the theatre. Paragraph 12 of the lease, the focal point of this lawsuit, provides:

> Lessee shall not sublet, assign, transfer or in any manner dispose of the said premises or any part thereof, for all or any part of the term hereby granted, without the prior written consent of the Lessor, such consent shall not be unreasonably withheld.

Joseph Luria, the principal for Branmar Shopping Center testified at trial that he negotiated the lease agreement with Isador Rappaport; that he made inquiries about Rappaport's ability to manage a theatre and satisfied himself that Rappaport had the competence and the important industry connections to successfully operate the theatre. It appears that Rappaport and his son operate a successful theatre in Cleveland, Ohio and have owned and operated theatres elsewhere.

Following execution of the lease the Rappaports were approached by Muriel Schwartz and Reba Schwartz, operators of ten theatres in the Delaware and neighboring Maryland area, with an offer to manage the theatre for the Rappaports who had no other business interests in the Wilmington area. This offer was not accepted but the Schwartzes subsequently agreed with the Rappaports to purchase the lease from plaintiff and have it assigned to them. An assignment was executed by plaintiff to the Schwartzes. Defendant rejected the assignment under the power reserved in Paragraph 12 of the lease. On May 29, 1969 the Schwartzes purchased the outstanding shares of plaintiff from the Rappaports. Upon receipt of notice of the sale defendant advised plaintiff that it considered the sale of the shares to the Schwartzes to be a breach of Paragraph 12 of the lease and the lease to be null and void.

The theatre building is now substantially completed and ready for occupancy. The Schwartzes are ready and willing to perform under the lease agreement. Defendant intends to substitute a new tenant, Sameric Theatres, for the corporate plaintiff, contending that Sameric is a better qualified operator than the Schwartzes.

Defendant argues that the sale of stock was in legal effect an assignment of the lease by the Rappaports to the Schwartzes, was in breach of Paragraph 12 of the lease, and that it was, therefore, justified in terminating plaintiff's leasehold interest. That in the absence of fraud, and none is charged here, transfer of stock of a corporate lessee is ordinarily not a violation of a clause prohibiting assignment is clear from the authorities. Defendant contends, however, that this is not the ordinary case. Here, it says, due to the nature of the motion picture business, the performance required was by the Rappaports personally. But while defendant's negotiations were with a member of the Rappaport family when the lease was executed it chose to let the theatre to a corporation whose stock might foreseeably be transferred by the then stockholders. In the preparation of the lease, a document of sixteen pages, defendant was careful to spell out in detail the rights and duties of the parties. It did not, however, see fit to provide for forfeiture in the event the stockholders sold their shares. Had this been the intent it would have been a simple matter to have so provided.

Defendant suggests that since "the Rappaports" could not assign the lease without its consent they should not be permitted to accomplish the same result by transfer of their stock. But the rule that precludes a person from doing indirectly what he cannot do directly has no application to the present case. The attempted assignment was not by the Rappaports but by plaintiff corporation, the sale of stock by its stockholders. Since defendant has failed to show circumstances to justify ignoring the corporation's separate existence reliance upon the cited rule is misplaced.

I find that the sale of stock by the Rappaports to the Schwartzes was not an assignment within the terms of Paragraph 12 of the lease and that the same remains in full force and effect.

PPG INDUSTRIES, INC. V. GUARDIAN INDUSTRIES CORP.

UNITED STATES COURT OF APPEALS, SIXTH CIRCUIT (LIVELY J.)
597 F.2D 1090 (1979)

The question in this case is whether the surviving or resultant corporation in a statutory merger acquires patent license rights of the constituent corporations. The plaintiff, PPG Industries, Inc., appeals from a judgment of the district court dismissing its patent infringement action on the ground that the defendant, Guardian Industries, Corp., as licensee of the patents in suit, was not an infringer. Guardian cross-appeals from a holding by the district court that its alternate defense based on an equipment license agreement was ineffective.

Prior to 1964 both PPG and Permaglass, Inc., were engaged in fabrication of glass products which required that sheets of glass be shaped for particular uses. Independently of each other the two fabricators developed similar processes which involved "floating glass on a bed of gas, while it was being heated and bent." This process is known in the industry as "gas hearth technology" and "air float technology"; the two terms are interchangeable. After a period of negotiations PPG and Permaglass entered into an agreement on January 1, 1964 whereby each granted rights to the other under "gas hearth system" patents already issued and in the process of prosecution.

311

Eleven patents are involved in this suit. Nine of them originated with Permaglass and were licensed to PPG as exclusive licensee under Section 3.2, subject to the non-exclusive, non-transferable reservation to Permaglass set forth in Section 3.3. Two of the patents originated with PPG. Section 4.1 granted a non-exclusive, non-transferable license to Permaglass with respect to the two PPG patents.

As of December 1969 Permaglass was merged into Guardian pursuant to applicable statutes of Ohio and Delaware. Guardian was engaged primarily in the business of fabricating and distributing windshields for automobiles and trucks. It had decided to construct a facility to manufacture raw glass and the capacity of that facility would be greater than its own requirements. Permaglass had no glass manufacturing capability and it was contemplated that its operations would utilize a large part of the excess output of the proposed Guardian facility.

The "Agreement of Merger" between Permaglass and Guardian did not refer specifically to the 1964 agreement between PPG and Permaglass. However, among Permaglass' representations in the agreement was the following:

> (g) Permaglass is the owner, assignee or licensee of such patents, trademarks, trade names and copyrights as are listed and described in Exhibit "C" attached hereto. None of such patents, trademarks, trade names or copyrights is in litigation and Permaglass has not received any notice of conflict with the asserted rights of third parties relative to the use thereof.

Listed on Exhibit "C" to the merger agreement are the nine patents originally developed by Permaglass and licensed to PPG under the 1964 agreement which are involved in this infringement action.

Shortly after the merger was consummated PPG filed the present action, claiming infringement by Guardian in the use of apparatus and processes described and claimed in eleven patents which were identified by number and origin. The eleven patents were covered by the terms of the 1964 agreement. PPG asserted that it became the exclusive licensee of the nine patents which originated with Permaglass under the 1964 agreement and that the rights reserved by Permaglass were personal to it and non-transferable and non-assignable. PPG also claimed that Guardian had no rights with respect to the two patents which had originated with PPG because the license under these patents was personal to Permaglass and non-transferable and non-assignable except with the permission of PPG.

One of the defenses pled by Guardian in its answer was that it was a licensee of the patents in suit. It described the merger with Permaglass and claimed it "had succeeded to all rights, powers, ownerships, etc., of Permaglass, and as Permaglass' successor, defendant is legally entitled to operate in place of Permaglass under the January 1, 1964 agreement between Permaglass and plaintiff, free of any claim of infringement of the patents."

312

Questions with respect to the assignability of a patent license are controlled by federal law. It has long been held by federal courts that agreements granting patent licenses are personal and not assignable unless expressly made so. This has been the rule at least since 1852 when the Supreme Court decided *Troy Iron & Nail v. Corning*. The district court recognized this rule in the present case, but concluded that where patent licenses are claimed to pass by operation of law to the resultant or surviving corporation in a statutory merger there has been no assignment or transfer.

The district court held that the patent licenses in the present case were not transferred because they passed by operation of law from Permaglass to Guardian. This conclusion is based on the theory of continuity which underlies a true merger. However, the theory of continuity relates to the fact that there is no dissolution of the constituent corporations and, even though they cease to exist, their essential corporate attributes are vested by operation of law in the surviving or resultant corporation. It does not mean that there is no transfer of particular assets from a constituent corporation to the surviving or resultant one.

The Ohio merger statute provides that following a merger all property of a constituent corporation shall be "deemed to be *transferred* to and vested in the surviving or new corporation without further act or deed." This indicates that the transfer is by operation of law, not that there is no transfer of assets in a merger situation. The Delaware statute, which was also involved in the Permaglass-Guardian merger, provides that the property of the constituent corporations "shall be vested in the corporation surviving or resulting from such merger or consolidation." The Third Circuit has construed the "shall be vested" language of the Delaware statute as follows: "In short, the underlying property of the constituent corporations is *transferred* to the resultant corporation upon the carrying out of the consolidation or merger."

In his opinion in *Koppers*, Judge Biggs disposed of arguments very similar to those of Guardian in the present case, based on the theory of continuity. Terming such arguments "metaphysical" he found them completely at odds with the language of the Delaware statute. Finally, on this point, the parties themselves provided in the merger agreement that all property of Permaglass "shall be deemed transferred to and shall vest in Guardian without further act or deed." A transfer is no less a transfer because it takes place by operation of law rather than by a particular act of the parties. The merger was effected by the parties and the transfer was a result of their act of merging.

The judgment of the district court is reversed on appeal and affirmed on cross-appeal, and the cause is remanded for further proceedings.

merger means they get to keep the licenses

HEILBRUNN V. SUN CHEMICAL CORPORATION

SUPREME COURT OF DELAWARE (SOUTHERLAND,C.J.)
150 A.2D 755 (1959)

This suit is brought by stockholders of Sun Chemical Corporation, a Delaware corporation, against Ansbacher-Siegle Corporation, a New York corporation, and Norman E. Alexander, President of Sun and owner of Ansbacher. Plaintiffs attack the validity of the purchase by Sun of all the assets of Ansbacker. The complaint states two grounds or causes of action: (1) that the transaction constituted a *de facto* merger and is unlawful since the merger provisions of the Delaware law were not complied with; and (2) that the transaction 'was tainted with self-interest', i. e., is unfair to Sun stockholders.

Defendants moved to dismiss the complaint. The Vice Chancellor held that the transaction was one of purchase and sale and not a merger. He dismissed the complaint as to the first cause of action. He denied the motion to dismiss the second cause of action. Plaintiffs appeal, and contend here, as they did below, that the transaction was by its nature a *de facto* merger.

Although the transaction has been consummated, it is convenient to state many of the facts as they appeared on November 8, 1957, when the proxy statement was sent to the Sun stockholders. They are as follows:

Sun is engaged in the business of manufacturing ink and pigments for ink. It owns a plant at Harrison, New Jersey. It has outstanding 19,000 shares of preferred stock and 1,196,283 shares of common stock. Its balance sheet shows total assets of over $24,000,000. The defendant Alexander is its president, and owns about 2.8 per cent of the common shares.

Ansbacher is engaged in the manufacture of organic pigments. Its products are used in the manufacture of ink, cosmetics, textiles, plastics, and other similar products. Its balance sheet shows total assets of about $1,786,000. The defendant Alexander is its sole beneficial stockholder.

In April of 1956 Alexander, then the owner of about 7,000 shares of Sun, suggested to Sun's then president the possible acquisition of Ansbacher by Sun. Nothing came of the suggestion.

In January, 1957, Alexander advised the Sun management that he and five friends and associates owned substantial amounts of Sun shares, and requested representation on the board. Negotiations followed, as a result of which five of the Sun directors resigned, and Alexander and four others named by him were elected to Sun's board. Alexander became president.

In June, 1957, a special committee of Sun's board was appointed to consider whether Sun should own and operate a pigment plant, and if so whether it should rehabilitate its Harrison plant or should acquire or build a new plant. The committee found that Sun's Harrison plant was old, inefficient, and incapable of expansion because of its location. It recommended the acquisition of Ansbacher.

An agreement for the purchase was entered into between Sun and Ansbacher on October 2, 1957. It provides, among other things, as follows:

1. Ansbacher will assign and convey to Sun all of Ansbacher's assets and property of every kind, tangible and intangible; and will grant to Sun the use of its name or any part thereof.
2. Sun will assume all of Ansbacher's liabilities, subject to a covenant that Ansbacher's working capital shall be at least $600,000.
3. Sun will issue to Ansbacher 225,000 shares of its common stock.
4. As soon as possible after the closing of the transaction Ansbacher will dissolve and distribute to its shareholders, pro rata, the shares of the common stock of Sun (subject to an escrow agreement relating to one-fourth of the shares).
5. Ansbacher will use its best efforts to persuade its employees to become employees of Sun.
6. Sun's obligation to consummate the transaction is subject to approval by the holders of a majority of Sun's voting stock, exclusive of shares owned or controlled by Alexander, at a special stockholders' meeting to be thereafter called.

The agreement was approved by the boards of directors of both corporations. A special meeting of Sun's stockholders was called for November 29, 1957. The proxy statement set forth detailed information with respect to the plan of acquisition.

On November 6, 1957, a ruling was obtained from the Commissioner of Internal Revenue that the transaction would constitute a tax-free reorganization under the applicable provisions of the Internal Revenue Code. Prior to the meeting plaintiffs filed written objections to the transaction, and gave notice of their intention to take legal action. The approval of the necessary majority of Sun's stockholders was obtained, and the transaction was consummated.

Plaintiffs contend that although the transaction is in form a sale of assets of Ansbacher it is in substance and effect a merger, and that it is unlawful because, the merger statute not having been complied with, plaintiffs have been deprived of their right of appraisal and have also suffered financial injury.

The argument that the result of this transaction is substantially the same as the result that would have followed a merger may be readily accepted. As plaintiffs correctly say, the Ansbacher enterprise is continued in altered form as a part of Sun. This is ordinarily a typical characteristic of a merger. Moreover the plan of reorganization *requires* the dissolution of Ansbacher and the distribution to its stockholders of the Sun stock received by it for the assets. As a part of the plan, the Ansbacher stockholders are compelled to receive Sun stock. From the viewpoint of Ansbacher, the result is the same as if Ansbacher had formally merged into Sun.

This result is made possible, of course, by the overlapping scope of the merger statute and the statute authorizing the sale of all the corporate assets. This possibility of overlapping was noticed in our opinion in the *Mayflower* case.

There is nothing new about such a result. For many years drafters of plans of corporate reorganization have increasingly resorted to the use of the sale-of-assets method in preference to the method by merger. Historically at least, there were reasons for this quite apart from the avoidance of the appraisal right given to stockholders dissenting from a merger. For example, if an interstate merger was not authorized by the statute, a sale of assets could be resorted to.

The doctrine of *de facto* merger has been recognized in Delaware. It has been invoked in cases of sales of assets for the protection of creditors or stockholders who have suffered an injury by reason of failure to comply with the statute governing such sales. The contention that it should be applied to cases of the kind here involved depends for its force upon the proposition that the stockholder has been forced against his will to accept a new investment in an enterprise foreign to that of which he was a part, and that his right to an appraisal under the merger statute has been circumvented.

Our Court of Chancery has said that the appraisal right is given to the stockholder in compensation for his former right at common law to prevent a merger. By the use of the sale-of-assets method of reorganization, it is contended, he has been unjustly deprived of this right.

As before stated, we do not reach this question, because we fail to see how any injury has been inflicted upon the Sun stockholders. Their corporation has simply acquired property and paid for it in shares of stock. The business of Sun will go on as before, with additional assets. The Sun stockholder is not forced to accept stock in another corporation. Nor has the reorganization changed the essential nature of the enterprise of the purchasing corporation.

Nor is it a case in which the seller can be said to have acquired the purchaser. Sun's net worth is ten times that of Ansbacher. Sun has simply absorbed another company's assets which are needed in its own business.

The diminution in the proportional voting strength of the Sun stockholder is not a ground of complaint. Such a consequence necessarily follows any issuance of stock to acquire property.

Plaintiffs made the further point that their proportional interest in the assets has also been diminished. This is, in effect, a charge that the terms of the acquisition are unfair to the Sun minority. Thus it is said that Ansbacher's net worth is about $1,600,000, and the issuance to Ansbacher of 225,000 shares of Sun stock of the market value of $10.125 a share results in the payment by Sun of a grossly excessive price and in the unjust enrichment of Alexander. It is also said that the report of the committee of Sun's directors admits that the earnings of Ansbacher do not justify the price paid.

These are arguments appropriate to the second cause of action, which the Vice Chancellor refused to dismiss. The legal power to authorize the transaction is one thing. The fairness of its terms and conditions is another. Only the first issue is before us. Plaintiffs are in no way foreclosed from pressing the above contentions when the second cause of action is tried.

Plaintiffs appear to concede that if the dissolution of Ansbacher and the distribution of Sun stock had not been *required* by the plan—that is, if Ansbacher had continued as a holding company—the doctrine of *de facto* merger would not apply. This concession exposes the weakness of plaintiffs' case.

How can a Sun stockholder have any concern with what Ansbacher does with the Sun stock after it receives it? Surely the presence or absence of injury to him cannot depend on Ansbacher's decision whether to dissolve and distribute the Sun stock or to continue as a holding company.

Whatever may be the case for giving the right of appraisal to a dissenting stockholder of a selling corporation, as many states have done, there seems little reason, at least in cases like the instant one, to accord it to the stockholders of the purchaser. At all events, no state appears to have done so by statute. And we find no basis in the facts of this case for the granting of such relief in equity on the theory of a *de facto* merger.

Plaintiffs say that the calling of a stockholders' meeting of Sun is in effect an admission that a merger was involved. On the contrary, the natural inference is that approval of the stockholders was sought because the transaction is one between the corporation and its president.

Some point is sought to be made of the fact that the plan and agreement do not use the words 'purchase' or 'sale'. Nor do they use the word 'merger'. We attach no significance to this omission. One may surmise that the choice of language was influenced by the necessity of devising a tax-free reorganization. But it does not matter what the reason was. The contract was in legal effect one of purchase and sale.

The judgment of the Court of Chancery is affirmed. —not a merger

PART B **ADVANCED DEAL STRUCTURES**

RAUCH V. RCA CORPORATION

UNITED STATES COURT OF APPEALS, SECOND
CIRCUIT (MAHONEY, C.J.)
861 F.2D 29 (1988)

Plaintiff Lillian S. Rauch appeals from a judgment of the United States District Court for the Southern District of New York dismissing her class action complaint challenging the propriety of a merger effected by defendants for failure to state a claim upon which relief can be granted. The district court held that Rauch's action was barred by Delaware's doctrine of independent legal significance. We affirm.

This case arises from the acquisition of RCA Corporation ("RCA") by General Electric Company ("GE"). On or about December 11, 1985, RCA, GE and Gesub, Inc. ("Gesub"), a wholly owned Delaware subsidiary of GE, entered into an agreement of merger. Pursuant to the terms of the agreement, all common and preferred shares of RCA stock (with one exception) were converted to cash, Gesub was then merged into RCA, and the common stock of Gesub was converted into common stock of RCA. Specifically, the merger agreement provided (subject in each case to the exercise of appraisal rights) that each share of RCA common stock would be converted into $66.50, each share of $3.65 cumulative preference stock would be converted into $42.50, and each share of $3.50 cumulative first preferred stock (the stock held by plaintiff and in issue here, hereinafter the "Preferred Stock") would be converted into $40.00. A series of $4.00 cumulative convertible first preferred stock was called for redemption according to its terms prior to the merger.

On February 27, 1986, plaintiff, a holder of 250 shares of Preferred Stock, commenced this diversity class action on behalf of a class consisting of the holders of Preferred Stock. It is undisputed that this action is governed by the law of Delaware, the state of incorporation of both RCA and Gesub. Plaintiff claimed that the merger constituted a "liquidation or dissolution or winding up of RCA and a redemption of the Preferred Stock," as a result of which holders of the Preferred Stock were entitled to $100 per share in accordance with the redemption provisions of RCA's certificate of incorporation, that defendants were in violation of the rights of the holders of Preferred Stock as thus stated; and that defendants thereby wrongfully converted substantial sums of money to their own use. Plaintiff sought damages and injunctive relief.

Defendants moved to dismiss the complaint and plaintiff cross-moved for summary judgment. The district court concluded that the transaction at issue was a *bona fide* merger carried out in accordance with the relevant provisions of the Delaware General Corporation Law.

Accordingly, the district court held that plaintiff's action was precluded by Delaware's doctrine of independent legal significance, and dismissed the complaint.

According to RCA's Restated Certificate of Incorporation, the owners of the Preferred Stock were entitled to $100 per share, plus accrued dividends, upon the redemption of such stock at the election of the corporation. Plaintiff contends that the merger agreement, which compelled the holders of Preferred Stock to sell their shares to RCA for $40.00, effected a redemption whose nature is not changed by referring to it as a conversion of stock to cash pursuant to a merger. Plaintiff's argument, however, is not in accord with Delaware law.

It is clear that under the Delaware General Corporation Law, a conversion of shares to cash that is carried out in order to accomplish a merger is legally distinct from a redemption of shares by a corporation. Section 251 of the Delaware General Corporation Law allows two corporations to merge into a single corporation by adoption of an agreement that complies with that section. The merger agreement in issue called for the conversion of the shares of the constituent corporations into cash. The statute specifically authorizes such a transaction:

> The agreement shall state the manner of converting the shares of each of the constituent corporations into shares or other securities of the corporation surviving or resulting from the merger or consolidation and, if any shares of any of the constituent corporations are not to be converted solely into shares or other securities of the surviving or resulting corporations, *the cash which the holders of such shares are to receive* in exchange for, or upon conversion of such shares, *which cash may be* in addition to or *in lieu of shares* or other securities of the surviving or resulting corporation.

Thus, the RCA-GE merger agreement complied fully with the merger provision in question, and plaintiff does not argue to the contrary.

Redemption, on the other hand, is governed by sections 151(b) and 160(a) of the Delaware General Corporation Law. Section 151(b) provides that a corporation may subject its preferred stock to redemption "by the corporation at its option or at the option of the holders of such stock or upon the happening of a specified event." In this instance, the Preferred Stock was subject to redemption by RCA *at its election*. Nothing in RCA's certificate of incorporation indicated that the holders of Preferred Stock could initiate a redemption, nor was there provision for any specified event, such as the Gesub-RCA merger, to trigger a redemption.

Plaintiff's contention that the transaction was essentially a redemption rather than a merger must therefore fail. RCA chose to convert its stock to cash to accomplish the desired merger, and in the process chose not to redeem the Preferred Stock. It had every right to do so in accordance with Delaware law. As the district court aptly noted, to accept plaintiff's argument "would render nugatory the conversion provisions within Section 251 of the Delaware Code."

We note in this regard that plaintiff's complaint nowhere alleges that the $40.00 per share conversion rate for the Preferred Stock was unfair. Rather, "plaintiff is complaining of a breach of contractual rights, entirely divorced from the purported 'fairness' of the transaction." Moreover, as the district court stated: "Delaware provides specific protection to shareholders who believe that they have received insufficient value for their stock as the result of a merger: they may obtain an appraisal under § 262 of the General Corporation Law." Plaintiff, however, explicitly disavows any appraisal theory or remedy, consistent with her position that fairness is not the issue.

The judgment of the district court dismissing the complaint is affirmed.

BOYER V. CROWN STOCK DISTRIBUTION, INC.

UNITED STATES COURT OF APPEALS, SEVENTH CIRCUIT (POSNER, C.J.)
587 F.3D 787 (2009)

These appeals arise from the Chapter 7 bankruptcy of Crown Unlimited Machine, Inc. The trustee in bankruptcy filed an adversary action charging the defendants—a defunct corporation and its shareholders, members of a family named Stroup—with having made a fraudulent conveyance in violation of the Uniform Fraudulent Transfer Act, a statute enforceable in a bankruptcy proceeding. After an evidentiary hearing, the bankruptcy judge awarded the trustee $3,295,000 plus prejudgment interest. The district judge affirmed and the defendants have appealed. The trustee has cross-appealed, seeking an additional $590,328.

Crown was a designer and manufacturer of machinery for cutting and bending tubes. Most of the machinery it made was custom-designed to the buyer's specifications, and only two other companies manufactured custom-designed machinery of that type. In January 1999 the defendants agreed to sell all of Crown's assets to Kevin E. Smith, the president of a company in a similar line of business. The price was $6 million. Crown agreed to employ Smith until the closing, so that he could assure himself of the value of the business before committing to buying it.

He decided to go through with the deal. At the closing, on January 5, 2000, Crown received from a new corporation, formed by Smith, $3.1 million in cash and a $2.9 million promissory note. The new corporation (also named Crown Unlimited Machine, Inc., the name being among the assets sold to the new Crown) had borrowed the $3.1 million from a bank. Although the loan was secured by all of Crown's assets, the annual interest rate (a floating rate) initially exceeded

9 percent. The rate suggests—since inflation expectations were low at the time—that the bank considered the risk of default nontrivial.

The promissory note was payable on April 1, 2006, with interest at an annual rate of 8 percent. Although that translates into an interest expense of $232,000 a year, the agreement of sale specified that the new corporation would be required to pay only $100,000 a year on the note, with the first payment due in April 2001, unless new Crown's sales exceeded a specified high threshold. The note, like the bank loan, was secured by all of Crown's assets, but the promisee's (old Crown's) security interest was subordinated to the bank's. Although the interest rate on the note was lower than the interest rate on the bank loan, even though the note was not as well secured, there was, as we'll see, little chance that the note would ever be paid; and after the first two $100,000 interest payments, it wasn't.

Smith's personal assets were meager. He contributed only $500 of his own money toward the purchase.

Just prior to the closing, old Crown transferred $590,328 from its corporate bank account to a separate bank account so that it could be distributed to Crown's shareholders as a dividend. This was done pursuant to an understanding of the parties that, depending on the company's performance between the initial agreement and the closing, the Stroups would be permitted to keep some of Crown's cash that would otherwise have been transferred to the new corporation as part of the sale; the sale, since it was of all of Crown's assets, included whatever money was in the corporation's bank account.

After the closing, old Crown (renamed Crown Stock Distribution, Inc.) distributed the entire $3.1 million in cash that it had received to its shareholders, and ceased to be an operating company.

New Crown was a flop. It declared bankruptcy in July 2003, and its assets were sold pursuant to 11 U.S.C. § 363 (which authorizes a sale, if approved by the bankruptcy judge, of assets of the debtor) for $3.7 million. The buyer was a new company of which Smith is now the president. Most of the money realized in the sale was required for paying off the bank; very little was left over to pay the claims of new Crown's unsecured creditors, who were owed some $1.6 or $1.7 million and on whose behalf the trustee in bankruptcy brought the adversary action. The action was timely.

We begin our analysis with the trustee's argument for recharacterizing the transaction. In a conventional LBO, an investor buys the stock of a corporation from the stockholders with the proceeds of a loan secured by the corporation's own assets. It follows that if all the assets are still fully secured when the corporation declares bankruptcy, the unsecured creditors cannot satisfy any part of their claims from a sale of the assets. If the trustee loses this suit, the unsecured creditors will have recovered only $150,000—less than 10 cents on the dollar.

Should the acquired company be doomed to go broke after and because of the LBO—if the burden of debt created by the transaction was so heavy that the corporation had no reasonable prospect of surviving—the payment to the shareholders by the buyer of the corporation is deemed a fraudulent conveyance because in exchange for the money the shareholders received they provided no value to the corporation but merely increased its debt and by doing so pushed it over the brink. A corporate transfer is "fraudulent" within the meaning of the Uniform Fraudulent Transfer Act, even if there is no fraudulent intent, if the corporation didn't receive "reasonably equivalent value" in return for the transfer and as a result was left with insufficient assets to have a reasonable chance of surviving indefinitely.

Some courts have been reluctant to apply the Act as written to leveraged buyouts. They sympathize with minority shareholders who have no power to prevent such a deal. They may also agree with the scholars who have argued that many LBOs are welfare-enhancing transactions because by making the managers owners (managers are often the buyers in an LBO) and thus fusing ownership with control, an LBO increases the managers' incentive to operate the corporation with a view to maximizing its value rather than their salaries and perks. These scholars also argue that devices that facilitate transfers of corporate control increase the mobility of capital.

The reluctance of the courts is not easy to square with the language of the Uniform Fraudulent Transfer Act. And anyway the "equities," as we shall see, do not favor lenient treatment in this case. Moreover, although before the LBO Smith was briefly a member of Crown's management, the LBO did not close a gap between managers and shareholders. LBOs, though by burdening the acquired corporation with additional debt they increase the risk of bankruptcy (because debt is a fixed cost, and therefore unlike a variable cost does not shrink when the debtor's output shrinks), can indeed have redeeming economic value when the corporation is publicly held and the managers have a low equity stake prior to the transaction. In a publicly held corporation there is a separation of ownership from control, and the managers may use their control to manage the company in a way that will increase their personal wealth rather than maximize the profits of the corporation; the conflict of interest is eliminated by making the managers the owners. But this rationale for an LBO is missing from this case because both old and new Crown were closely held corporations. And while the economic literature also argues that the increased risk of bankruptcy that an LBO creates concentrates the minds of the managers (just as, according to Samuel Johnson, the prospect of being hanged concentrates the mind of the condemned person), this is hard to take seriously in the present case; for the owner-manager had only a $500 stake in the company.

But the critical difference between the LBO in this case and a bona fide LBO is that this LBO was highly likely to plunge the company into bankruptcy. There was scant probability that the transaction would increase the firm's value; on the contrary, it left the firm with so few assets that it would have had to be extremely lucky to survive.

The transaction differed, however, in two formal respects from a conventional LBO: the buyer bought the assets of the corporation, rather than stock in the corporation; and despite a load of debt and a dearth of cash, the corporation limped along for three-and-a-half years before collapsing into the arms of the bankruptcy court. The defendants urge these as grounds for not reclassifying the asset purchase as an LBO.

New Crown staved off bankruptcy for several years and might have staved it off longer had it not been for mistakes made by Smith in running the business. (His biggest mistake was shifting from the production of custom-designed to standardized machinery, a market in which new Crown faced competition from hundreds of firms rather than from just two.) But to assess the significance of this point one must distinguish between insolvency and the acknowledgment of insolvency and between insolvency and a lack of adequate capital. A firm might be insolvent in the bankruptcy sense of negative net worth—its liabilities exceeded its assets—yet it might continue operating as long as it was able to raise enough money to pay its debts as they became due, or even longer if its creditors were forbearing.

By encumbering all the company's assets, the sale reduced its ability to borrow on favorable terms, as it could offer no collateral to lenders. And by surrendering most of old Crown's cash (the cash that was paid as a dividend) and obligating itself to pay $100,000 a year to the defendants and $495,000 a year to service the $3.1 million bank loan, without receiving anything in return except Smith's $500, new Crown was forced to engage in continual borrowing during its remaining life, and on unfavorable terms. Seven months before it declared bankruptcy it had run up $8.3 million in debt and its assets were worth less than half that amount.

New Crown thus had made payments and incurred obligations without receiving "reasonably equivalent value" in return. Even if it was not actually insolvent *ab initio*, as a result of the lack of equivalence it began life with "unreasonably small" assets given the nature of its business. That was what the bankruptcy judge meant when he said that new Crown survived as long as it did only on "life support." That was a finding of fact to which we defer.

The difference between insolvency and "unreasonably small" assets in the LBO context is the difference between being bankrupt on the day the LBO is consummated and having at that moment such meager assets that bankruptcy is a consequence both likely and foreseeable. Focusing on the second question avoids haggling over whether at the moment of the transfer the corporation became "technically" insolvent, a question that only accountants could relish having to answer.

But one has to be careful with a term like "unreasonably small." It is fuzzy, and in danger of being interpreted under the influence of hindsight bias. One is tempted to suppose that because a firm failed it must have been inadequately capitalized. The temptation must be resisted. But new Crown started life almost with no assets at all, for all its physical assets were encumbered twice over, and the dividend plus new Crown's interest obligations drained the company of virtually all its cash. It was naked to any financial storms that might assail it. So the statutory condition for a fraudulent conveyance was satisfied—or so at least the bankruptcy judge could and did find without committing a clear error.

The fact that mistakes by the buyer hastened the company's demise is not a defense. Whether a transfer was fraudulent when made depends on conditions that existed when it was made, not on what happened later to affect the timing of the company's collapse. Not that the length of the interval between the LBO and the collapse is irrelevant to determining the effect of the transfer. It is pertinent evidence. The longer the interval, the less likely that the collapse was fated at the formation of the new company, although we are skeptical of cases that can be read to suggest that ten or twelve months is a long enough interval to create a presumption that the terms of the LBO were not responsible for the company's failure. An inadequately capitalized company may be able to stagger along for quite some time, concealing its parlous state or persuading creditors to avoid forcing it into a bankruptcy proceeding in which perhaps only the lawyers will do well.

The interval was longer than in previous cases, but the defendants are unable to sketch a plausible narrative in which new Crown could have survived indefinitely despite being cash starved as a result of the terms of the LBO that brought it into being. The fact that Smith made mistakes in running the company does not weigh as strongly as the defendants think. Everyone makes mistakes. That's one reason why businesses need adequate capital to have a good chance of surviving in the Darwinian jungle that we call the market.

The "dividend" was an integral part of the LBO, although the trustee stumbled by failing to present evidence concerning old Crown's dividend policy. Family-owned companies rarely pay dividends, but instead channel profits into salary in order to avoid double taxation. Had this been shown to be true of old Crown it would have clinched the case for the trustee. But we do know that at least four of old Crown's shareholders were officers or directors and so presumably were salaried. We know as well that the dividend represented 50 percent of Crown's 1999 profits, which was unreasonably high given the cash needs of the business. Crown's owners drained it of cash—all unbeknownst to the corporation's present and future unsecured creditors. These indications that the dividend was part of the fraudulent transfer rather than a normal distribution of previously earned profits—that it wasn't an ordinary dividend but rather the withdrawal of an asset vital to the acquiring firm—were sufficient to place a burden on the defendants of producing evidence that it was a bona fide dividend, a burden they failed to carry.

The defendants make some other arguments, but they do not require discussion. The trustee is entitled to the judgment awarded by the bankruptcy judge, plus the $590,328 dividend. After the claims of all creditors have been satisfied and the costs of administering the bankruptcy paid, any money remaining in the hands of the trustee must be returned to the defendants. The judgment of the district court is therefore affirmed in part and reversed in part (the part relating to the dividend), and the case remanded for further proceedings consistent with this opinion.

DISSENTERS' RIGHTS OF PART C APPRAISAL

WEINBERGER V. UOP, INC.

COURT OF CHANCERY OF DELAWARE (BROWN, V.C.)
426 A.2D 1333 (1981)

This is a decision after trial in a class action brought on behalf of certain former shareholders of a Delaware corporation. The plaintiff, William B. Weinberger, is a former shareholder of the defendant, UOP, Inc. The defendant, the Signal Companies, Inc., is the former majority shareholder of UOP. It is also a Delaware corporation. On May 26, 1978, a merger was effectuated between UOP and Sigco Incorporated, the latter corporation then being a wholly-owned subsidiary of Signal. As a result of the merger, UOP, as the surviving entity, became the wholly-owned subsidiary of Signal, and UOP's former minority shareholders were paid the sum of $21 per share for their former interests in UOP.

Plaintiff attacks the validity of that merger transaction on the theory that the price of $21 per share paid to the minority shareholders of UOP was grossly inadequate and that as a consequence the merger was unfair and should be set aside. In the event that the now-completed transaction is too involved to undo, plaintiff, as an alternative, seeks what he would term an "equitable rescission" in the form of either an award of money damages to the former UOP minority shareholders or an award to each member of the class of an appropriate stock interest in Signal.

Signal is a diversified, technologically based company operating through various subsidiaries. UOP is a diversified industrial company which, as of the beginning of 1978, was engaged in six major lines of business, including petroleum and petrochemical services and related products.

In 1974, friendly negotiations were initiated between representatives of Signal and UOP. Signal proposed $19 per share as a fair price to pay to obtain a controlling interest in UOP. The representatives of UOP sought $25 per share. In the arm's length bargaining that followed, an understanding was reached between the two companies whereby Signal agreed to purchase from UOP 1.5 million of UOP's authorized but unissued shares for a price of $21 per share. This purchase, however, was made contingent upon Signal making a successful cash tender offer for 4.3 million publicly held shares of UOP, also at a price of $21 per share. The combined acquisition in this manner of 5.8 million shares was designed to give Signal a 50.5 per cent stock ownership interest in UOP.

On March 6, 1978 meetings of both Signal's board and UOP's board were convened. Telephone communications were maintained between the two meetings. First, Signal's board unanimously adopted a resolution which authorized Signal to propose to UOP a cash merger at $21 per share as outlined in a certain merger agreement and other supporting documents. Of significance, Signal's proposal required that the merger would have to be approved by a majority of UOP's outstanding minority shares voting at the shareholders meeting at which the merger would be considered and, in addition, that the minority shares voting in favor of the merger, when coupled with Signal's 50.5 per cent interest, would have to comprise at least two-thirds of all UOP shares. Otherwise the proposed merger would be deemed disapproved.

UOP's board then proceeded to consider the proposal. On the advice of counsel, UOP's five Signal directors abstained from voting. All five indicated, however, that if they had voted they would have voted in favor of the resolution. The remaining UOP directors all voted in favor of the resolution, and thus approved the merger on terms proposed by Signal.

Despite the foregoing swift action taken by the boards of the two companies, the vote on the merger was not submitted to UOP's shareholders until UOP's annual meeting on May 26, 1978. At the meeting only 56 per cent of the minority shares were voted. Of the minority shares voted, the merger was approved by a ratio of nearly 12 to 1. When Signal's shares were added to the minority shares voting in favor, a total of 76.2 per cent of UOP's outstanding shares voted for the merger while only 2.2 per cent opposed it.

Under the terms of the agreement, the merger became effective on May 26, 1978, and each share of UOP stock, other than those owned by Signal, was automatically converted into a right to receive $21 in cash.

Based upon these facts, plaintiff contends that Signal has unfairly used its majority stock ownership position in UOP to cash out UOP's 49.5 per cent minority at a price per share which is grossly inadequate to the minority shareholders. Specifically, plaintiff charges that there was no legally proper purpose for the merger since it was brought about by Signal solely to further its own economic interests, and thus to rid itself of the minority shareholders.

Finally, plaintiff contends that the true value of UOP's minority shares at the time of the merger was not less than $26 per share, and accordingly he argues that, all other factors aside, the price paid to the minority was grossly inadequate, and thus unfair. To this end, plaintiff offered expert testimony in support of his position that $26 was the minimum price that Signal should have been required to pay in return for the right to acquire 100 per cent ownership of UOP.

This position of the plaintiff, if I have perceived it correctly, stems from the Supreme Court's admonishment that a majority shareholder cannot be absolved from the scrutiny of the courts simply because minority shareholders who are unhappy with the cash out price have the right to seek judicial determination of the value of their shares under the Delaware appraisal statute. As a consequence, plaintiff seems to be contending that the factors which go into a determination of the value of stock under a § 262 appraisal proceeding are not those which apply in a proceeding such as this wherein a minority shareholder is attacking the fairness, and thus the validity of the merger itself, on the grounds that the price paid for the minority interests is grossly inadequate. Thus, plaintiff seems to be suggesting that in evaluating the fairness of the merger terms to the minority in such a proceeding as this, one must look to what it is reasonably worth to the former majority shareholder to be rid of all other shareholders so as to become the sole owner of the enterprise, and then, using that as a basis or starting point, determine what is a fair amount for it to have paid the minority for the right to become sole shareholder. The resulting figure the plaintiff, through the approach employed by his expert, would transform into the fair value of the minority shares in the context of a cash out merger.

This approach assumes that a stock has more than one value in the hands of a minority shareholder. That is to say, if he has no complaints as to how the merger came about and no complaints as to the good faith effort of those in a fiduciary position to discharge their duties, but if he nonetheless has an honest difference of opinion as to the price and for that reason desires an appraisal under § 262, then the Court hears evidence and values his shares under one standard. But if the same shareholder feels that those in a fiduciary position to his interests have acted in disregard of their duty, or if he feels that a concentration of all the corporate stock in the hands of the former majority shareholder will unjustly enrich the former majority shareholder when compared against that which he is paying for it, then the Court is to hear evidence and value his shares under a different standard. I cannot believe that the policy of our law contemplates the application of such a dual standard.

Thus, to the extent that plaintiff is suggesting that in the context of a cash out merger the fairness of the price paid to the minority is to be determined by reference to that which the former majority shareholder will have immediately after the merger as a result of being the 100 per cent owner of the corporation, I reject the argument as being unsound and not in accord with the existing law.

At the same time, it is presumably proper to view the benefits that may flow to the majority shareholder as a result of becoming the 100 per cent owner as one of the elements to be considered in determining the fairness of the transaction. The value of the minority shares to the majority shareholder is the standard to be applied.

For the purposes of trial, the defendants retained the investment banking firm of Dillon, Read & Co., Inc. to review the financial terms and conditions relating to the merger and to give an opinion as to whether they were fair and equitable to the holders of common stock of UOP other than Signal.

The Dillon, Read report approached the task in the manner generally approved by the Delaware case decisions dealing with appraisal actions. It considered market value, net asset value and investment value, including UOP's dividend record. It examined these elements for the five-year period prior to and including the merger and compared them against the performance of certain companies selected as being reasonably comparable to UOP in their business activities.

Dillon, Read also considered the structure of the merger, i.e., the vote being left to a majority of the minority shareholders with its added requirement that a sufficient number of minority shareholders vote in favor of the merger so that, when coupled with Signal's 50.5 per cent vote, at least two-thirds of all outstanding shares gave their approval to the transaction. Dillon, Read also considered the so-called premium paid by Signal over the market price existing on the day preceding the announcement of the merger.

From all of the foregoing, as well as the supporting statistics and documentation provided in the Dillon, Read report, there is a reasonable basis for finding that the merger price of $21 per share represented a price which was fair to the minority shareholders of UOP.

no t enough evidence for any of ∏'s claims

In summary, there is no indication that Signal's purpose in proposing the merger was legally improper; there is no convincing proof that there was any misrepresentation or omission of material facts in the dissemination of information by UOP or Signal; there is no evidence which indicates by a preponderance that UOP's board abdicated its fiduciary responsibility; and there is an evidentiary basis for concluding that the merger price agreed upon was fair to the minority under the circumstances. In addition, even though others may have held a differing view, and despite the arguable nature of all of the foregoing, the final say was still submitted to the decision of UOP's minority shareholders and those who cared enough to vote gave the transaction their overwhelming approval.

Viewed overall, I find that the terms of the merger were legally fair to the plaintiff and the other minority shareholders of UOP.

PART D HOSTILE TAKEOVERS

PARAMOUNT COMMUNICATIONS, INC. V. TIME, INC.

SUPREME COURT OF DELAWARE (HORSEY, J.)
571 A.2D 1140 (1989)

Paramount Communications, Inc. and two other groups of plaintiffs, shareholders of Time Incorporated, separately filed suits in the Delaware Court of Chancery seeking a preliminary injunction to halt Time's tender offer for 51% of Warner Communication, Inc's outstanding shares at $70 cash per share. The court below consolidated the cases and, following the development of an extensive record, after discovery and an evidentiary hearing, denied plaintiffs' motion. In a 50-page unreported opinion and order entered July 14, 1989, the Chancellor refused to enjoin Time's consummation of its tender offer, concluding that the plaintiffs were unlikely to prevail on the merits.

The principal ground for reversal, asserted by all plaintiffs, is that Paramount's June 7, 1989 uninvited all-cash, all-shares, "fully negotiable" (though conditional) tender offer for Time triggered duties under *Unocal Corp. v. Mesa Petroleum Co.*, and that Time's board of directors, in responding to Paramount's offer, breached those duties. As a consequence, plaintiffs argue that in our review of the Time board's decision of June 16, 1989 to enter into a revised merger agreement with Warner, Time is not entitled to the benefit and protection of the business judgment rule.

Applying our standard of review, we affirm the Chancellor's ultimate finding and conclusion under *Unocal*. We find that Paramount's tender offer was reasonably perceived by Time's board to pose a threat to Time and that the Time board's "response" to that threat was, under the circumstances, reasonable and proportionate. Applying *Unocal*, we reject the argument that the only corporate threat posed by an all-shares, all-cash tender offer is the possibility of inadequate value.

Time is a Delaware corporation with its principal offices in New York City. Time's traditional business is publication of magazines and books; however, Time also provides pay television programming through its Home Box Office, Inc. and Cinemax subsidiaries. In addition, Time owns and operates cable television franchises through its subsidiary, American Television and Communication Corporation. During the relevant time period, Time's board consisted of sixteen directors. Twelve of the directors were "outside," nonemployee directors.

In late spring of 1987, a meeting took place between Steve Ross, CEO of Warner Brothers, and Nicholas of Time. Ross and Nicholas discussed the possibility of a joint venture between the two companies through the creation of a jointly-owned cable company. Time would contribute its cable system and HBO. Warner would contribute its cable system and provide access to Warner Brothers Studio. The resulting venture would be a larger, more efficient cable network, able to produce and distribute its own movies on a worldwide basis. Ultimately the parties abandoned this plan, determining that it was impractical for several reasons, chief among them being tax considerations.

The board's consensus was that a merger of Time and Warner was feasible, but only if Time controlled the board of the resulting corporation and thereby preserved a management committed to Time's journalistic integrity.

From the outset, Time's board favored an all-cash or cash and securities acquisition of Warner as the basis for consolidation. Bruce Wasserstein, Time's financial advisor, also favored an outright purchase of Warner. However, Steve Ross, Warner's CEO, was adamant that a business combination was only practicable on a stock-for-stock basis. Warner insisted on a stock swap in order to preserve its shareholders' equity in the resulting corporation.

Eventually Time acquiesced in Warner's insistence on a stock-for-stock deal, but talks broke down over corporate governance issues. Time, and particularly its outside directors, viewed the corporate governance provisions as critical for preserving the "Time Culture" through a pro-Time management at the top.

Warner and Time resumed negotiations in January 1989.

On March 3, 1989, Time's board, with all but one director in attendance, met and unanimously approved a stock-for-stock merger with Warner. Warner's board likewise approved the merger. The agreement called for Warner to be merged into a wholly-owned Time subsidiary with Warner becoming the surviving corporation. The common stock of Warner would then be converted into common stock of Time at the agreed upon ratio. Thereafter, the name of Time would be changed to Time-Warner, Inc.

The rules of the New York Stock Exchange required that Time's issuance of shares to effectuate the merger be approved by a vote of Time's stockholders. The Delaware General Corporation Law required approval of the merger by a majority of the Warner stockholders. Delaware law did not require any vote by Time stockholders. The Chancellor concluded that the agreement was the product of "an arms-length negotiation between two parties seeking individual advantage through mutual action."

At its March 3, 1989 meeting, Time's board adopted several defensive tactics. Time entered an automatic share exchange agreement with Warner. Time would receive 17,292,747 shares of Warner's outstanding common stock (9.4%) and Warner would receive 7,080,016 shares of Time's outstanding common stock (11.1%). Either party could trigger the exchange. Time also agreed to a "no-shop" clause, preventing Time from considering any other consolidation proposal, thus relinquishing its power to consider other proposals, regardless of their merits. Time did so at Warner's insistence. Warner did not want to be left "on the auction block" for an unfriendly suitor, if Time were to withdraw from the deal.

By the end of May, the Time-Warner merger appeared to be an accomplished fact.

On June 7, 1989, these wishful assumptions were shattered by Paramount's surprising announcement of its all-cash offer to purchase all outstanding shares of Time for $175 per share. The following day, June 8, the trading price of Time's stock rose from $126 to $170 per share. Paramount's offer was said to be "fully negotiable."

Time found Paramount's "fully negotiable" offer to be in fact subject to at least three conditions. First, Time had to terminate its merger agreement and stock exchange agreement with Warner, and remove certain other of its defensive devices, including the redemption of Time's shareholder rights. Second, Paramount had to obtain the required cable franchise transfers from Time in a fashion acceptable to Paramount in its sole discretion. Finally, the offer depended upon a judicial determination that the Delaware Anti-Takeover Statute was inapplicable to any Time-Paramount merger. While Paramount's board had been privately advised that it could take months, perhaps over a year, to forge and consummate the deal, Paramount's board publicly proclaimed its ability to close the offer by July 5, 1989.

Over the following eight days, Time's board met three times to discuss Paramount's $175 offer. The board viewed Paramount's offer as inadequate and concluded that its proposed merger with Warner was the better course of action. Therefore, the board declined to open any negotiations with Paramount and held steady its course toward a merger with Warner.

At these June meetings, certain Time directors expressed their concern that Time stockholders would not comprehend the long-term benefits of the Warner merger. Large quantities of Time shares were held by institutional investors. The board feared that even though there appeared to be wide support for the Warner transaction, Paramount's cash premium would be a tempting prospect to these investors.

The board's prevailing belief was that Paramount's bid posed a threat to Time's control of its own destiny and retention of the "Time Culture." Even after Time's financial advisors made another presentation of Paramount and its business attributes, Time's board maintained its position that a combination with Warner offered greater potential for Time. Warner provided Time a much desired production capability and an established international marketing chain.

Time's board decided to recast its consolidation with Warner into an outright cash and securities acquisition of Warner by Time; and Time so informed Warner. Time accordingly restructured its proposal to acquire Warner as follows: Time would make an immediate all-cash offer for 51% of Warner's outstanding stock at $70 per share. The remaining 49% would be purchased at some later date for a mixture of cash and securities worth $70 per share. To provide the funds required for its outright acquisition of Warner, Time would assume 7–10 billion dollars worth of debt, thus eliminating one of the principal transaction-related benefits of the original merger agreement.

On June 23, 1989, Paramount raised its all-cash offer to buy Time's outstanding stock to $200 per share. Paramount still professed that all aspects of the offer were negotiable. Time's board met on June 26, 1989 and formally rejected Paramount's $200 per share second offer. The board reiterated its belief that, despite the $25 increase, the offer was still inadequate. The Time board maintained that the Warner transaction offered a greater long-term value for the stockholders and, unlike Paramount's offer, did not pose a threat to Time's survival and its "culture." Paramount then filed this action in the Court of Chancery.

Paramount contends that the Chancellor, in applying the first part of the *Unocal* test, erred in finding that Time's board had reasonable grounds to believe that Paramount posed both a legally cognizable threat to Time shareholders and a danger to Time's corporate policy and effectiveness. Paramount further claims that the court erred in applying *Unocal*'s second part in finding Time's response to be "reasonable." Paramount points primarily to the preclusive effect of the revised agreement which denied Time shareholders the opportunity both to vote on the agreement and to respond to Paramount's tender offer. Paramount argues that the underlying motivation of Time's board in adopting these defensive measures was management's desire to perpetuate itself in office.

We turn now to plaintiffs' *Unocal* claim.

Time's decision in 1988 to combine with Warner was made only after what could be fairly characterized as an exhaustive appraisal of Time's future as a corporation.

In *Unocal*, we held that before the business judgment rule is applied to a board's adoption of a defensive measure, the burden will lie with the board to prove (a) reasonable grounds for believing that a danger to corporate policy and effectiveness existed; and (b) that the defensive measure adopted was reasonable in relation to the threat posed. Directors satisfy the first part of the *Unocal* test by demonstrating good faith and reasonable investigation.

Unocal involved a two-tier, highly coercive tender offer. In such a case, the threat is obvious: shareholders may be compelled to tender to avoid being treated adversely in the second stage of the transaction. In subsequent cases, the Court of Chancery has suggested that an all-cash, all-shares offer, falling within a range of values that a shareholder might reasonably prefer, cannot constitute a legally recognized "threat" to shareholder interests sufficient to withstand a *Unocal* analysis. In those cases, the Court of Chancery determined that whatever threat existed related only to the shareholders and only to price and not to the corporation.

From those decisions by our Court of Chancery, Paramount and the individual plaintiffs extrapolate a rule of law that an all-cash, all-shares offer with values reasonably in the range of acceptable price cannot pose any objective threat to a corporation or its shareholders. Thus, Paramount would have us hold that only if the value of Paramount's offer were determined to be clearly inferior to the value created by management's plan to merge with Warner could the offer be viewed—objectively—as a threat.

Implicit in the plaintiffs' argument is the view that a hostile tender offer can pose only two types of threats: the threat of coercion that results from a two-tier offer promising unequal treatment for nontendering shareholders; and the threat of inadequate value from an all-shares, all-cash offer at a price below what a target board in good faith deems to be the present value of its shares. Since Paramount's offer was all-cash, the only conceivable "threat," plaintiffs argue, was inadequate value. We disapprove of such a narrow and rigid construction of *Unocal*, for the reasons which follow.

The usefulness of *Unocal* as an analytical tool is precisely its flexibility in the face of a variety of fact scenarios. *Unocal* is not intended as an abstract standard; neither is it a structured and mechanistic procedure of appraisal. Thus, we have said that directors may consider, when evaluating the threat posed by a takeover bid, the "inadequacy of the price offered, nature and timing of the offer, questions of illegality, the impact on 'constituencies' other than shareholders, the risk of non-consummation, and the quality of securities being offered in the exchange." The open-ended analysis mandated by *Unocal* is not intended to lead to a simple mathematical exercise: that is, of comparing the discounted value of Time-Warner's expected trading price at some future date with Paramount's offer and determining which is the higher.

In this case, the Time board reasonably determined that inadequate value was not the only legally cognizable threat that Paramount's all-cash, all-shares offer could present. One concern was that Time shareholders might elect to tender into Paramount's cash offer in ignorance or a mistaken belief of the strategic benefit which a business combination with Warner might produce. Moreover, Time viewed the Paramount offer as uncertain. Further, the timing of Paramount's offer to follow issuance of Time's proxy notice was viewed as arguably designed to upset, if not confuse, the Time stockholders' vote. Given this record evidence, we cannot conclude that the Time board's decision of June 6 that Paramount's offer posed a threat to corporate policy and effectiveness was lacking in good faith or dominated by motives of either entrenchment or self-interest.

We turn to the second part of the *Unocal* analysis. As applied to the facts of this case, the question is whether the record evidence supports the Court of Chancery's conclusion that the restructuring of the Time-Warner transaction, including the adoption of several preclusive defensive measures, was a *reasonable response* in relation to a perceived threat.

Paramount argues that, assuming its tender offer posed a threat, Time's response was unreasonable in precluding Time's shareholders from accepting the tender offer or receiving a control premium in the immediately foreseeable future. Once again, the contention stems, we believe, from a fundamental misunderstanding of where the power of corporate governance lies. Delaware law confers the management of the corporate enterprise to the stockholders' duly elected board representatives. The fiduciary duty to manage a corporate enterprise includes the selection of a time frame for achievement of corporate goals. That duty may not be delegated to the stockholders. Directors are not obliged to abandon a deliberately conceived corporate plan for a short-term shareholder profit unless there is clearly no basis to sustain the corporate strategy.

Although the Chancellor blurred somewhat the discrete analyses required under *Unocal*, he did conclude that Time's board reasonably perceived Paramount's offer to be a significant threat to the planned Time-Warner merger and that Time's response was not "overly broad." We have found that even in light of a valid threat, management actions that are coercive in nature or force upon shareholders a management-sponsored alternative to a hostile offer may be struck down as unreasonable and non-proportionate responses.

Here, on the record facts, the Chancellor found that Time's responsive action to Paramount's tender offer was not aimed at "cramming down" on its shareholders a management-sponsored alternative, but rather had as its goal the carrying forward of a pre-existing transaction in an altered form. Thus, the response was reasonably related to the threat. The Chancellor noted that the revised agreement and its accompanying safety devices did not preclude Paramount from making an offer for the combined Time-Warner company or from changing the conditions of its offer so as not to make the offer dependent upon the nullification of the Time-Warner agreement. Thus, the response was proportionate. We affirm the Chancellor's rulings as clearly supported by the record. Finally, we note that although Time was required, as a result of Paramount's hostile offer, to incur a heavy debt to finance its acquisition of Warner, that fact alone does not render the board's decision unreasonable so long as the directors could reasonably perceive the debt load not to be so injurious to the corporation as to jeopardize its well being.

Applying the test for grant or denial of preliminary injunctive relief, we find plaintiffs failed to establish a reasonable likelihood of ultimate success on the merits. Therefore, we affirm.

REVLON, INC. V. MACANDREWS & FORBES HOLDINGS, INC.

SUPREME COURT OF DELAWARE (MOORE, J.)
506 A.2D 173 (1986)

In this battle for corporate control of Revlon, Inc., the Court of Chancery enjoined certain transactions designed to thwart the efforts of Pantry Pride, Inc. to acquire Revlon.[1] The defendants are Revlon, its board of directors, and Forstmann Little & Co. and the latter's affiliated limited partnership. The injunction barred consummation of an option granted Forstmann to purchase certain Revlon assets (the lock-up option), a promise by Revlon to deal exclusively with Forstmann in the face of a takeover (the no-shop provision), and the payment of a $25 million cancellation fee to Forstmann if the transaction was aborted. The Court of Chancery found that the Revlon directors had breached their duty of care by entering into the foregoing transactions and effectively ending an active auction for the company. The trial court ruled that such arrangements are not illegal *per se* under Delaware law, but that their use under the circumstances here was impermissible. We agree. Thus, we granted this expedited interlocutory appeal to consider for the first time the validity of such defensive measures in the face of an active bidding contest for corporate control. Additionally, we address for the first time the extent to which a corporation may consider the impact of a takeover threat on constituencies other than shareholders.

In our view, lock-ups and related agreements are permitted under Delaware law where their adoption is untainted by director interest or other breaches of fiduciary duty. The actions taken by the Revlon directors, however, did not meet this standard. Moreover, while concern for various corporate constituencies is proper when addressing a takeover threat, that principle is limited by the requirement that there be some rationally related benefit accruing to the stockholders. We find no such benefit here.

Thus, under all the circumstances we must agree with the Court of Chancery that the enjoined Revlon defensive measures were inconsistent with the directors' duties to the stockholders. Accordingly, we affirm.

---

1   The nominal plaintiff, MacAndrews & Forbes Holdings, Inc., is the controlling stockholder of Pantry Pride. For all practical purposes their interests in this litigation are virtually identical, and we hereafter will refer to Pantry Pride as the plaintiff.

The somewhat complex maneuvers of the parties necessitate a rather detailed examination of the facts. The prelude to this controversy began in June 1985, when Ronald O. Perelman, chairman of the board and chief executive officer of Pantry Pride, met with his counterpart at Revlon, Michel C. Bergerac, to discuss a friendly acquisition of Revlon by Pantry Pride. Perelman suggested a price in the range of $40–50 per share, but the meeting ended with Bergerac dismissing those figures as considerably below Revlon's intrinsic value. All subsequent Pantry Pride overtures were rebuffed, perhaps in part based on Mr. Bergerac's strong personal antipathy to Mr. Perelman.

Thus, on August 14, Pantry Pride's board authorized Perelman to acquire Revlon, either through negotiation in the $42–$43 per share range, or by making a hostile tender offer at $45.

On August 19, the Revlon board met specially to consider the impending threat of a hostile bid by Pantry Pride.[2] At the meeting, Lazard Freres, Revlon's investment banker, advised the directors that $45 per share was a grossly inadequate price for the company. Felix Rohatyn and William Loomis of Lazard Freres explained to the board that Pantry Pride's financial strategy for acquiring Revlon would be through "junk bond" financing followed by a break-up of Revlon and the disposition of its assets. Martin Lipton, special counsel for Revlon, recommended two defensive measures: first, that the company repurchase up to 5 million of its nearly 30 million outstanding shares; and second, that it adopt a Note Purchase Rights Plan. Under this plan, each Revlon shareholder would receive as a dividend one Note Purchase Right (the Rights) for each share of common stock, with the Rights entitling the holder to exchange one common share for a $65 principal Revlon note at 12% interest with a one-year maturity. The Rights would become effective whenever anyone acquired beneficial ownership of 20% or more of Revlon's shares, unless the purchaser acquired all the company's stock for cash at $65 or more per share. In addition, the Rights would not be available to the acquiror, and prior to the 20% triggering event the Revlon board could redeem the rights for 10 cents each. Both proposals were unanimously adopted.

Pantry Pride made its first hostile move on August 23 with a cash tender offer for any and all shares of Revlon at $47.50 per common share subject to (1) Pantry Pride's obtaining financing for the purchase, and (2) the Rights being redeemed, rescinded or voided.

On August 29, Revlon commenced its own offer for up to 10 million shares, exchanging for each share of common stock tendered one Senior Subordinated Note (the Notes) of $47.50 principal at 11.75% interest, due 1995, and one-tenth of a share of $9.00 Cumulative Convertible Exchangeable Preferred Stock valued at $100 per share. Lazard Freres opined that the notes

---

2 There were 14 directors on the Revlon board. Six of them held senior management positions with the company, and two others held significant blocks of its stock. Four of the remaining six directors were associated at some point with entities that had various business relationships with Revlon. On the basis of this limited record, however, we cannot conclude that this board is entitled to certain presumptions that generally attach to the decisions of a board whose majority consists of truly outside independent directors.

would trade at their face value on a fully distributed basis. Revlon stockholders tendered 87 percent of the outstanding shares (approximately 33 million), and the company accepted the full 10 million shares on a *pro rata* basis. The new Notes contained covenants which limited Revlon's ability to incur additional debt, sell assets, or pay dividends unless otherwise approved by the "independent" (non-management) members of the board.

At this point, both the Rights and the Note covenants stymied Pantry Pride's attempted takeover. The next move came on September 16, when Pantry Pride announced a new tender offer at $42 per share, conditioned upon receiving at least 90% of the outstanding stock. Pantry Pride also indicated that it would consider buying less than 90%, and at an increased price, if Revlon removed the impeding Rights. While this offer was lower on its face than the earlier $47.50 proposal, Revlon's investment banker, Lazard Freres, described the two bids as essentially equal in view of the completed exchange offer.

The Revlon board held a regularly scheduled meeting on September 24. The directors rejected the latest Pantry Pride offer and authorized management to negotiate with other parties interested in acquiring Revlon. Pantry Pride remained determined in its efforts and continued to make cash bids for the company, offering $50 per share on September 27, and raising its bid to $53 on October 1.

In the meantime, Revlon's directors unanimously agreed to a leveraged buyout by Forstmann. The terms of this accord were as follows: each stockholder would get $56 cash per share; management would purchase stock in the new company by the exercise of their Revlon "golden parachutes";[3] Forstmann would assume Revlon's $475 million debt incurred by the issuance of the Notes; and Revlon would redeem the Rights and waive the Notes covenants for Forstmann or in connection with any other offer superior to Forstmann's. The board did not actually remove the covenants at the October 3 meeting, because Forstmann then lacked a firm commitment on its financing, but accepted the Forstmann capital structure, and indicated that the outside directors would waive the covenants in due course. Part of Forstmann's plan was to sell Revlon's Norcliff Thayer and Reheis divisions to American Home Products for $335 million. Before the merger, Revlon was to sell its cosmetics and fragrance division to Adler & Shaykin for $905 million. These transactions would facilitate the purchase by Forstmann or any other acquiror of Revlon.

When the merger, and thus the waiver of the Notes covenants, was announced, the market value of these securities began to fall. The Notes, which originally traded near par, around 100, dropped to 87.50 by October 8. One director later reported a "deluge" of telephone calls from irate noteholders, and on October 10 the Wall Street Journal reported threats of litigation by these creditors.

---

3   In the takeover context "golden parachutes" generally are understood to be termination agreements providing substantial bonuses and other benefits for managers and certain directors upon a change in control of a company.

Pantry Pride countered with a new proposal on October 7, raising its $53 offer to $56.25, subject to nullification of the Rights, a waiver of the Notes covenants, and the election of three Pantry Pride directors to the Revlon board.

Again privately armed with Revlon data, Forstmann met on October 11 with Revlon's special counsel and investment banker. On October 12, Forstmann made a new $57.25 per share offer, based on several conditions. The principal demand was a lock-up option to purchase Revlon's Vision Care and National Health Laboratories divisions for $525 million, some $100–$175 million below the value ascribed to them by Lazard Freres, if another acquiror got 40% of Revlon's shares. Revlon also was required to accept a no-shop provision. There would be a $25 million cancellation fee to be placed in escrow, and released to Forstmann if the new agreement terminated or if another acquiror got more than 19.9% of Revlon's stock. Finally, there would be no participation by Revlon management in the merger. In return, Forstmann agreed to support the par value of the Notes, which had faltered in the market, by an exchange of new notes.

On October 22, Pantry Pride again raised its bid, with a cash offer of $58 per share conditioned upon nullification of the Rights, waiver of the covenants, and an injunction of the Forstmann lock-up.

On October 15, the Court of Chancery prohibited the further transfer of assets, and eight days later concluded that the Revlon directors had breached their duty of loyalty by making concessions to Forstmann, out of concern for their liability to the noteholders, rather than maximizing the sale price of the company for the stockholders' benefit.

We turn first to Pantry Pride's probability of success on the merits. The ultimate responsibility for managing the business and affairs of a corporation falls on its board of directors. In discharging this function the directors owe fiduciary duties of care and loyalty to the corporation and its shareholders. These principles apply with equal force when a board approves a corporate merger, and of course they are the bedrock of our law regarding corporate takeover issues. While the business judgment rule may be applicable to the actions of corporate directors responding to takeover threats, the principles upon which it is founded—care, loyalty and independence—must first be satisfied.

If the business judgment rule applies, there is a "presumption that in making a business decision the directors of a corporation acted on an informed basis, in good faith and in the honest belief that the action taken was in the best interests of the company." However, when a board implements anti-takeover measures there arises "the omnipresent specter that a board may be acting primarily in its own interests, rather than those of the corporation and its shareholders." This potential for conflict places upon the directors the burden of proving that they had reasonable grounds for believing there was a danger to corporate policy and effectiveness, a burden satisfied by a showing of good faith and reasonable investigation. In addition, the directors must analyze the nature of the takeover and its effect on the corporation in order to ensure balance—that the responsive action taken is reasonable in relation to the threat posed.

The first relevant defensive measure adopted by the Revlon board was the Rights Plan, which would be considered a "poison pill" in the current language of corporate takeovers—a plan by which shareholders receive the right to be bought out by the corporation at a substantial premium on the occurrence of a stated triggering event. The board clearly had the power to adopt the measure. Thus, the focus becomes one of reasonableness and purpose.

The Revlon board approved the Rights Plan in the face of an impending hostile takeover bid by Pantry Pride at $45 per share, a price which Revlon reasonably concluded was grossly inadequate. Lazard Freres had so advised the directors, and had also informed them that Pantry Pride was a small, highly leveraged company bent on a "bust-up" takeover by using "junk bond" financing to buy Revlon cheaply, sell the acquired assets to pay the debts incurred, and retain the profit for itself. In adopting the Plan, the board protected the shareholders from a hostile takeover at a price below the company's intrinsic value, while retaining sufficient flexibility to address any proposal deemed to be in the stockholders' best interests.

To that extent the board acted in good faith and upon reasonable investigation. Under the circumstances it cannot be said that the Rights Plan as employed was unreasonable, considering the threat posed. Indeed, the Plan was a factor in causing Pantry Pride to raise its bids from a low of $42 to an eventual high of $58.

Although we consider adoption of the Plan to have been valid under the circumstances, its continued usefulness was rendered moot by the directors' actions on October 3 and October 12. At the October 3 meeting the board redeemed the Rights conditioned upon consummation of a merger with Forstmann, but further acknowledged that they would also be redeemed to facilitate any more favorable offer. On October 12, the board unanimously passed a resolution redeeming the Rights in connection with any cash proposal of $57.25 or more per share. Because all the pertinent offers eventually equalled or surpassed that amount, the Rights clearly were no longer any impediment in the contest for Revlon. This mooted any question of their propriety under *Moran* or *Unocal*.

The second defensive measure adopted by Revlon to thwart a Pantry Pride takeover was the company's own exchange offer for 10 million of its shares. The directors' general broad powers to manage the business and affairs of the corporation are augmented by the specific authority conferred under 8 Del. C. § 160(a), permitting the company to deal in its own stock. However, when exercising that power in an effort to forestall a hostile takeover, the board's actions are strictly held to the fiduciary standards outlined in *Unocal*. These standards require the directors to determine the best interests of the corporation and its stockholders, and impose an enhanced duty to abjure any action that is motivated by considerations other than a good faith concern for such interests.

The Revlon directors concluded that Pantry Pride's $47.50 offer was grossly inadequate. In that regard the board acted in good faith, and on an informed basis, with reasonable grounds to believe that there existed a harmful threat to the corporate enterprise. The adoption of a defensive measure, reasonable in relation to the threat posed, was proper and fully accorded with the powers, duties, and responsibilities conferred upon directors under our law.

However, when Pantry Pride increased its offer to $50 per share, and then to $53, it became apparent to all that the break-up of the company was inevitable. The Revlon board's authorization permitting management to negotiate a merger or buyout with a third party was a recognition that the company was for sale. The duty of the board had thus changed from the preservation of Revlon as a corporate entity to the maximization of the company's value at a sale for the stockholders' benefit. This significantly altered the board's responsibilities under the *Unocal* standards. It no longer faced threats to corporate policy and effectiveness, or to the stockholders' interests, from a grossly inadequate bid. The whole question of defensive measures became moot. The directors' role changed from defenders of the corporate bastion to auctioneers charged with getting the best price for the stockholders at a sale of the company.

This brings us to the lock-up with Forstmann and its emphasis on shoring up the sagging market value of the Notes in the face of threatened litigation by their holders. Such a focus was inconsistent with the changed concept of the directors' responsibilities at this stage of the developments. The impending waiver of the Notes covenants had caused the value of the Notes to fall, and the board was aware of the noteholders' ire as well as their subsequent threats of suit. The directors thus made support of the Notes an integral part of the company's dealings with Forstmann, even though their primary responsibility at this stage was to the equity owners.

The original threat posed by Pantry Pride—the break-up of the company—had become a reality which even the directors embraced. Selective dealing to fend off a hostile but determined bidder was no longer a proper objective. Instead, obtaining the highest price for the benefit of the stockholders should have been the central theme guiding director action. Thus, the Revlon board could not make the requisite showing of good faith by preferring the noteholders and ignoring its duty of loyalty to the shareholders. The rights of the former already were fixed by contract. The noteholders required no further protection, and when the Revlon board entered into an auction-ending lock-up agreement with Forstmann on the basis of impermissible considerations at the expense of the shareholders, the directors breached their primary duty of loyalty.

A lock-up is not per se illegal under Delaware law. Its use has been approved in an earlier case. Such options can entice other bidders to enter a contest for control of the corporation, creating an auction for the company and maximizing shareholder profit. Current economic conditions in the takeover market are such that a "white knight" like Forstmann might only enter the bidding for the target company if it receives some form of compensation to cover the risks and costs involved. However, while those lock-ups which draw bidders into the battle benefit shareholders, similar measures which end an active auction and foreclose further bidding operate to the shareholders' detriment.

The Forstmann option had a destructive effect on the auction process. Forstmann had already been drawn into the contest on a preferred basis, so the result of the lock-up was not to foster bidding, but to destroy it. The board's stated reasons for approving the transactions were: (1) better financing, (2) noteholder protection, and (3) higher price. As the Court of Chancery found, and we agree, any distinctions between the rival bidders' methods of financing the proposal were nominal at best, and such a consideration has little or no significance in a cash offer for any and all shares. The principal object, contrary to the board's duty of care, appears to have been protection of the noteholders over the shareholders' interests.

While Forstmann's $57.25 offer was objectively higher than Pantry Pride's $56.25 bid, the margin of superiority is less when the Forstmann price is adjusted for the time value of money. In reality, the Revlon board ended the auction in return for very little actual improvement in the final bid. The principal benefit went to the directors, who avoided personal liability to a class of creditors to whom the board owed no further duty under the circumstances. Thus, when a board ends an intense bidding contest on an insubstantial basis, and where a significant by-product of that action is to protect the directors against a perceived threat of personal liability for consequences stemming from the adoption of previous defensive measures, the action cannot withstand the enhanced scrutiny which *Unocal* requires of director conduct.

In addition to the lock-up option, the Court of Chancery enjoined the no-shop provision as part of the attempt to foreclose further bidding by Pantry Pride. The no-shop provision, like the lock-up option, while not per se illegal, is impermissible under the *Unocal* standards when a board's primary duty becomes that of an auctioneer responsible for selling the company to the highest bidder. The agreement to negotiate only with Forstmann ended rather than intensified the board's involvement in the bidding contest.

It is ironic that the parties even considered a no-shop agreement when Revlon had dealt preferentially, and almost exclusively, with Forstmann throughout the contest. After the directors authorized management to negotiate with other parties, Forstmann was given every negotiating advantage that Pantry Pride had been denied: cooperation from management, access to financial data, and the exclusive opportunity to present merger proposals directly to the board of directors. Favoritism for a white knight to the total exclusion of a hostile bidder might be justifiable when the latter's offer adversely affects shareholder interests, but when bidders make relatively similar offers, or dissolution of the company becomes inevitable, the directors cannot fulfill their enhanced *Unocal* duties by playing favorites with the contending factions. Market forces must be allowed to operate freely to bring the target's shareholders the best price available for their equity. Thus, as the trial court ruled, the shareholders' interests necessitated that the board remain free to negotiate in the fulfillment of that duty.

The court below similarly enjoined the payment of the cancellation fee, pending a resolution of the merits, because the fee was part of the overall plan to thwart Pantry Pride's efforts. We find no abuse of discretion in that ruling.

In conclusion, the Revlon board was confronted with a situation not uncommon in the current wave of corporate takeovers. A hostile and determined bidder sought the company at a price the board was convinced was inadequate. The initial defensive tactics worked to the benefit of the shareholders, and thus the board was able to sustain its *Unocal* burdens in justifying those measures. However, in granting an asset option lock-up to Forstmann, we must conclude that under all the circumstances the directors allowed considerations other than the maximization of shareholder profit to affect their judgment, and followed a course that ended the auction for Revlon, absent court intervention, to the ultimate detriment of its shareholders. No such defensive measure can be sustained when it represents a breach of the directors' fundamental duty of care. In that context the board's action is not entitled to the deference accorded it by the business judgment rule. The measures were properly enjoined. The decision of the Court of Chancery, therefore, is

AFFIRMED.

CHAPTER TEN

INTRODUCTION TO SECURITIES REGULATION

INTRODUCTION

Although corporate law initially developed in the nineteenth century as a concern of state lawmakers, it has become increasingly federalized in response to a series of scandals and crashes, most notably the Great Depression. The result has been that American corporations—both large and small—must follow not only state corporation statutes but also federal securities regulations. With this in mind, this chapter provides a brief introduction to the federal law governing the offer and sale of securities.

The most important aspect of federal business regulation that all lawyers must understand is that the definition of a "security" is far broader than one might expect. Indeed, it has famously been extended to include the sale of orange groves, whiskey warehouse receipts, and even chinchillas (a kind of expensive fur coat). Thus, every business lawyer must be constantly on the lookout for transactions that could be deemed to be sales of securities and hence subject to federal regulation. In Part A, we explore the breadth of the definition.

In Part B, we turn our attention to the basic equation that underpins all of federal securities laws —the requirement that all offers and sales of securities be either registered with the Securities and Exchange Commission (most commonly in a transaction known as an "IPO") or exempt from such registration pursuant to one of a list of specified exemptions. Although many casual observers assume that securities law is a subject of importance only to big corporations, this requirement applies equally to all business firms, whatever the type or size.

In Part C, we consider the relationship between public companies—those whose stock is listed for trading on a national stock exchange like Nasdaq or the NYSE—and their shareholders. Specifically, we examine the disclosure rules that govern communications between such corporations and their shareholders. Because of the omnipresent specter of fraud, the SEC requires that all such communications be subject to certain standards of quality and made publicly available for all investors to access.

In Part D, we take a look at the system of periodic reporting that is required of all publicly traded corporations. In order to ensure that investors are not defrauded, federal securities laws require such companies to make frequent disclosures to the public. This ensures that any potential buyer or seller of stock will be in possession of all material information relevant to their investment decision.

Finally, in Part E, we briefly examine the law regarding securities fraud and insider trading. Here again, we have a simple equation that serves as the foundation for a more complex scheme—those in possession of material nonpublic information must either disclose that information to the public or refrain from trading. Anything else constitutes securities fraud and may subject the parties to criminal liability.

Note that we will not attempt in this chapter to address state regulations known as "blue sky" laws. As a political compromise, Congress explicitly opted not to preempt state regulation of securities when it adopted the federal scheme in the 1930s. Thus, sales of securities must be registered (or exempt) not only federally but also with each state in which an offer or sale is made. This is generally a simple process that serves mostly to provide revenue for the states in the form of filing fees. However, this dual regulatory structure means that allegations of securities fraud may be prosecuted at either, or both, the national and state level.

Even more so than with M&A, we recommend that students interested in practicing securities law enroll in an upper-level course that devotes ample time to these and other complex topics. Like tax law, securities law carries the potential for criminal liability and is not a subject in which it is wise to dabble. That being said, at the end of this chapter, you will be familiar with the basic outlines of the federal regulation of corporations. This will enable you to recognize a sale of securities and thus help your clients avoid liability by engaging competent co-counsel. Most importantly, you will understand the two-tiered nature of business law, whereby corporations must follow not only state corporation statutes but federal securities laws and regulations as well.

DEFINITION OF A "SECURITY" PART A

GREAT LAKES CHEMICAL CORP. V. MONSANTO CO.

UNITED STATES DISTRICT COURT, DISTRICT OF DELAWARE (MCKELVIE, J.)
96 F. SUPP. 2D 376 (2000)

This is a securities case. Plaintiff Great Lakes Chemical Corporation is a Delaware corporation with its principal place of business in Indianapolis, Indiana. Defendants Monsanto Company and its wholly owned subsidiary, Sweet Technologies, Inc., are Delaware corporations with their principal places of business in St. Louis, Missouri.

On May 3, 1999, Great Lakes purchased NSC Technologies Company, LLC, from Monsanto and STI. NSC is a Delaware limited liability company with its principal place of business in Mount Prospect, Illinois.

On January 4, 2000, Great Lakes filed the complaint in this action, alleging that Monsanto and STI violated § 10(b) of the Securities Exchange Act of 1934 and Rule 10b-5 promulgated thereunder by failing to disclose material information in conjunction with the sale of NSC. Great Lakes also alleges that defendants are liable for violating Indiana securities law, engaging in common law fraud, and breaching the sale contract, and that defendants must indemnify Great Lakes for all costs arising from the breaches of their representations and warranties in the purchase agreement.

On March 9, 2000, Monsanto and STI moved to dismiss the complaint for failure to plead fraud with specificity and for failure to state a claim upon which relief may be granted. Among their assertions, Monsanto and STI argue that the interests sold to Great Lakes were not "securities," as defined by § 2(a)(1) of the Securities Act of 1933.

In approximately 1985, Monsanto created the NSC Unit within its NutraSweet division to develop specialized pharmaceutical intermediates and pharmaceutical active compounds derived from L-phe. In 1995, Monsanto reorganized its NutraSweet division and established the NSC Unit as a separate reporting division of Monsanto Growth Enterprises.

On September 25, 1998, Monsanto entered into an agreement with STI to establish the NSC Unit as a limited liability company called NSC Technologies Company, LLC, pursuant to the Delaware Limited Liability Company Act.

In Delaware, LLCs are formed pursuant to the Delaware Limited Liability Company Act. LLCs are hybrid entities that combine desirable characteristics of corporations, limited partnerships, and general partnerships. LLCs are entitled to partnership status for federal income tax purposes under certain circumstances, which permits LLC members to avoid double taxation, i.e., taxation of the entity as well as taxation of the members' incomes. Moreover, LLCs members, unlike partners in general partnerships, may have limited liability, such that LLC members who are involved in managing the LLC may avoid becoming personally liable for its debts and obligations. In addition, LLCs have greater flexibility than corporations in terms of organizational structure. The Delaware Limited Liability Company Act, for example, establishes the default rule that management of an LLC shall be vested in its members, but permits members to establish other forms of governance in their LLC agreements.

To prevail in its claim that defendants engaged in securities fraud under § 10(b) of the Securities Exchange Act of 1934, Great Lakes must demonstrate that: (i) defendants made a misstatement or omission; (ii) of a material fact; (iii) with scienter; (iv) in connection with the purchase or sale of securities; (v) upon which plaintiffs relied; and (vi) that reliance proximately caused plaintiffs' losses. A threshold question in this matter is whether defendants' alleged misconduct involved a purchase or sale of securities. Defendants contend that plaintiff's claim fails as a matter of law because the Interests in NSC do not constitute securities.

Section 2(a)(1) of the Securities Act of 1933 lists financial instruments that qualify as securities, as follows:

The term "security" means any note, stock, treasury stock, bond, debenture, evidence of indebtedness, certificate of interest or participation in any profit-sharing agreement, collateral-trust certificate, preorganization certificate or subscription, transferable share, investment contract, voting trust certificate, certificate of deposit for a security, fractional undivided interest in oil, gas, or other mineral rights, any put, call, straddle, option, or privilege on any security, certificate of deposit, or group or index of securities (including any interest therein or based on the value thereof), or any put, call, straddle, option, or privilege entered into on a national securities exchange relating to foreign currency, or, in general, any interest or instrument commonly known as a "security", or any certificate of interest or participation in, temporary or interim certificate for, receipt for, guarantee of, or warrant or right to subscribe to or purchase, any of the foregoing.

Among the securities enumerated in § 2(a)(1) of the Securities Act, Great Lakes contends that the Interests in NSC constitute either "stock," an "investment contract," or "any interest or instrument commonly known as a 'security.'"

The Supreme Court defined the parameters of an "investment contract" for the purposes of federal securities law in the case of *SEC v. W.J. Howey Co. Howey* concerned a Florida corporation, the Howey Company, that sold small tracts of land in a citrus grove to forty-two purchasers, many of whom were patrons of a resort hotel. For the most part, the purchasers lacked the knowledge, skill, and equipment necessary for the care and cultivation of citrus trees. They invested in the enterprise for profit. The purchasers were free to contract with a number of companies to service the tracts, but the sales contract stressed the superiority of Howey-in-the-Hills Service, Inc., which the purchasers chose to service 85% of the acreage sold. The service contracts granted Howey-in-the-Hills full and complete possession of the acreage, and the individual purchasers had no right of entry to market the crop. Purchasers of tracts shared in the profits of the enterprise, which amounted to 20% in the 1943-44 growing season. The Howey Company did not register the interests in the enterprise as securities.

The Securities and Exchange Commission brought an action pursuant to § 5(a) of the Securities Act seeking to enjoin the Howey Company from using interstate mail to offer and sell interests in the enterprise. Because the interests at issue did not constitute any of the traditional kinds of securities enumerated in § 2(a)(1) of the Securities Act, the SEC argued that the interests were "investment contracts." Noting that the term "investment contract" was not defined by Congress, but that the term was widely used in state securities laws, the Court largely adopted the definition used at the time by state courts. The Court stated that "an investment contract for purposes of the Securities Act means a contract, transaction or scheme whereby a person invests his money in a common enterprise and is led to expect profits solely from the efforts of the promoter or a third party." Thus, the three requirements for establishing an investment contract are: (1) "an investment of money," (2) "in a common enterprise," (3) "with profits to come solely from the efforts of others." In articulating this test, the Supreme Court stated that this definition "embodies a flexible rather than a static principle, one that is capable of adaptation to meet the countless and variable schemes devised by those who seek the use of the money of others on the promise of profits."

The Supreme Court established guidelines for whether non-traditional instruments labeled "stock" constitute securities in *United Housing Foundation, Inc. v. Forman. Forman* concerned a nonprofit housing cooperative that sold shares of "stock" to prospective tenants. The sole purpose of acquiring the shares was to enable the purchaser to occupy an apartment in the cooperative. The shares essentially represented a recoverable deposit on the apartment. The shares were explicitly tied to the apartment, as they could not be transferred to a non-tenant. Nor could they be pledged or encumbered. No voting rights attached to the shares.

After the housing cooperative raised rental charges, the residents sued the cooperative under § 17(a) of the Securities Act asserting that the cooperative falsely represented that it would bear all subsequent cost increases due to factors such as inflation. The Supreme Court held that the "stock" issued by the cooperative did not constitute a security. The shares, the Court found, lacked the five most common features of stock: (1) the right to receive dividends contingent upon an apportionment of profits; (2) negotiability; (3) the ability to be pledged or hypothecated; (4) voting rights in proportion to the number of shares owned; and (5) the ability to appreciate in value. Finding that the purchasers obtained the shares in order to acquire subsidized low-cost living space, not to invest for profit, the Court ruled that the "stock" issued by the cooperative was not a security.

Following the issuance of *Forman*, a number of lower courts began to apply the Howey test to distinguish between investment transactions, which were covered by the securities laws, and commercial transactions, which were not. In *Landreth Timber Co. v. Landreth*, the Ninth Circuit addressed whether a single individual who purchased 100% of the stock in a lumber corporation, and who had the power to actively manage the acquired business, could state a claim under the securities laws for alleged fraud in the sale of the business. The Ninth Circuit found that the purchaser bought full control of the corporation, and that the economic reality of the transaction was the purchase of a business, and not an investment in a security. The court held that the sale of 100% of the stock of a closely held corporation was not a transaction involving a "security."

Reversing the Ninth Circuit, the Supreme Court reasoned that it would be burdensome to apply the *Howey* test to transactions involving traditional stock. The Court held that, insofar as a transaction involves the sale of an instrument called "stock," and the stock bears the five common attributes of stock enumerated in *Forman*, the transaction is governed by the securities laws. The Court noted that stock is specifically enumerated in § 2(a)(1) of the Securities Act as a security, and that stock is so "quintessentially a security" that it is unnecessary to apply the *Howey* test to determine if it is a security. The financial instrument involved in the case, the Court reasoned, "is traditional stock, plainly within the statutory definition." "There is no need here," the Court continued, "to look beyond the characteristics of the instrument to determine whether the Securities Acts apply." The Court stated that the *Howey* test should only be applied to determine whether an instrument is an "investment contract," and should not be applied in the context of other instruments enumerated in § 2(a)(1) of the Securities Act.

Great Lakes contends that NSC is the functional equivalent of a corporation, and that the Interests in NSC should be treated as stock. Great Lakes notes that the LLC Agreement refers to the Interests as "equity securities," and that the LLC Agreement prohibits the transfer of the Interests in such a way as would "violate the provisions of any federal or state securities laws."

Monsanto and STI, on the other hand, contend that the Interests cannot be stock because NSC is not a corporation.

As noted by plaintiffs, the attributes of stock also characterize, at least to some degree, the Interests in NSC. NSC's Members are entitled to share, *pro rata*, in distributions of Net Cash Flow, contingent upon its distribution by the Board of Managers. The Interests are negotiable and may be pledged or hypothecated, subject to approval by the Board of Managers. Members in NSC have voting rights in proportion to their Percentage Interest in the company. And, the Interests in NSC have the capacity to appreciate in value. The Interests in NSC are undoubtedly stock-like in character, but the question remains if the Interests can be characterized as "stock" for the purposes of the federal securities laws.

The primary goal of the securities laws is to regulate investments, and not commercial ventures. In transactions involving traditional stock, lower courts had attempted to distinguish between investment transactions and commercial transactions. The Supreme Court, as discussed above, held that it is unnecessary to attempt to distinguish between commercial and investment transactions when the financial instrument in question is traditional stock. Because stock is listed in § 2(a)(1) of the Securities Act as a security, and because people trading in traditional stock are likely to have a high expectation that their activities are governed by the securities laws, the Court ruled that all transactions involving traditional stock are covered by the securities laws, regardless if the transaction is of an investment or commercial character. The Court expressly limited this rule to transactions involving traditional stock.

In the present case, the LLC Interests, although they are "stock-like" in nature, are not traditional stock. Landreth, thus, is inapplicable to this case, and the court must determine whether the sale of NSC was essentially an investment transaction, in which case the securities laws apply, or whether it was a commercial transaction, in which case they do not. To make this determination, the court will apply the Howey test for investment contracts. The court will also consider whether the Interests can be characterized as "any interest or instrument commonly known as a security."

Monsanto and STI argue that Great Lakes' purchase of the Interests in NSC fails the second prong of the Howey test, which requires that an investor invest its money in a "common enterprise." According to defendants, Great Lakes bought the entirety of NSC without pooling its contributions with those of other investors.

In this case, Great Lakes bought 100% of the Interests of NSC from Monsanto and STI. Great Lakes, accordingly, did not pool its contributions with those of other investors, as is required for horizontal commonality. After the sale, Monsanto and STI retained no interest in NSC, so it cannot be said that the fortunes of Great Lakes were linked to those of defendants, as is required for vertical commonality.

Monsanto and STI argue that the profits in NSC did not come solely from the efforts of others, as would support a finding that the Interests in NSC were securities. Rather, defendants contend that Great Lakes had the power to control NSC through its authority to remove managers with or without cause, and to dissolve the entity.

Great Lakes had the authority to remove NSC's managers without cause. Because Great Lakes was the sole owner of NSC, its power to remove managers was not diluted by the presence of other ownership interests. Great Lakes' authority to remove managers gave it the power to directly affect the profits it received from NSC. Thus, the court finds that Great Lakes' profits from NSC did not come solely from the efforts of others.

Finally, Great Lakes argues that, even if the Interests in NSC do not otherwise satisfy the Howey test for investment contracts, they should be deemed to be "any interest or instrument commonly known as a security," as provided for in § 2(a)(1) of the Securities Act. Great Lakes notes that the LLC Agreement refers to the Interests at issue as "equity securities," and that the LLC Agreement prohibits the transfer of the Interests in such a way as would "violate the provisions of any federal or state securities laws." Moreover, Great Lakes contends, ten states have defined interests in LLCs as securities, including Indiana, where NSC has its principal place of business.

The Supreme Court has indicated that the term "any interest or instrument commonly known as a security" covers the same financial instruments as referred to by the term "investment contract." In *United Housing Foundation, Inc. v. Forman* the Court stated that "we perceive no distinction, for present purposes, between an 'investment contract' and an 'instrument' commonly known as a 'security.' In either case, the basic test for distinguishing the transaction from other commercial dealings is 'whether the scheme involves an investment of money in a common enterprise with profits to come solely from the efforts of others.'" The *Howey* test, the Court explained, "embodies the essential attributes that run through all of the Court's decisions defining a security."

In sum, the court finds that the Interests in NSC constitute neither "stock," nor an "investment contract," nor "any interest or instrument commonly known as a security." The court will grant defendants' motion to dismiss Count I of Great Lakes' complaint.

PART B REGULATION OF OFFERS AND SALES

SECURITIES AND EXCHANGE COMMISSION V. RALSTON PURINA CO.

SUPREME COURT OF THE UNITED STATES (CLARK, J.)
346 U.S. 119 (1953)

Section 4(2) of the Securities Act of 1933 exempts "transactions by an issuer not involving any public offering" from the registration requirements of § 5. We must decide whether Ralston Purina's offerings of treasury stock to its "key employees" are within this exemption. On a complaint brought by the Commission seeking to enjoin respondent's unregistered offerings, the District Court held the exemption applicable and dismissed the suit. The Court of Appeals affirmed. The question has arisen many times since the Act was passed; an apparent need to define the scope of the private offering exemption prompted certiorari.

Ralston Purina manufactures and distributes various feed and cereal products. Its processing and distribution facilities are scattered throughout the United States and Canada, staffed by some 7,000 employees. At least since 1911 the company has had a policy of encouraging stock ownership among its employees; more particularly, since 1942 it has made authorized but unissued common shares available to some of them. Between 1947 and 1951, the period covered by the record in this case, Ralston Purina sold nearly $2,000,000 of stock to employees without registration and in so doing made use of the mails.

In each of these years, a corporate resolution authorized the sale of common stock "to employees who shall, without any solicitation by the Company or its officers or employees, inquire of any of them as to how to purchase common stock of Ralston Purina Company." A memorandum sent to branch and store managers after the resolution was adopted, advised that "The only employees to whom this stock will be available will be those who take the initiative and are interested in buying stock at present market prices." Among those responding to these offers were employees with the duties of artist, bakeshop foreman, chow loading foreman, clerical assistant, copywriter, electrician, stock clerk, mill office clerk, order credit trainee, production trainee, stenographer, and veterinarian. The buyers lived in over fifty widely separated communities scattered from Garland, Texas, to Nashua, New Hampshire and Visalia, California. The lowest salary bracket of those purchasing was $2,700 in 1949, $2,435 in 1950 and $3,107 in 1951. The record shows that in 1947, 243 employees bought stock, 20 in 1948, 414 in 1949, 411 in 1950, and the 1951 offer, interrupted by this litigation, produced 165 applications to purchase. No records were kept of those to whom the offers were made; the estimated number in 1951 was 500.

The company bottoms its exemption claim on the classification of all offerees as "key employees" in its organization. Its position on trial was that "A key employee is not confined to an organization chart. It would include an individual who is eligible for promotion, an individual who especially influences others or who advises others, a person whom the employees look to in some special way, an individual, of course, who carries some special responsibility, who is sympathetic to management and who is ambitious and who the management feels is likely to be promoted to a greater responsibility." That an offering to all of its employees would be public is conceded.

The Securities Act nowhere defines the scope of § 4(2)'s private offering exemption. Nor is the legislative history of much help in staking out its boundaries.

Decisions under comparable exemptions in the English Companies Acts and state "blue sky" laws, the statutory antecedents of federal securities legislation, have made one thing clear – to be public, an offer need not be open to the whole world. In Securities and Exchange Comm. v. Sunbeam Gold Mines Co., this point was made in dealing with an offering to the stockholders of two corporations about to be merged. Judge Denman observed that:

> In its broadest meaning the term "public" distinguishes the populace at large from groups of individual members of the public segregated because of some common interest or characteristic. Yet such a distinction is inadequate for practical purposes; manifestly, an offering of securities to all redheaded men, to all residents of Chicago or San Francisco, to all existing stockholders of the General Motors Corporation or the American Telephone & Telegraph Company, is no less "public", in every realistic sense of the word, than an unrestricted offering to the world at large. Such an offering, though not open to everyone who may choose to apply, is none the

less "public" in character, for the means used to select the particular individuals to whom the offering is to be made bear no sensible relation to the purposes for which the selection is made. To determine the distinction between "public" and "private" in any particular context, it is essential to examine the circumstances under which the distinction is sought to be established and to consider the purposes sought to be achieved by such distinction.

The courts below purported to apply this test. The District Court held, in the language of the Sunbeam decision, that "The purpose of the selection bears a 'sensible relation' to the class chosen," finding that "The sole purpose of the 'selection' is to keep part stock ownership of the business within the operating personnel of the business and to spread ownership throughout all departments and activities of the business." The Court of Appeals treated the case as involving "an offering, without solicitation, of common stock to a selected group of key employees of the issuer, most of whom are already stockholders when the offering is made, with the sole purpose of enabling them to secure a proprietary interest in the company or to increase the interest already held by them."

Exemption from the registration requirements of the Securities Act is the question. The design of the statute is to protect investors by promoting full disclosure of information thought necessary to informed investment decisions. The natural way to interpret the private offering exemption is in light of the statutory purpose. Since exempt transactions are those as to which "there is no practical need for the Act's application," the applicability of § 4(2) should turn on whether the particular class of persons affected need the protection of the Act. An offering to those who are shown to be able to fend for themselves is a transaction "not involving any public offering."

The Commission would have us go one step further and hold that "an offering to a substantial number of the public" is not exempt under § 4(2). We are advised that "whatever the special circumstances, the Commission has consistently interpreted the exemption as being inapplicable when a large number of offerees is involved." But the statute would seem to apply to a "public offering" whether to few or many. It may well be that offerings to a substantial number of persons would rarely be exempt. Indeed, nothing prevents the commission, in enforcing the statute, from using some kind of numerical test in deciding when to investigate particular exemption claims. But there is no warrant for superimposing a quantity limit on private offerings as a matter of statutory interpretation.

The exemption, as we construe it, does not deprive corporate employees, as a class, of the safeguards of the Act. We agree that some employee offerings may come within § 4(2), e.g., one made to executive personnel who because of their position have access to the same kind of information that the act would make available in the form of a registration statement. Absent such a showing of special circumstances, employees are just as much members of the investing "public" as any of their neighbors in the community. Although we do not rely on it, the rejection in 1934 of an amendment which would have specifically exempted employee stock offerings supports this conclusion. The House Managers, commenting on the Conference Report, said that "the participants in employees' stock-investment plans may be in as great need of the protection afforded by availability of information concerning the issuer for which they work as are most other members of the public."

Keeping in mind the broadly remedial purposes of federal securities legislation, imposition of the burden of proof on an issuer who would plead the exemption seems to us fair and reasonable. Agreeing, the court below thought the burden met primarily because of the respondent's purpose in singling out its key employees for stock offerings. But once it is seen that the exemption question turns on the knowledge of the offerees, the issuer's motives, laudable though they may be, fade into irrelevance. The focus of inquiry should be on the need of the offerees for the protections afforded by registration. The employees here were not shown to have access to the kind of information which registration would disclose. The obvious opportunities for pressure and imposition make it advisable that they be entitled to compliance with § 5.

Reversed.

COMMUNICATIONS WITH PART C SHAREHOLDERS

MILLS V. ELECTRIC AUTO-LITE CO.

SUPREME COURT OF THE UNITED STATES (HARLAN, J.)
396 U.S. 375 (1970)

This case requires us to consider a basic aspect of the implied private right of action for violation of §14(a) of the Securities Exchange Act of 1934. As in J.I. Case Co. v. Borak the asserted wrong is that a corporate merger was accomplished through the use of a proxy statement that was materially false or misleading. The question with which we deal is what causal relationship must be shown between such a statement and the merger to establish a cause of action based on the violation of the Act.

Petitioners were shareholders of the Electric Auto-Lite Company until 1963, when it was merged into Mergenthaler Linotype Company. They brought suit on the day before the shareholders' meeting at which the vote was to take place on the merger, against Auto-Lite,

Mergenthaler, and a third company, American Manufacturing Company, Inc. The complaint sought an injunction against the voting by Auto-Lite's management of all proxies obtained by means of an allegedly misleading proxy solicitation; however, it did not seek a temporary restraining order, and the voting went ahead as scheduled the following day. Several months later petitioners filed an amended complaint, seeking to have the merger set aside and to obtain such other relief as might be proper.

Petitioners alleged that the proxy statement sent out by the Auto-Lite management to solicit shareholders' votes in favor of the merger was misleading, in violation of §14(a) of the Act and SEC Rule 14a-9 thereunder. Petitioners recited that before the merger Mergenthaler owned over 50% of the outstanding shares of Auto-Lite common stock, and had been in control of Auto-Lite for two years. American Manufacturing in turn owned about one-third of the outstanding shares of Mergenthaler, and for two years had been in voting control of Mergenthaler and, through it, of Auto-Lite. Petitioners charged that in light of these circumstances the proxy statement was misleading in that it told Auto-Lite shareholders that their board of directors recommended approval of the merger without also informing them that all 11 of Auto-Lite's directors were nominees of Mergenthaler and were under the "control and domination of Mergenthaler." Petitioners asserted the right to complain of this alleged violation both derivatively on behalf of Auto-Lite and as representatives of the class of all its minority shareholders.

On petitioners' motion for summary judgment, the District Court for the Northern District of Illinois ruled as a matter of law that the claimed defect in the proxy statement was, in light of the circumstances in which the statement was made, a material omission. The District Court concluded, from its reading of the Borak opinion, that it had to hold a hearing on the issue whether there was "a causal connection between the finding that there has been a violation of the disclosure requirements of §14(a) and the alleged injury to the plaintiffs" before it could consider what remedies would be appropriate.

After holding such a hearing, the court found that under the terms of the merger agreement, an affirmative vote of two-thirds of the Auto-Lite shares was required for approval of the merger, and that the respondent companies owned and controlled about 54% of the outstanding shares. Therefore, to obtain authorization of the merger, respondents had to secure the approval of a substantial number of the minority shareholders. At the stockholders' meeting, approximately 950,000 shares, out of 1,160,000 shares outstanding, were voted in favor of the merger. This included 317,000 votes obtained by proxy from the minority shareholders, votes that were "necessary and indispensable to the approval of the merger." The District Court concluded that a causal relationship had thus been shown, and it granted an interlocutory judgment in favor of petitioners on the issue of liability, referring the case to a master for consideration of appropriate relief.

The Seventh Circuit affirmed the District Court's conclusion that the proxy statement was materially deficient, but reversed on the question of causation. The court acknowledged that, if an injunction had been sought a sufficient time before the stockholders' meeting, "corrective measures would have been appropriate." However, since this suit was brought too late for preventive action, the courts had to determine "whether the misleading statement and omission caused the submission of sufficient proxies," as a prerequisite to a determination of liability under the Act. If the respondents could show, "by a preponderance of probabilities, that the merger would have received a sufficient vote even if the proxy statement had not been misleading in the respect found," petitioners would be entitled to no relief of any kind.

The Court of Appeals acknowledged that this test corresponds to the common-law fraud test of whether the injured party relied on the misrepresentation. However, rightly concluding that "reliance by thousands of individuals, as here, can scarcely be inquired into," the court ruled that the issue was to be determined by proof of the fairness of the terms of the merger. If respondents could show that the merger had merit and was fair to the minority shareholders, the trial court would be justified in concluding that a sufficient number of shareholders would have approved the merger had there been no deficiency in the proxy statement. In that case respondents would be entitled to a judgment in their favor.

As we stressed in *Borak*, §14(a) stemmed from a congressional belief that "fair corporate suffrage is an important right that should attach to every equity security bought on a public exchange." The provision was intended to promote "the free exercise of the voting rights of stockholders" by ensuring that proxies would be solicited with "explanation to the stockholder of the real nature of the questions for which authority to cast his vote is sought." The decision below, by permitting all liability to be foreclosed on the basis of a finding that the merger was fair, would allow the stockholders to be bypassed, at least where the only legal challenge to the merger is a suit for retrospective relief after the meeting has been held. A judicial appraisal of the merger's merits could be substituted for the actual and informed vote of the stockholders.

The result would be to insulate from private redress an entire category of proxy violations — those relating to matters other than the terms of the merger. Even outrageous misrepresentations in a proxy solicitation, if they did not relate to the terms of the transaction, would give rise to no cause of action under §14(a). Particularly if carried over to enforcement actions by the Securities and Exchange Commission itself, such a result would subvert the congressional purpose of ensuring full and fair disclosure to shareholders.

Further, recognition of the fairness of the merger as a complete defense would confront small shareholders with an additional obstacle to making a successful challenge to a proposal recommended through a defective proxy statement. The risk that they would be unable to rebut the corporation's evidence of the fairness of the proposal, and thus to establish their cause of action, would be bound to discourage such shareholders from the private enforcement of the proxy rules that "provides a necessary supplement to Commission action."

Such a frustration of the congressional policy is not required by anything in the wording of the statute or in our opinion in the *Borak* case. Section 14(a) declares it "unlawful" to solicit proxies in contravention of Commission rules, and SEC Rule 14a-9 prohibits solicitations "containing any statement which is false or misleading with respect to any material fact, or which omits to state any material fact necessary in order to make the statements therein not false or misleading." Use of a solicitation that is materially misleading is itself a violation of law, as the Court of Appeals recognized in stating that injunctive relief would be available to remedy such a defect if sought prior to the stockholders' meeting. In Borak, this Court limited its inquiry to whether a violation of §14(a) gives rise to "a federal cause of action for rescission or damages." In the present case, there has been a hearing specifically directed to the causation problem. The question before the Court is whether the facts found on the basis of that hearing are sufficient in law to establish petitioners' cause of action, and we conclude that they are.

Where the misstatement or omission in a proxy statement has been shown to be "material," as it was found to be here, that determination itself indubitably embodies a conclusion that the defect was of such a character that it might have been considered important by a reasonable shareholder who was in the process of deciding how to vote. This requirement that the defect have a significant propensity to affect the voting process is found in the express terms of Rule 14a-9, and it adequately serves the purpose of ensuring that a cause of action cannot be established by proof of a defect so trivial, or so unrelated to the transaction for which approval is sought, that correction of the defect or imposition of liability would not further the interests protected by §14(a).

There is no need to supplement this requirement, as did the Court of Appeals, with a requirement of proof of whether the defect actually had a decisive effect on the voting. Where there has been a finding of materiality, a shareholder has made a sufficient showing of causal relationship between the violation and the injury for which he seeks redress if, as here, he proves that the proxy solicitation itself, rather than the particular defect in the solicitation materials, was an essential link in the accomplishment of the transaction. This objective test will avoid the impracticalities of determining how many votes were affected, and, by resolving doubts in favor of those the statute is designed to protect, will effectuate the congressional policy of ensuring that the shareholders are able to make an informed choice when they are consulted on corporate transactions.

Our conclusion that petitioners have established their case by showing that proxies necessary to approval of the merger were obtained by means of a materially misleading solicitation implies nothing about the form of relief to which they may be entitled. A determination of what relief should be granted in Auto-Lite's name must hinge on whether setting aside the merger would be in the best interests of the shareholders as a whole. In short, the merger should be set aside only if a court of equity concludes, from all the circumstances, that it would be equitable to do so.

Monetary relief will, of course, also be a possibility. If commingling of the assets and operations of the merged companies makes it impossible to establish direct injury from the merger, relief might be predicated on a determination of the fairness of the terms of the merger at the time it was approved. These questions, of course, are for decision in the first instance by the District Court on remand, and our singling out of some of the possibilities is not intended to exclude others.

For the foregoing reasons, we conclude that the judgment of the Court of Appeals should be vacated and the case remanded to that court for further proceedings consistent with this opinion.

It is so ordered.

PERIODIC DISCLOSURE PART D
REQUIREMENTS

IN THE MATTER OF HEWLETT-PACKARD COMPANY

SECURITIES AND EXCHANGE COMMISSION
RELEASE NO. 55801 (2007)

This matter involves Hewlett-Packard's failure to disclose the circumstances surrounding a board member's resignation amidst the company's controversial investigation into boardroom leaks. On May 18, 2006, HP's Board of Directors learned the findings of the company's leak investigation and voted to request the resignation of a director believed to have violated HP's policies by providing confidential information to the press. Silicon Valley venture capitalist and fellow director Thomas Perkins (not the source of the leak) voiced his strong objections to the handling of the matter, announced his resignation, and walked out of the Board meeting. Contrary to the reporting requirements of the federal securities laws, HP failed to disclose to investors the circumstances of Mr. Perkins' disagreement with the company.

Under the Securities Exchange Act of 1934, a public company must file with the Securities and Exchange Commission a report on Form 8-K when a director resigns from the board. If a director has resigned because of a disagreement with the company, known to an executive officer, on any matter relating to the company's operations, policies, or practices, the company must, among other things, disclose a brief description of the circumstances of the disagreement. In addition, the company must give the director the opportunity to timely review and respond to the company's disclosure about the director's resignation, and the company is required to file any letter written by the director to the company in response to the company's disclosure. Absent such a disagreement, the company must report the resignation, but need not provide the reasons.

In or around January 2006, in response to apparent unauthorized disclosures of confidential information about HP Board meetings to the press, HP initiated an investigation to determine the source of the leaks. HP Board member Thomas Perkins, Chairman of the Board's Nominating and Governance Committee (which was responsible for, among other things, establishing board member qualifications and evaluating board operations), was generally informed of the inquiry. Mr. Perkins believed that he and HP's Chairman had agreed that, upon completion of the investigation, they would approach any individual implicated privately, obtain an assurance that it would not happen again, and inform the full Board that the matter had been resolved without identifying the source of the leak.

By April 2006, HP investigators tentatively concluded that a long-standing HP director had leaked information in connection with a January 23, 2006 press article. After consulting with HP's Chief Executive Officer, General Counsel, outside counsel, and Chairman of the Audit Committee, the Chairman of the Board determined that the leak investigation findings should be presented to the full Board.

HP's Board of Directors met beginning at 12:30 p.m. on May 18, 2006 at HP's headquarters in Palo Alto, California. All but one of the directors attended, including the CEO (who is a director), as did the company's General Counsel (acting as the Board secretary).

At the start of the meeting, the head of HP's Audit Committee discussed the leak investigation and its findings. After some discussion, the identity of the director who provided information for the January 2006 article was revealed. The director addressed the Board, explained his actions, and left the room to permit additional deliberations. The Board discussed HP's policy on unauthorized public disclosures, and considered measures that could be taken in response to the director's actions, including asking him to resign.

During the course of the Board's deliberations, which lasted approximately 90 minutes, Mr. Perkins voiced his strong objections to the manner in which the matter was being handled. Among other things, he repeatedly told the Board that the source of the leak should have been approached "off-line" for an explanation and a warning, rather than identified to the whole Board. He affirmed his belief that the matter should have been handled confidentially by the Chairman of the Board and himself as Chairman of the Nominating and Governance Committee. He also questioned the wisdom of requesting the director to resign over what he perceived to be a relatively minor offense, noting that the director had made significant contributions to HP.

Mr. Perkins then resigned from the Board and departed the meeting at approximately 2:00 p.m. The director identified by the leak investigation was asked to resign following the vote, but declined to resign at that time.

On May 22, 2006, HP filed a report on Form 8-K, pursuant to Item 5.02(b) of Regulation S-K, reporting Mr. Perkins' resignation, but did not comply with Item 5.02(a) by failing to disclose that there had been a disagreement with the company. HP also filed with the Form 8-K a May 19 press release, which announced that Mr. Perkins had resigned without disclosing the circumstances of his disagreement.

HP concluded, with the advice of outside legal counsel and the General Counsel, that it need not disclose the reasons for Mr. Perkins' resignation because he merely had a disagreement with the company's Chairman, and not a disagreement with the company on a matter relating to its operations, policies, or practices. Contrary to HP's conclusion, the disagreement and the reasons for Mr. Perkins' resignation should have been disclosed. Mr. Perkins resigned as a result of a disagreement with HP on the following matters: (1) the decision to present the leak investigation findings to the full Board; and (2) the decision by majority vote of the Board of Directors to ask the director identified in the leak investigation to resign. Mr. Perkins' disagreement related to important corporate governance matters and HP policies regarding handling sensitive information, and thus constituted a disagreement over HP's operations, policies or practices.

Section 13(a) of the Exchange Act and Rule 13a-11 promulgated thereunder require issuers of securities registered pursuant to Section 12 of the Exchange Act to file with the Commission current reports on Form 8-K upon the occurrence of certain events, including the departure of directors or principal officers. Item 5.02(a) of Form 8-K specifies that if a director has resigned because of a disagreement with the registrant, known to an executive officer of the registrant, on any matter relating to the registrant's operations, policies, or practices, the registrant must, among other things, disclose a brief description of the circumstances representing the disagreement that the registrant believes caused, in whole or in part, the director's resignation. In addition, the registrant must provide the resigning director with a copy of the disclosure no later than the day the company files the disclosure with the Commission. Also, the registrant must provide the director with the opportunity to furnish a response letter stating whether the director agrees with the disclosure in the registrant's Form 8-K. In the event that the registrant receives a response letter from the former director, the letter must be filed by the registrant as an amendment to its Form 8-K within two business days of its receipt. No showing of scienter is required to establish a violation of Section 13(a) of the Exchange Act.

On May 18, 2006, director Thomas Perkins resigned because of a disagreement with HP regarding the decision to present the leak investigation findings to the full Board and the decision by the Board to ask the director identified in the leak investigation to resign. The disagreement was known to HP executive officers. Mr. Perkins' disagreement with HP related to the operations, policies, or practices of HP. Consequently, HP was required by Item 5.02(a) of Form 8-K to disclose a brief description of the circumstances representing the disagreement, and was required to provide Mr. Perkins with a copy of this disclosure no later than the day of filing. By disclosing the resignation of Mr. Perkins pursuant to Item 5.02(b) in a Form 8-K filed on May 22, 2006, HP failed to disclose the circumstances of Mr. Perkins' disagreement with HP and also failed to provide the director with a copy of such a filing. As a result, HP violated Section 13(a) of the Exchange Act and Rule 13a-11 thereunder.

In view of the foregoing, the Commission deems it appropriate to impose the sanctions agreed to in Respondent HP's Offer.

Accordingly, it is hereby ORDERED that Respondent HP cease and desist from committing or causing any violations and any future violations of Section 13(a) of the Exchange Act and Rule 13a-11 thereunder.

PART E SECURITIES FRAUD AND INSIDER TRADING

BASIC INCORPORATED V. LEVINSON

SUPREME COURT OF THE UNITED STATES (BLACKMUN, J.)
485 U.S. 224 (1988)

This case requires us to apply the materiality requirement of § 10(b) of the Securities Exchange Act of 1934 and the Securities and Exchange Commission's Rule 10b-5.

Prior to December 20, 1978, Basic Incorporated was a publicly traded company primarily engaged in the business of manufacturing chemical refractories for the steel industry. As early as 1965 or 1966, Combustion Engineering, Inc., a company producing mostly alumina-based refractories, expressed some interest in acquiring Basic, but was deterred from pursuing this inclination seriously because of antitrust concerns it then entertained. In 1976, however, regulatory action opened the way to a renewal of Combustion's interest.

Beginning in September 1976, Combustion representatives had meetings and telephone conversations with Basic officers and directors, including petitioners here, concerning the possibility of a merger. During 1977 and 1978, Basic made three public statements denying that it was engaged in merger negotiations. On December 18, 1978, Basic asked the New York Stock Exchange to suspend trading in its shares and issued a release stating that it had been "approached" by another company concerning a merger. On December 19, Basic's board endorsed Combustion's offer of $46 per share for its common stock, and on the following day publicly announced its approval of Combustion's tender offer for all outstanding shares.

Respondents are former Basic shareholders who sold their stock after Basic's first public statement of October 21, 1977, and before the suspension of trading in December 1978. Respondents brought a class action against Basic and its directors, asserting that the defendants issued three false or misleading public statements and thereby were in violation of § 10(b) of the 1934 Act and of Rule 10b-5. Respondents alleged that they were injured by selling Basic shares at artificially depressed prices in a market affected by petitioners' misleading statements and in reliance thereon.

The District Court adopted a presumption of reliance by members of the plaintiff class upon petitioners' public statements that enabled the court to conclude that common questions of fact or law predominated over particular questions pertaining to individual plaintiffs. The District Court therefore certified respondents' class. On the merits, however, the District Court granted summary judgment for the defendants. It held that, as a matter of law, any misstatements were immaterial: there were no negotiations ongoing at the time of the first statement, and although negotiations were taking place when the second and third statements were issued, those negotiations were not "destined, with reasonable certainty, to become a merger agreement in principle."

The United States Court of Appeals for the Sixth Circuit affirmed the class certification, but reversed the District Court's summary judgment, and remanded the case. The court reasoned that while petitioners were under no general duty to disclose their discussions with Combustion, any statement the company voluntarily released could not be "so incomplete as to mislead." In the Court of Appeals' view, Basic's statements that no negotiations were taking place, and that it knew of no corporate developments to account for the heavy trading activity, were misleading. With respect to materiality, the court rejected the argument that preliminary merger discussions are immaterial as a matter of law, and held that "once a statement is made denying the existence of any discussions, even discussions that might not have been material in absence of the denial are material because they make the statement made untrue."

The Court of Appeals joined a number of other Circuits in accepting the "fraud-on-the-market theory" to create a rebuttable presumption that respondents relied on petitioners' material misrepresentations, noting that without the presumption it would be impractical to certify a class under Federal Rule of Civil Procedure 23(b)(3).

We granted certiorari to resolve the split among the Courts of Appeals as to the standard of materiality applicable to preliminary merger discussions, and to determine whether the courts below properly applied a presumption of reliance in certifying the class, rather than requiring each class member to show direct reliance on Basic's statements.

The 1934 Act was designed to protect investors against manipulation of stock prices. Underlying the adoption of extensive disclosure requirements was a legislative philosophy: "There cannot be honest markets without honest publicity. Manipulation and dishonest practices of the market place thrive upon mystery and secrecy." This Court "repeatedly has described the 'fundamental purpose' of the Act as implementing a 'philosophy of full disclosure.'"

The Court previously has addressed various positive and common-law requirements for a violation of § 10(b) or of Rule 10b-5. The Court also explicitly has defined a standard of materiality under *TSC Industries, Inc. v. Northway, Inc.*, concluding in the proxy-solicitation context that "an omitted fact is material if there is a substantial likelihood that a reasonable shareholder would consider it important in deciding how to vote." It further explained that to fulfill the materiality requirement "there must be a substantial likelihood that the disclosure of the omitted fact would have been viewed by the reasonable investor as having significantly altered the 'total mix' of information made available." We now expressly adopt the TSC Industries standard of materiality for the § 10(b) and Rule 10b-5 context.

The application of this materiality standard to preliminary merger discussions is not self-evident. Where the impact of the corporate development on the target's fortune is certain and clear, the *TSC Industries* materiality definition admits straightforward application. Where, on the other hand, the event is contingent or speculative in nature, it is difficult to ascertain whether the "reasonable investor" would have considered the omitted information significant at the time. Merger negotiations, because of the ever-present possibility that the contemplated transaction will not be effectuated, fall into the latter category.

Petitioners urge upon us a Third Circuit test for resolving this difficulty. Under this approach, preliminary merger discussions do not become material until "agreement-in-principle" as to the price and structure of the transaction has been reached between the would-be merger partners. By definition, then, information concerning any negotiations not yet at the agreement-in-principle stage could be withheld or even misrepresented without a violation of Rule 10b-5.

We find no valid justification for artificially excluding from the definition of materiality information concerning merger discussions, which would otherwise be considered significant to the trading decision of a reasonable investor, merely because agreement-in-principle as to price and structure has not yet been reached by the parties or their representatives.

Even before this Court's decision in TSC Industries, the Second Circuit had explained the role of the materiality requirement of Rule 10b-5, with respect to contingent or speculative information or events, in a manner that gave that term meaning that is independent of the other provisions of the Rule. Under such circumstances, materiality "will depend at any given time upon a balancing of both the indicated probability that the event will occur and the anticipated magnitude of the event in light of the totality of the company activity." Interestingly, neither the Third Circuit decision adopting the agreement-in-principle test nor petitioners here take issue with this general standard. Rather, they suggest that with respect to preliminary merger discussions, there are good reasons to draw a line at agreement on price and structure.

In a subsequent decision, the late Judge Friendly, writing for a Second Circuit panel, applied this Texas Gulf Sulphur probability/magnitude approach in the specific context of preliminary merger negotiations. After acknowledging that materiality is something to be determined on the basis of the particular facts of each case, he stated:

> Since a merger in which it is bought out is the most important event that can occur
> in a small corporation's life, to wit, its death, we think that inside information, as

regards a merger of this sort, can become material at an earlier stage than would be the case as regards lesser transactions – and this even though the mortality rate of mergers in such formative stages is doubtless high.

We agree with that analysis.

Whether merger discussions in any particular case are material therefore depends on the facts. Generally, in order to assess the probability that the event will occur, a factfinder will need to look to indicia of interest in the transaction at the highest corporate levels. Without attempting to catalog all such possible factors, we note by way of example that board resolutions, instructions to investment bankers, and actual negotiations between principals or their intermediaries may serve as indicia of interest. To assess the magnitude of the transaction to the issuer of the securities allegedly manipulated, a factfinder will need to consider such facts as the size of the two corporate entities and of the potential premiums over market value. No particular event or factor short of closing the transaction need be either necessary or sufficient by itself to render merger discussions material.

As we clarify today, materiality depends on the significance the reasonable investor would place on the withheld or misrepresented information. The fact-specific inquiry we endorse here is consistent with the approach a number of courts have taken in assessing the materiality of merger negotiations. Because the standard of materiality we have adopted differs from that used by both courts below, we remand the case for reconsideration of the question whether a grant of summary judgment is appropriate on this record.

We turn to the question of reliance and the fraud-on-the-market theory. Succinctly put: "The fraud on the market theory is based on the hypothesis that, in an open and developed securities market, the price of a company's stock is determined by the available material information regarding the company and its business. Misleading statements will therefore defraud purchasers of stock even if the purchasers do not directly rely on the misstatements. The causal connection between the defendants' fraud and the plaintiffs' purchase of stock in such a case is no less significant than in a case of direct reliance on misrepresentations."

Our task, of course, is not to assess the general validity of the theory, but to consider whether it was proper for the courts below to apply a rebuttable presumption of reliance, supported in part by the fraud-on-the-market theory.

This case required resolution of several common questions of law and fact concerning the falsity or misleading nature of the three public statements made by Basic, the presence or absence of scienter, and the materiality of the misrepresentations, if any. In their amended complaint, the named plaintiffs alleged that in reliance on Basic's statements they sold their shares of Basic stock in the depressed market created by petitioners. Requiring proof of individualized reliance from each member of the proposed plaintiff class effectively would have prevented respondents from proceeding with a class action, since individual issues then would have overwhelmed the common ones. The District Court found that the presumption of reliance created by the fraud-on-the-market theory provided "a practical resolution to the problem of balancing the substantive requirement of proof of reliance in securities cases against the procedural requisites of Federal Rule of Civil Procedure 23." The District Court thus concluded that with reference to each public statement and its impact upon the open market for Basic shares, common questions predominated over individual questions, as required by Federal Rules of Civil Procedure 23(a)(2) and (b)(3).

Petitioners and their *amici* complain that the fraud-on-the-market theory effectively eliminates the requirement that a plaintiff asserting a claim under Rule 10b-5 prove reliance. They note that reliance is and long has been an element of common-law fraud and argue that because the analogous express right of action includes a reliance requirement, so too must an action implied under § 10(b).

We agree that reliance is an element of a Rule 10b-5 cause of action. Reliance provides the requisite causal connection between a defendant's misrepresentation and a plaintiff's injury. There is, however, more than one way to demonstrate the causal connection. Indeed, we previously have dispensed with a requirement of positive proof of reliance, where a duty to disclose material information had been breached, concluding that the necessary nexus between the plaintiffs' injury and the defendant's wrongful conduct had been established. Similarly, we did not require proof that material omissions or misstatements in a proxy statement decisively affected voting, because the proxy solicitation itself, rather than the defect in the solicitation materials, served as an essential link in the transaction.

The modern securities markets, literally involving millions of shares changing hands daily, differ from the face-to-face transactions contemplated by early fraud cases, and our understanding of Rule 10b-5's reliance requirement must encompass these differences.

"In face-to-face transactions, the inquiry into an investor's reliance upon information is into the subjective pricing of that information by that investor. With the presence of a market, the market is interposed between seller and buyer and, ideally, transmits information to the investor in the processed form of a market price. Thus the market is performing a substantial part of the valuation process performed by the investor in a face-to-face transaction. The market is acting as the unpaid agent of the investor, informing him that given all the information available to it, the value of the stock is worth the market price."

The presumption is also supported by common sense and probability. Recent empirical studies have tended to confirm Congress' premise that the market price of shares traded on well-developed markets reflects all publicly available information, and, hence, any material misrepresentations. It has been noted that "it is hard to imagine that there ever is a buyer or seller who does not rely on market integrity. Who would knowingly roll the dice in a crooked crap game?" Indeed, nearly every court that has considered the proposition has concluded that where materially misleading statements have been disseminated into an impersonal, well-developed market for securities, the reliance of individual plaintiffs on the integrity of the market price may be presumed. Commentators generally have applauded the adoption of one variation or another of the fraud-on-the-market theory. An investor who buys or sells stock at the price set by the market does so in reliance on the integrity of that price. Because most publicly available information is reflected in market price, an investor's reliance on any public material misrepresentations, therefore, may be presumed for purposes of a Rule 10b-5 action.

The judgment of the Court of Appeals is vacated, and the case is remanded to that court for further proceedings consistent with this opinion.

It is so ordered.

UNITED STATES V. O'HAGAN

SUPREME COURT OF THE UNITED STATES (GINSBURG, J.)
521 U.S. 642 (1997)

This case concerns the interpretation and enforcement of § 10(b) of the Securities Exchange Act of 1934 and Rule 10b-5. Is a person who trades in securities for personal profit, using confidential information misappropriated in breach of a fiduciary duty to the source of the information, guilty of violating § 10(b) and Rule 10b-5? Our answer is yes.

Respondent James Herman O'Hagan was a partner in the law firm of Dorsey & Whitney in Minneapolis, Minnesota. In July 1988, Grand Metropolitan PLC, a company based in London, England, retained Dorsey & Whitney as local counsel to represent Grand Met regarding a potential tender offer for the common stock of the Pillsbury Company, headquartered in Minneapolis. Both Grand Met and Dorsey & Whitney took precautions to protect the confidentiality of Grand Met's tender offer plans. O'Hagan did no work on the Grand Met representation. Dorsey & Whitney withdrew from representing Grand Met on September 9, 1988. Less than a month later, on October 4, 1988, Grand Met publicly announced its tender offer for Pillsbury stock.

On August 18, 1988, while Dorsey & Whitney was still representing Grand Met, O'Hagan began purchasing call options for Pillsbury stock. Each option gave him the right to purchase 100 shares of Pillsbury stock by a specified date in September 1988. Later in August and in September, O'Hagan made additional purchases of Pillsbury call options. By the end of September, he owned 2,500 unexpired Pillsbury options, apparently more than any other individual investor. O'Hagan also purchased, in September 1988, some 5,000 shares of Pillsbury common stock, at a price just under $39 per share. When Grand Met announced its tender offer in October, the price of Pillsbury stock rose to nearly $60 per share. O'Hagan then sold his Pillsbury call options and common stock, making a profit of more than $4.3 million.

The Securities and Exchange Commission initiated an investigation into O'Hagan's transactions, culminating in a 57-count indictment. The indictment alleged that O'Hagan defrauded his law firm and its client, Grand Met, by using for his own trading purposes material, nonpublic information regarding Grand Met's planned tender offer. According to the indictment, O'Hagan used the profits he gained through this trading to conceal his previous embezzlement and conversion of unrelated client trust funds. O'Hagan was charged with 20 counts of mail fraud; 17 counts of securities fraud; 17 counts of fraudulent trading in connection with a tender offer; and 3 counts of violating federal money laundering statutes. A jury convicted O'Hagan on all 57 counts, and he was sentenced to a 41-month term of imprisonment.

A divided panel of the Court of Appeals for the Eighth Circuit reversed all of O'Hagan's convictions. Liability under § 10(b) and Rule 10b-5, the Eighth Circuit held, may not be grounded on the "misappropriation theory" of securities fraud on which the prosecution relied. The Eighth Circuit further concluded that O'Hagan's mail fraud and money laundering convictions rested on violations of the securities laws, and therefore could not stand once the securities fraud convictions were reversed.

Decisions of the Courts of Appeals are in conflict on the propriety of the misappropriation. We granted certiorari and now reverse the Eighth Circuit's judgment. In pertinent part, § 10(b) of the Exchange Act provides:

> It shall be unlawful for any person, directly or indirectly, by the use of any means or instrumentality of interstate commerce or of the mails, or of any facility of any national securities exchange—
>
> (b) To use or employ, in connection with the purchase or sale of any security registered on a national securities exchange or any security not so registered, any manipulative or deceptive device or contrivance in contravention of such rules and regulations as the Securities and Exchange Commission may prescribe as necessary or appropriate in the public interest or for the protection of investors.

The statute thus proscribes (1) using any deceptive device (2) in connection with the purchase or sale of securities, in contravention of rules prescribed by the Commission. The provision, as written, does not confine its coverage to deception of a purchaser or seller of securities; rather, the statute reaches any deceptive device used "in connection with the purchase or sale of any security."

Pursuant to its § 10(b) rulemaking authority, the Commission has adopted Rule 10b-5, which, as relevant here, provides:

> It shall be unlawful for any person, directly or indirectly, by the use of any means or instrumentality of interstate commerce, or of the mails or of any facility of any national securities exchange,

(a) To employ any device, scheme, or artifice to defraud, [or]

(c) To engage in any act, practice, or course of business which operates or would operate as a fraud or deceit upon any person, "in connection with the purchase or sale of any security.

Under the "traditional" or "classical theory" of insider trading liability, § 10(b) and Rule 10b-5 are violated when a corporate insider trades in the securities of his corporation on the basis of material, nonpublic information. Trading on such information qualifies as a "deceptive device" under § 10(b), we have affirmed, because "a relationship of trust and confidence exists between the shareholders of a corporation and those insiders who have obtained confidential information by reason of their position with that corporation." That relationship, we recognized, "gives rise to a duty to disclose or to abstain from trading because of the 'necessity of preventing a corporate insider from taking unfair advantage of uninformed stockholders.'" The classical theory applies not only to officers, directors, and other permanent insiders of a corporation, but also to attorneys, accountants, consultants, and others who temporarily become fiduciaries of a corporation.

The "misappropriation theory" holds that a person commits fraud "in connection with" a securities transaction, and thereby violates § 10(b) and Rule 10b=5, when he misappropriates confidential information for securities trading purposes, in breach of a duty owed to the source of the information. Under this theory, a fiduciary's undisclosed, self-serving use of a principal's information to purchase or sell securities, in breach of a duty of loyalty and confidentiality, defrauds the principal of the exclusive use of that information. In lieu of premising liability on a fiduciary relationship between company insider and purchaser or seller of the company's stock, the misappropriation theory premises liability on a fiduciary-turned-trader's deception of those who entrusted him with access to confidential information.

The two theories are complementary, each addressing efforts to capitalize on nonpublic information through the purchase or sale of securities. The classical theory targets a corporate insider's breach of duty to shareholders with whom the insider transacts; the misappropriation theory outlaws trading on the basis of nonpublic information by a corporate "outsider" in breach of a duty owed not to a trading party, but to the source of the information. The misappropriation theory is thus designed to "protect the integrity of the securities markets against abuses by 'outsiders' to a corporation who have access to confidential information that will affect the corporation's security price when revealed, but who owe no fiduciary or other duty to that corporation's shareholders."

In this case, the indictment alleged that O'Hagan, in breach of a duty of trust and confidence he owed to his law firm, Dorsey & Whitney, and to its client, Grand Met, traded on the basis of nonpublic information regarding Grand Met's planned tender offer for Pillsbury common stock. This conduct, the Government charged, constituted a fraudulent device in connection with the purchase and sale of securities.

The Court of Appeals rejected the misappropriation theory primarily on two grounds. First, as the Eighth Circuit comprehended the theory, it requires neither misrepresentation nor nondisclosure. However, deceptive nondisclosure is essential to the § 10(b) liability at issue. Concretely, in this case, "it was O'Hagan's failure to disclose his personal trading to Grand Met and Dorsey, in breach of his duty to do so, that made his conduct 'deceptive' within the meaning of § 10(b)."

Second and "more obvious," the Court of Appeals said, the misappropriation theory is not moored to § 10(b)'s requirement that "the fraud be 'in connection with the purchase or sale of any security.'" According to the Eighth Circuit, three of our decisions reveal that § 10(b) liability cannot be predicated on a duty owed to the source of nonpublic information: Chiarella v. United States, Dirks v. SEC, and Central Bank of Denver, N.A. v. First Interstate Bank of Denver, N.A. "Only a breach of a duty to parties to the securities transaction, or, at the most, to other market participants such as investors, will be sufficient to give rise to § 10(b) liability." We read the statute and our precedent differently, and note again that § 10(b) refers to "the purchase or sale of any security," not to identifiable purchasers or sellers of securities.

Chiarella involved securities trades by a printer employed at a shop that printed documents announcing corporate takeover bids. Deducing the names of target companies from documents he handled, the printer bought shares of the targets before takeover bids were announced, expecting (correctly) that the share prices would rise upon announcement. In these transactions, the printer did not disclose to the sellers of the securities (the target companies' shareholders) the nonpublic information on which he traded. For that trading, the printer was convicted of violating § 10(b) and Rule 10b-5. We reversed the Court of Appeals judgment that had affirmed the conviction.

The jury in *Chiarella* had been instructed that it could convict the defendant if he willfully failed to inform sellers of target company securities that he knew of a takeover bid that would increase the value of their shares. Emphasizing that the printer had no agency or other fiduciary relationship with the sellers, we held that liability could not be imposed on so broad a theory. There is under § 10(b), we explained, no "general duty between all participants in market transactions to forgo actions based on material, nonpublic information." Under established doctrine, we said, a duty to disclose or abstain from trading "arises from a specific relationship between two parties."

The Court did not hold in *Chiarella* that the only relationship prompting liability for trading on undisclosed information is the relationship between a corporation's insiders and shareholders. That is evident from our response to the Government's argument before this Court that the printer's misappropriation of information from his employer for purposes of securities trading – in violation of a duty of confidentiality owed to the acquiring companies – constituted fraud in connection with the purchase or sale of a security, and thereby satisfied the terms of § 10(b). The Court declined to reach that potential basis for the printer's liability, because the theory had not been submitted to the jury.

Chiarella thus expressly left open the misappropriation theory before us today. Certain statements in Chiarella, however, led the Eighth Circuit in the instant case to conclude that § 10(b) liability hinges exclusively on a breach of duty owed to a purchaser or seller of securities. The Court said in *Chiarella* that § 10(b) liability "is premised upon a duty to disclose arising from a relationship of trust and confidence between parties to a transaction," and observed that the printshop employee defendant in that case "was not a person in whom the sellers had placed their trust and confidence." These statements rejected the notion that § 10(b) stretches so far as to impose "a general duty between all participants in market transactions to forgo actions based on material, nonpublic information," and we confine them to that context. The statements highlighted by the Eighth Circuit, in short, appear in an opinion carefully leaving for future resolution the validity of the misappropriation theory, and therefore cannot be read to foreclose that theory.

Dirks, too, left room for application of the misappropriation theory in cases like the one we confront. *Dirks* involved an investment analyst who had received information from a former insider of a corporation with which the analyst had no connection. The information indicated that the corporation had engaged in a massive fraud. The analyst investigated the fraud, obtaining corroborating information from employees of the corporation. During his investigation, the analyst discussed his findings with clients and investors, some of whom sold their holdings in the company the analyst suspected of gross wrongdoing.

The SEC censured the analyst for, *inter alia*, aiding and abetting § 10(b) and Rule 10b-5 violations by clients and investors who sold their holdings based on the nonpublic information the analyst passed on. In the SEC's view, the analyst, as a "tippee" of corporation insiders, had a duty under § 10(b) and Rule 10b-5 to refrain from communicating the nonpublic information to persons likely to trade on the basis of it. This Court found no such obligation, and repeated the key point made in *Chiarella:* There is no "general duty between all participants in market transactions to forgo actions based on material, nonpublic information."

No showing had been made in *Dirks* that the "tippers" had violated any duty by disclosing to the analyst nonpublic information about their former employer. The insiders had acted not for personal profit, but to expose a massive fraud within the corporation. Absent any violation by the tippers, there could be no derivative liability for the tippee. Most important for purposes of the instant case, the Court observed in *Dirks:* "There was no expectation by the analyst's sources that he would keep their information in confidence. Nor did the analyst misappropriate or illegally obtain the information." *Dirks* thus presents no suggestion that a person who gains nonpublic information through misappropriation in breach of a fiduciary duty escapes § 10(b) liability when, without alerting the source, he trades on the information.

Last of the three cases the Eighth Circuit regarded as warranting disapproval of the misappropriation theory, *Central Bank* held that "a private plaintiff may not maintain an aiding and abetting suit under § 10(b)." We immediately cautioned in *Central Bank* that secondary actors in the securities markets may sometimes be chargeable under the securities Acts: "Any person or entity, including a lawyer, accountant, or bank, who employs a manipulative device or makes a material misstatement (or omission) *on which a purchaser or seller of securities relies* may be liable as a primary violator under 10b-5, assuming the requirements for primary liability under Rule 10b-5 are met." The Eighth Circuit isolated the statement just quoted and drew from it the conclusion that § 10(b) covers only deceptive statements or omissions on which purchasers and sellers, and perhaps other market participants, rely. It is evident from the question presented in *Central Bank*, however, that this Court, in the quoted passage, sought only to clarify that secondary actors, although not subject to aiding and abetting liability, remain subject to primary liability under § 10(b) and Rule 10b-5 for certain conduct.

Furthermore, *Central Bank's* discussion concerned only private civil litigation under § 10(b) and Rule 10b-5, not criminal liability. *Central Bank's* reference to purchasers or sellers of securities must be read in light of a longstanding limitation on private § 10(b) suits. In particular, *Blue Chip* Stamps recognized the abuse potential and proof problems inherent in suits by investors who neither bought nor sold, but asserted they would have traded absent fraudulent conduct by others. Criminal prosecutions do not present the dangers the Court addressed in *Blue Chip* Stamps, so that decision is "inapplicable" to indictments for violations of § 10(b) and Rule 10b-5.

In sum, the misappropriation theory, as we have examined and explained it in this opinion, is both consistent with the statute and with our precedent. Vital to our decision that criminal liability may be sustained under the misappropriation theory, we emphasize, are two sturdy safeguards Congress has provided regarding scienter. To establish a criminal violation of Rule 10b-5, the Government must prove that a person "willfully" violated the provision. Furthermore, a defendant may not be imprisoned for violating Rule 10b-5 if he proves that he had no knowledge of the Rule. O'Hagan's charge that the misappropriation theory is too indefinite to permit the imposition of criminal liability thus fails not only because the theory is limited to those who breach a recognized duty. In addition, the statute's "requirement of the presence of culpable intent as a necessary element of the offense does much to destroy any force in the argument that application of the statute" in circumstances such as O'Hagan's is unjust.

The Eighth Circuit erred in holding that the misappropriation theory is inconsistent with § 10(b). The Court of Appeals may address on remand O'Hagan's other challenges to his convictions under § 10(b) and Rule 10b-5.

Based on its dispositions of the securities fraud convictions, the Court of Appeals also reversed O'Hagan's convictions for mail fraud. We need not linger over this matter, for our rulings on the securities fraud issues require that we reverse the Court of Appeals judgment on the mail fraud counts as well.

The judgment of the Court of Appeals for the Eighth Circuit is reversed, and the case is remanded for further proceedings consistent with this opinion.

It is so ordered.

CPSIA information can be obtained
at www.ICGtesting.com
Printed in the USA
BVHW092103100920
588455BV00002B/67